THE

IRISH

IN

AUSTRALIA

Other books by Patrick O'Farrell

Harry Holland: Militant Socialist

The Catholic Church in Australia: A Short History 1788–1967

Documents in Australian Catholic History, 1788–1968

Ireland's English Question. Anglo-Irish Relations 1534–1970

England and Ireland Since 1800

The Catholic Church and Community in Australia: A History

Letters from Irish Australia 1825–1929

The Catholic Church and Community. An Australian History

Vanished Kingdoms: Irish in Australia and New Zealand. A Personal Excursion

Through Irish Eyes. Australian and New Zealand Images of the Irish 1788–1948

UNSW: A Portrait

Professor Patrick O'Farrell, a New Zealander, first came to the University of New South Wales in 1959 with degrees from the University of Canterbury and a doctorate from the Australian National University. He was awarded a Personal Chair in History at UNSW in 1972 and elected to the Australian Academy of the Humanities in 1976. In 1998 he was appointed Scientia Professor. He held visiting professorships in Dublin—at University College, Dublin, and Trinity College, Dublin—for two years, 1965–66 and 1972–73.

Professor O'Farrell's historical expertise and reputation have been wide and various. His international reputation was built initially by two provocative and influential books on Anglo-Irish relations, published in the early 1970s, *Ireland's English Question. Anglo-Irish Relations 1534–1971* and *England and Ireland Since 1800*. He also wrote a series of pioneering books on Australian Catholicism, including the still-standard history *The Catholic Church and Community. An Australian History* (UNSW Press 1992). Professor O'Farrell went on to write five major books on the history of the Australian-Irish, including *The Irish in Australia*, which won the NSW Premier's Literary Award and the Ernest Scott prize. Both that book and *Vanished Kingdoms* (UNSW Press 1990) were recognised by the National Book Council and Australian history bodies as pathfinders in their professional field. He has also written the history of the University of New South Wales *UNSW: A Portrait* (UNSW Press 1999).

the IRISH in AUSTRALIA

1788 TO THE PRESENT

CORK **cup** UNIVERSITY PRESS

Patrick O'Farrell

First published in 1986 by
University of New South Wales Press

Published in Ireland in 2001 by
Cork University Press
Crawford Business Park
Crosses Green
Cork

British Library Cataloguing in Publication Data
A CIP catalogue record for this book is available
from the British Library.

ISBN 1 85918 321 2 paperback

Title pages 1798 rebellion monument, in Waverley
Cemetery, Sydney, Australia. *Richard O'Farrell*

Printed in Singapore

CONTENTS

PREFACE

The Irish in Australia is an impossible subject, too vast, too various, too complex, and certainly too elusive. Why attempt it when some degree of failure is assured? Obviously, for the sake of achieving whatever can be managed of success, and to draw attention to the neglected area of historical concern: the contribution of the Irish to Australian national life and character is of a scale of importance and interest as to demand close attention. It has been particularly bedevilled by what happens when historians fail to do their job: the growth—in the place of serious scholarship—of myths, prejudices, bigotries, stupidities, hagiography and fables. This book does not aspire to cleansing Australia of fairy stories about the Irish. It will not dispel the most powerful in those quarters where they exist and will survive for their own reasons: the contradiction of mere evidence will not shift them. Nor would I, in many cases, wish to do so. In a tame world good stories and wild inventions have their place and function, and the Irish are prolific generators of such and other magical benefactions.

But it is certainly my hope that this book will give the invincibly ignorant some pause and, particularly, that it will improve the level of discussion of the subject. Perhaps more importantly, I would like to think that this will act as a stimulating framework for further debate.

Traditionally, the American Irish urban experience has been the measure of all Irish emigrant things. Recent research has thrown that harsh image into serious question, with research not only in America itself but also into the very different experiences of the Irish in Canada, Britain, New Zealand, and South Africa. Anyone who has lived in, or even visited those countries will be aware of the contrasts with the atmosphere and realities of Irish Australia. What this research does offer, in addition to comparisons, is recent lessons in the kinds of historical and sociological investigations which might be applied, to great advantage, to the Irish in Australia.

Such is work which might inform the future, but I should explain some past considerations that have influenced the making of this particular book. Having written extensively on the history of Australian Catholicism, I am keenly aware of the overlap and confusion in the Australian situation between what is Catholic and what is Irish. I do not claim to have made any exact distinction in this matter but, as a simple fact of relevance, I have previously written a history of the Catholic Church in Australia, and this present work is a subsequent and different enterprise. My *The Catholic Church and Community. An Australian History* is readily available (UNSW Press, Sydney 1993) and I have deliberately avoided reproducing material from it in the present book. I have imposed the same self-denying ordinance on my other relevant books, all of which are accessible to those who wish to pursue related material.

My *Letters from Irish Australia 1825–1929* (UNSW Press, Sydney 1984) presents direct testimony from Irish immigrants, mainly Protestant, whose letters survive.

And in 1990, having traversed the ground in general terms, I saw the need to approach the area in a historical way radically different and very personal—specific, anecdotal, particularised. *Vanished Kingdoms: Irish in Australia and New Zealand. A Personal Excursion* (UNSW Press, Sydney 1990) was the outcome. I see that as the reverse of this book's coin; the one the compass and orbit of individual lives, the other—this book—the wide span and the *longue durée*.

In relation to the background of Irish history and to Anglo-Irish relations, my *England and Ireland Since 1800* (Oxford University Press, London 1975) is particularly concerned with English images of Ireland as forces in their historical relations, while my *Ireland's English Question. Anglo-Irish Relations 1534–1970* (Batsford, London 1971) argues a religious interpretation of their relationship and of Irish history generally. For the author of a book such as this present one an obvious question is: how much explanation of Irish events and persons is necessary? Given the ready availability of my own and other relevant Irish treatments, and my assumptions about the familiarity most readers are likely to already have, I have kept such background to a minimum. I have sought to avoid the obvious and well-known, so as not to lengthen the book needlessly.

My debts in the research and writing of the book are well beyond full specific acknowledgement, in that they go back to 1964 and are both Australia-wide and Ireland-wide. In 1964 Dr Eoin MacWhite, then Irish ambassador to Australia, encouraged and made it possible for me to study Irish history in Ireland itself, through the generosity of University College, Dublin: I would like to think that both the embassy and the college, and the individuals those general terms cover, feel that their trust and breadth of vision has had some repayments in results. Despite the obvious origins of my name, it was not until then, when I was thirty, that I developed any interest in, or knowledge of the history of the Irish. My association with both the embassy and the college has continued most happily since that time in the freest and most co-operative fashion, so that I am now not so much listing debts as acknowledging long and various friendships.

The role of the Irish ambassadors to Australia and the Irish Department of Foreign Affairs in assisting me with this book has been vital. From the 1980s those ambassadors—their Excellencies Joseph Small, James Sharkey, Martin Burke, Richard O'Brien—have provided me with enormous practical help and co-operation, on the basis of trust and with full respect for scholarly freedoms. So has the Irish Department of Foreign Affairs, assisting with trips to Ireland and America in 1985, and subsidising the initial publication of this book.

Living in Ireland in 1965–66, and 1972–73, and on numerous visits since, and on many research trips around Australia, my wife and I have built up a network of friends and indebtedness. It would be impossible to list twenty years' worth of helpful people: my theory is that the subject brings out the best in all those associated with it. Nevertheless, some help has been continuous and quite vital to the whole project, in particular that of my wife, who helped me with research, read the manuscript, argued about it, and is responsible for comment here and there. She also set the entire book on word-processor. Various members of our family have helped in different, but essential ways—Clare, Gerard, Virginia, Richard, Justin. Tony Cahill of the University of Sydney read this typescript. I have been helped by two great editors, Venetia Nelson and Roderic Campbell. At UNSW Press I am particularly grateful to Doug Howie, Di Quick, and Robin Derricourt.

A few more general acknowledgements. My thanks for the support of my own university at all levels and over many years. Recently I have benefited from Australian Research Council assistance, Arts Faculty research grants and from leave arrangements that reflect not only the university's consideration but the tolerance of my colleagues in the School of History. Those colleagues, and others in a wider research framework, together with some of my students, have made their unpublished work available to me. In Ireland I have had the assistance of University College, Dublin, Trinity College, Dublin, the National Library of Ireland, the Public Record Office of Northern Ireland, the State Paper Office in Dublin, the Ulster Historical Foundation, the National Museum of Ireland, the Department of Foreign Affairs, Bord Failte, the Ulster Museum, and the many archives of institutions of the Catholic Church. In Australia my debts are to my own university library, the National Library of Australia, the Mitchell Library, Sydney, the La Trobe Library, Melbourne, St Mary's Cathedral Archives, Sydney, and the Melbourne Archdiocesan Historical Commission.

Most of the illustrations came from my own collection, now held by the National Library in Canberra. Other material from that collection was published in 1994 in my *Through Irish Eyes. Australian and New Zealand Images of the Irish 1788–1948* (Aurora Books, Melbourne 1994). For additional illustrative material for this book, I am indebted to the National Library of Ireland, the Ulster Museum, Sir James Langham of Tempo Manor (Tempo, County Fermanagh), the Public Record Office of Northern Ireland, the Melbourne Diocesan Historical Commission, St Mary's Cathedral Archives, Sydney, the Hibernian Society, Sydney, the National Library of Australia, the Mitchell Library, Sydney, the La Trobe Library, Melbourne. To these institutions I add several individual debts: Dr Brian Trainor in Belfast, Dr W.A. Maguire of the Ulster Museum, Fr F.A. Mecham of Haberfield, New South Wales, and Les McCarthy and Fr J. Kearney of Melbourne. Laurie Dunne of the University of New South Wales did most of the copying work. Richard O'Farrell took the contemporary photographs.

A final word on the present edition of the book. In large part it reprints the first edition, but with a substantial, concluding section on 'Being Irish in Australia', which brings the book up to the present time and puts it into contemporary focus. The 1993 revised edition was a factual updating; but the final section of this book not only subsumes and further updates that previous edition, it also attempts to make some sense out of recent developments, an approach in harmony with the structuring of the whole book. After the elapse of the best part of a decade, matters then in train, and what has happened since, offer a much clearer picture.

The previous editions had substantial bibliographies. These have been replaced by a brief guide to selected further reading, intended for the general reader rather than for the academic. This procedure was suggested by the availability in libraries of the earlier editions and by the fact that those earlier bibliographies were designed in a pioneering situation, to assist interested scholars: no such need exists now. Indeed, a present bibliography of Irish Australia—books, articles, theses—merits a book-size treatment of its own: since 1980 the subject has become one of significant Australian academic interest.

History is supposedly a serious pursuit. It is; but serious is not solemn. I have found the Irish a vastly entertaining, perplexing and inexhaustible subject, for which capacities to amuse—in the best sense—I am immensely grateful. I hope I have been able to pass on some of the joys and sorrows of their past that they have conveyed to me.

Patrick O'Farrell
Emeritus Scientia Professor of History
University of New South Wales

I N T R O D U C T I O N

Precisely who, and what, shall be called up from the ranks of the dead? Those Irish and that Irishness that came to Australia? that Irish Australia they found and made there? their descendants? Within the moving swirl of that evocation, all precision vanishes: an elusive complexity rules.

Who were the Irish? Those who said they were—and some of those who said they were not, and others who were silent on the matter? If only it were so easy. Obviously, those who came from Ireland. But these came from three very different cultural traditions—Gaelic Catholic, Anglo-Irish, Ulster Protestant; to say nothing of Irish Jews and Quakers. And they came from very different Irelands; Donegal was a world away from Cork; Galway or Mayo were foreign lands in the streets of Dublin. And the Ireland of 1900 was a whole creation away from that of 1800, a creation of anglicisation, education, communication, and the habit of emigration, to say nothing of history and economics. At any time, these were ambivalent, ambiguous people, thinking Irish, talking English; hating the tyranny, serving the tyrant. At any time, they came riven by class divisions; the few 'gentlemen', the mass of 'peasants' and everything in between. In Australia each arriving Irish generation brought a new phase of Irish experience, its Ireland frozen for it at the moment of departure, to be overlaid by that of the next influx, so that within Australia a procession of Irish histories, Irish comprehensions, proceed at once; to be confused further by the camera images (and fantasies) generated in Australian-born descendants. Nor is this a simple line of obedient descent: for all the children tutored at 12 000 miles remove in the glories of holy Erin, would not as many have scorned the Irish message as paid heed? To pursue the phrase 'Irish Catholic' through Australian history (it lives still) is to discover a marvel of continuity and successful parenthood as children are posited replicas of their parents (themselves ever stalwart) in their deference to Irish origins and Catholic religiosity. Fairytales.

But surely Irish birth is a firm criterion? Not so: the Duke of Wellington is said to have dissociated himself from Irishness as any necessary consequence of his Irish birth with a telling analogy: being born in a stable does not make one a horse. Gavan Duffy gave this point Australian application: 'To strangers at a distance who read of Murphys, Barrys, MacMahons and Fitzgeralds in high places, it seemed a paradise of the Celt—but they were Celts whose forefathers had broken with the traditions and creed of the island.' Duffy's was a narrow reading—he meant the *Gaelic* traditions and *Catholic* creed dominant numerically in the island—but the observation had general validity: many of those of Irish descent, and even of Irish birth, did not consider themselves Irish. They acknowledged nothing meaningfully Irish in their identity or sense of self. In some cases this was a deliberate and conscious act of repression, the denial of origins judged a liability or an embarrassment, but in the cases to which Duffy refers it was more a matter of Irish birth or lineage being accidental to a secure cultural formation which was not Irish, perhaps even anti-Irish.

But obviously, those of Irish birth are the central subjects of this study. What caused some to affirm or assert Irishness while others did not, or did so less vigorously? There were various Australian ways of being Irish. Archbishop Daniel Mannix did not become aggressively Irish until he came to Australia. The reason seems clear: in Ireland there was no need for the vigorous affirmation—defence—of Ireland's character, demanded by the hostile situation in Australia. Under siege, under threat and attack, such Irish felt a strong need to assert the value of their culture, indeed claiming for it, in natural reaction, superior worth, which, in the circumstances of power, had to be moral worth. With them Ireland embodied a counter-culture of morality and religion superior to the dominant material Empire of Britain. Often linked to this was Irishness as a principle, more a sense of distinctive identity, of being separate, as coming from a particular place which conferred a personal sense of meaning and identity unique to that origin. This had no necessary religious application or limitation: it was more a sense of place.

The Mannix example draws attention to Ireland in Australia as the symbol of other local causes or grievances. Ireland was both warning and inspiration. Australia must never be allowed to fall victim to the tyrannies that had enslaved Ireland. Yet Ireland, persecuted, unfree, heroic and rebellious, seemed to many Irish and Irish Australians to represent, in the great arena of nations, their own position as underdogs and outcasts. Ireland was their personal predicament writ large. In weeping for the sorrows of Erin, they wept for themselves.

Here, disentangling the Irish impulses from the Australian is an obvious problem. A further complication springs from those Irish immigrants who came not from Ireland direct, but via a sojourn, perhaps years, in some British city, situations which make problematic reactions to the dominant English culture of Australia. So, expressions of Irishness might be merely the frantic clinging to what was familiar, known, in the midst of strangeness and isolation—this, of course, whatever the route from Ireland, direct or circuitous. How much professions of Irishness cloak reactions to being lonely and confused in a strange land is impossible to calculate. But the thought should give pause. Several of Irish Australia's most active Irishmen arrived in Australia as infants, or children: as adults they held most vigorously to a culture whose habitat they had hardly known.

There are other ways of relating to a point of reference than that of embracing it. The Irish Australian experience also encompassed those who rejected it vehemently. Some Irish—of Anglo-Irish or Ulster Protestant background—were so anxious to prove the acceptability of being Irish, on criteria of English Tory imperial standards of behaviour and ideology, that they were in the vanguard of manifestations of loyalty to Crown and Empire—and led the attack on those Irish who questioned or repudiated such things. Less frontal, more uneasy, were those who knew themselves to be apostates and renegades, who avoided and denied Irishness imposed on them by birth or descent, but who yet accepted Irishness as central to their concerns—the importance of being not Irish. The convolutions of these 'ex-Irish' twist down the generations and live still. They harbour deep well-springs of self-loathing, loathing that they should be so weak as to hate themselves, so open to being vulnerable to Irish-baiting, full of anger and self-contempt at being trapped in a stereotype they both accept and deny. Contrary and perverse, nothing pleases them, for they are caught between realisation of the Irishman within and rejection of the consequences: they are in suspended—all hostile—animation, sensitive to all the shafts and abrasions of a non-Irish world. Their impulse is simply reversed in the case of the 'super-

Irish', those who parody themselves to proclaim belligerently that the boozy bog Irish have a monopoly of Irish identity. All others are imposters—especially the respectable, the decent, the affluent, the non-Catholic, indeed the non-ex-Catholic: these are not 'real' Irish, but pale imitations.

So limp through the corridors of Irish Australia the casualties of culture conflict, bearing their wounds and neuroses. Who said that the battlefield for a fair occupancy of Australia's territories would not be littered with the lame and the halt, few corpses though there were? Or that the war would not take its toll in tensions and treacheries?

Nor was everything clear-cut. There were those to whom being Irish was a secondary allegiance. Australian-born E.W. O'Sullivan adopted the term Anglo-Celt to compound his loyalties. There were Australian Irish and Irish Australians, who blended or combined the two allegiances in some way, perhaps in different ways at different times and circumstances. In theory, and no doubt usually in practice, Irish churchmen, Protestant and Catholic, put their God before their nationality. And to many Irish their Irishness in Australia was confused and erratic, an emotion which fluctuated according to whim and convenience, and according to the reaction of others to Irish outpourings. The Irish engineer C.Y. O'Connor, designer of Fremantle harbour and the Coolgardie water scheme in the 1890s, had an Irishness emotional and symbolic: his racing colours were shamrock green emblazoned with Irish harps, he employed Irish horse boys and treated them as family. Raw Australian criticism proved too much: he killed himself. Sir Terence Aubrey Murray, pioneer landholder in the Monaro region, gloried in ambivalence and confusion. He moved from Catholicism to Anglicanism as it suited his inclination and convenience, played the Irish patriarch when he felt like it, and combined Irishness with imperial pride. All this was tenable eccentricity in the 1840s and 1850s, but its sour legacy to his son Hubert, governor of New Guinea, was tortured sensitivity, and a virtual obsession with Ireland and Catholicism as giving meaning and guidance to his life.

Which leads on to the question of Ireland as filling a psychological need. What of the cases where commitment to Ireland seems to spring, not from the principles of the cause itself, but from individual requirements? The question is important in the Australian case where Ireland was an issue both remote and unpopular. To illustrate. In 1918, several members of the Irish National Association, including its founder in 1915, Albert Dryer, were interned in Darlinghurst gaol for alleged sedition in supporting Irish independence. Dryer had never been to Ireland. Neither had the two men most instrumental in launching the processes whose momentum eventually landed him in gaol—the Prime Minister W.M. Hughes, and the prominent Melbourne loyalist, Herbert Brookes. Dryer was an austere and selfless romantic idealist, a man to whom Ireland was an inspiration, a dream, the fount of all that was moral, good and religious. To Brookes and Hughes Ireland was a nightmare, the epitome of all that was evil and destructive; it was the friend of the Hun, the home of superstition and disloyalty which had spawned that arch-fiend Mannix. In Dryer's case Ireland was the dedication and driving force of his life; for Brookes it was the obsessive focus for his bigotry, and Hughes turned on it his fury and frustration over the defeat of conscription. In none of these cases did these visions of Ireland confront experience of Irish reality in Ireland itself.

Yet, there is an argument which says such direct experience is irrelevant: the Irish carried Ireland with them—they *were* Ireland. Such arguments make much of allotted roles, and society as a confrontationist mechanism. The Irish were The Enemy. In their various forms—convicts, Catholics, rebels, workers, Fenians, Sinn Feiners—they were the despised and rejected, the outcast, the feared, the hated. They were hated and they hated in return. Their history in Ireland and Australia demanded the continued existence of an Enemy, an exploiter, an oppressor; and of course the British, and their Tory colonial lackeys in Australia, filled that role.

So Irish Australia can be explained as searching for completion in confrontation: I fight, therefore I am. What of Irishness as the nineteenth century saw it, the summation and expression of racial characteristics? As B.R. Wise put this in relation to the Australian Irish in 1889, 'There are differences of opinion against which no wise man would think of arguing, because they originate in differences of race, training or temperament which lie beyond the reach of argument'. There were natural racial characteristics inherent in national groups, traits which could not be changed. The French were passionate, the English phlegmatic; the Irish—by which Wise meant Roman Catholics of Gaelic culture—had two characteristics of peculiar significance in Australian politics: they tended to isolate themselves from all other nationalities, and to cohere together. This illustration makes the point that such racial analyses usually served some particular judgemental interest. To employers 'the Irish' were lazy, dirty, drunken, and so on. To their friends they were religious, sentimental, generous. These were taken to be, not individual matters, but expressions of a common behavioural stereotype assumed to be racially inherent: 'the Irish are always rebels' is a common generalisation of this kind.

Such racial stereotyping is no longer intellectually fashionable, indeed it is now deemed discreditable, but it lives still at a popular level and in other forms; it is too convenient and satisfying an explanatory tool to be utterly banished. So resort is made to the immigrants' alleged habits and dispositions when no other explanation for complex historical processes or questions is readily available. Events in which immigrants or even the children of immigrants seem to obtrude lend themselves to causal analysis in which explanations can be moved back to the obscure remoteness of distant country of origin, about which information is often thin, and prejudiced. Ireland was particularly convenient in this regard, and Manning Clark's explanation of Ned Kelly a classic case: 'Mad Ireland had fashioned Ned.' The questions begged are legion: was Ireland 'mad'? how had it fashioned Australian-born Ned? why had the Irish of northern Victoria fallen hosts to such insanity and not the equally Irish of Queensland's Darling Downs? The answers are available, but not in stereotype.

All precision vanishes. Generalisations must be made to shepherd the particular into the structures of the comprehensible. The Irish impact on Australia is not necessarily or simply related to the Irish population proportion, to matters of size and numbers. Nor do the dynamic forces at work need to express the dispositions of the entire community: an extreme determined element within a broader minority can impose its narrow convictions against the inclinations of the whole group if it stresses and exploits traditional themes central to the group experience and identity—nationalism and religion. The extremists play on tradition, conscience and group loyalty to coerce support. In Australia, Catholicism and Irish nationality were used to foster aggressive separateness among those whose preferences were essentially toward conformity and anglicisation.

A minority group is seldom one on all issues, at all times; rather, it is one on particular issues, consolidating only for some occasions, on some grievances. A major factor in its continuing vitality are the expectations or fears of the majority. So with Irish Catholics, caught in a self-fulfilling prophecy. The public conviction that, whatever the appearances, there must be Irish plots, created a degree of Irish solidarity by way of reaction to such allegations: the Irish banded together to defend themselves against the charge that they tend to band together. In fact, all kinds of internal divisions, conflicts and ambivalences remained obvious in the Irish camp. Only certain issues, at certain times, generated sufficient sense of external pressure to bring about a temporary reaction of Irish unity. And what the general community construed as Irish attack, the Irish saw as legitimate and imperative defence. The climate of continuing hostility to the Irish in Australia induced conformity, but also generated, as a reaction, an Irish determination to assert a separate and distinctive identity.

On the mechanics of social interaction, it may be observed that there is a critical size for minority groups. The Irish in Australia were a group big enough to encourage assertion and self-confidence, and to compel serious attention. But while they were too large to be disregarded, they were too small, too dispersed, too ill-disciplined, to get their way. Hence the protracted stand-off confrontation that threads Australian history. Not that the size of the Irish component was the overriding determinant: witness the differing historical situations and atmospheres in Victoria and Queensland where proportions of Irish Catholics were similar, but where leadership factors (that in Victoria being markedly more aggressive) were particularly important.

Fortunately in all this, when the logic is exhausted and the machinery of social analysis creaks to a halt, a refreshing core of irrationality and unpredictability remains. At its very origins the migration process refused to obey simple expectations. Thus, in Ireland 'peasants in the poorest areas were the most reluctant to leave'; 'the non-economic value of remaining in Ireland on the family land took precedence over economic concerns'. Sometimes. And sometimes the anticipated and the obvious took place: the poorest emigrated. There are no immutable laws.

There are, however, some patterns—designs grand and otherwise. The incorporation of Irish elements into Australia's character was, historically, a matter of continuing controversy and conflict, often bitter, sometimes violent. The Australian establishment, and the non-Irish generally, was often hostile, and sometimes most indignant in its refusal to accept the Irish as true and proper Australians. Such attitudes amounted to the demand that particularly the Catholic Irish reject their consciousness of distinctive national origin and differing religion, or, in other words, abandon their identity. That they would not do. Hence the conflict and controversy that surrounds their history. What they were prepared to do—and that happily—was to compromise, to accept their new environment and fit in to it. But not entirely on terms dictated by the English-oriented majority. No: the Irish demanded a definition of Australia and of being Australian which was broad and flexible enough to include them as they were, which would embrace or accept, at least to the degree of tolerance, those aspects of their character they held to be most important.

Australia was founded as an English penal colony, a gaol—very unpromising beginnings. What followed from this negative start, by way of freedoms, humane developments, tolerance, self-questioning, the cultivation of goodness, did not just happen, was not inevitable. They had to be fought for and constructed against the natural dark grain of prison walls. Good things had to be made to happen against the inbuilt tendencies of the early colonial situation towards evil, corruption, hopelessness, authoritarianism (even tyranny), a deadening obsession with conformity, and rampant persecuting prejudice. Australia was gradually and painfully created out of a stagnant English prison. Such is historical hindsight that this growth and liberation seem natural and even inevitable, viewed from the present. Closer scrutiny suggests not such necessity: it need not have happened, or at least so quickly. Why did it? The Irish are central to an explanation.

Until very recently, the Irish have been the dynamic factor in Australian history, that is, the galvanising force at the centre of the evolution of our national character.

Is this an extravagant claim? It only seems so because of the falsely unified way in which Australian history has been presented—one people from the beginning. Yet there were no Australians from the beginning (save Aborigines), only those who had come to Australia from Britain and Ireland: after forty years of settlement the 1828 census revealed less than a quarter local-born. Yet the history books brim with unifying assumptions. Their chapter headings tell their story—'Convicts', 'New Settlers', 'Gold Diggers', 'Squatters' and the like, which impose on an immigrant population categories derived entirely from their new Australian circumstances. It is as if stepping ashore in Australia was sufficient to obliterate the immigrants' past history and national backgrounds.

Why has this absurdity occurred? Because it was convenient to lazy historians, because it was the accepted fashion to assume that history was the story of the ruling classes, and because it posits a consoling sense of unity in national experience and endeavour. But it avoids, disguises and minimises basic facts of Australian history; that it was composed from the beginning of diverse peoples; and that its major internal formative force was tension and conflict, ultimately of a most creative kind, between minority and majority groups.

What has ruled in Australian history hitherto has been the unconscious and unfettered dictatorship of place, the unquestioned assumption that the Australian environment, this harsh, isolated land, has imperiously determined and contained from arrival, the concerns and horizons of its white inhabitants. More than influenced—it certainly did that—determined and contained. This historical orthodoxy is clearly revealed for the impersonal geographic and economic determinism that it is, by the practice of presenting Australia's population as best comprehended in categories related to economic function, or occupation—convicts, farmers, trade unionists or whatever—that is, categories derived from what people did for a living. What about what they were as people, human beings of diverse backgrounds, beliefs, and cultural traditions? The traditional accounts deal with only one of the roles in which people in Australia acted, the economic facet of their lives, a very narrow conception of the boundaries of human existence—and one naturally contained by Australia's geographic confines. The whole truth is much wider, more human.

The real history of Australia, monstrously neglected, is the history of the gradual growth and development, through confrontation and compromise, of a people of distinctive quality and character, derived from and produced by cultures—majority and minority—in conflict. The story is not a narrow one of man versus the land or nature, or of class versus class, or the solitary individual against flaws and limitations in the self; no, the broad outlines in which all these things are contained, their context, is that of culture conflict, interaction, ferment. The basic premise of this view of Australian history is that it is not self-contained. What we find in Australia are issues and conflicts of local importance substantially derived from and sustained by the outside.

In this situation of culture conflict, the Irish were the key dynamic factor, not entirely in themselves of course (it would be silly to suggest that) but in the provocative and liberating impact of their role as a powerful minority, aggressive enough to contest for a significant say in determining the character of Australian life and institutions. Whereas the smaller minorities—Germans, Italians—tended to be content with tolerance within a dominant British system, the Irish rejected or questioned the system, or at least demanded that it be adjusted to meet their requirements, with the effect of creating a new, modified system, a unique Australian blend and compromise which fitted the character of a mixed and interacting group of people, on the basis of equity.

This is the sense in which white Australia has had not one history but two, majority and minority, in which decisive, character-forming movement has been produced by, and substantially consists of, the tension, abrasion and sometimes collision, between two cultural forces.

Two histories, not one. If it is conceived as one, it is that of the conflict, interaction, between the two; if it is envisaged as a multitude, these two were the broad opposing structures which contained them. The boundaries and parameters of Australia's attitudes and concerns were marked by an English extreme on the one hand, an Irish on the other. These extremes were certainly inhabited by small fanatic minorities, but the main historical activity takes place in the space between, swinging sometimes towards one pole, another time towards the other, the poles attracting and repelling as events steer between, following an uncharted course of tendencies and corrections, swerves and swings, adjustments and compromises, drifts and eddies that navigators plot, dispute and contest. The nautical analogy leaves room to identify the landmarks—England and Ireland—and to suggest that officers and crew were engaged in constant debate about the course to be taken.

Perhaps the language of sociology is more to the point. Majorities seldom if ever act against their own power and privilege: they move reluctantly and only when compelled. Australia's English-oriented majority—or those in power who acted on its behalf—were quite happy to ignore (or exploit) outsiders, underdogs, and generally those not of their own kind. The Irish refused to accept this exclusion. The very existence of a substantial and insubordinate Irish minority deflated and confused the English majority. Their refusal to act out a deferential role discomfited the elite, eroded their superior certainties, provided a constant liberalising creative irritant, and gave notice that the old-world social order could not be reproduced in Australia. This produced not only pressure towards specific changes, but a general atmosphere in which exclusion, discrimination and rigid hierarchies became increasingly less possible to sustain. Certainly the pressures of the Irish accorded with tendencies present in the overall colonial situation: Australia was open to movement in the direction the Irish wished to go. Yet, that the favourable opportunities were taken is substantially due to Irish initiative. The direct Irish contribution to Australian liberties is very great, in terms of effective protest against religious and political monopolies, refusal to accept discriminatory laws, and demands for social equality. Perhaps even more vital is the impact of their energetic activities and independent opinions on liberalising and humanising the climate of Australian life, on freeing the atmosphere of authoritarianism, pretence, and cultural tyranny. The Irish had no philosophic notion of an open pluralistic society. It might even be argued that their preferences were ideally the opposite. Yet an open society in Australia was the effect of their determination to prise apart a society which threatened to become closed.

The contest between Irish-oriented minority and English-oriented majority, far from being divisive, became the main unifying principle of Australian history. What held this country's people together, in a constructive and productive social and political relationship, was a continuing debate, always vigorous, often bitter, and sometimes even violent, about what kind of country this should be. The tension and conflict between minority and majority was not, in its essence or effects, a fundamentally destructive one, but a creative exchange which compelled Australia's inhabitants, of all kinds and persuasions, to take stock of the nature of their society. Australia had room and resources enough to indulge such activity in reasonable peace. Elsewhere close urban or rural living might exacerbate confrontations; here a comparatively vacant land both fostered people's tolerance of each other and permitted them a degree of freedom to live apart and be themselves. Australian distances both separated people and drew them together, as did its pioneering newness, so that disputes over the character of an appropriate Australian society tended to be in the nature of family quarrels, rather than of warfare between strangers. The fundamental restraining Australian fact, in matters of disputation, was that people needed each other. The land was too vast, too empty, to be a mere backdrop to social questions: it conditioned those questions and the way they were pursued. The absurdity of a few people, marooned on a large, rich and—to European eyes—vacant desert island quarrelling to the point of schism, or violence, was obvious. This did not stop them quarrelling, for the matters at stake were important and deeply felt, but it muted their quarrels, often reducing them to mere bickering, and in the long run issued in reasonable compromise.

What were these great debates and issues in which the Irish contested with the English over the character of Australian society? All were crucial to that character. All involved the Irish centrally. All resulted in some form of liberalisation, some plurality, some wider accommodation. Hence the argument that the Irish were the force that made things change.

These contentious matters? The longest continuing divisive issue in Australian history, Catholic education; religion in politics, beginning in the 1840s; the great matter of freer access to Australia's land; the conscription referenda of 1916–17; the debate over immigration, from the 1830s; the sectarian battle between Catholics, Protestants and secularists. And, of course, in the other great dispute which has run through Australia's history—labour versus capital—Irish prominence is no less obvious. These are not merely the dramatic episodes of Australian history; they are the fundamental themes, the long-term issues on which generations of men and women are disagreed. They might be agreed on their war against land and climate, and, sadly, against the Aborigines, but on these other great issues—who should come here, how should they worship, how should they behave, who should own and control, what should be their loyalty and allegiance—there was division between the polarities of Irish Catholicism and British Protestantism. The Irish embodied, focused and sustained the principle of protest. Not that it would have been absent without them, but it would have been less strident, continuous and effective: it would have been protest within an agreed social structure, not controversy about the structure itself. As it was, the claims of pluralism, of an open varied society, were asserted against the demand of homogeneity, the idea of a closed, uniform society.

Australia was not merely the context of this dynamic. It was the outcome. The English assumption was that Australia would be a little Britain of the south. It was the Irish minority that was compelled to entertain the matter of an Australian nationalism which would repudiate the extremes of Tory Britain, hierarchical, conservative, rigorist. The distinctive Australian identity was not born in the bush, nor at Anzac Cove: these were merely situations for its expression. No; it was born in Irishness protesting against the extremes of Englishness.

Why should the Irish push for an Australian identity? Why not an Irish one? Most Irish saw this as a minority cause bound to fail. To stress Australian identity had obvious logic, drew on local support, was removed from the odium of self-interest associated with any directly Irish claim, and avoided the liabilities of an openly anti-British stance—and represented the true Irish Australian mind: here was the new place in which they now lived, and let it be free of slavish old-world imitations. The development of Australian nationalism can be seen, not as some wondrous natural and spontaneous outgrowth of climate and soil, pride and self-consciousness, but rather as a device invented and nurtured as a means of preventing an overwhelming growth of Englishness generated by the colonial governing classes. Again, not that the Irish held any monopoly of 'Australian' views, but they were central to their championing, and conditioned Australia's cultural climate in such a way as to allow other deviations from Englishness to appear and flourish.

The pivot of this thesis of Irish dynamic influence is the Catholic Gaelic Irish. What of Ulster Protestants and the Anglo-Irish? At the beginnings of settlement around 10 percent of Irish convicts were Protestants, and at some later periods, around 20 percent of assisted Irish migrants. Both in percentage and actual numbers this was not insignificant, and in any case the impact of this variety of Irish immigration went well beyond its size. These Irish shared Protestantism with the majority of the Australian population, but were often intensely conscious of their Irishness and proud of it. They seemed to fall into the 'Irish' camp, complete with brogue, yet their Protestantism put them in the English. The resultant duality and confusion worked against Irish stereotyping and towards broadening of colonial social attitudes as did the tendency of the Protestant Irish towards better education and greater skills. The superior socio-economic attainments of the Protestant Irish tended to create a greater openness to all Irish, provided they could demonstrate the capacities and abilities needed by colonial society. Of course the Anglo-Irish professional elite had these skills in an abundance that was crucial to colonial development, particularly in Victoria from the 1850s to the 1880s, but vital to the administration of Greater Britain at all stages.

Travelling across this varied Irish Protestant terrain, one eventually reaches its extreme fringes, also Irish in their way: while some Protestant Irish kept their Irishness to themselves, others saw it as a proud dimension of Britishness, conscious of separate identity in a regional and cultural sense that was a distinctive part of an imperial whole. Others still were ultra-English. Did they seek to expiate their Irishness, to compensate for a profound sense of inferior national origins by embracing the most agressive and superior English Tory values and attitudes? These extremists, who tended to group around the non-conformist and evangelical religions, and to be of the middle class, were militantly insistent on the virtues of British imperialism, the English Crown and the Protestant religion, but their energies were even more vigorously expressed in their shrill and total opposition to all the values and aspirations of the Gaelic and Catholic Irish in Australia.

Hence arose the situation in which the extremes of cultural opposition in Australia were both occupied by Irishmen of opposing conviction: Irish republicans confronted Irish super-loyalists. The outcome was the education of the main body of Australians—including Irish Australians—in the positive demerits of both alternative extreme positions, and of the whole notion and territory of extremism. The lesson was bred deep into the national character to appear in various forms and degrees of apathy, indifference, suspicion of passionate ideological commitment, and general scepticism.

To move back to the Irish as dynamic: the claim goes beyond what they wanted for themselves—to belong. Both J.F. Hogan's *The Irish in Australia* (1888) and P.S. Cleary's *Australia's Debt to the Irish Nation Builders* (1933) were efforts to assert the Irish role in the Australian enterprise, conceived as one story. Both were a jumping on the traditional bandwagon, driven by the establishment, with the cry 'The Irish are here too!', the demand to be included. Real history was what the governors and the wealthy did, and both books were bids to show that in this the Irish were contributing, conforming. Both books were rebellions against exclusion from the establishment's self-promoting games, but they are also testimony to the acceptance of rules and standards which were foreign and inappropriate. And the price was the neglect and minimising of their own very different contributions to Australia, by way of protest, and of affirmation of spiritual, humane, and imaginative values. They moulded themselves to what was dominant and superficial, bleaching, and eroding with uncertainty and misgiving, their own unique character which was different but not inferior. Despite their knowledge of belonging to a different Australia, they politely conspired in the pretence that its real history took place somewhere above their world. Of course, they had another history—Irish—the proud history of their ancestors to which they could retreat—heady but sustaining stuff, a powerful, mysterious injection to strengthen Irish Australian resolve already there. The efforts of both Hogan and Cleary to get the Irish into Australian history were greeted with hostility, derision and ridicule, or ignored: their audiences were of their own Celtic kind. So the Irish were forced out, into just that foreign real Irish historical territory which would inspire, justify and sustain their challenging and protesting role in Australia. And so the illusion of unity and self-containment remained. Australia was for a very long time not so much a nation as an assemblage of assorted immigrants, living out of the cultural and psychological baggage they had brought with them—but this has remained a hidden history, a subsoil which lay unprobed beneath the historical landscape obvious to the eye.

J.F. Hogan, journalist, author of
The Irish in Australia *(1887)*
M.P. for Mid-Tipperary in the
British Parliament 1893—1900

Why did this Irish factor not obtrude beyond the colourful and the incidental? Irish-Australian self-assertion was directed towards a resolution of its identity in Australia, a quest in which it was divided and unsure, and which was so close to a local exploration as to lose its Irish character in its Australian context. In Australia, neither Gaelic nor Anglo-Irish cultures revolted against English culture to anything like the same degree they did in Ireland: destructive hates did not develop as they did at home. The reasons are many, but a key one is the paucity, among Irish immigrants to Australia, of intellectuals, of the disaffected middle class, of classic troublemakers in the revolutionary tradition. Or if they came, Australia bought them off with quick satisfactions and they vanished into prosperity. Only one major Irish revolutionary leader, and he a moderate, enamoured of Australia, came here voluntarily—Charles Gavan Duffy: the considerable commotion that surrounded him opens the question of what might have happened had there been more of his kind, or those more radical. But the Australian Irish leadership was that of churchmen, pacific, and fully occupied with a missionary task of enormous urgency and magnitude—converting their own people to the practice of religion. Until the end of the century—too late—clerics had little time or energy left to combat (had they wished) the rule of the dominant English culture, except where its power intruded on what they regarded as the province of Irish religion. The clerical crusade against an English culture deemed base, materialist, corrupt, which was a feature of Ireland from the 1890s, had no Australian counterpart. Nor would it have been popular: the momentum of an upwardly mobile Australian Irish population was towards greater anglicisation, not less.

The absence of alienated lay leadership, of anti-English clerical cultural pressure, and those key aspects of Irish-Australian life—dispersion and mobility: these all worked to reduce Irish separatism, but also to direct Irish energies towards leavening the mainstream aspects of Australian affairs. A concentrated Irish community might have been more 'Irish', more interested in Irish affairs, but in very consequence, less dynamic within the general Australian situation. As it was, Irish Australia was in constant movement. That did not prevent it from being profoundly regional, like the rest of the Australian population. Irish organisations and newspapers tended to operate, at the very widest, on a State basis. Even those few organisations which built, of necessity, an Australian structure, such as the Hibernian Australasian Catholic Benefit Society, normally operated on a State level. There was no national Irish nationalist organisation or newspaper. As to that constant ferment of movement, it was both horizontal and vertical, geographic and socioeconomic. Perhaps more than other immigrants, the Irish moved about the colonies, not merely in search of labouring work which was itself mobile, as roads and railways explored the continent, but from sheer restlessness. And they moved up. The shearer became a selector; the coach driver managed a pub. Although this might introduce geographical stability in the lives of those who had hitherto moved often, it also broke down group solidarity by introducing socioeconomic distinctions, if not barriers, and enhanced natural individualism. The Irish thrived on this movement—to and fro, up and sometimes down. It was, after all, a basic exercise of freedom, a simple and precious delight to those hitherto imprisoned by the constrictions of poverty or of a rigid traditional social order: to come or to go as one pleased was a luxury beyond price which Australia could indulge as a matter of course. Little wonder that there was no desperate Irish assault on the whole fabric of society, or growth of a ghetto mentality. There well might be pockets of intense resistance to the Irish, but they could move elsewhere, and such pockets were small in comparison with general Australian tolerance—and space: 'Clancy's gone to Queensland droving, and we don't know where he are' captures the Irish Australian ideal and some of the reality. Ideally the Irish could not have much quarrel with such a society. Such a situation was linked to lack of leadership among them. Undoubtedly, in matters of leadership there is some operation of the law of supply and demand: the relative absence of enduring grievances among the Irish—as Irish —meant that Irish leadership was hardly in demand, and that efforts to supply it, via the manufacturing of issues that the few Irish extremists in Australia thought should rouse the Irish rank and file, invariably failed. As the Australian Irish saw them, the contentious issues were religious and economic; and it was leadership in those directions, that of the Catholic Church and the Labor Party, that they accepted and supplied.

All these factors bear noting as explaining the level and direction of Irish activity in Australia, that is, not as some separatist or alienated revolutionary force, but as a dynamic, an internal energising element, a leaven.

The importance of the family in Irish social and economic structures, and its extension to wide networks of kindred, gave it particular power in atomised colonial Australia to hold its members together in coherence against the world. Practically, it provided avenues of accommodation, employment and friendship. It met emotional needs, offering an environment in which the individual was known and cared for, conferring a sense of belonging, giving help, perhaps lending money. And it provided continuity between generations, acting as a stabilising conservative influence which passed on traditional attitudes and practices. The point here is not that all such influences were necessarily positive or socially healthy, but that the institution itself acted as a cohesive force. Nor was it one on which the Irish held any monopoly. The most that can be argued for the Irish family is significance of degree, in conjunction with other factors marking off the Irish community. Obviously, the family was of fundamental importance in the whole Australian community, and many non-Irish families were indistinguishable from Irish. Yet the society from which the ordinary English immigrants came was being rapidly remodelled by the Industrial Revolution, its traditional ways of life being disrupted by the new factories and the new cities. In contrast, most of the Irish came from a pre-industrial—pre-modern—rural society, where both tradition and religion remained very strong, as did a peculiarly intense sense of kinship and family life. The much greater incidence of chain migration patterns among Irish immigrants tends to suggest stronger family and kinship ties than among other groups: the Victorian ideal of family—epitomised by the Queen herself—held sway among the middle classes of all ethnic origins, but the Irish seem to have taken this down to the lower levels of ordinary working society. Not that their model was the Queen: it was tradition, heavily reinforced in the case of the Catholic Irish, by the pro-family teaching of their church. By direct teaching, marriage regulations, and its educational provisions, the Catholic Church fostered a cohesion already latent, indeed operative, in the traditional social structures of the Irish community.

The very word 'dynamic' carries radical connotations which require clarification—and qualification: here are the Irish, harbingers of change, source of social unrest, agitators, wanderers. This is deceptive. Few were natural radicals. They protested not so much against the system, but against their exclusion from its benefits. Give them a modest share of prosperity and the conservatism of a peasant and religious people asserts itself. Even this is overlaid and distorted by their gravitation to the dramatic, the colourful and spectacular. Where the action was in Australian history, there also were the Irish, in positions that gave them the influence which notoriety generates. Tiny groups of extremists exerted disproportionate influence through arousing the consciences of friends and the fear of enemies: the

Irish influence on Australian history is not only what it was, but what its opponents thought it might become.

In assessing this judgement, it is easy to forget the extent to which the nineteenth-century Irish seem 'foreign' in Australia. Prejudice and hostility towards the Catholic Irish cannot be explained merely as religious bigotry, although that was certainly present. Rather it was generated by a whole range of differences which, compounded together, was unacceptable—and many English immigrants had not encountered the Irish before: they had never been to Ireland, and it was not until the 1830s that Irish immigrants became significant in parts of Britain. As to their Catholicism, it needs to be remembered that until Catholic emancipation in 1829, the visible external signs of Catholicism—a distinctively garbed priesthood, nuns, convents, processions—had not been seen in Britain since the seventeenth century. ('You are a Catholic, sir!' cried the lady who saw A.W.N. Pugin, the English neo-Gothic architect, cross himself in a railway compartment; 'Guard, let me out—I must get into another carriage!') To this foreign religion, the Irish added, if not a foreign language in Gaelic, then foreign-sounding English in the brogue, and often distinctive dress, clay pipes, odd hats, to say nothing of other characteristics, real or alleged: poverty, absence of skills, dirt. All this added up to a total impression of 'foreignness', a distinctive minority to be viewed as such, sometimes with amusement, by others with dimensions of suspicion and fear. In Australia the Irish dropped as much as they could of their 'foreignness' as a liability, and their numbers gradually accustomed the non-Irish to their presence. To some degree, the continuing presence of an Irish-born priesthood acted as a brake on their 'Australianisation', perhaps encouraging a kind of split cultural personality among Irish Catholics who remained Irish-oriented in religion, but increasingly Australian in general culture. Yet whether such a split was healthy, even creative, or otherwise, is a matter both problematical and vexatious. Whatever the superficialities of appearances, whatever the tensions and ambivalences, by the 1880s the 'Irish' minority was rapidly changing in demographic character to a group whose predominantly Australian birth gave it a sense of belonging to Australia as a right denied the original Irish migrant; or whose children of Australian birth conferred the same sense of commitment and involvement as of right. The change in Irish conceptions of Australia, from someone else's country in which they were made to feel unwelcome guests, to a sense of rightful occupancy and possession as being their country, is impossible to date precisely, and varied with individuals, but it was well advanced by the 1880s. It is this affronted consciousness of full belonging which lies behind the aggressive assertion of 'Irish Catholics' in 1916–17: indeed by that stage they were ceasing to think of themselves as a minority, but as the real, true Australians.

No less imponderable would be the location in time of the stage when Irish immigrants ceased thinking of Ireland as 'home', with all that implied in attitudes to Australia. Never, in the case of the Irish priesthood? When they had property and children in the case of the ordinary immigrant? Perhaps much earlier, for there is a case for arguing, despite the myths and the sentiment, that the real love of the Irish man or woman was not so much for home as a geographic place (which might be harsh, poor, repellent) but home as a focal point for the people they knew and loved, home as a familiar society. No doubt in many cases the two were woven together, but for many Irish, people were more important than place. When so many emigrated, in some instances to the complete desertion of former settlements, when in some cases of eviction or farm consolidation, old habitations were razed from the earth, the human attractions of home simply vanished. When, as chain migration so often made the case, those he or she knew, the human constituents of home, joined the emigrant in the colonies, the sense of being 'at home' took on a colonial location, acquired some local meaning.

Could the migrant forget 'being Irish'? The answer seems to have been yes, if he or she was allowed to do so. Reminders came not so much from within their own ranks, from enthusiasts within, but from critics and opponents who persisted in seeking to exclude them from Australian society, to call their character and loyalty in question, and to treat them as lesser, inferior persons, outsiders. This hostility to difference was more than religious, more than economic and political, but like the religious, the economic factor was of great importance—and in both spheres the Australian environment was, when put to the test, sufficiently flexible. In matters of religion, Australia skirted potential sectarian catastrophe, perhaps because its inhabitants did not believe deeply enough, or in sufficient numbers, in the importance of the old world's traditional enmities, those generated by questions of belief, faith, truth, the catchcries of the old religious camps. Australia's foundation was heir to the Enlightenment and the American and French Revolutions, with their secular issues of liberty, equality and fraternity, and the pursuit of happiness, rather than a product of the divisions of the Reformation, which still haunted Europe and not least Britain and Ireland. Were these old religious—or irreligious—feuds worth replicating in the colonies at the cost of social disintegration or major division? For all the sound and fury, the answer was no. Nor would the economy permanently repress the Irish. Their determined upward economic thrust through the resistant layers of the dominant socio-economic structures was accommodated without major conflict. Opposed certainly, but the economy was open and prosperous enough, and sufficiently fluid in structure, to allow opportunity and movement: there was resistance, but not consistent frustration and denial. Australia adjusted to absorb, as part of itself, the thrust of Irish energies so that these became not some separate activity, but an integral part of a common endeavour.

Loss and gain. A bland account of events will not convey the dimensions of the Irish Australian experience. And the encounter between Ireland and Australia has hardly been an exercise in the ordinary. To this distant tip for human garbage, this refuge for refuse, this utilitarian colonial experiment, came the archaic, melancholy, humorous, religious, contradictory and occasionally indomitable Irishry, maddeningly pre-modern, non-conformist and volatile, dividing and hesitating in the face of possible destinies. Into a society whose rationale was merely that it work, function (as a gaol, a sheep-run, a mine) came a people who wanted—and did not want—it to have some meaning, some higher purpose. Their Irishness was more than an allegiance: it was a spirit, an attitude, a sensitivity, a set of mental and moral equipment, a quickness. It was an element that went against the English grain of progress, compromise and moderation, unity and homo-geneity. The outcome was ambivalence and confusion as the Irish were both dazzled and repelled by Empire, by the attractions of material gain and comfort, by the inducements of respectability and conformity, by the lures of this world versus the next.

In their rebellion against modernity, the Irish—by accident, as a by-product—extended the limits of freedom. In creating new horizons, they outreached themselves into a con-dition of pale emptiness: Australia gradually leached and bleached their substance. In Australia the Irish searched, or deliberately failed to search, for that which was not there—a sense of meaning and purpose. Not for identity. The emigrant Irish knew who they were. It is no accident that the Australian stereotype image of the tall, tanned, bushman/digger/lifesaver presented a physical idealisation of non-Irish characteristics: the quick, dark Celt, pale, short and wiry, intense and individualist, defied generic inflation. The constant Australian occupation of image-building went on without Irish participation. Sun-bronzed, masculine, hedonist but a devotee of the cult of mateship, military, wholesome, non-intellectual, a son of sand and surf—Irish qualities are hard to detect in such a mixture. Yet the assumed qualities of national character (as distinct from physique) draw heavily on the Irish: independence, lawlessness; stereotypes that were easy-going, anti-hierarchy and authority, generous, fun-loving, boozy, and as game as Ned Kelly. The Irish might not look the epitome of a large and self-confident colonial independence, but they acted it: the frame and flesh of the typical Australian were not Irish but his disposition was. Not so his mind and heart. Those the Irish kept to themselves, rendering the archetypal Australian as a hollow man.

Vague and contentious ground. Yet the argument of Irish as galvanic factor, as dynamic, is truncated if confined to social mechanics. The Irish are not only the source of movement, but the creators of atmospheres, the generators of aura, 'feel', style: the Catholic Irish have been the main Australian enemies of undue solemnity, pomposity, repression, sourpussery and wowserism. They have been the 'fun factor', ranging from innocent merriment, through deliberate mischief, to the kind of serious mad escapade attempted with foolhardy honour and passionate tragedy by Robert O'Hara Burke. Their priorities exalted neither work nor wealth and their ideas about enjoying this world—and of preparing for the next—contrasted, and often conflicted, with those of their fellow citizens.

What troubled the Irish in Australia was not the question of who they were, but why they were there. In contrast with the American belief in special providence, haven of refuge, or manifest destiny, Australia had no destiny or higher purpose, no self-justifying ethos: it was born of convenience, not hope. Immigrants had no faith or hope other than in the future prospect of material well-being. For the Irish in particular, wedded to an ancient spiritual community of people and place, this was often not enough. Their Australian experience set up a painful opposition between material well-being and their traditional human values. Part of this was the inevitable consequence of moving from old world to new, from a historical, peopled and nostalgic landscape to a new and vacant place. But part was a consequence of Australia's character. Its immigrants faced the jeopardy of a complex and profound personal deprivation. Lacking all other justification, such as the pursuit of freedom, or the quest for some new Jerusalem, they had to believe (why else had they deserted their homes?) that the improvement in their material world was sufficient to make them happy. Electing for materialism they thus became compulsory materialists, compelled in self-justification to exalt the obvious external things of life. They had to devise a connection between themselves and the new land because they had to justify not simply being there, but leaving their known and meaningful home to be there. The American Irish had an easier task: they could blame the Famine and make lives from the legacy of hate. Perhaps the Australian Irish could also delude themselves they had to leave. But, however managed, they needed to construct another sense of home. By and large they failed. Australia defeated them, and they defeated themselves.

In extenuation it should not be forgotten that the Irish had been trained by centuries of British rule to blame others, and to look outside themselves for solutions to their problems. Australian colonial experience confirmed what was an Irish habit of mind, a profound orientation towards reliance on the machinery of the state as this grew. Supplicating or manipulating the state for sectional or individual purposes became a commonplace of Irish-Australian social disposition, as distinct from self-reliance and individual initiative.

Perversely conjoined with this was hostility to the state, and suspicions of and contempt for its officials and politicians. Their view of the state and its apparatus was combative.

Instead of a home, Australia offered a condition akin to pilgrimage, the route and destination vacillating, uncertain, obscure. The Australian Irish found themselves constantly unsettled by distant echoes, heard from afar. Some were reverberations of death and infinity, suggesting that in empty getting and spending they laid waste their days. The Ulster Protestants among them lived in awe of the stern Creator, the Catholics were more softly ruled by a crucified God and His weeping mother, but both were conscious of the world's transitory sham and the shadow of the day of reckoning. Other echoes were those of distant conflicts and the troubled hum of old enmities. Lacking its own furniture to fill the immigrant mind, Australia's condition of emptiness invited the newcomer to import his familiar interests to fill the vacuum. The wonder is that they did this so little—the benefit of ordinariness, the boon of a lack of great minds and hearts, the favour of the absence of passionate intensity?

Yet, the unease is there. Was Ireland a prison, or Australia? Australia was rich and free—but empty, a dull, shrivelling environment. Ireland was poor and unfree—but full, of familiar people, of sustaining causes, of meaning, mystery, interest. Material relief and the challenge of the unmoulded new fought history, homesickness and spiritual destitution. So grew the living tension between remembering and forgetting, between fat fun and lean melancholy, between generosity and hardness of heart, between affirmation and betrayal. Remembering was more important, more real, than any futile effort to imitate or re-create what had existed at home. Home was home: Australia was different. An Irish Australia? Rubbish. In the minds of the Australian Irish, a thousand Irelands lived on unchanged, changeless, the pivot and meaning of personal worlds sealed off in the heart away from the contamination of the real.

What of the real? How could the Irish relate to an Australian scene more crassly worldly than any ever created before? Very well: its bounty afforded and indulged their peculiarities and seeming stupidities, the wasters as much as the saints. There was plenty for all to live on the earth's sunny surface. And why not? Foolish in the eyes of the world (and of some bishops of the Church), many Irish—partly in keeping with the slow rhythms of their past lives, or ideal lives, partly perhaps in shock—elevated a wandering footloose irresponsibility into an art form close to God in its silent protest against the secular values of wealth, security, caution, respectability. And won their way into men's grudging esteem—the bemused Sydney *Gazette* of the 1830s, looking with tolerance, affection even, at the outrageous antics of 'Patlanders', merry-drunk, singing, exploiting their reputation for fun and games. They won their way too in showing contempt for money and possessions. Mere things were of no real consequence, but objects to be used, consumed, not really valued. Australia itself was in the category of a thing, something metaphysically inadequate: they denied it their full commitment.

For the most part, Australia's Irish were poor, and more than poor, for their poverty was not a simple condition of deprivation, but a way of life, a structure of accepted values, a personal and social order not easily abandoned or overthrown: it was as if the life of the poor man bound him to a destiny beyond his control or even wish to change. Indeed, to change it was betrayal, and probably sin. The consequence was not only indifference to worldly progress as exhibited by some, but the limited ambition shown by others, the concept of enough being sufficient, without the pursuit of surplus, much less massive wealth. It was a reaction in which contempt was admixed with fear, a mind-frame inimical to capitalist aggregation. A people so long denied wealth and the opportunity to pursue it, so long inured to hardship and deprivation, had made a virtue of this necessity and they believed their religion confirmed such values. Australia made little impact on the nature of these convictions and expectations other than to adjust their level: an Irishman might rest content in conditions of modest comfort and equality. The cheat of Australian wealth was that it was promised so crudely, so bereft of the ideals, the style, the expansive grandeur, that would have recommended it to the Irish. They concluded that small and equal achievement was more fitting than great. While the non-Irish rich and powerful pursued individual eminence and personal possessions and built commercial and industrial empires that grasped small men by the throat, the poor and virtuous Irish preferred anonymity, equality, and the comfort of their own kind as their vision of a tolerably human life. It was a coherent, morally defensible stand for the underdog, but its danger lay in sanctifying and perpetuating the role of underdog; in courting the construction of a world in which only the underdog ruled, with his strange fatalism, his pessimism, his denial of self, his suspicion of excellence, his sense of grievance.

Who were the Irish in Australia? All kinds and conditions of men and women who came from Ireland. They continue to come and the history of those who came, and are now vanished, has hardly begun to be told, has still to be discovered, and will long continue to remain, in meaning and influence, obscure. What follows is a very little of their story, so far.

C H A P T E R
T W O

P R I S O N E R S

The first fleet of convict ships which began the settlement of Australia reached Sydney Harbour in the colony of New South Wales in January 1788. Some of those aboard this fleet and the second—convicts, crew, officers and guards—were Irish-born. The Catholic Irish element, noted by J.D. Lang in the 1840s as evident in regiments in service in the colony, was no doubt there from the beginning, as were the 'North of Ireland' men referred to by Joseph Holt in 1800. And the Irish were also present among the more prominent; for example, D'Arcy Wentworth of Portadown, founder of an Australian dynasty of wealth and conservatism, and the Anglo-Irishman Thomas Jamison, First Fleet surgeon.

But these were unremarked as 'Irish': they were (and the theme remains muted yet constant for the next century) a virtually indistinguishable facet of the British imperial and colonial enterprise. The first convicts sent direct from Ireland—133 males and 22 females—arrived from Cork on the *Queen* on 26 September 1791. The youngest convict aboard was David Fay of Dublin. He was eleven. The oldest was Patrick Fitzgerald at sixty-four. How far the clank of convict origins echoed into the future of Irish Australia is suggested by the life-span of Michael Lamb, eighteen when arriving on the *Queen*, dying aged eighty-six, in 1860.

Significant also for the future was the first image these Irish generated in the tiny colony: here were fools, simpletons, clowns of no account—and lazy as well. Several contemporary journals, notably that of Judge-Advocate Colonel David Collins (himself Irish) in November 1791, and that of Captain Watkin Tench in the same month, refer to attempts by various of the *Queen* convicts to escape, with, as Collins put it 'the chimerical idea of walking to China, or of finding in this country a settlement wherein they would be received and entertained without labour ...' This 'absurd' enterprise earned the escapees the ridicule of the colony, to which general merriment and derision they reacted with intense shame, proffering the excuse that they had been driven to it by overwork and harsh treatment. Nor was this the last time that scorn for the ignorance of such simple men and women was to goad them further into anger and frustration with their immediate lot and feed their longings for freedom. Governor Hunter was not without sympathy for these Irish, whose simplicity made them 'the sport of more wicked or designing knaves', and permitted convict expeditions of exploration which might convince them of the absurdity of this idea of interior paradise and of the deadly folly of trying to reach it. Tench saw behind these Irish 'Chinese travellers' 'folly stimulated to desperation'—at least he sensed its dimensions of despair and its child-like utopianism—but he too saw it as a joke, if a sad one for those who perished in their quest. And Tench also, in describing this imbecile behaviour, had no doubts in regard to its origins and attribution. Declaring his continued respect for the Irish brother officers he had encountered in his military profession (some of my best friends ...) and wishing not 'to cast an illiberal national reflection', yet he felt compelled to observe that 'it is certain that all these people are Irish'.

The Australian parameters for the Irish were set within two months of the *Queen*'s arrival. There were some good Irishmen—one's equals, certainly—(Collins and Tench were agreed on that) but, oh dear, there were also among that nation some dreadfully silly fellows, ignorant to the point of incomprehensible absurdity. China indeed! None paused to ponder the existence of that unfettered dreamworld that infused the imaginations of these people who knew hardly the rudiments of any world outside their own. For Collins the fact that these Irish convicts were forever trying to escape said nothing about them other than give persistent witness to their ignorance and temerity.

But then Collins was judging the Irish, as so many had done before and would do after, by standards different from those applicable to normal men. The Irish were not men, but surely, he thought, rather 'a race of beings (for they do not deserve the appellation of men) so extremely ignorant, and so little humanized as they were ...' To him—and he was typical—here were convicts 'nearly as wild themselves as the cattle', still obsessed (in 1798) by the unsubdued delirium of their search for the road to China, constantly restless, forever credulous, foremost in every mischief and discontent, even harbouring, in January 1799, that fantastic and dangerous idea 'that Ireland had shaken off its connection with England, and that they were no longer to be considered as convicts under the British government'. That was their most pernicious continuing illusion, but they were, on Collins' account, abubble constantly with myths and rumours about impending freedom, such as that of April 1798 when an old woman prophesied the arrival of French warships to liberate the colony. This 'ridiculous tale' unhinged an Irish convict in a gang at Toongabbie: he 'threw down his hoe, advanced before the rest, and gave three cheers for liberty'—for which he was, of course, flogged. To Collins, all this signified not, as it might seem now, a genuine thirst for freedom, but madness and stupidity, an Irish failure to recognise the realities of power. It might be a matter of regret that the exact sentences of such prisoners might be unknown, (through administrative incompetence) but this was no excuse for rebellious behaviour. Besides, even kindness to such persons went amiss. At the conclusion of the harvest at Toongabbie later in that year, the Irish harvesters, men and women, each received a small quantity of spirits and water. This produced 'at first cheerfulness and play, but terminated in riot and ill-humour; a circumstance not uncommon with that class of people'.

By the 1820s and 1830s such Irish convicts were arriving at an average rate of about 1000 a year. By the time transportation to Australia's eastern colonies ended in 1853, just on 40 000 convicts (29 466 males and 9104 females) had been sent direct from Ireland. Of those convicts sent from England, estimates suggest that somewhere about 8000 were Irish-born and perhaps a similar number of Irish descent. Indeed the Irish were dominant in some areas of English and Scottish criminal disturbance, among machine-breaking weavers for instance. In all, the Irish-born element represented about a quarter of all convicts transported, though this proportion was not evenly distributed across time. For instance, of convict women arriving in the years 1815–21, nearly 55 percent were from Ireland, and over the period 1788–1828, over 40 percent of female convicts were Irish. Such concentration, as with certain periods of free immigration later, helps explain both the Irish impact on colonial life and the outbursts of hostility it provoked.

Irish-Australian historical tradition has depicted these Irish convicts as honourable victims of gross injustice, social oppression and national persecution, or as heroic rebels. The facts seem otherwise. In the strictly nationalist sense, political rebels among the Irish convicts seem relatively few, about 1.5 percent, that is, less than 600 in the entire history of transportation, of whom nearly 500 arrived in the very early years of the colony, up to 1806: if this early concentration of 'politicals' is the basis of the legend of injured Irish innocence, it also set the official image of the Irish convicts in the cast of sedition and incipient terrorism. Social rebels—those convicted of crimes of violent protest against poverty and landlordism—have been estimated at about a fifth. Yet, despite research, the picture is by no means clear or settled. In Ireland itself wide differences exist in estimates of the size of the major revolutionary organisation associated with the disturbances that culminated in, and followed from, the rebellion of 1798—the United Irishmen. Some say it was tiny. Others claim that in some counties—Carlow is cited—it took in virtually the entire adult population, a suggestion that seems highly improbable. What is certain is that revolutionary organisations were not confined to Catholics, or the lower orders. One of the best known of the Irish political transportees, Joseph Holt—his *Memoirs* contribute to both the history of the 1798 rebellion, and of early colonial New South Wales—was both a Protestant and 'a farmer of considerable property and respectability'. To complicate the revolutionary matter further, the extent and degree of its nationalist ideology is questionable and obscure. Even the educated Holt described himself as 'not very well up to republican notions', and seems to have been a moderate man driven into rebellion by the persecution of irresponsible ultra-loyalists.

All of these complications and diminishments hardly registered in the minds of the authorities of colonial New South Wales: the Irish convicts were a pack of dangerous, low, Papist rebels, a general principle which neither exceptions nor evidence to the contrary could alter. In fact, about four-fifths of Irish convicts can be described properly as ordinary criminals, mostly thieves. Of the women, many were prostitutes as well. Yet it is true that all research suggests that—and this is also true of the Western Australian convict scene half a century later—generally, the Irish were a better type of convict, less criminally inclined, more likely to completely reform, less inclined to turn to crime in Australia. They were taller, healthier, their stealing more likely to be of farm animals, their criminal impulses those of the destitute and desperate. But the general, broader, comparative picture does not invalidate the specifics, or diminish the moral absolutes. Here also were men and women dishonest and cunning, often violent and dissolute, no less so than their English counterparts—and no more interested in revolutionary politics. Thieves made up about three-quarters of all convicts, English and Irish. Of Irish convicts, about a third had previous convictions, and multiple convictions were quite common. Nor were the Irish an older and more responsible element: less than one-fifth of them were over thirty. Even that minority describable as political or social rebels was not necessarily of a different stamp from the mere criminals. The respectable Holt described the men who accepted his command in the 1798 rebellion as

> a band of ruffians ... many of the men were inclined to become robbers ... they were desperate and bloody minded ... religion ... was a pretext and excuse for their deceit ... The political feeling, or sense of injury which brought them out in the first instance, was forgotten; and living so long at free-quarters, made them think robbery and murder lawful.

Nor can their Catholicism be necessarily presumed a civilising restraint. Holt recounts the occasion of his men cramming into a mountain chapel: upon the priest protesting at their bringing in weapons, one man threatened to kill him at the altar if he did not proceed with Mass. And there was ample confirmation within the convict colony of the violent criminality of the Irish. If one discounts Sir Thomas Brisbane's report in 1824 that 'every murder or diabolical crime, which has been committed in the colony since my arrival, has been perpetrated by Roman Catholics,' there is still the letter of the free settler and future bank manager, John O'Sullivan to Archbishop Murray of Dublin in 1830:

> some of our unfortunate and wretched countrymen are foremost in perpetrating the shocking crimes that mark this colony . . . I did not think the Irish character capable of performing the villainous deeds that are daily blazoned forth . . . the blood-thirsty and treacherous acts of the ruffians are enough to make the genuine Irishman hide his face in shame.

With one area of convict vice the Irish were explicitly not associated; that described in the language of the time as 'unnatural offences'. In 1843 Sir George Gipps reported to Lord Stanley on the incidence of homosexuality in the convict population; it was variously estimated as affecting one man in eight to one in twenty, and was punishable, when proved, by the lash. Gipps added: 'The Crime is said to prevail almost exclusively among the Prisoners of English birth . . . and the Irish are (to their honour) generally acknowledged to be untainted by it.'

However, if the murderous and violent Irish in early New South Wales were a tiny minority, it was a very spectacular one, which fed and confirmed the pre-existing public image of the Irish. The Irish of good life and respectable position found themselves saddled with a national reputation generated by the worst elements of Irish society. And so it continued to be.

For the Irish, as ever, stood apart: even in felony they tend to be a distinctive group. A section of the Irish, small but significant in its prominence, were men of integrity, guilty of political or social protest, not common criminals. The Irish were mostly Catholics, whereas the English and Scots were Protestants. Most of the Irish were peasants (though about a third possessed skills of some kind), while most of the English came from towns. Though the literacy rate of Irish males was not markedly different from that of English males (about 60 percent could read and between 40 and 50 percent could also write), many of the Irish did not speak English among themselves, but Gaelic.

The existence of this separate language, with a long and rich oral—as distinct from written—tradition, points to key elements of Irish difference in Australia. It was no quaint folk survival, but the bearer of a distinctive cultural tradition, world-view, historical experience and sense of values—all of which were not merely different from, but hostile to, those of the English and Scots majority. Nor was this relationship one of tiny minority overwhelmed by vast majority. Its importance, difficulty and intensity is best judged by the population balance in the British Isles at the beginning of the nineteenth century. The Irish were not, as now, one in twelve, but one in three, a very different arbiter of relations. At the time of the foundation of Australia, the Gaelic world, if in decline, was still a significant aspect of the culture of the British Isles.

The matter of survival of Gaelic culture among the convict Irish, and among the free immigrants who followed them, is a complex and obscure question. Certainly a basic assumption must be that, as many Irish in Australia came from Gaelic-speaking areas in Ireland, they must have brought that language and culture with them. Yet the old Irish culture was in the process of decline, indeed disintegration, well before the period of massive emigration. This rapid erosion reflected the spread of the English language and culture in Ireland, added to the effects of Ireland's extraordinary population explosion (from 2.5 million in 1753 to 8.2 million in 1841), compounded by the disruptive effects of the emigration process itself. Not for nothing, or for mere poetry, have migrants been dubbed 'the uprooted', for they leave behind their familiar soil. In the Irish-Australian case, overwhelmingly it was the individual who migrated, not the group; that is, a fragment, not the whole community; the available materials of life were now timber, not Irish stone, and the climate and environment were that of a mild or semi-tropical southern hemisphere. It is not surprising that the material culture was little transferred: Mannion's study finds the same in Eastern Canada. The demands of a new situation and economy were dead against it. From a position of ample labour and little land, the Irish in Australia had migrated to the reverse. Their old culture in Ireland was not a quaint and colourful—or immutable—lifestyle designed for tourist, antiquarian or nationalist purposes: it had evolved over centuries as a series of practical or emotionally necessary responses to a given Irish environment and economy. When that changed—and it changed radically with migration to Australia—the culture, the response, changed. Indeed it was imperative that it should. The immigrant had to discard or adjust his old culture, and acquire an appropriate new one, to survive: he could not spend vital time and energy attempting, even if it was possible, to construct an Irish cabin of mud or stone in the midst of an abundant Australian forest. The Irish, one might say, were compulsorily anglicised by the materials of the physical environment in Australia. And when they, say, grew potatoes, as they did in large quantities up from Warrnambool in south-west Victoria, they did so not out of habit, or sentiment, or compulsion, or because they knew nothing else, but because there was a large and lucrative Melbourne market, because potatoes could be transported there readily—and, of course, because they knew how to grow potatoes: thus they prospered.

Those now who expect much culture transfer with Irish immigrants are romantics, and the implication of their interest a fixation on the Australian failures. To blame Irish immigrants for abandoning what was a hindrance, or simply irrelevant, is to tax them with not maintaining museums. Yet the antiquarians of the 1980s have something resembling that expectation: the new multi-culturalism must have a traditional culture, an ancient ethnic character, to lament the destuction of. What presently passes for Gaelic culture was the re-creation of the later nineteenth century, when there were resources for that luxury. What was Gaelic continuous, what was preserved, nurtured, passed on, was not language, or modes of building, or curious folkways, but something more elusive, much less tangible, more central—mind-sets, mentality, values, mental furniture, ways of thought, attitudes, dispositions, slants and tangents. In those deep fastnesses of mind and heart the real Gaelic person long continued to live.

All that being understood and given, what are the Gaelic public evidences? The first Catholic chaplains in 1820, Fathers Therry and Conolly, sought the recruitment of Irish-speaking priests from home as a preference for the confessional. Occasional isolated cases can be found, particularly within the legal system, of those who claimed to speak Gaelic only—an instance in an Ipswich court in the 1860s, or a murder trial in 1847 at Hartley, New South Wales, in which one of the witnesses had to be provided with an interpreter from the Gaelic. There is ample suggestion that many of the pioneer Irish in Victoria's western districts spoke Gaelic among themselves. These cases raise the question of the degree to which those whose first language was Gaelic had mastery of English, and in many it must not have been easy or complete. Recently detailed comparative analysis of convict skills and literacy in the period 1817–39 has convincingly demonstrated that Irish convicts who had been living in England itself had skills and literacy not significantly different from their English counterparts. The traditional English libel that the Irish were less intelligent, stupid, is disprovable from Australia's beginnings; but the demand that they not merely understand, but master English, placed many at an initial disadvantage. The facts of Australian life in regard to Gaelic are best illustrated by an incident in 1800 when a group of Irishmen who had been talking in Gaelic were brought to trial on this basis alone: in the hysterical climate of that time it was assumed by uncomprehending English eavesdroppers that this was inevitably the language of seditious plotting. In Ireland itself, by the end of the eighteenth century, Gaelic had become a clear liability for getting on in the world, and the sensible modern Irishman or woman increasingly used English—Gaelic was the badge of poverty and failure. In Australia the same applied, with the additional danger that its use might be construed as covering crime. Little wonder that the language, already dying in Ireland, promptly vanished in Australia; in Ireland, its preservation and eventual revival were for long the preserve of leisured Protestant antiquaries—a stimulus both non-existent and tainted in the eyes of Gaelic Australia. How total the shedding of their language is evident in the proud tombstones of the Australian Irish, where they might proclaim beyond their time their origins, identity and allegiance. They are innocent of Gaelic. Name, family, county of Irish origin, often when they came, a pious phrase—all in English. Betrayal? Not so: common sense (who would read?), pride in achievement, conquering the language of the conquerors. Whatever may be thought of it now, since the Gaelic revival, the Australian Irish of the early nineteenth century saw the Gaelic language as another means by which they were isolated and subdued. It was a bar to the world of power, dominated by the English, a double imprisonment for the Irish convicts of New South Wales. And it was seen, at best, as a joke: the influence of Gaelic idioms and linguistic structures when carried over into English were seen generally as funny, laughable. In fact, Langker's research into the vocabulary of convictism and Flash in early New South Wales shows that the Irish had a 'disproportionately small influence on Australian English' (indeed virtually none at all). While many Irish arrived almost completely ignorant of English, they abandoned their Gaelic and took up English as soon as they possibly could, a situation which permitted little if any linguistic interaction. In America some residual Gaelic usages lingered ('Shebeen' for drinking place is a case), but in Australia the only carryovers from the Irish scene appear to be English words of joke or opprobrium—thus 'croppy' to signify Irish Catholic rebel (the derivation was from hair cut short in sympathy with the French Revolution), or the *Sydney Gazette*'s benign 'Patlander', or the more enduring 'Sheila' and 'Paddy'—the Sydney *Monitor* (22 March 1828) remarked of a fracas in Sydney's Hyde Park in which the Irish were involved, 'many a piteous Shela stood wiping the gory locks of her Paddy'. 'Sheila' had a generic use in Ireland, from where also derived 'live off the smell of an oilrag', 'go bail' and 'barrack'—but all these are phrases in English, testimony to the anglicising process.

Other expressions of the old Irish culture got similar short shrift. In July 1791 Collins noted that the carelessness of those Irish engaged in a wake—the traditional Irish festive celebration for the dead—had led to the burning down of a hut and the scorching of the corpse. His comments on a later Parramatta Irish community wake, in October 1794, leave no doubt about his attitude to strange Irish folk practices, which 'celebrated the funeral rites in a manner and with orgies suitable to the deceased, his widow, and themselves'. The Irish wake was to continue, but it was quickly privatised and modified: the Irish were not going to exhibit their rituals to the taunts of a hostile and uncomprehending audience. Besides, the dispersion of settlement worked against communal occasions, while the Catholic Church, as it grew from the 1820s, was strenuously opposed to the continuation of practices seen as remnants of primitive paganism: as late as in the catechism approved by the Plenary Council of 1885, wakes of a certain kind came under prohibition—those which included not only the usual drinking, and perhaps games, but parodies of religious ceremonies and mimes and dances with strong sexual symbolism. Whether this censure was necessary in Australia, such features were aspects, if minor ones, of the traditional Irish scene.

But a whole range of pressures operated against the continuance in Australia of Irish folk beliefs and customs, the mental world of magic and superstition, fairies, spells and portents, that were intertwined with the daily round and with Christian beliefs. There were the constraints of the convict situation, and the wide geographic dispersal of the Australian Irish. A large body of traditional custom and belief in Ireland centred on holy places and seasonal festivals. The holy places had been left behind, and in Australia the hemisphere (reversing the seasons), the warmer climate in which seasonal transitions were nothing so marked, and an agricultural economy very different from Ireland's, all conspired against celebration of the Irish folk calendar. Nevertheless, Father Therry, when he arrived in 1820, found a congregation with many 'curious beliefs', including the crediting to him of what amounted to magical powers, an attribution not uncommon in Ireland. Individuals may have long preserved folk practices and beliefs, their obscurity usually escaping the detection of history. Into the 1860s, Sarah Tully, daughter of the Durack clan, followed the example of her grandmother in Ireland, by placing her offspring 'soon after birth, on the fresh tilled soil, to receive the goodness and strength of their mother earth'. Mother Earth was herself, in Australia as in Ireland. It is possible too—stories of matchmaking in the Kirkstall area of Victoria suggest this—that some of the first generation of Irish settlers in areas of Irish concentration may have retained the old procedures governing formal arrangement of marriages. And of course an inherited brogue long lingered in the children of Irish areas; it was common in the Catholic schools of the western districts of Victoria into the 1930s, in children of the third or fourth Australian generation. In matters of tradition and habit, the Irish combined a fluid attitude to their previous preferences, with a willingness to accept or adapt as suited the scene. The Wexford rebel Michael Hayes, turned Sydney store- and hotelkeeper, seeking in 1817 to arrange with his family in Ireland a shipment of liquor, told them not to send much whiskey, 'it not being used but by the Irish, and only retained as a novelty'. Rum or porter would sell well.

This commentary on the Gaelic Catholic peasantry is not to imply that the early Australian Irish were a homogeneous group. They were not. According to Peter Cunningham in 1825, the Irish convicts saw themselves as divided into 'Cork boys', 'Dublin boys' and 'North boys'—the last, on account of their accent, being commonly called Scotchmen by the others. Within this crude geographic polarity were refinements of county and region, family and cousinage. The particular location in Ireland of outbreaks of violence might determine regional or even family groupings as all participants were swept up in a net of law and order. Some counties constantly verged on criminal anarchy; Tipperary consistently led the convict tallies as policing forays nibbled at its core of ungovernables. Not all those caught were equally convict. So various and haphazard was the Irish machinery of apprehension, conviction and transportation that, particularly at times of maximum public disorder, it resembled more a lottery than a judicial system. There were, in earlier years, cases of transportation without trial, of the wrong person through malice, mistake or confusion; of others without record of sentence. John Hogan from Tipperary was saddled with the wrong sentence, which he could eventually prove; he took action for unlawful detention and in 1838 was awarded £50 damages. At the other extreme, there were, apparently, those who had been transported as an official obligement. An Irish labourer in Tasmania deposed that he had been 'laying about the streets and went to the police and told them I should like to be transported'. The authorities relieved his boredom and assuaged his sense of aimlessness with the adventure of seven years' transportation for vagrancy. There were wide social and moral gulfs among the Irish. A few (only 500 by 1828) had come to the colony as free settlers. Of the convicts, some were violent and vicious, while others were not. Some emancipated convicts had utterly reformed; there were remarkable transformations like that of Elizabeth Mulhall, 25-year-old Kilkenny murderess, who became the wife of a successful ex-convict trader, eventually managing his business. Others faded into hardworking respectable obscurity. Some returned to crime or its shady environs. There were Irish who achieved considerable prosperity, and the failures, and all the economic grades between. There were also Catholics and Protestants. Up to 10 percent of Irish convicts were Protestants, a proportion which rose to 20 percent for some later periods of free assisted migration. And there were discernible differences in skill and English literacy between those Irish-born convicted in England and those sent from Ireland.

A varied picture, but among the Irish convicts the small group of acknowledged political rebels has captured most historical attention, their unusual characteristics tending, in Irish-Australian mythology, to typify the whole. The most prominent rebels were often men of some previous substance, educated, high-principled, and quite often Protestants. Some English politicians (Sir Robert Peel, for instance) believed that this 'educated' 'gentleman' convict was the worst type of criminal: they knew what they were doing and further trouble might be anticipated from them. But the practice of colonial governors was not to treat such men as ordinary convicts: such would have been both insensitive and a waste of desperately needed skills and accomplishments. Some, like James Meehan the surveyor, were absorbed into the government service; others, like Joseph Holt, were employed as farm managers; some, such as Michael Dwyer, had not been convicted and were allowed to become settlers; all were pardoned or emancipated relatively quickly.

Michael Dwyer, 'the Wicklow Chief', had been a prominent leader in the 1798 rebellion. He and a group of companions—Martin Burke, Hugh Byrne, Arthur Devlin and John Mernagh—had surrendered voluntarily in 1803 following the collapse of Robert Emmet's rebellion: not all were 1798 veterans; Devlin was a deserter from the English army who was related to both the Dwyer and Byrne families. Their initial surrender, after five years on the run, had been on their understanding that they would be pardoned and sent to America. Regarded not as convicts, but state prisoners, they were placed in separate unrestricted quarters (the legend has them in chains) on the convict transport *Tellicherry*, sailing from Cork in August 1805. Dwyer was given £200 and his companions £100 by the Irish Chief Secretary: they took the view that they were wronged exiles. Governor King had general distrust of the Irish character, intensified by these men's proven 'turbulent disposition', but their legal situation was such that he felt obliged to treat them as free settlers: he made them land grants of 100 acres each in the Cabramatta area, centred on Warwick Farm. Far from staying together, the Dwyer group tended to go individual ways in the colony, to grow apart and indeed fall out; there was a curious incident in March 1811 when Dwyer, elevated to be constable at Parramatta, arrested Devlin on larceny charges, which were unproven. But to the authorities their good behaviour itself was suspicious: it must mask deep plotting. King could not bring himself to believe that such famous rebels

Michael Dwyer, hero of 1798

could stop rebelling, or that their very presence would not incite trouble among the volatile Irish. Governor Bligh went further. In March 1807 he imprisoned Dwyer and his companions on suspicion of fomenting treason. They were tried, and, to Bligh's chagrin, acquitted. Nevertheless, he banished Dwyer to Norfolk Island and the others to various outposts. It seems quite clear that the treason charges were fabricated by Irish informers who knew that such stories would be instantly believed by colonial authorities in constant fear of the wild Irish, stories whose invention might be used to purchase their own freedom. Soon restored to the colony, and never once fulfilling his rebel reputation, Dwyer died in respectable prosperity in 1826.

From his arrival in 1806, through the century that followed, Dwyer epitomised Irish rebellion in Australia: he personified in the colony the period of archetypal Irish rebellion, 1798–1803. The effects of this were curious indeed. One is conjectural. Documents associated with the Sheedy family in Sydney suggest that James Meehan, former 1798 rebel, turned government surveyor, and Dr Daniel McCallum who had been transported for tending 1798 rebels, were, in 1803, in touch with the revolutionary Society of the United Irishmen in Ireland. If this was in fact so, the government were not aware of it, diverted from all other suspicions by their obsession with the obvious but innocent Dwyer.

The other effect of the focus on Dwyer was more complex and long-term. Historians of the Irish convicts have spent much time and energy estimating the number of Irish political rebels and social protestors; A.G.L. Shaw says one in eight in either category, that is, about 5000; George Rudé says half that number—2250. Seen in one crucial light, the question is indeed academic, as the operative historical image was not a question of precise numbers, but of perceived impression—and the dominant, virtually exclusive, Irish image, from 1798, was created by the rebel element. It was an agreed image, held both by the Irish prisoners (and those Irish who followed them historically) and their gaolers. And its eventual effect was not provocative or unsettling, but the opposite, a pacifying one.

The 1798–1803 rebels were a colonial cynosure: their fellow Irish hero-worshipped them; the authorities feared them and exaggerated their numbers and influence. Governors had a potentially rebellious role marked out for them: their vision of Ireland was of a country seething with violence, its populace maddened by discontents, plots, and popery, in the grip of secret societies with designs and power beyond measure. Given this nebulous landscape of fear, the actual number of proven rebels was irrelevant: all Irish were rebels, an assumption confirmed by a scare in 1800 and the Castle Hill convict rising of 1804. This situation invited not only coercion, but also—particularly from authorities vulnerable and weak, and in a tandem to become familiar in later nineteenth-century Ireland—conciliation, stick and carrot. One way of dealing with the threat the Irish were constantly presumed to present was to repress it, but another way was to buy it off with concessions and compromise.

Both the brutality and the concessions of the convict system reflect the terror of the settlement's authorities: it was a prison, but, much worse, an Irish prison. The English belief was that the Irish were beyond redemption, lawless and ungovernable; their lower orders were depraved and violent. English rule and law in Ireland were partial, fluctuating, arbitrary and inefficient. Many convicts from the rebellion areas had been transported without legal process, or through confusion, malice or mistake. Thus the incendiary potential of the Irish penal situation in Australia seemed enormous and volatile. It was defused by conciliation—specifically, tickets of leave, emancipation, land grants—and by Australian circumstances.

Of first importance were the divisions among political prisoners. The known leaders, such as Holt and Dwyer, were more exiles than prisoners. They were, or were very soon, free in the colony, separate from the lower orders they once led. But above all they were gentlemen, of a class with their gaolers. Transportation to Australia may have been a dreadful sentence for the lowly, but for the gentleman leaders, and even those of middling status, it could serve as a reprieve and an opportunity: the 1798 rebels in Australia were a fairly successful, enterprising lot, featuring some prominent success stories, even among the illiterate.

Why? Because they accepted the government's conciliatory terms, particularly under Macquarie's governorship (1810–1821), which they regarded as benevolent, and a great improvement on the petty tyrannies that preceded it. But even as early as 1802 Michael Hayes was sending back to Ireland for three small firkins of best salt butter (a great delicacy) to give as presents to the Governor and other officials. These rebels took their land grants, conformed and prospered. They adopted a low public profile in response to their seditious reputations and devoted themselves to work, and those good lives noted in Catholic history.

Thus was established a duality vital to the practicalities of Irish behaviour in the colony. Rebels conformed in peace, setting up a marvellous tension between myth and reality which gave the Australian Irish the best of both worlds—the proud and fearsome reputation for rebellion, heroism, and devotion to principles of freedom; and a quiet profitable stake in the new country. The rebel 'chiefs' and 'generals' had done sufficient in Irish rebel history to assure them of automatic dominance of the Australian Irish scene and to ensure that whatever they did locally would be consecrated as a proper and acceptable course. They opted into the Australian colonial enterprise, and their previous revolutionary eminence not only made this conformism the Irish norm, but a posture unchallengeable by the extremism of wild nonentities: the heroes had taken the quiet path.

Why did they choose it? The exiles of 1848 were not to do so. Fundamentally because the 1798 men had been reluctant, some even accidental, rebels in Ireland. They were not dedicated revolutionary ideologues, but conservative middle-class farmers, with a keen eye, as the letters (1799–1825) of Michael Hayes show, for good land, high farm prices, and the extraordinary opportunities offered by free land grants. Hayes, a Wexford participant in the 1798 rebellion, is an excellent illustration of the 'Australianisation' processes at work on 'gentleman' rebels. His letters witness not only to genuine piety and concern for the good of religion, but to a drive towards an almost snobbish respectability which identified at least initially with the liberality and morality of Macquarie. He is conscious of liberal civilising class, has a taste for the refinements of civilisation (he had Latin and Greek), is deferentially disposed towards authority, and is obsessed with personal freedom, rather than any wider form. He is typical too of the rebel group in being gradually embroiled in local society. He begins trading, buying land, incurring obligations and debts, being owed money, establishing contacts, embarking on plans, eventually acquiring a wife and family – all of which, as he wrote home in 1812, conspired against his returning to Ireland. By 1816 Hayes had eight children, hardly revolutionary equipment. In fact, even twelve years after his transportation, he remained a highly repentant rebel; his 'misfortune' had disgraced and gravely disadvantaged his family in Wexford, and this continued to plague him with worry and regret. It did not occur to those who took the heroic view of the 1798 rebels that some at least—perhaps most—saw themselves very differently—with shame; they had acquired the stigma of criminality, and had been banished by their own doing from their land and family to share the company of evil men. They were not heroes but failures who had deserted their families and caused them great distress, and they were determined to make amends and toe the line of respectability in future. Thus Michael Hayes. As to the heroic Michael Dwyer, living off the land of Wicklow for five years, was his surrender a response to the likely effect of a £500 reward on a local community very resentful of his levies? Heroism paid no bills. In Australia the ex-heroes practised and preached contentment. By 1816 Hayes was writing, 'There is room here for some millions [of the Irish tenantry] if they were allowed to emigrate'. There were no rents or tithes. 'What a happiness it would be to the unfortunate Irish tenantry were they here to participate in these blessings.' Yet the heroes remained heroes, then, and for subsequent history. Others had canonised them as heroes, because they needed them to be able to live with 1798 with self-esteem: the celebration of the men of '98 became hallowed rhetoric, inspiring respect among the Irish, dread among others, at no cost.

So, paradoxically, the prominence of the 1798 rebellion in the Irish tradition in Australia ensured that it would not be a rebellious tradition but a pacific one, a process furthered by the discontinuity between that rebellion and those that followed it in Irish history. Seventeen ninety-eight was the last of the primitive Irish rebellions. Its dominance in Australian Irish history tended to insulate that history from the currents of romantic nationalism which pervaded the Irish revolutionary tradition from 1848 onward. For Irish Australia, Irish rebellion meant Michael Dwyer and his like, practical, commonsense, middling farmers who had tilled and were buried in its own soil, not the romantic nationalist literateurs of 1848 and thereafter. The long-term effects of 1798 were to protect Australia from subsequent Irish nationalisms, to dampen their local fires. This subduing process derived not only from its chronological dominance but from its nature. Because of its timing, and links with France, it has been assumed that the 1798 Irish rebellion was in the tradition of the then new and modern popular demand for liberty, equality and fraternity, a radical nationalist demand for freedom. In reality it was an anachronism, a harking back to the desperate and primitive uprisings of seventeenth-century Ireland, riddled with localism, sectarianism, and sheer savagery: essentially it was an outbreak, in various parts of Ireland, with some French assistance, of barbarous rural anarchy. The surge of rural violence in Ireland, peaking in 1798 but continuing on and off into the 1830s—the generator of the 'best' Irish convicts sent to Australia—was denounced and repudiated as shameful, vicious and degrading by those few in Ireland who did have nationalist ideals. What the 1798 rebellion and its immediately prior and subsequent upheavals transported to Australia was not the products of a noble radical nationalism, but in the main, at a popular level, the squalid vestiges of an old peasant world crumbling towards a messy end: rebel Ireland was a backwards-looking pre-modern society in collapse whose primitive fragments were captured and flung out to New South Wales and Van Diemen's Land.

Not surprisingly, for this ancient peasant society was powerful in numbers and energy, and these colonies were vulnerable to internal threat, all this created an atmosphere of terror, and the very consciousness of threat had a remarkably solvent effect on colonial life. One obvious protection was to disperse the Irish as widely as possible—a policy to have important repercussions for Irish Australia. Another was for authority to buy off Irish leadership where it could, grateful for what support it could get, if only passively, against an Irish mob which inspired panic. Without leadership, and lacking a real revolutionary spirit, those lower orders had little cause to revive in Australia their tradition of rebellious rural violence. The myth of 1798 was a powerful stabiliser: the Irish in Australia were sustained, given self-respect and honour in their own estimate, and the oppressors checked, intimidated, and brought to concession, by the reputation of past rebellion elsewhere—although 1804 at Castle Hill was a salutary local reminder. While violence was to cling long to the image of the colonial Irish, and they continued to appear to embody the threat of outrage and disorder, this was increasingly seen, by all involved, as a posture, real enough to breed caution and distrust on one side, pride on the other, but an unlikely basis for action.

Of the 1798 rebels, some returned to Ireland. Joseph Holt, and the Catholic priests, Dixon, O'Neil and Harold are examples. (Harold, dining on the harbour on the evening of his arrival in Sydney in 1800, entertained his Protestant clergyman host with a rendition of 'The Exile of Erin'. Heard by a crowd of Irish on the beach, who shouted 'Encore!', he sang it again.) In his *Memoirs* (1800–14) Holt left a highly individual account of his compulsory sojourn in New South Wales, centred on himself as a loyal Protestant gentleman, above and apart from the affairs of the ordinary Catholic Irish. Others—the great majority—remained to become the most prominent and prosperous Irishmen in Sydney Town: James Meehan, William Davis, James Dempsey, Edward Redmond and Michael Hayes were all '98 veterans. Seventeen ninety-eight veterans, centring around the group of Wicklow rebels, formed such a landholding concentration to the south-west of Sydney as to attract to the district the initial name of Irishtown (now Bankstown). This concentration, from 1809, was apparently contrived by Meehan as government surveyor, and, spreading from the Liverpool to the Illawarra districts, acted as a continuing magnet for further Irish concentration; others were attracted to the vicinity by the prosperity and society of their countrymen, or were employed on their farms. So the '98 men pioneered a socioeconomic path many Irish were to follow—from convict status through emancipation to land acquisition or commercial activity to modest prosperity and social respectability.

Given the nature and opportunities of the early Australian pioneering economy, it is hardly surprising that the Irish should also take the path towards land and livestock. But comprehension of their rural role may be threatened by the influence of images generated elsewhere—by their preponderance in the urban ghettoes of America and England (their major role in Canadian farming being hitherto overlooked) suggesting a role as essentially city immigrants; and the conflicting but derogatory connotations of the popular concept of 'peasant'. Australia's Irish immigrants—bond and free—came from all levels of a stratified Irish rural world, not necessarily from its lower echelons. Recent studies of pre-Famine Ireland, from whence Australia's early Irish population derived, show considerable variants in social status and economic activity, and complex internal relations between various levels of landlord and tenant, employer and employee. A simple 'landlord-peasant' division ignores the realities: the land occupiers fell into four obvious divisions—farmers, smallholders, cottiers and labourers, and farm servants, with vast economic and social gulfs *within* as well as between these categories, dependent on whether land was rented or owned, how large or prosperous, regional factors and so on. Such gradations and subtleties of a highly stratified rural society were not left behind in Ireland, though they were invisible, or largely so, to outsiders in Australia: the convict system and later contemptuous estimation lumped the 'non-gentleman' Irish into what Samuel Marsden dismissed as 'the lowest Class of the Irish Nation'. But these vital social distinctions and social hierarchies remained and operated in the knowledge and consciousness of the Irish themselves. It can be assumed that Michael Dwyer expected to be, and was, called 'Mister' by his Irish farm servants, though that was not a title he would have been accorded by colonial officials. The Irish farming concentrations which grew up in south-western New South Wales from Irish convict land grants were heavily stratified, and evidence suggests that they significantly replicated, at least initially and to some extent, the socioeconomic divisions and hierarchies of the old Irish rural world. Some of that evidence is in durable stone: the graveyard at the centre of Edward Ryan's rural empire at Galong is an assemblage of multiple relationships, superiors and inferiors, of gradations and subordinations both stark and subtle, carved out in judgements of height, substance, quality of stone, ornamentation, placement. From Ned Ryan as king, with plinth and pinnacle, towering over all, the procession descends, through lesser relations, down to the simple slab of the retainer, the loyal farm labourer. There are not only internal hierarchies, but separate groupings. All the Ryans crowd together in the company of the dead. Then, at a little distance, so do the Whelans; a distinct family, yet related. And so on: the little community that once was, their status symbolised in stone.

These are also monuments of another sort, for another purpose: they affirm the dignity of triumph over the stigma of penal servitude. Ned Ryan was a free man: he had a Certificate of Freedom (dated 29 June 1830) and his own monument (dated 26 February 1871) to prove it. His opulent grave was no stone fist shaken against the last tyrant, death, but a proclamation of victory over those lesser but substantial foes—imprisonment, poverty, drought, flood, and the ordinary mistakes of man. What is to be made of this extraordinary collection of grandiose Irish Australian dolmen, remote and shimmering in the heat-hazed middle of a bleached Australian nowhere? It is a peasant Irish affirmation that all flesh is not grass, but that kings who were once prisoners may command legends with their ruins, and with depositions written on the land.

Few were that ambitious. The ordinary pre-Famine Irish 'peasant', be he farmer or landless labourer back home, had vacated his special place in that world, but he brought from it general attitudes and values important to the new. Until perhaps the 1850s, the Irish emigrating classes (convict or free) were not the Irish nationalist classes. The world of the Irish rural immigrant is not one of radical nationalism. The Irish peasant had little direct contact with the central government before the 1820s and 1830s—a situation probably with implications for the way in which the Irish viewed the state in Australia; their Irish experience was too often that of weak and intermittent government of which they always felt the coercive edge. Their key disposition was conservatism: in Ireland they had sought to preserve an old order against new and improving landlords, whom they saw as destroying the traditional world. Their main worries were land and rents, and the tithes of the Anglican church. These land matters were by far the greatest cause of disturbance—and thus of the crimes that led to transportation.

The Irish land situation explains much Irish-Australian history. Irish peasants lived in dread that if they lost their land they would be starving wanderers through their world; threats to their occupancy turned them frantic and wild—'the mind gets changed', observed a Tipperary shopkeeper in the 1830s. Any notion that the Irish peasant lived in tranquil, humdrum, even-tempered poverty, is gravely astray. Multiple demands and threats daily menaced their tenure and subsistence. Many lived on a knife-edge of tension, prey to extreme psychological pressures.

Understood thus, the reactions of such people to Australian conditions are not surprising. Some basked in a kind of lyrical daze at their good fortune—access to land, which they were accustomed to see as the key to security and happiness, and freedom from the appalling weight of worry: Australia could liberate them from the oppression of the basic facts of Irish peasant life. Their whole personalities sighed with patent relief, and many lapsed irresponsibly into the available comforts, one of which was wage employment. In Ireland most farm work was done by unpaid relatives, and temporary labour often paid in kind or by return services—wages, particularly regular and adequate wages, were a rarity in Ireland. Australia offered a wonderful contrast—by comparison, ready, constant, lucrative wage labour.

This situation of choice revealed an important hidden characteristic of the ordinary Irish. The ownership of land was not always their first priority, when they could be carefree travelling men, or labourers without responsibility. This was a feature of Irish-Australian life from the beginning: some of the Irish were labourers not—or not only—from unskilled necessity, but from preference of lifestyle. To some observers, this seemed incomprehensible, sheer laziness or irresponsibility. It was in fact a reflex of the tensions of the Irish rural economy. Robert Dunne, Archbishop of Brisbane in the 1880s and 1890s, was a rural dreamer with a vision of an Irish Catholic farming community in Queensland of prosperous respectable settlers. His efforts to encourage the realisation of this Arcadia foundered on the resistant fact that the Irish immigrant ideal was not a farm, but rather 'a job on the railway, a beat as a policeman, or a billet under Government'. In the earlier years of the century, such luxuries of employment choice lay far ahead—and besides, free land grants, good land, a booming rural economy were attractive enough. But the later realities soon asserted themselves. A farm was a first priority in Ireland because there it offered security, status, some substance. And for the lower orders it was such a remote impossible ideal as to be the stuff of dreams. Certainly some, indeed many, saw and took the chance Australia offered to realise that ambition; yet as a realisable Australian goal, the reality of a farm promised worry, hard work, debt, and the prospect of defeat by drought, flood, or inexperience; a return to the realm of tensions and responsibilities from which the migrant, compulsory or free, had just escaped by leaving Ireland, and from which he could continue to escape by taking the readily available, well-paid, footloose wage labour available in the colonies. The wonder is that so many tried farming, not that they gravitated to the daily mindlessness of hard labour.

The rural scene left behind in Ireland, with its anarchy, violence, and appalling stress, is also a factor in explaining what was from the beginning of settlement a considerable Irish overrepresentation in the statistics for crime, drunkenness and insanity. The high proportion of Irish among Australian society's casualties has usually been attributed to the trauma of migration (or transportation) and to their lower socioeconomic position. It is more likely a legacy of the world from which they came, a world which maimed some of them for life. It would have been impossible for all personalities to have survived untouched the harsh pressures of that frantic, troubled countryside. Many must have been damaged, and the less resilient set to crumble and disintegrate.

Again, what is remarkable is their overall success in the early colony. The 1828 census of New South Wales, when the population was under 40 000, makes this clear. The Catholic population was about a quarter of this—10 000—of whom nearly 20 percent were colonial-born, thus giving an Irish-born section of about 8000. Of these, about a third were convicts. Of the 5000 Irish who were then free, only one in ten had come to the colony free: the rest were emancipated convicts. And they were a relatively prosperous lot. Up to a quarter of free Irishmen in the colony held land or livestock or both. Some were among the leading landholders or flock masters in their districts. Still others were well established in the middling areas of commerce. The 1828 census substantially qualifies the traditional historical depiction of the early Australian Irish as poverty-stricken. If few were wealthy, many were reasonably affluent, comfortable, a conclusion also reflected in the middling but numerous donations to St Mary's Catholic Chapel. To some extent, the success stories replicated gradations in the Irish world left behind: those who came with experience of initiative and enterprise tended to make best use of new opportunities. But this was far from an invariable rule, and many Irish nobodies had risen to be at least modest Australian somebodies. The 1828 census highlights a feature of colonial society that was to be the basis of relatively easy Irish assimilation in Australia: however hostile the environment, however disadvantaged their initial position, however resistant the Anglo-Saxon Protestant majority, it was still possible for the Irish to make their way up in the Australian world.

Circumstances in early New South Wales were peculiarly advantageous to this. The Irish were a sufficiently large section of the initial population, present from the beginning, and favoured by an economy that demanded their labour and an administration conscious of their threat, to claim a role as a founding people. Their situation in the other early Australian colony, Tasmania, was markedly different. Over a third of New South Wales convicts were Irish, but only a fifth of Tasmania's—and most of these came later, after 1840 when transportation ceased to New South Wales; in the decisive period of early settlement, the Irish-born element was probably less than 10 percent. Further, Tasmania's Irish convicts of the 1840s tended to be, in a sense, Famine victims; not hardened criminals, but those forced into crime through destitution. Perhaps it was the enervation of the Famine, perhaps lack of the energy and enterprise so often rewarded by penal servitude at this time; more likely it was because the founding opportunities had been taken, but by mid-century, in contrast to New South Wales, very few Tasmanian Irish had obtained land or succeeded in business. Richard Dry, whose son Sir Richard was to become premier of Tasmania 1866–69, was exceptional in arriving early (1807), being Anglican, having a head for business, and achieving wealth and prominence. The ordinary and Catholic Irish tended to conform strongly to the cliché stereotype, congregating in the major towns, mostly unskilled labourers, and almost totally excluded from the social or economic establishment.

Irish success in New South Wales was achieved in the face of considerable suspicion and hostility. This derived from two main sources—old attitudes and prejudices brought out from the British Isles, and the simple fact that New South Wales was a convict colony. So far as the governors and local administration were concerned, the chief factor governing their attitudes towards the Irish seems not so much racial or religious prejudice as fear of violence and sedition. In the words of Governor Hunter to the Duke of Portland in January 1798, 'if so large a proportion of these lawless and turbulent people, the Irish convicts, are sent into this country, it will scarcely be possible to maintain the order so highly essential to our well-being'. It was a worrying fact that there was a large number of Irish among the Nore and Spithead mutineers of 1797, a situation which not only raised questions about the loyalty of Britain's armed forces but located military experience within the ranks of the convicts. The fear that the tiny garrison of the prison colony might be overwhelmed by an Irish uprising appears very early in the history of New South Wales, certainly before 1798. The rebellion of that year, and those transported because of it, heightened such fears to the level of near hysteria. They were confirmed by the reputation Irish convicts speedily acquired within the settlement for being insolent, turbulent, unco-operative, and for ever conspiring and attempting to escape. The image of the Irish as fools, 'China travellers', was not so much supplanted as massively supplemented and overlaid by the belief that they were all dangerous rebels: the idiot and simpleton took on a terrifying aspect.

This belief seemed vindicated by the discovery in 1800 of what was taken to be United Irish plotting. A severe scare ensued. Then, in March 1804, a convict rebellion occurred at Castle Hill, on the outskirts of Sydney, panicking the settlement. Led by the Irishmen Philip Cunningham and William Johnston, over 300 men assembled to march on Sydney. They were outwitted and routed by the military, and the rebellion quickly and bloodily repressed.

Although the rebellion involved English as well as Irish convicts, it was both officially and popularly given an Irish identity. This is true enough to its general character, but the particulars of the affair are obscure and the numerous accounts contradictory. Were, as alleged, Joseph Holt and Father Dixon involved in the plotting? Holt, in dissociating himself from it said, 'The lower people, convicts and other, both English and Irish ... conceived an opinion that they could overpower the army, possess themselves of the settlement, and make their escape from it ...'. Certainly some of the Irish trusted 'General' Holt, if not with their plans, with their general intentions. His name and rebel reputation were used. According to him, he warned the plotters against any such action, and against informers, the bane of all Irish plots. But despite his denials of complicity he was exiled to Norfolk Island. Conclusive in his mind of his lack of involvement was his claim that had he led the rebellion he would have 'made short work of it', an hour's work in his estimate to capture 'magazine, army and all ...'.

What did these Irish convict rebels want? Apparently not revenge, for they killed virtually no one, or political objectives, but what they shouted for: 'Death or Liberty' and (a contemporary account adds, with plaintive practicality) 'a ship to take them Home'. Escape. Home—and all that those things meant to the mind and heart. For the leaders were, as R. W. Connell remarks, 'not the bottom dogs of the convict system, but ... men of some experience and responsibility, possibly some education ... men, in short, on whom the cruelties incidental to transportation, degradation, uprooting, and separation from families, might have weighed more heavily than the direct burdens of forced labour'. These rebels were of a different caste from those of their fellow countrymen who saw transportation as a boon. Death or Liberty was a choice of their own contrivance. Some of them were seven-year men who could have worked out the remainder of their sentences. Cunningham was a skilled workman acting as overseer of stonemasons; he had a house of his own, as had other leaders of the rising. They had something real to lose; why throw it—and life—away? Theirs was not the rebellion of crushed desperation, but of sentiment and hope, forlorn maybe; an affirmation of spirit that, in less spectacular forms, continued to echo down the lower corridors of Australian history: death or liberty was an alternative which was to be either seriously and sympathetically understood—or, more usually, dismissed by observers as plain silly. What drove the Irish was not only ideologies and dreams, but frustrations, sickness of heart, and impulses of affront: in a word, pride, which in the circumstances of convictism—not very different in style from the looser yoke permanently affixed by England to Ireland—expressed itself in grim determination not to be broken. The seventeenth-century Irish poet has its flavour and edge:

> May we never taste of death nor quit this vale of tears
> Until we see the Englishry go begging down the years
> Packs on their backs to earn a penny pay
> In little leaking boots, as we went in our day.

This convict Irishry would have known its poets, and the sentiments of one of their own rural number, the itinerant farm labourer Eoghan Rua Ó Súilleabháin (1748–84), would have echoed in New South Wales.

> Tis not the poverty I most detest
> Nor being down forever
> But the insult that follows it
> Which no leeches can cure.

Such poets, in an essentially oral tradition, moved at the bottom of Irish rural society, in a hidden Ireland where their audience was cultured in the literature of pride and deprivation: it was a world whose sounds were unintelligible to its rulers, until they burst out in the clamour of violence. To this was added a special Australian dimension reflected in that afterthought—'and a ship to take them home'. There was an aspect of Irish violence, and some Irish dispositions generally, that rebelled against the very fact of Australia. They had been banished (by their own will, in later emigrations) to this distant hell, vacant, strange and pitiless. True, they might do well there, be comfortable in the flesh, but it was not Ireland, not home, not nearly sufficient.

All this was too far below the surface for colonial perception, which had neither inclination nor aptitude for fanciful speculation. The plain fact was that the Irish convicts had acquired an image which virtually monopolised turbulent tendencies and rebellious intentions. Anything could be believed, even expected of them. Their 1802 plot included the idea of putting English convicts in front of the rebel phalanx, so that they would be compelled to fight, or be put to death by the Irish behind them—a plan deemed by officialdom to be truly and contemptibly Irish. The discovery of an illicit still was taken officially as evidence that the Irish sought to contrive 'every moral and political evil'—as if the Irish were not likely to consume its production entirely themselves. By 1804 an enduring theme of Australian history had been very firmly established—suspicion of the loyalty of the Irish.

But what had they, in those early colonial days, to be loyal to? Their Catholic religion was proscribed by law, any assembly by them was forbidden, and their very existence seen as a threat to civilisation. In 1807, the Reverend Samuel Marsden, Anglican chaplain in New South Wales, contended that 'if the catholic religion was ever allowed to be celebrated by authority . . . the colony would be lost to the British empire in less than one year'. Marsden reasoned thus:

> The number of catholic convicts is very great in the settlement; and these in general composed of the lowest class of the Irish nation, who are the most wild, ignorant and savage race . . . men that have been familiar with robberies murders and every horrid crime from their infancy . . . governed entirely by the impulse of passion and always alive to rebellion and mischief they are very dangerous members of society . . . They are extremely superstitious artful and treacherous . . . They have no true concern whatever for any religion nor fear of the Supreme Being: but are fond of riot drunkenness and cabals; and was the catholic religion tolerated they would assemble together from every quarter not so much from a desire of celebrating mass, as to recite the miseries and injustice of their punishment, the hardships they suffer, and to enflame one another's minds with some wild scheme of revenge.

Marsden's proposed remedy to the Irish threat was simple: prohibit Catholicism and impose Protestantism, so producing industry, prosperity and peace. This remedy was not adopted. On the contrary, the arrival of official Catholic chaplains, Fathers Therry and Conolly, from 1820 begins an increasing official tolerance of the religion of the Irish. But the judgements and attitudes expressed so candidly by Marsden were long to remain deeply ingrained in the Australian community.

They held elements of truth. It could hardly be expected that the Irish convicts should not be depraved and brutalised with the rest, and that their Catholicism, without priests for thirty years and with very few for another twenty, should not be in many cases merely nominal—or in the worse cases, hideously twisted into blasphemous cursing of religion, its works, ministers, and God. Before 1820, Catholicism survived as a devotional system and moral code, only among the best of the men of '98, practised probably by less than a hundred persons. They saw themselves as a tiny island barely surfaced in a sea of vice. Writing home in 1802, Michael Hayes was vehement in his opposition to his sister's proposal to join him. Of 1100 women in the colony he was unable to count twenty virtuous: all manner of lewdness, bigamy, shameless behaviour and crime flourished among them. The picture of the '98 men as the only vestige of religion and decency is confirmed by Father Philip Conolly on his arrival in 1820. He was eloquent on the contagious depravity of the environment and particularly on the effects of the tyranny of sexual distance. Writing on 22 August 1822 to Bishop Poynter in London he reported:

> Bigamy has been very frequent here: it continues so still. With few exceptions, to be found, almost universally amongst those who have been transported for the Irish rebellion, there were hardly any who did not, as soon as they obtained any degree of freedom, form new connections: some got married in the Protestant Church—others lived together without any form of marriage; having husbands or wives in England or Ireland made little exception.

Conolly found brazen open bigamists, and those who tried to conceal former marriages; some ignored such discovery, others circumvented his opposition. As to the progeny of such unions, he was pleasantly surprised: he found the local-born children 'smart and intelligent', but with 'a certain degree of unusual levity and wildness about them', which he (and others) attributed to their associating with the Aborigines. And Father Conolly, like generations of priests to follow him, and with pre-echoes of *Around The Boree Log* found virtue and value best preserved in the seclusion of the interior country, well away from the corruption of the towns. As to his own reception in this society, he found that the worst possessed the most, and that a general disposition was to say that the priest was money-grubbing instead of preaching the Gospel. He could not bring himself to seek aid from such a people—they repelled and revolted him with their cynicism, hardness and lack of deference.

All this is scarcely surprising, and the apathy, indifference and dereliction characteristic of the great majority of the first Irish Catholics was to persist as a feature of that community until the 1860s at least. For the brutal fact was that most of the Irish Catholic convicts in Australia were real criminals, with all that meant in relation to the rejection of religion and moral codes. The piety and good moral conduct of the tiny fragment of '98 men was no doubt genuine, but it was also an affirmation of distinction from the majority criminal classes, a public denial of depravity, a claim to respectability, and an implicit assertion of the injustice of their sentences, all of which were necessary to their self-esteem. Small wonder too that this pious fragment swiftly grew in subsequent historical imagination to blot out and exclude the darker reality and come to dominate, as founding fathers, the received version of the Irish Catholic past.

Like all myths it has its truth: the early New South Wales church was built around and on this core by its first priest, the aggressive Irishman John Joseph Therry who arrived, with Father Conolly, in 1820. But the fact that Therry's construct grew rapidly beyond this respectable nucleus to draw in and become relevant to the irreligious and disreputable residue of Irish criminality owes much to his personal style and to his constant politicising of religious issues: Therry made Catholicism a crusade against the status quo, a cause in which many aggrieved Irish were delighted to enlist—while incidentally resuming the practice of religion. It was not a deliberate ploy on Therry's part (it would have been brilliant had it been conscious policy) but its effect was to link Catholicism with the sociopolitical protests and sense of exclusion and grievance of the Irish lower orders, a marriage which was both to endure long and benefit both parties. In the early 1820s the interreligious atmosphere was harmonious, reflecting the small size and quiet discreet ways of the active Irish Catholic group—as well as the general deferential and co-operative temper of Catholicism in the British dominions before the various bars and disabilities applying to Catholics were removed in the Emancipation Act of 1829. However, as the impatient (indeed belligerent) Therry pursued his missionary work energetically, he moved into a constant state of abrasion with authority and the colonial establishment. By the late 1820s he was well known as a friend of the most prominent critics of the administration—the colony's democratic politicians—and was something of a symbol of opposition to authority. In the process he split the Catholic community into pro- and anti-Therry factions, acquiring among the majority (the lower orders, not the respectable) an immense popular following and a reputation for himself as a saint—and, in the process, bringing many back into some semblance of the practice of religion: it is difficult to believe that any antiseptic urging of the benefits of religion would have succeeded, given the raw intractable material on which Therry had to work, without the presence of this 'political' dimension. So Therry became the venerated leader of an Irish Catholic tribe, valued both for his challenges to the administration and for his ministry. Irish Catholicism therefore became identified with the challenge to a status quo composed of English social conservatism and the Anglican religion; its relations with authority declined accordingly. In Tasmania, Conolly's stance was more respectable and conformist, less entangled with a convict and emancipist class he saw as depraved, needing stern and remote spiritual treatment: he was highly critical of the 'firebrand' Therry, particularly of his efforts to get his people to give him money and cattle. Conolly was above such things. But Therry talked the language of his people—which was money and cattle—and they understood him. And they also understood, and shared, his instinctive confrontationist reaction when coping with the English establishment—stand up and fight. This Catholic truculence and intransigence set the stage for sectarian conflict, which was becoming evident by the late 1830s. At first, Catholic agitation was for religious causes—freedom and equality in worship, and the defence of Catholic doctrines. But by the time of the laying of the foundation stone of Sydney's second Catholic church, St Patrick's, Church Hill, in August 1840, Catholic assertiveness had taken on an Irish nationalist aspect.

Father John Joseph Therry in the 1830s

That aspect already existed in the colony in a mild and convivial form in the celebration of St Patrick's Day—national rather than nationalist, the one social expression of Irishness tolerated in the penal colony. The first report of festivities was in 1795 when David Collins remarked in his journal: 'On the 17th St Patrick found many votaries in the settlement . . . libations to the saint were so plentifully poured that at night the cells were full of prisoners.' Joseph Holt, writing of his Australian farm in 1803, made an aside along similar lines, explaining 'my usual time to commence to sow was the first Monday after St Patrick's Day: it requiring a few days to get my men sober'. This explanatory addendum suggests, with Collins, that the day was merely an excuse for quasi-tribal drinking and riotous behaviour. As such it had its uses as a safety valve and occasion for unwinding in a peculiar and primitive settlement, and since it was already established as a community occasion, and would profit by some civilising, it was taken up by Governor Macquarie in 1810: he recognised the day by providing entertainment for government artificers and labourers. St Patrick's Day was acceptable to the colony's authorities probably because its connotations were then mild, ecumenical, and subordinate to the United Kingdom. It was not a separatist or religious day and Macquarie's blessing was to ensure that it would not become so: Irish Protestant and Catholic might join with all comers in common and convivial loyal celebration. And such was to continue into the 1840s, with dignified celebrations at the highest levels of colonial society. The first formal dinner appears to be that of 1827, with D'Arcy Wentworth and Dr Douglas as committee members and Chief Justice Forbes as honoured guest. The 1832 celebration, organised by the Sons of St Patrick, with Roger Therry prominent, invited the Governor, and a hundred gentlemen attended. Similar elegance and national ecumenism prevailed in 1835, but no dinner was held in 1836, because by then Therry had made himself politically unpopular, as had Governor Bourke, as composing, in the eyes of establishment conservatism, an Irish faction identified with mob rule and the interests of emancipated convicts. Thereafter the colony's conservatives went rapidly sour on Ireland and all things Irish. The mere word began to trigger off hostility. Said the *Herald* in July 1836: 'Being Englishmen, we do not like the name Irish system of education . . .'—the type of reaction that made Bourke's plans to use Irish educational models instantly contentious without reference to their content. But up to that time Ireland and St Patrick's Day had united, not divided the upper echelons of colonial society. In the same spirit, Melbourne's first St Patrick's Society of Australia Felix was founded in 1842 as a non-denominational and non-political association of Irish 'gentlemen' or those who aspired so to be.

But the evidence suggests that the lower levels of Irish Catholic society in the colony saw the day differently, cramming into the official tolerance of festivities on this one day all they could of the traditional Irish folk occasion, the village 'pattern'. In country areas, as Holt indicates, it was extended into a protracted bout of the kind of pre-industrial idleness and merrymaking—and drinking—that the Church in Ireland was then denouncing. It was reported to Father Therry from Bathurst on 27 March 1833: 'They have been keeping St Patrick's Day since the 12th inst. and not ended it yet.' By the 1840s the term 'keeping up St Patrick' was a euphemism for getting blind drunk, a pursuit which had no necessary national boundaries on the saint's day, but which did lead to distinctive forms of violence. What the Melbourne *Austral Light* termed in 1908, 'the spirit of Donnybrook Fair, "who meets with a friend and for love knocks him down"' can be found exactly implemented on St Patrick's eve in Sydney in 1834: Terence Maloney spent three hours in the stocks for breaking the heads of about half a score of His Majesty's Hibernian subjects 'just for love'. This sounds a relatively mild and benevolent form of the faction fighting between families and regional groups which occasionally took vicious and deadly forms in Ireland (and, for example, common in Canada) but was not noted in Australia. Irish reference can be found in the language of Australian street violence—later, 'hooligan' but in the 1830s 'three year olds' as a term for the three-pound stones used by currency lads in fights with sailors—but in the early colony remarkable community tolerance seems to have been extended to the more picturesque and vigorous forms of Irish low-life behaviour. Perhaps it was colour in a dull world. Perhaps the reporters were Irish. Perhaps they had been inured to Irish eccentricities by incidents such as that of Sir Henry Brown Hayes' importation in 1803 of 500 tons of snake-repellent turf from his beloved Ireland with which to surround his Vaucluse House: only genuine Irish convicts were allowed to dig the soil in. And certainly they reacted well to the stage Irishman: Sydney's Theatre Royal opened in 1833 with the popular farce 'The Irishman in London'. Whatever the reason, in early Sydney, Irish drinking, fighting for fun, and noisy carousing, seems to have been regarded as an expected and whimsically tolerated aspect of the St Patrick's Day scene. Indeed, marked improvement in such conduct seems to have been noted with a tinge of regret: Irish antics were a source of diversion and entertainment Australia-wide. So the South Australian *Register* noted of St Patrick's Day 1862: 'Pat in Adelaide seldom breaks the law or a friend's head; he has lost half his fun, but has doubled his industry.'

It was among the Irish themselves that St Patrick's Day was a source of concern and division. Some shared the concern of the *Australasian Chronicle*, Australia's first Irish Catholic newspaper, which, on St Patrick's Day, 1840, looked in vain 'for a proof that Irishmen have not forgot their country, save in tavern and taproom'. At the same time, simmering beneath the Irish surface, looking for an outlet, were Irish energies that had forgotten nothing. Some had also learnt nothing; but most applied their sense of grievance to the Australian rather than the Irish situation. In August 1840 they got their chance to make their point: they would be prisoners no longer.

Their opportunity occurred in this way. The colony's English Benedictine bishop, John Bede Polding, who had arrived in 1835, and his vicar-general, Dr William Ullathorne, were strenuously opposed to the non-denominational education system proposed by the Governor, Sir George Gipps. When he put to them that he doubted they had significant support, they decided upon a public demonstration, choosing the laying of the foundation stone of St Patrick's Church as the occasion. The site had been donated by William Davis, a veteran of 1798 who had become a wealthy man, and was distant from the official quarter of town which included St Mary's: for these and other reasons (the Irish priest John McEncroe was to be parish priest, whereas St Mary's was the centre of the English Benedictines) St Patrick's was a symbol of emergent Irishness. And the laying of its foundation brought to public view the basic realities of the Catholic situation in Australia. By the late 1830s a Whig–Catholic–Irish connection existed. Irish Catholics, under English Benedictine leadership, were claiming and asserting religious equality against Anglican dominance. At the same time, Irish Catholics who were emancipated convicts were joining the 'democratic' popular movement which sought to break the monopoly of political social and economic power enjoyed by the colonial establishment. At first these Catholic pressures had no specifically Irish content; indeed they were matters of principle shared with the other non-Anglican denominations, notably Presbyterians. But Catholic claims to equality were of their nature (in that they were claims with civil implications that had to be urged and defended in the public arena) tantamount to political demands made in the face of powerful established interests and prejudiced resistance. However reasonably and moderately these claims might be urged by Catholicism's articulate (and English) leadership, their ultimate backing was the Catholic body and that was predominantly Irish. Any action which enlisted the energies of that body would have to take the Irish with the Catholic: given the tendency of confrontation situations to reduce themselves to the basic simplicities of power—us versus them—it must engage the bitter resentment, latent aggression, and quasi-tribal unity of the Irish proletariat.

It is appropriate to note here a curious consequence of the English caste, personnel and authority of the early Australian Catholic church. In Ireland itself the old pre-Christian Irish culture was to an extent sustained and continued by the variety of Catholicism with which it had long lived and accommodated. In Australia, English rule in religion meant that the religious was separated from the traditional elements of Irish culture, leaving the traditional to atrophy in a way no purely Irish church establishment could have contrived: the death of the old Irish world had the effect of strengthening the new Irish religion—deprived of their dual cultural allegiance to pagan and Christian worlds, the

Australian Irish took up their religion with a zeal that was proprietorial and exclusive.

Before the projected St Patrick's Church demonstration in August 1840, as Ullathorne wrote, 'national distinctions had been instinctively avoided in the colony; all prided themselves on being Australians'. Now 'a warm national feeling' appeared among the Irish Catholics, who resolved to make the ceremony a national demonstration, with green banners and scarves and other Irish emblems. The government was alarmed, fearing an Orange counter-demonstration and violence. Ullathorne persuaded the organisers to abandon the Irish emblems, but the procession was the largest and by far the most impressive seen in Australia up to that time—bands, 300 girls in white, thousands of marching Catholics. The emblems may have been put aside, but the Irish were on the march in Australia. They were not to stop for nearly a century.

A sketch of Church Hill in the 1840s, St Patrick's on the right

But their marching was not all together, or in the one direction. St Patrick's Day 1841 saw the first formal celebration of that day, a procession which ended with High Mass, then dinner in the evening for a hundred gentlemen. Its purpose was not aggressive, or to protest, but on the contrary, to demonstrate the respectability, loyalty and community spirit of affluent Irish emancipists, both Protestant and Catholic: the same impulse in Melbourne, among those of non-convict background, led the following year to the formation of a St Patrick's Society. In Sydney in 1841 the stimulus and control were clerical, centring on Father Francis Murphy, then vicar-general, later Bishop of Adelaide. Murphy proposed the first toast at the dinner—to the Queen, in words which went far beyond any polite formality: 'As Irishmen we owe her a special debt of gratitude, which we can never repay, for the kindness and justice with which she has treated a long suffering and persecuted people (cheers).' Though Daniel O'Connell, The Liberator, then at the height of his Irish power, received later mention, the occasion was innocent of anything resembling Irish nationalism or indeed grievance: for these Irish ex-convict gentlemen in distant New South Wales everything Irish and about Ireland was lovely.

The St Patrick's Day dinner in Sydney 1841 sets out clearly some major themes in the history of the Irish in Australia. First is the constant effort of the Irish clergy to mobilise and control the Irish, and Irish nationalism, for their own religious purposes—on this occasion the dinner was in relation to fund-raising to build St Patrick's Church. Second is the assertion of pride in national origins and identity, allied with the quest among the prosperous Irish for respectability and social acceptance. This alliance was to prove very difficult to maintain, and the wealthy Australian Irish were often confronted in the years to follow with the need to choose between Irish causes and community acceptance. In 1841 two major influences were at work in forming the dispositions of successful Irish ex-prisoners. One was the traditional Irish Catholic stance. Father Murphy was essentially a pre-Emancipation Irishman, that is, brought up in an Irish atmosphere which favoured quietude and deference to British authority. This was also the environment shared by many of the transportees, now emancipists; their immediate Catholic inclination was to conform, be good citizens. And the same kind of influence was generated by their experience of the penal system. These rebels—or criminals—had paid an awesome price for their transgressions, but they had contrived to build success from that disaster and shame. It is a romantic illusion to think of transportation as a recipe for producing stalwart permanent rebels; it was an experience more likely to produce, in emancipists, determination to put it, and the behaviour which had led to it, behind them. With complications. Some wealthy Irish emancipists demonstrated early, in matters of 'political', division, that principles or ideology meant little or nothing to them; they put economic interest or political convenience first, siding in matters of extension of the franchise with exclusives against the democracy as suited their own position. Simply, many Irish acted, thought, voted, in terms of local self-interest or personal involvement: Irish (or Catholic) loyalties came a very distant second. Many of this first Irish emancipist generation were of this kind, semi-literate, with no understanding of principle, contradictory, factional, selfish, unpredictable, and Irish in no sense other than a primitive loyalty to tribe of origin. And so it was to continue with many Irish thereafter—Irish when it suited them, if ever.

But another theme obtrudes in relation to the 1841 St Patrick's Day dinner: that reaction of criticism and rejection in Australian society which provided a constant goad and pressure to push the most reluctant Irishman back into the Irish camp. The Irish diners and their supporters were affronted and enraged when the *Sydney Morning Herald* went out of its way to insist that those attending the dinner were not 'gentlemen' as they claimed, but 'respectable citizen-artizans'. This was simply another, indeed mild, shot in the campaign to keep the Irish in their place; the generation of an atmosphere and reputation which had, by the 1830s, even percolated into the value judgements of the Aboriginal population. English tutelage had been sufficiently precise and powerful on the point of the general deficiency of all things Irish as to cause Rev. Gunther, Anglican missionary, to note in his diary on 30 December 1837: 'our Natives commonly attach some idea of inferiority to what is Irish & to Ir[e]land', the occasion of his observation being the efforts of tribal elders to prejudice Aborigines against wearing cloaks made from government blankets by telling them that they were 'Irish cloaks'.

All these were serious matters, and themes for the future, but so was a theme less solemn but no less continuous and powerful. A major element in the life of Irish societies was their capacity to provide entertainment—in the widest social sense—for their members: meetings could be immensely enjoyable and diverting occasions, as well as providing the opportunity to attend to business. A reminiscence by Andrew Byrne of the Sydney St Patrick's Society in the 1840s captures some of this magic effervescence: 'I can well remember the Archdeacon [McEncroe] standing on his platform with the busts . . . of O'Connell and Emmet on each side of him, and a banner with the harp behind him, telling side-splitting stories and eliciting every particle of fun from those around them . . .' The promise of fun in a dull world was a significant factor in the attractive power of Irish societies, but this did not insulate them from division and criticism.

Scorned by the establishment to which they aspired above, the 1841 St Patrick's Day diners also came under criticism from below as renegades and toadies, traitors to the cause of dear old Ireland. An enduring division was revealed between wealthier and conservative Irish elements that wished to blend harmoniously with their Australian environment, and the Irish working classes, often truculent, radical, aggrieved with their lot, resentful of barriers and exclusions, prone to see Irish national causes as deeply symbolic and expressive of their own sense of local oppression. In 1843 there were two simultaneous St Patrick's Day dinners in Sydney, one for the top of the Irish Australian social pyramid, the other for those less well placed.

This tension, often amounting to a division but seldom to a gulf, continued to exist among the Irish in Australia. In its earliest phase the emancipists, the transportees, tended to become the conformists, the integrators; while the free immigrants, increasing through the 1830s, coming from O'Connell's emancipated Ireland, tended to be the ultra-Irish. However it did not become structurally established, for its components changed, both with immigration and the continued upward mobility of the lower elements. Transportation of convicts to New South Wales ended in 1840, to Tasmania in 1853. Up to 1840, almost all the convicts from Ireland had been sent to New South Wales, with the result noted in 1837 by that hostile observer, Presbyterian minister J.D. Lang, that no less than a third of the colony's population were Irish Catholics, nearly all of whom were convicts or emancipated convicts, or, he might have added, their children; in 1840 W.A. Duncan, the Scots Catholic who edited the *Australasian Chronicle*, claimed that more than half the white inhabitants of the colony were Irish, either by birth or descent.

Archdeacon McEncroe

Then, in the 1840s came an acceleration of Irish free migration, a flood by the 1850s and 1860s. This virtually submerged the tiny group of established Irish transportees who sought the community's regard as gentlemen, and overwhelmed the conformist tone that had come to dominate the early Irish: aggressive confrontation, never dead, revived again as the favoured stance. But the tension remained, the pull to conform working against the impulse to protest. The next, very famous, batch of Irish prisoners cut across all the local Australian Irish structures in such a way as to render their brief presence virtually irrelevant: they were the big names of the 1848 Irish rising, real 'gentlemen', intellectuals, romantics, revolutionaries who had fallen out with Irish Australia's hero, O'Connell because of their extremism. Obviously they must be heroes, but beyond that, Irish Australia remained bewildered and detached in the face of the men of '48.

It was an attitude reciprocated. In 1849 the leaders of the Young Ireland rising of the previous year were transported as gentleman prisoners to Tasmania—William Smith O'Brien, John Mitchel, Thomas Francis Meagher, Patrick O'Donohoe, Terence Bellew McManus, Kevin Izod O'Doherty and John Martin. Much more than the transportees of 1798, the 1848 rebels were men of standing in business, professions or politics, educated, intellectual; three were Protestants. They regarded themselves as temporary exiles, bent on returning as soon as they could to the centres of Irish affairs—Ireland or America. They all did. O'Doherty was the only one to have a substantial Australian career, in medicine in Brisbane after his return in 1860. And perhaps O'Doherty later wished he had done otherwise: his Australian life, for all its distinction, was sad. His transportation in 1849 had been in the midst of a fairy-tale romance with Mary Eva Kelly who had already won fame as nationalist poet—'Eva' of the Dublin *Nation*. On his release O'Doherty, with an Australian Irish gift of 200 sovereigns, but having had no luck on a venture into the goldfields, returned to marry Eva: the ceremony was performed by Cardinal Wiseman. The romantic dream shrank to drab and protracted reality. Of eight children, those who survived infancy died young: the only grandson was killed in the First World War. Knowing Bishop Quinn from Ireland, they went to Brisbane in 1862, there to share the odium Quinn generated. Despite election to the Queensland parliament in 1867, and the British parliament in 1885 as Irish member for North Meath, O'Doherty fell increasingly short of the story-book romantic legendary which had grown up to enshrine 1848. Anything coming after that high point of Young Ireland risked being anti-climax. Everything was, not only for the essentially cautious and pedestrian O'Doherty, but for dreamy Eva, now married to her aging and very ordinary former idol, marooned in a primitive colony a world distant from Ireland. Banished. Melancholy. Her poetry tells the surface of the story.

> Lone as a spectre straying
> My days are passing away
> Cold and grey, and voiceless,
> Nor passion nor hope; nor fear,
> But the footstep of memory falling
> All drearily on the ear.

And, from 1890, to add to disappointment came illness and poverty, stretching on for fifteen years to O'Doherty's death in 1905, then on another five to Eva's in 1910.

O'Doherty should have known better. The comments of the brilliant Mitchel typify their attitude to Australia: beautiful scenery, nothing else . . . 'there is no action, no living, properly so to speak, in a country so remote from all the great centres of the world's

Kevin Izod O'Doherty   *Mrs O'Doherty: 'Eva' of* The Nation

business'. 'Whether I was truly in Australia at all, or whether in the body or out of the body—I cannot tell; but I have had bad dreams.' 'I usually find our condition here to be a kind of syncope or trance, our movements to be somnambulatory, and our apparent doings and sayings to be sick men's dreams . . .' And they were all still living in a daze of romantic nationalism, dramatising their relative freedom in the penal colony (they had their own houses, and districts through which they might move around, and several even brought out wives and children) with notions of honour, paroles, tickets of leave and appropriate gentlemanly behaviour. Said O'Meagher (who appropriated an 'O' in his restlessness), 'The sentence which has led me to this strange clime has not separated me from my own beautiful sad old country. I am with her still. Her memories, her sorrows, and her hopes mingle with my own . . .'. Unike the others, who had private means, O'Donohue needed a livelihood. Against the advice of all the others he launched in January 1850 a newspaper, *The Irish Exile and Freedom's Advocate*, appropriately named, which led him into conflict with the penal colony's administration, but attracted a remarkable 800 subscribers before it was closed in April 1851. O'Donohue's newspaper briefly spread his influence Australia-wide, but otherwise the exiles kept their nationalism to themselves across the five-year period until the last of them—O'Brien and Martin and O'Doherty—were pardoned in 1854: Meagher, McManus, O'Donohue, and Mitchel had earlier, and at various times, escaped to America. There was no danger that these men would infect the Australian Irish, quite apart from Tasmania's remoteness and its small Irish population, for these men were in no way attracted to Australia. In Tasmania they had been welcomed by the better class of settler, almost all non-Irish, who would play 'The Shan Van Vocht' or 'The Wearing of the Green' just to please them: such generous and considerate hospitality was also witness to the Tasmanian irrelevance of such revolutionary Irish sentiments. Moreover all of the exiles felt the strongest repugnance for the Tasmanian penal scene in which they felt degraded and oppressed. Martin wrote home, '. . . we are branded convicts here at the uttermost end of the earth in this loathsome den of the depravity of the whole Empire, by the relentless Enemy, and alas as yet triumphant Enemy, of our country'. America was freedom, Australia was tyranny. And as for any idea of fomenting rebellion among the convicts and emancipists, O'Donohue dismissed this as unthinkable: '. . . it would be contemptible to be mixed up with the petty cabals of colonial rogues and rapparees—I look upon an Irish rebel in too respectable a light for that . . . God help me among such bloody curious medley of queer fellows . . .' If Mitchel had had his way the early Irish population of Australia would have been small indeed: observing the convicts he remarked, 'What a blessing to these creatures, and to mankind, both in the northern hemisphere and the southern, if they had been hanged'.

Yet the brief sojourn in Australia of these leaders of Young Ireland is too lightly dismissed as a romantic irrelevance. In part it was. Australia was too far away, too British, and its Irish too few and too convict to attract the leaders of Irish nationalism at this stage. This had its advantages. If it deprived Irish Australia of Irish leaders of stature, it also spared it the divisive consequences, and the depredations of some of the lesser and less honourable figures that hovered around the American Irish scene. The negative reactions of the Young Irelanders published abroad, particularly through Mitchel's *Jail Journal*, probably promoted the image of Australia as a dread prison long after it was in any way accurate. But the overall effect was positive, so far as the image and repute of Irish nationalism was concerned. The *Launceston Examiner* expressed a general reaction when it said that O'Brien's presence in the Tasmanian community gave them all a sense of inspiration: they beheld 'in him the accomplished gentleman—the man of unspotted honour, pure and devoted patriotism'. O'Brien in fact went beyond Irish interests to contribute to Australian, publishing in the *Examiner* in 1853 a draft constitution for

Mitchel spent some of his time sketching: Lake Sorrell and Meagher's Cottage

William Smith O'Brien. In 1854 the
Irish gold miners of Ballarat presented him
with a gold cup, now in the National
Museum of Ireland

John Mitchel

Tasmania and also one for an Australian federation. Exile in Tasmania had the effect of immensely enhancing the international reputation of Young Ireland, but, in addition to that, it helped to transform the local image of Irish patriotism from that of the refuge of rough rebels and criminals to a noble pursuit, worthy of gentlemen. It also formed the core of an Irish revolutionary masterpiece, John Mitchel's *Jail Journal*, first published in 1854 and in print ever since. Mitchel invested his exile with an extraordinary mythical power which clung in the mind to its Australian setting, but which also seemed to capture the sense of internal exile, even within their own country, which tormented many Irishmen. The *Jail Journal's* phenomenal and electric intensity blazed down the years, such that a Sydney Irish priest might write, on 13 May 1922, on his copy of the 1921 edition (it had a preface by Arthur Griffith, then President of Ireland): 'Re-read this Journal, lest my hatred of England be in the least diminished after $21\frac{1}{2}$ years absence from my dear Native Land.'

That last group of Irish prisoners, sixty-two Fenian convicts transported to Western Australia on the *Hougoumont*, arriving in January 1868, had an Australian relevance similar to that of the Young Irelanders, distant, partial, fluctuating. The most famous of them, John Boyle O'Reilly, escaped to America in February 1869. It was from America that the *Catalpa* expedition was organised, that most famous and daring of the Fenian escapades which rescued six prisoners from Western Australia in 1876 and took them to America. Some few of these Fenian prisoners were, on their release, to stay in Australia, but most regarded it as 'this most miserable of all miserable places'. Like the Young Irelanders, though a step below them on the social scale, the leaders of the Fenian group were superior convicts, travelling with the privileges of political prisoners, and gentlemen, producing a handwritten newspaper on board ship, educated, cultivated, and very hostile to their

Australian environment. John Casey, in letters home, articulated their disgust: Western Australia was an 'infernal Country', a desperate fraud offering false inducements to immigrants. The colonists themselves sickened him: these were people who poisoned and shot Aborigines, 'men perhaps endowed by God with talents which if properly developed would be found superior to the thick-skulled & narrow minded bigotry of the colonists of W.A.'. They were humbugs and pseudo-democrats. The rest of Australia was hardly better: 'Melbourne and Sydney are worthy of each other & of old England.' The Australian Irish were generous, collecting money to enable released Fenian prisoners to return home, but they were people of little consequence or principle, demeaned by lowly origins and the contagion of an environment dominated by sympathy with England.

This Irish image of Australia as a dumping ground for the refuse of the British Isles was strengthened when it became known in the late 1870s that a significant number of informers in the Fenian trials of the late 1860s had been quietly settled in Australia, their fares and lump sums being provided by the British administration in Ireland. In 1883 a plan to ship five such Irish 'approvers' to Australia became public, sparking colonial protests which were eventually successful, but it is unlikely that this was the last Australian traffic of Irish informers; strong rumours suggest that more arrived after IRA trials in Northern Ireland in the 1980s and it seems likely that such an Australian escape—or banishment—route was something of an historical constant.

Seen from the superior standpoint of the Young Irelanders and the Fenians imprisoned there, Australia was a very inferior place. This view was obviously conditioned by the fact that it represented exile and imprisonment to them, and contained a good deal of the contempt and patronising disdain the sophisticated metropolitan felt naturally for the rough colonial. But there was more to it than that. Australia had long been a penal colony; until 1868, Western Australia still was. It was assumed therefore to harbour the scum of the earth—Irish earth as well as English. Moreover such an assumption suited the book of Irish nationalist martyrs, transported for their devotion to country to this distant and degraded hell, there compelled to consort with the 'wretches' and 'wild beasts' that were the criminals. Casey's scalding appraisal of Western Australia in the *Irishman*, 4 June 1870, puts in extreme form a general Fenian (and Young Ireland) reaction to Australia:

> 'The population of Western Australia may be divided into two classes—those actually in prison, and those who more richly deserve to be there' . . . all are equally dishonest. What more can be expected from a nation of felons. Murder and murderous assaults are manly sports to the colonists . . . they live and die like dogs . . . More real depravity, more shocking wickedness, more undisguised vice and immorality is to be witnessed at midday in the most public thoroughfares of Perth, with its population of 1,500, than in any other city of fifty times its population, either in Europe or America.

And so on. As to the Australian Irish, though some of them were generous, many had no wish to be associated with Fenians or Fenianism, attitudes which drew the Fenians' contempt.

Indeed, disdain and contempt were central to the attitudes of both the Young Irelanders and the Fenians to Australia and those who lived there. Small wonder that the Australian Irish turned to the rebels of 1798 as founding fathers around whom to weave purifying myths. If convict origins and reputedly criminal legacies could neither be denied nor forgotten, they might—interpreted positively—be transformed into assets to serve the interests of a triumphalist apologia for Irish Catholicism as it developed throughout the nineteenth century. The Irish had risen in Australia from the catacombs of 1798: in 1898 the centenary of the rebellion became the occasion for celebration by Irish Australian notables in every State—politicians, professional men, men of church and commerce, success stories all. And in Sydney an imposing monument was erected over the exhumed and relocated remains of Michael Dwyer, in Waverley Cemetery. After a little initial clerical uncertainty and indecision in 1898 (1798 was, after all, a rebellion, generically frowned on by the Church) by 1921 the condition of the 1798 myth was such that Arch-bishop Kelly of Sydney could claim as beyond dispute that the 1798 rebellion was forced on the Irish people by the English as an excuse to impose their Union with Ireland 1800; and that the subsequent transportees to Australia (the implication was, all of them) were largely political offenders 'high-minded, industrious and progressive'.

This was the end point of a number of interpretations of its convict origins which had been developing within the Australian Irish Catholic community over the previous century. The nucleus of this mythology can be seen in the observation by the Sydney *Freeman's Journal* on 14 July 1855 that '. . . the only radiance that illumines the darkness of Australia's early history was reflected from bright Irish names—the glorious names of the patriots of '98'. It would be easy to disregard this as vacant rhetoric, and to miss the sting of that distancing and distinguishing adjective—'the *only* radiance': in fact the claim implied was, that the Australian Irish were not merely equal to, but immeasurably better than, other colonists. The stilted phrasing cloaked a sweeping claim to moral superiority, not merely self-promotion. By 1903 this was being said frontally and with historical apparatus. In the Melbourne *Austral Light* Father J.A. Knowles asserted that the Irish prisoners of '98 (an 'almost successful' rebellion) had been sent to Australia in revenge by Britain, in a vain attempt to deliberately degrade them by compelling them to associate with the lowest strata of English criminals, 'her own degenerate offspring'. But 'she had been thwarted in her fell design . . . These very men whom she had fondly hoped to see descend to the lowest depths of shame and infamy, became, in time the brightest ornaments and most respected citizens of her colonial empire'. The natural adjunct to this interpretation of Australia's origins was spelt out boldly in the *Austral Light* of June 1906. Australia's English majority were 'tainted citizens'. Only the descendants of the Irish were free from the hateful stains, because their forbears were not real criminals. English Australians had corrupt convict origins, and—the interpretation came up to date—their children were sustained in corruption by secular education. As to glosses on 1798, in 1905 Cardinal Moran had gone even further in fantasy, claiming that 'the great body of the people were genuine Martyrs. Hatred of the Faith was the motive of those who forced them into rebellion, & they freely died for their Faith'.

So was the Australian Irish world turned downside up, declared innocent and pure, with the vigorous assistance and blessing of its major social institution, the Catholic Church—and this long before Professor G.A. Wood of Sydney University put the idea of convicts better than their gaolers before the general Australian public in 1922. The sins of the Irish convicts had been wiped away by the myth-making efforts of their church, which thus consecrated as saintly its origins in a penal settlement that was heir to 1798. So criminality was transformed into martyrdom, evil into good—and who is to say that the new descriptions did not more justly fit the forgotten realities?

This relabelling reversal filled obvious functions within the Irish Catholic community, whose inferior position was both explained and made heroic, whose pride in race and identity was confirmed, and those hatreds and resentments were thereby justified. The

Australian Irish stood forth as a victim people, persecuted saints and heroes, whose socioeconomic subjection was due to old wrongs, and whose suspicions about their hostile environment were amply justified: given these origins, their achievements were all the more great.

But the implications of rebel reinterpretation of Australian history by a prisoner people were much more profound than simply providing social therapy and comfort for the Irish. It reversed the moral authority positions of the major occupiers of social roles in Australia: the gaolers, the rulers, the possessors of power, the nominal authorities, were transformed in this view into oppressors and tyrants, the real wrongdoers; while the prisoners, the powerless, the little people, were the innocent victims. The Catholic Church, as champion of the Irish view of Australia's origins, became central to a fundamental reappraisal of the established aggregations of power. Its stance had the effect of calling into question the traditional concepts of authority, and of bringing the existing social hierarchy into contempt, for it encouraged among its members a corrosive egalitarianism in which police, judge and gaoler, and the structures, values, and machinery they represented, were rated no better than those they imprisoned—indeed worse. Thus was fostered a climate of cynicism and distrust, the expectation of low standards from established authority, the resigned tolerance of stupidity, venality and corruption. So it was that the Catholic Church, that bastion of hierarchical conservatism in the old world (though less in Ireland) came in Australia to sanctify and promote the convict view of authority, that of disrespect, rejection and subversion. Instead of buttressing the social order, that church worked to loosen its bonds. From early in its Australian history, that church, and its predominantly Irish members, developed a view of English authority as repressive, unjust, brutal, persecuting, immoral, the sort of shackles from which the real Australia must escape. It was a dynamic perspective, committed to principles of challenge and change, restless with any position less than full Australian independence from old ways, alive with the erratic and contradictory energies of those being slowly set free.

CHAPTER THREE

IMMIGRANTS

Who emigrated? And why to Australia? As the most important continuing fact of Irish life in the nineteenth and twentieth centuries, emigration has been both the subject of unquestioning acceptance, and of conflicting interpretations and understandings: it remains both elusive and contentious—and contradictory. Before the Famine, the main champions of emigration from Ireland were Anglo-Irish, Trinity College intellectuals, who shared the view that it was Britain's duty and responsibility to populate the world, and who believed that Ireland was overpopulated, the cause of agrarian disturbances. But even they were in two minds about it, as they believed—correctly before the 1840s—that it was the Protestants who were emigrating to North America—175 000 in the period 1825–1834 was the estimate of the *Dublin University Magazine* in July 1834. That is, in their variant of the answer to the question of the quality of emigrants, the best, the loyal, the industrious were leaving Ireland in the hands of papists and rebels. As to Australia, until the late 1830s it was an unthinkable destination. In 1839 the *Dublin University Magazine* was promoting emigration to South Australia, stressing its non-convict nature: New South Wales it judged had 'no power of recovering from the baneful effects of its first origin' in turpitude, since convicts still kept arriving.

Given the encouragement of Irish emigration by Britain and Irish Protestants, it is hardly surprising that the orthodox Irish nationalist line was that emigration was the consummate evil, draining the nation's life-blood, cause of misery to those left at home, corrupter of those forced abroad. The emigrant is seen as driven out unwillingly from his homeland, a victim and unwilling exile: this is part of an obsessive population imagery culminating in the horrors of the 1845–49 Famine (a British plot to exterminate the Irish) but stretching back to Cromwell's seventeenth-century Irish massacres (seen as deliberate purges) and beyond.

This mournful orthodoxy, with its fulsome melodramatic sentimentalising, might strain modern credulity were it not for impeccable documentation. Those keen observers of the Irish scene Mr and Mrs S.C. Hall witnessed, on the wharf at Cork, a group of emigrants leaving for Australia in June 1840. The emotions verge on the theatrical or hysteric, but the occasion rings true.

> The band of exiles amounted to two hundred, and an immense crowd had assembled to bid them a long and lasting adieu ... Mothers hung upon the necks of their athletic sons; young girls clung to elder sister; fathers—old white-headed men—fell upon their knees, with arms uplifted to heaven, imploring the protecting care of the Almighty on their departing children. 'Och', exclaimed one aged woman, 'all's gone from me in the wide world when you've gone ... Oh Dennis, Dennis, never forget your mother—' ... Men, old men too, embracing each other and crying like children. Several passed bearing most carefully little relics of their homes ... a strong man, whose features were convulsed with emotion, while he grasped his children tightly to his

The harbour at Cork: mid-nineteenth century engravings

The Emigration Depot, Cork
National Library of Australia

bosom. 'And remember your promise, Mogue, remember your promise; not to let my bones rest in the strange country, Mogue,' said his wife; 'but to send me home when I'm dead to my own people in Kilcrea—that's my consolation.' . . . Shrieks and prayers, blessings and lamentations, mingled in 'one great cry' from those on the quay and those on shipboard . . .

Nor were such emotions much changed a decade later. In 1852, John Forbes described emigrants for Australia leaving from Killaloe. He was particularly struck by the actions of a 'strong, rough, long-coated young fellow' who, in farewelling his two sisters, had been caught on the boat when it made its departure from the wharf. Awaiting the dropping of the pilot downstream,

he set to, with right good will and with all his might, to dance jigs before them! Poor fellow, it was at once laughable and melancholy to see the mingled grotesque and sorrowful expression of his countenance, more especially when, amid his formal mirth, he now and then caught a glance of his sisters rubbing their swollen eyes . . . when the final leave-taking was made . . . he took his departure from the ship, setting up, as soon as he descended into the boat, such another portentous howl, as had signalised the parting at Killaloe.

In contrast to such dismal departures is the happy-adventurer interpretation, which has the emigrant escaping from frustration and poverty, and by so doing also improving the lot of those left behind. And there is also ample documentation of that. Writing to Lord Monteagle from Geelong in Victoria on 2 February 1853, Patrick Danaher expressed, on behalf of all those from Foynes and Shanagolden, Co. Limerick, 'the liveliest sense of gratitude' for Monteagle's assistance towards their passages. The fact that Danaher expressed back to Monteagle a landlord's view of the benefits of emigrations, and of the good that might come from the Famine—he saw it, not as a fiendish contrivance of the British (that was a later nationalist view) but as divine punishment, does not necessarily impugn his sincerity:

I am glad to learn that the American as well as the Australian immigrants are taking away as much as they can of their own friends from a land which refused . . . them a livelihood. Should emigration continue on a large scale for a few years more, I hope poverty will be known only by name in our beloved Ireland. Perhaps this visitation of God to his people would be productive of more good in the end than it has hitherto been of evil.

Certainly the Famine wrought fundamental changes in Irish attitudes to emigration, from encouraging the belief that anywhere would be better than Ireland, to the creation of excessive expectations—'this country is not half so good as it is represented to [be] at home' complained Margaret Healy from Australia in 1855. Trite enough in the book of migrant experience. And perhaps the voyage wrought a sea-change in attitudes to leaving Ireland: sad to leave, but glad to be gone. However tearful the farewells, the overwhelming weight of testimony sent back to Ireland is thankful, amply sufficient to sustain, by the 1880s, an image that had the emigrant 'moved by a deep seated law of national life and vigour', impelled by 'wanderlust and fecundity', bound for Botany Bay or fair Americay full of enterprise and excitement, bursting with buoyancy, cheerfulness and hope. Seen thus, Ireland could take pride in the worldwide dispersion of the Irish race; it was a tribute to them, to their energy, adaptability, success; a triumph denied within Ireland itself by English oppression. At its most grandiose, this was a racial and imperial view of Irish emigration which saw it as the expansion of a spiritual empire, centred on the Irish Catholic Church, similar (and geographically wider) but superior to, the merely secular Empire of the British.

These paradigms of Irish migration waxed and waned as suited various purposes and interests, as well as reflecting phases in the process itself. They implied divergent views of the quality and character and motivation of the emigrants. In 1931, W.B. Yeats encapsulated the extreme negative view:

Out of Ireland have we come.
Great hatred, little room,
Maimed us at the start.
I carry from my mother's womb
A fanatic heart.

This perception was shared by many non-Irish at the receiving end, who regarded Irish migrants as twisted and unfitted undesirables, the discarded human refuse of their home society. More central was the tragic Irish view, in which emigration spelt melancholy disorientation, the end of wholeness, a range of emotional disablements whose variety could be traced through the history of Irish poetry and song.

Dead against this depiction of emigration as a torrent of poets and misfits, is the thesis of common sense. The best left, not the worst, leaving behind the broken, the dispirited, the ineffectual, those who could not, or would not leave. It took initiative, resourcefulness, capacity, to move—and also, obviously, money. Plain common sense in reasoning is borne out by, say, the district reports of 1849—from Castlebar 'the most respectable tradespeople & shopkeepers are leaving the country'; or Longford, 'The provident & energetic farmers have in very many cases emigrated'; or from Thurles, 'Emigration upon an extensive scale is going on among the farmers who have sufficient left to carry them away . . .'. All reports tell the same story: it was the 'comfortable' farmers, those 'with ample means', able to realise their assets or borrow, who were the emigrants. And these kind of people can be found at the Australian end, farmers with a little capital, usually not enough to survive

Emigrants on the quay at Cork, 1851
Illustrated London News 10 May 1851

Australian conditions, but not penniless refugees; rather, at their best, the bold explorers, adventurous, footloose, those unwilling to shrink at home, the enterprising. In this thesis, the real, vital, practical Irish emigrate; the rich and comfortable plus a stagnant residue remain. (A corollary proposition is that emigration created a cultural and intellectual vacuum in which the destinies of Ireland itself lapsed into the hands of romantics, fools, poets and extremists with tenuous Irish connections—Parnell and Pearse of English descent, de Valera, the Spanish American—with disastrous effects on Irish history.)

There is no calculating the Irish might-have-beens had there been no emigration: the actual social impact on Ireland was profound and a continuing influence on future migrant generations. Putting aside the question of whether it was the 'best' or 'worst' who left, it was certainly the youth: most migrants were between eighteen and twenty-five. The transference of such natural sources of energy and initiative from old country to new had incalculable repercussions for both. The very existence of emigration as an option of escape had a distorting and demoralising effect on the entirety of Irish society. It spawned utopian visions—of American streets paved with gold, of an Australia entirely populated with happy Irish—and frightening, paralysing nightmares, of a new world seething with sin, in contrast to a holy Ireland where the old world stood still, in simplicity and sanctity.

How did the emigrant, focus of this babel, react to it? Without pause they continued to leave, attitudes differing with their temperaments and circumstances and destinations. From England it was possible to return, eventually to virtually commute. America was the emigrant's measure of all things—wealth, opportunity, republican freedom. Australia and New Zealand were distant, remote to the mind, not too far for journeying, but too far for thinking. The 'American wake' confirms the concept of emigration as a kind of death, though Irish funereal celebrations tended to be happy affairs: both ceremonies marked and honoured the final passing to another world. But Australia was a farther world still: America had exhausted the distancing capacities of the Irish, and besides, too few of them went there at first to demand notice or comprehension.

And they were convicts, pariahs. This situation changed rapidly and radically in the 1840s, not merely from convict to free, but in terms of social range, nationalist disposition, and educational resource. By 1901, such was the efficacy of the Irish education system founded in 1831 that literacy in Ireland was 88 percent, higher than in either Britain or the United States. A simple assumption might suggest that the addition of free Irish to the convict foundation must have increased Irish-Australian strength and refined its quality. Not so. It brought divisions, and 'free' was not necessarily 'superior'.

As the 1828 census shows, the emancipist ex-convict Irish were remarkably well integrated into the middling orders of colonial society, with the men of '98 established as an accepted aristocracy. This elite was in fact socially superior in Irish terms, regarded themselves as 'gentlemen', and considered that their achievements, affluence, and recognised substance in the colony entitled them to pre-eminence and deference: further, they believed (and called on their experience to support this) that the proper Irish behaviour in the colony was integration and the pursuit of social harmony. However, among the new free Irish immigrants of the late 1830s and 1840s was an element, small but very significant, which would accept none of this. The received version of the Irish free immigrant flood that began to build up from the late 1830s is that it was composed of peasants, unskilled labourers and agricultural workers. This had its truth, but throughout, and particularly in the early forties, there was a leavening of the lower middle class and Irishmen of skill and attainment. It was from those prominent in this group (Mark Lyons has called them the 'forties generation' of Irish Catholics) that most of the local leadership of Irish national causes came for almost the rest of the century. To the emancipists and men of '98, these new Irish were hardly to be distinguished from the peasant mass, lacked proper respect for their betters and those who knew the Australian scene, and amounted to little better than upstart troublemakers. The new immigrants saw things very differently. They had come from an Ireland whose identity, strength, and national

Paying the passage money at the emigration agents office in Cork, 1851
Illustrated London News 10 May 1851

consciousness had been revived by O'Connell's agitation: they saw themselves as better and more truly Irish than their supine predecessors. They had received a hostile reception from the colonial press on their arrival, as being ignorant peasant Irish, and they were not going to forget that. And they were not going to defer to men who were, as they saw it, essentially uneducated convicts who had no real sense of nationality and pride. The names of these forties arrivals—tailors, shopkeepers, journalists, booksellers, accountants, middling men—Butler, Freehill, Hughes, Moore, O'Connor, perhaps a dozen in all, recur in the annals of Australian Irish organisations from the 1850s to the 1880s—and beyond, for in some cases their sons followed them. Nearly all of them were active in politics of some kind, if only at the municipal level, in the public affairs of the Catholic Church, building committees, charities and the like. With the Catholic clergy, they were the core figures of the Irish Catholic presence in the public life of New South Wales. Their relations with the old emancipist Irish generation were uneasy, but the division was essentially passive, the new generation soon taking the initiative and control in aggressive Irish affairs.

These middling, skilled men arrived as a trickle through the 1840s, a tiny stream in what was becoming an Irish flood. Their Australian importance came from their initiatives and leadership in local Irish affairs, but they also represent the changing character of Irish emigration, and that element within it which had considerable skills and accomplishments but sought greater opportunity than Ireland could provide: by the 1840s Australia had joined the options available to the thinking Irishman. Despite all the rhetoric and self-deception, and wailing and lamentation, Ireland was a country which many of its inhabitants wanted to leave. By the 1880s the image of emigration had evolved, through the idea of duty or obligation, to that of natural expectation by the young and ambitious. But for Australia all the basic motivations were operative by the 1840s. For many, emigration was a convenient escape—from strained family relations, from quarrels over ownership of land, from burdens and responsibilities: to such cases the cliché of exiled children hardly applies—nor to such as wrote to Lord Monteagle in 1856 desperate to go to Australia simply so as not to be left behind by friends and relations. Does it apply to those girls without dowries who set out for Australia in the hope of marriage?—like the O'Brien sisters, aged seventeen and eighteen in 1882, daughters of small farmers in Fermanagh, travelling for £2 in steerage with their own food (hard-boiled eggs, griddle oat cakes) assembled by family and neighbours. Happy the outcome too, for in Melbourne they married two Clare men, MacNamara and Purcell, eventually ending up in America. As K.H. Connell distils the process in a celebrated article, 'as more and more young men yearned to acquire clothes like the Yankee's and a voice so *bizarre* and a purse so full, their generation learned with new conviction that a life tied to the land of Ireland was a life tied to tedium, liable to be dark forever when set against the dazzle of what might have been'.

What might have been: emigration raised unbounded hopes and became a solvent which ate deep into the fabric of Irish society, so that nothing could be right with it. On board the *Australasian* en route to Brisbane in 1885, J.A. Froude questioned an Irish emigrant as to why he was leaving just when conditions were improving. The emigrant replied, 'The divil is in the country, there is no living in it in any way. There are good laws now. There is nothing to say against the laws; but do what you will with them, no one is any better'. As to what particularly had gone wrong for himself—'Well, your honour' (the courtesy title was an Irish politeness that was music to the ears of Froude and Englishmen like him)—and then followed an explanation: Manxmen had outfished him and he had borrowed too much from banks. But there need have been no specific reason: by then emigration was an

One who stayed: a potato picker named McCaffrey, near Tempo, Co. Fermanagh, on
1 November 1899
Ulster Museum, Langham collection

ordinary avenue of escape, fount of expectations and illusions. Emigrants were increasingly being viewed with envy and hostility by those left behind, as having the opportunity of access to the good things of the world, leaving behind the poverty, tedium, and fetters of family. Such 'exiled children' were not welcomed home. Those few emigrants who returned found they were permanent outsiders, not accepted back into the world they had left: Michael Corduff of Rossport, Ballina, Co. Mayo, recalled in the 1950s the isolation of a man who returned after many—fifty?—years. Known as 'The Australian', he saw his neighbours as superstitious and conservative; they regarded him as odd, eccentric, and wanting in religion. By the time of the Anglo–Irish War, 1919–21, in some extreme political circles, feeling against emigrants, always present among those left behind, had hardened to the degree of branding them traitors—those who had left Ireland when she needed them. Emigration, however exciting and hopeful, had always been guilt-ridden. The very fact that emigration was seen by the British as a cure for Ireland's ills, and by Irish nationalists as a disaster, induced something akin to penitence in many, certainly confusion.

Leaving family and friends was often painful, producing remorse, and placing on the emigrant a compulsion to succeed to justify his or her departure. This sometimes twisted and distorted attitudes to new home and old. Some saw leaving Ireland as an admission of personal failure, and thus everything Australian as the embodiment of the second-rate. Others compensated for their defection by being ultra-Irish in the colonies. Some migrants deliberately severed links with home, wishing to vanish and hear of it no more. For many, circumstances eased them out of Irish networks and drew them painlessly into the local scene. Some families emigrated entire, though usually in stages and not at once. Parents at home died, terminating links.

The variations are multifarious, but many, perhaps most, maintained some links with home, their lives influenced by a subtle, hidden and mysterious history of interaction between homes near at hand and homes far away.

Most of Ireland's overseas emigrants went to the United States of America: their history there offers insights which illuminate their countrymen's Australian place and experience. (The situation of the Irish in Britain—close to home, swallowed in the Industrial Revolution and urban slums—has much less comparative stimulus.) In American history the Irish came relatively late, mainly nineteenth-century immigrants to a country already settled and its power structures determined for several centuries, an environment much more closed against them than was Australia, where they came at the beginning of settlement and shared, if in an initially subordinate role, in the creation of the society and economy. In America the Irish tended to remain in the already established cities where work in building and industry was expanding. In pioneering Australia the opportunities and employment were on the land; in America the Irish pioneered the urban ghetto. That an Irish peasantry should gravitate to American cities relates in part to the distance, passage cost and convict reputation of Australia, but the crucial factor is that the vast Famine migration to America of 1845–50 established a pattern of family and friends too strong to be greatly affected by the promise of land in Australia. The magnet effect did operate from Australia as emancipated convicts sought to persuade family and friends to join them; but weakly—they were too few and Australia too far away to compete for Irish migrants without the stimulus of free or cheap passages. Such passages themselves were governed in number by the size of colonial economies and budgets: small begat small.

The seeming Irish preference for American cities as against the opening lands of the American West raises questions of Australian relevance, given the suggestion that the explanation is that the Irish lacked farming skills, particularly those techniques necessary to sustain large-scale American dry farming. It might seem that Australia offers a similar lesson: many Irish farmers went bankrupt. But then, so did many other farmers, and there are many exceptional and enduring successes, such as the Duracks, and the big names of south-western New South Wales. Moreover, Canadian studies have shown that there the Irish have been highly adaptable to local agricultural environment: in Canada they remained on the land and did not sell their farms. It is true that in Australia many Irish farmers preferred small high-yield areas and crops, but this often made best economic sense, producing for the Melbourne market for instance. And while many Irish left the land for the city, this was part of the general Australian urban drift. What seems a common factor in both the American and Australian Irish experiences is the gregarious, sociable, community-oriented bent of the Irish towards gathering together in groups: whereas in America the cities provided a ready-built and even coercive permanent context for this urge, in Australia the Irish were happy with a much looser form, focused on country towns and supplemented by patterns of constant interchange of visits for holidays and the like.

The balance of research now strongly favours the proposition that the United States not only got the most of the Irish, but the worst—or at least the worst affected: the massive outpourings of the Famine, desperate, embittered, defeated, penniless and powerless, bare survivors, plagued thereafter with feelings of inadequacy and inferiority, or of alienation and frustration. In Australia, in contrast, the emancipated convict Irish soon developed modest but significant entrepreneurial qualities; very few Famine refugees came to Australia; and its mass Irish population came from the 1850s to the 1880s in search of gold, land, fortune and adventure: they were a much more accomplished, venturesome and happy lot than those the Famine had dumped on America.

Indeed it can be argued that many of the evident distinctions between the character of the American and Australian Irish spring from their being established, in the main bulk, by different generations of Irish: America absorbed the Famine; Australia's Irish population was mainly post-Famine, those whose families had come through that period and who were better educated, less traumatised, with more 'English' ways. The emigration figures tell the story. In the Famine decade of 1841–50 under 2 percent of those who left Ireland came to Australia—23 000. In the 1851–60 decade Australia got almost five times that number of Irish—101 540, or 8.3 percent of the total; in 1861–70, it was 82 900 or 10 percent of the total who left Ireland; the seventies, 61 946 (11.4 percent); the eighties, 55 476 (7.55 percent), thereafter declining rapidly. The Irish emigrant totals for 1851–1921 make the United States/Australia contrast overwhelmingly evident for the post-Famine period. Nearly four million went to North America, just over one third of a million (342 842) went to Australia and New Zealand. But analysis of such figures spells out two salient features of Irish emigration to Australia—that it was marked both by elements prompted by a sense of adventure, and by those moved by enterprise and calculation. Patently it was the gold rushes which established Irish Australia—101 000 Irish immigrants in the 1851–60 decade. Many of these, as in later periods, were assisted, but many were not. Of the 6200 who came in 1854, 1200 to Victoria were unassisted—the lure of gold was attraction enough. Of those assisted it was often alleged, then and later, that they were the scum (or dregs) of Ireland, disproportionately (because of the fact of assistance) the absolute bottom of the scale of labourers, serving girls, Catholics, and illiterates. The fact is, that even for

The Irish Emigrant seen at his handsome best by S.T. Gill
Mitchell Library

those assisted, the journey was more expensive than that to the United States. For America it might be possible for emigrants to leave in the clothes they wore; the length of the journey to Australia, and the climatic variations, entailed the purchase of several outfits, as well as towels, utensils and incidentals. These were detailed on the emigration advertisements and would have entailed expenses beyond the capacity of the very poor. Assisted passages meant merely that, not that they were totally free. To illustrate from an advertisement in the *Irish People* of 7 May 1864. The Irish Emigration Committee would assist 'Fifty Young Married Couples and Fifty Single Young Women to Melbourne', married couples to contribute £12, single women £5. (There was a list of other conditions also, suggestive of a process likely to produce 'better' migrants. The single women to be not older than thirty, and all persons to have a baptismal certificate, if married, a marriage certificate, a medical certificate of 'robust health' and 'freedom from any bodily deformity', a vaccination certificate, and a certificate of moral fitness from a clergyman.) Migrants then, as in more recent times, took advantage of what assistance was available: why pay more than one need? Some even—as in later days—used free or assisted passages to travel to Australia—and then on to New Zealand or America.

So Australia's vast distance from Ireland, dictating little chance of return, implied two contrasting sets of migrant attitudes, that which looked on it as a great adventure, and that which saw it as a very deliberate and considered decision. Nor were the two impulses incompatible. The adventurers who paid their way in the search for gold in the 1850s formed a solid numerical base for nominations for assisted passages, and remittances of passage money in subsequent years. Above all, the fact of distance and the time patterns of Irish migration suggest that the Irish emigrant to Australia was a thoughtful one. Not necessarily well informed (landing in Adelaide in the 1850s some Irish girls thought they could walk to Melbourne or Sydney) but thoughtful in the sense that it represented a forward commitment and investment of life.

The concentration of Australian Irish immigration in the mid– to late century points to other characteristics. To these later immigrants, the Famine was history, not direct experience, nor was it subject to its embittered American interpretation. They came from a rapidly changing Ireland in which the arbiters of the quality of life—education, health, prosperity, religion—were all improving in character, becoming more 'English'—whatever nationalists might think, easing the integration of Irish immigrants into the Australian colonies.

There was another crucial difference between the Australian and American Irish experiences. Australian immigration was ordered, organised and protected in a way American immigration was not. Government regulation and control had begun with the convict transportation system, and colonial assisted immigration schemes meant the continuation of bureaucratic state direction. To this was added the invigilation of English philanthropists and reformers (Elizabeth Fry for instance took a close interest in the convict women sent from Cork, Caroline Chisholm in the free female migrants of the 1830s and forties) and the conscience and pride of English politicians and administrators who viewed migration to Australia as an internal imperial transaction to be conducted at the highest standards. Of course all this was not without political considerations. C.J. Bailey put it to Lord Monteagle in October 1848: 'we must be careful not to plant a New Ireland in any colony, where opportunity and contiguity may raise up new a ferment of antipathy against England,' a point others made differently—that Irish emigration must be diverted from America, where it generated political problems for Britain. Earl Grey was very much of this mind. Keenly aware of the large-scale operation of chain migration among the Irish, he sought to use the process by priming the pump, suggesting that Monteagle encourage other landlords to send groups to Australia that would bring out others. Also well aware of colonial prejudice against the Irish, Grey thought such a scheme would circumvent this as it would be self-generating, and bypass the political problems associated with assisted migration.

So, in consequence of state paternalism, high-minded private individuals, and the desperate need for labour in the colonies, Irish emigrants to Australia were looked after in a way their American counterparts were not. The whole Australian process was advertised, regulated and overseen by committees whose requirements were documented and publicised and open to public scrutiny. Ships were inspected, rations ensured adequate, doctors were on board, morals were safeguarded. In contrast, Irish emigrants to America were often cheated, maltreated, preyed upon and left to fend for themselves, in a way that made emigration a shattering and bitter experience, disposing them both to alienation from their new environment and to retreat into whatever semblance of the old structures of family or locality they could reassemble to protect them. The Australian system did not call for such supports. It did not foster the re-emergence in the new land of old arrangements which would locate, protect, employ, and provide identity and friendship for the immigrant: the actual immigration system provided these things for those who needed them, while the hardy and adventurous did not.

In consequence, the Australian immigration process was a conditioning process radically different from the American, rendering national protective arrangements superfluous, favouring rapid integration on arrival, and providing—as numerous seaboard diaries testify—a marvel-filled world tour and long sea holiday as a prelude.

For this wide range of reasons, America was at first an unfriendly environment, hostile to Irish Catholics, to which they reacted by grouping in ghettoes, havens against enemies. In contrast, Australia was more friendly, less closed, more tolerant. The Irish were not historically experienced city dwellers, and urban slum pressures brought out their worst, accentuating the reaction against them in America. In early Australia cities did not exist, and when they grew they did so with suburban sprawl, with room for gardens, a little living space. Besides, the Irish tended to move not only to the cities, but to the country towns: both suburbia and the country town offered the Australian compromise—sociability and some chooks of one's own. Yet it would be false to generalise. Some Australian Irish chose the inner city; or had it chosen for them by their employment. They could be found in Sydney or the bush, and all points in between. The parallels with the Irish in Canada appear strong, where the Irish came, not as families, but as individuals with links of kin. Despite the gregarious stereotype, their preference was for individualism. The Canadian Irish chose not to live in villages of the close Irish kind, but to live apart from each other, often adjacent, but not always. In Australia the same—and different, for some settlements had a very Irish look.

Two sociopolitical contrasts bear noting. In the United States the Irish were only one of several major competing, ethnic strands—the Germans and Italians even competed with them for occupancy of a Catholic Church to which the Irish presumed monopoly. Much Irish American energy went into surviving against such other immigrant competition, and of course in hostility towards those beneath them on the social scale, the blacks. In Australia, the Irish were the only significant 'ethnic' group until after 1947, and thus could devote all their energies to relating to the majority culture. (Or almost all. Australia had a significant other minority, the Chinese, from the 1850s to the 1880s and there is evidence that many Irish viewed them with antagonism, despite the liberality of Cardinal Moran, whose tolerance led the *Bulletin* to dub him, in 1888, 'The Chow's Patron.')

In addition, distance allowed Irish Australia to develop its own circumspect relationship with Mother Ireland. Irish America was under the constant influence of its closeness to Ireland, of the massive Irish concentrations in New York, Boston and Chicago, of itinerant Irish agitators, and of a historically anti-British American republican tradition. Hatred of Britain was both stronger and easier to express in the United States, where it tended to perform a scapegoat function for Irish failure in American society—had they not been driven out of Ireland by British tyranny...Nevertheless, the question of attitudes to Britain is no simple one. The Irish in America felt more free—or claimed they did—in that republic; but they were also more alien. In Australia, the Irish found familiar, if at times abrasive, English institutions. They knew how the structures of society operated and quickly set about using them for themselves: the sense of strangeness, being foreign outsiders, was less than in America. As well, despite sectarian clashes, Irish Catholicism in Australia had a character less offensive, less culturally repugnant to the host Protestant majority than the Catholicism of America. It was the extravaganzas of the Italian Catholics that drove Protestants to frenzy in England: in New England, the United States generally, it was the Italians plus the Germans. Some Protestants from Ulster noted this contrast en route to Australia. In 1888 Mrs Cherry, a shipboard diarist passing through Naples, encountered for the first time statues of the Blessed Virgin in the (filthy) streets, candles, religious processions, people crossing themselves, all in public: 'I thought the Catholics at home attended to their religious duties but nothing to what they do in this place.' Furthermore, 'there seems to be no sabbath with them, almost every 50th man you meet belongs to the priesthood in some way ... There was a display of fireworks in Naples after I came on board so I leave you to guess the kind of place it is.' Statues, public display, no sabbath, the place crawling with priests, fireworks—every Protestant susceptibility was offended: Australia would be blessed relief!

In contrast to these European Catholicisms, which embodied all that the English and their American imitators disliked about the Continent—emotion, show, noise, triumphalism—Irish Catholicism was virtually 'Protestant'—austere, quiet, dignified, low-key, with relatively undemonstrative liturgy. Especially from the 1850s, Irish priests were preoccupied with a reformatory puritanism close to the style and stance of Protestant evangelism: Victorian Protestantism with its emphasis on respectability, reserve, and decorum had an immense influence on the conventions of Irish Catholicism. In Australia, this 'Protestant' mode of Catholicism had the additional cultural advantage of its alliance, in the public mind, with the cultivated English Catholicism of the Benedictines—and no confusion with Italian or German varieties. All this does much to explain why there was relatively little culture clash in Australia and why religious divisions were not culturally divisive: all Australian religion was some brand or other of Victorian Protestantism; Catholics were sufficiently Protestant to be, ultimately, culturally tolerable. Of course, this was in the light of the lesser importance of religion in Australian life: in America religion was one of the principles of colonial foundation. In Australia there was a common faith that transcended religious divisions—in secular progress and prosperity.

There were contrasts; also similarities. Both American and Australian Irish experienced the hostility roused by the Irish everywhere. Their social failures induced constant moralising from the successful and established, and complaints about costs to the community. As labourers and servants they attracted the criticisms—lazy, stupid—usual to those classes, whatever their race. On the path upward, American Irish families frequently gave their daughters a better education than their sons: teaching or nursing were professions protected from an environment where men might take care of themselves. The need was less in Australia but the trend existed. Sport was a favoured avenue of escape, lucrative for the individual, illustrious for the community. The fame and fortune of the American boxer John L. Sullivan, and later of Jack Dempsey and Gene Tunney, had their Australian parallels in the careers of Larry Foley and Les Darcy. Boxing lent itself peculiarly well to the dispositions of a frustrated minority: of Darcy the popular Irish Catholic tag was 'The power in his fists came straight from God'.

Implied in the comparisons made above is the suggestion that the ghetto situation welded the American Irish together in a way not duplicated in the looser Australian situation. But the common drive upward, and towards respectability, also had divergent outcomes. In both countries the lower Irish classes were more interested in local bread-and-butter political issues than in Irish nationalism, but in America the emergent middle classes, aggressive, political, self-confident, saw affirmation of Irish nationalism as advantageous and respectable in the diverse American ethnic climate. For the equivalent groups in Australia—and they were, even relatively, much smaller and less powerful—the reverse was the case: the Australian orthodoxy of respectability and success was narrowly English, indeed specifically set against demonstrations of an Irishness seen as disloyal. The result—in contrast with the mass political machines, big names, and family dynasties of the American Irish—was a small, fluctuating, hesitant Irish Australian nationalism, willing enough in principle, but unsure of its basis and direction, while mass Irish energies eventually went to Australian issues via the Labor Party. As well, at the time of Daniel O'Connell, founder of modern Irish nationalism from the 1820s to the 1840s, the Australian Irish were too few and too convict to take this up in any powerful way, had they wished—and they did not. For while the closed and oligarchical nature of American politics compelled the Irish to organise concentrated pressure groups, Australian politics were initially fluid and unformed in such a way as to be relatively open to the percolation, across the spectrum, of Irish with inclination and ability.

To dwell at this length on the Irish in America highlights by contrast some of the features of the Irish in Australia. But it is also appropriate because the American Irish exercised a hypnotic influence on the horizons and imaginations of the Irish in Australia. Their numbers, wealth, power, and strident Irishry, their dominance of the popular Irish world through song, their newspapers, their constant parading of Irish agitators, all dominated the thinking of the Australian Irish and kept them worried about what they saw as their own inferiority. Yet American example usually proved to be confusing or misleading. The nature and scale of the Australian Irish enterprise were very different. For instance, Australia would not support Irish bookshops: in theory, or principle, it should, but the moral imperative did not produce sales and such bookshops continued to fail. American appearances could be deceptive and ignorance of the realities was widespread. In 1903 the Hibernian Australasian Catholic Benefit Society sought to join forces with the Ancient Order of Hibernians in America on the strength of their shared name, unaware of the Ancient Order's connections with the secret and violent Molly Maguires. American models continually produced false starts, wrong directions, and divisive frustrations in Australia as efforts were made to ape US Irish organisations that were independent of, or even anti-church—and powerful enough to get away with it. The basic fact of Australian Irish life—however it might be otherwise in America—was that it was dominated by the Catholic Church, sustained by that church, and in the last resort, at very minimum, dependent on that church's tolerance.

Before the 1850s and gold, free Irish immigration was substantially government-assisted migration, that is, financed from the sale of colonial lands by individual Australian colonies that sought a labour force for development: R.B. Madgwick calculates that 48 percent of assisted immigrants, from 1829 when schemes started, to 1851, were Irish—37 306. Relatively few at this early stage (less than 1000 a year) paid their own passage out: an Australian voyage cost five times an American one, £10–15 to Australia as against £2–6 to America. The gold discoveries revolutionised Australia's attractive power, but various forms and degrees of assistance remained crucial to Irish immigration. Colonial government schemes remained central, and these were used (some said exploited) by the Irish more heavily than other nationalities. Where such assistance could not be found, or was insufficient, nominated chain migration operated strongly: many Irish immigrants owed their passage money to those who had preceded them, relatives, friends, paid back from wages after arrival. Nomination schemes, such as that operative in Victoria 1856–61, allowed local Irish to deposit cash in relation to specified migrants, for whom the colonial government paid the rest (most) of the passage. There was a strong sense of Irish kin obligation, even when the kin were personally disliked. To this was added a whole variety of private schemes and ventures, operating in limited times and places. In the 1840s Lord Monteagle helped many of his Limerick tenants to Australia. He was properly believed a benevolent landlord, but his motivation was not entirely altruistic. He explained to Lord Grey in October 1846 that emigration would help both his tenants and himself. As an innocent landlord he was tired of criticism. If he left his estates for his tenants to run, they became pauper warrens, attracting cries of Shame! If he consolidated them into economic units, against the traditional practice, he was accused of inhumanity. Emigration, he believed, would solve the problem, providing an option which , even if not taken, would give the people a sense of freedom and thus produce contentment. Other, privately sponsored schemes ranged from the ambitious plans of Bishop Quinn which brought 4000 Irish to Queenland in 1862–65, to small kinship arrangements such as that of Bishop Lanigan of Goulburn who brought out nine of his nephews. The Famine period saw significant sums raised in the colonies. In mid-1846, Father Geoghegan remitted £1362 he had collected in three months to the Protestant and Catholic archbishops of Dublin. That indefatigable collector Archdeacon McEncroe did the same in October 1847 with £3560 from New South Wales. (But then McEncroe was always collecting: in February 1855 he sent Cardinal Cullen nearly £500 for the widows and orphans of those Irish soldiers who had fallen in the Crimean War.) These sums were for either emigration or relief: if they went to emigration—which is unlikely—it would have been to America. Specifically directed toward making possible emigration to Australia was the work of the Donegal Relief Fund Committee, another of McEncroe's projects, from May 1858. McEncroe planned to make systematic use of the colonies' assisted passage scheme: he would deposit money, the government provided a related number of passages to persons between twelve and forty years of age, selected by an agent in Ireland.

In 1859 nearly 1000 emigrants on three ships were sponsored by this fund, and 160 in 1861: this represented Australian donations of around £5000 (perhaps $200 000 on today's

The famous sketch of the priest's blessing of emigrants as they leave home, 1851
Illustrated London News 10 May 1851

equivalents). This scheme was revived in 1861 to respond to what had happened in April that year at Derryveigh, in North East Donegal. There the landlord of a vast estate, John George Adair, had become involved in conflict with his tenants. Subsequent to the murder of one of his stewards, Adair, with the aid of 200 police and 30 soldiers, carried through one of the most notorious mass evictions of Irish history, demolishing the cabins and driving from his land about fifty families. Australian funds were raised to assist 140 of these people to emigrate to Australia and their departure in January 1862 was made the occasion of a dinner in their honour and an address by the well-known nationalist journalist and politician, A.M. Sullivan. Their priest spoke to them in Gaelic: 'And, boys, don't forget poor old Ireland (intense emotion, and cries of "Never—never, God knows!")—don't forget the old people at home, boys. Sure they will be counting the days till a letter comes from you. And they'll be praying for you . . .' On their way to the railway station en route to the Liverpool ferry, they passed their ancient burial ground, grass-grown. Sullivan recounts: 'Here in a body they knelt, flung themselves on the graves of their relatives, which they reverently kissed again and again, and raised for the last time the Irish *caoine* or funeral wail. Then—some pulling tufts of grass which they placed in their bosoms—they resumed their way on the road to exile'—that is, Sydney. Here was an emigrant departure harrowing enough to gladden the most sentimental nationalist heart, but it can be doubted if it was typical by the 1860s—or at least for the country as a whole. A decade of goldfield emigration had made the process matter-of-fact and an occasion for anticipation and excitement among many young Irish; but perhaps transformation of attitudes was least advanced in the West, and in the remotenesses of Donegal.

Whatever the atmosphere that surrounded their leaving Ireland, the atmosphere on their arrival in Australia was almost invariably full of contention and hostility. The colonies wanted British settlers, but English and Scots were not forthcoming, so the emigration commissioners in the British Isles were compelled to send Irish, mainly the poor and destitute, particularly from Cork, Clare, Limerick and Tipperary: the typical Irish emigrants to Australia in the late 1830s and 1840s tended to be semi-skilled farm workers forced off the land by the contraction of tillage in those areas. The result was a succession of colonial complaints that Australia was being flooded with ignorant, uncivilised, degraded Catholic paupers. The loudest and longest critic was the Scots Presbyterian minister, Rev. J.D. Lang, in Sydney, but such criticism was voiced Australia-wide, still being strident in Queensland when it was settled in the 1860s.

Hostility predated Lang's onslaughts, surfacing first in 1836–37 with adverse comparisons by the Sydney *Herald* of the Irish with Chinese coolies, and anti-Catholic diatribes. Some of this hostility was a corollary of the *Herald*'s anti-convict position, as is evident in its comments on the arrival of free Irish female immigrants on the *Duchess of Northumberland* in October 1836: 'They too frequently sink down into the Convict class. They marry Convicts. Their children are educated with convict feelings and principles, hostile to good institutions and at enmity with the character and feelings of free Emigrants . . .' The *Herald* conceded that this might also happen with the English, but it was far more likely among the 'low, depraved and bigotted classes who are selected from the south of Ireland'—'Popish serfs'. The Anglican Bishop Broughton took a similar stance. This first expression of animus was so evidently anti-Irish Catholic as such as to draw criticism from other responsible colonists, who prided themselves on a society both liberal and tolerant: Broughton's chairmanship of the Legislative Council's Immigration Committee was successfully protested in 1839. Still, there was a sense in which this first wave of opposition was not specific to the Irish. The exclusivist view of society was of a hierarchical structure under their control, with convict or coolie labour: an influx of Irish Catholics merely represented the worst possible outcome of the large-scale free immigration to which they objected on principle. Intelligent conservatives, seeing that the assertion that Irish Catholics contaminated Australian society would not win any general support, changed their ground to that of objection to the number of such immigrants. Here they were on much firmer ground: 37 percent of assisted migrants in 1837–40 were Irish and this proportion was rising rapidly so that the New South Wales figure across the period 1837–50 was almost half the total.

Precise figures for Irish immigration have always been uncertain. Margaret Kiddle's generalisation provides an indicative basis: 'over the whole nineteenth century 35% of the immigrants coming to Australia were Irish. Between 1831–51 . . . 48% of the immigrants were Irish'. But she goes on to suggest that such figures are less than actuality, given the many Irish who lived in England (nearly half a million in 1841) and who emigrated from there and were counted as English, as well as those who were transhipped. She instances J.D. Lang's case of the *Glenswilly* in 1841, sailing from London and Plymouth, with 310 emigrants returned as English; all were Irish, having been brought across to join the ship in Plymouth. Transference of the basis of criticism of Irish immigration to the numbers area had several advantages: it was irrefutable, yet subject to the inflation of a vague but appropriately worrying 'Irish in England' factor, and allowed selective use of figures to maximise the feelings of threat and concern in an audience: Lang was fond of the period January 1841–July 1842 when, of 25 330 assisted immigrants, 16 892 were from Ireland and only 8438 from England and Scotland. And, of course, the assisted area was where the figures game told most heavily against the Irish, who were not nearly so prominent among immigrants who paid for themselves. But that, so the hostile argument went, was irrelevant: the colonists were paying to import excessive numbers of these inferior people. Were they inferior? Earlier, perhaps some, yes; and that may have set a colonial image. For the colonists had a constant vision of hordes of Irish barbarians clamouring to be let emigrate to marvellous Australia, a notion which did not fit at least the earlier facts. In the early 1830s it was almost impossible to get women of good character to emigrate, and some ships—one certainly in 1834 with 226 girls—had extreme difficulty in filling their quota; resort was had to 'the sweeping of the streets', as the cliché had it.

By the 1840s, the higher level of anti-Irish argument concentrated on their immigrant numbers, but another major strand remained vigorously racial and anti-Catholic, sometimes with some ingenuity. It was trite for the *Australian* in March 1841 to complain that Protestant money was being used to bring out bigoted Catholics, but crafty of the Sydney *Gazette* of the previous September to hold that it was in the interests of the Catholic Church to encourage the Irish to migrate: in Ireland they were too poor to pay Peter's Pence, in Australia quite able to.

In racist vein, there was an obvious standard for derogatory comparison—the Aborigine. In 1843, Dr Alexander Thompson claimed that the Irish were intellectually inferior to Aborigines, 'utterly useless'. It was a comment that went to the heart of one aspect of the rejection of the Irish. They—or rather, some—were pre-modern, pre-industrial, their very existence superseded by progress, commerce, science, invention, the arrogances of the nineteenth century: like the Aborigine, the Irish were primitive, backward, outmoded, the butt of impatience and contempt. Comparison with the Aborigine lingered on as a dismissive device: in the 1870s the English traveller Mrs Baxter deemed native huts a decided improvement on those she had seen in Ireland. (Relations between the Irish and Aborigines were generally of the kind indicated by the Aboriginal writer Faith Bandler, recalling her childhood in northern New South Wales. In contrast to Protestant paternalist or exploitative whites, Irish Catholics treated the Aborigines as human beings, as equals, an equality extending to marriage, as distinct from the sexual exploitation common in white relations with Aborigines: the 'shamrock/Aboriginal' names prominent among contemporary Aboriginal activists testifies to that relationship.) Racial comparisons were the then matter-of-alleged-fact language of normal discussion, not intended as offensive, merely as clarification of labour needs and realities. They could even be expressed in an exact formula, a precise working ratio. Thus the *Australian* of 13 April 1846: 'We rate these three different races as follows:- Three first rate lowland Scotch or English labourers or shepherds . . . to seven west and mountain Irish or highlanders; and to ten coolies . . . We mean no offence in this to the Irish as a nation . . .'

To return to the higher ground of the anti-Irish argument, that dominated by the tireless crusader J.D. Lang, his thesis is cogently and vehemently set out in his 1841 pamphlet *The Question of Questions!* with its uncompromising subtitle 'Is this colony to be transformed into a Province of the Popedom?' Its main points were to be reiterated until his death in 1878. Lang's basic proposition was that Protestants, although a numerical majority, were divided: Catholics were united and therefore must eventually prevail politically. And they were pouring in, an Irish deluge, three-quarters of all assisted immigrants. Ireland was itself demonstrably non-productive, requiring an expensive government, yet still 'a grand nursery or university of crime and criminals', with the counties from whence most emigrants came—Dublin, Cork, Galway and Tipperary—'the strongest holds of popery, bigotry, superstition and immorality, in the British Empire'. These emigrants were 'the most ignorant, the most superstitious, and the very lowest in the scale of European civilisation', and of these Australia got the worst: the best went to America. Australia was a pastoral sheep-farming country, but the only animal the Irish knew anything about was the pig, their only cultivation the potato. And they were dangerous. Australia was a convict country: free Irish immigrants would form revolutionary brotherhoods with the Irish convicts. Why were these dreadful Irish coming? In general Lang held that it was all a plot to convert Australia into a dominion of the Man of Sin; on the practical machinery he believed that they were preferred by emigration speculators because, being eager to join their convict cousins, they were easier to collect, and, having little luggage, they were cheaper to transport to Britain and thereafter to Australia.

Lang was at pains to insist that he was not hostile to these people, and quick to concede that their condition was the result of centuries of misgovernment. But why import their problems to Australia? Indeed his pamphlet of 1848 *Repeal or Revolution, or A Glimpse of the Irish Future* urged on Britain imperative reform as appropriate justice and preferable to revolution. But in the early 1840s the Irish began behaving as Lang had predicted and feared, as a tyrannical mob, intimidating citizens. Even teetotalism, with its ostentatious and frequent processions, he saw as a vehicle for exhibiting the threat of physical force. And they soon showed that they were infected by the O'Connell virus. A branch of O'Connell's Repeal Association was formed in Sydney 1842 and the elections of the following year—the first elections in the colony—saw 'Tipperary boys' (a curiously constant phenomenon in Australian public history) on the rampage.

While it is academically correct to point out that there was never any such thing in Australia as a monolithic Catholic or Irish vote, that is not to say that there were not consistent efforts to secure such a vote, or firm beliefs that it existed or was about to. The whole impact of Australia's first election campaigns—for the Sydney Municipal Council in 1842 and the Legislative Council (particularly the Melbourne campaign) in 1843—suggested an Irish Catholic political menace. These campaigns were accompanied by scenes close to riot, in which recent immigrants from Ireland were vigorously prominent. Viewed dispassionately, here was merely a rough pioneering society enjoying the entertaining novelty of popular elections, but such sociological analysis was not foremost in the minds of those who knew these immigrants had come from an Ireland where the new and exciting O'Connellite elections were a focus and outlet for mass power. The prospect, indeed sight, of O'Connellite mobs on Sydney and Melbourne streets prompted fear—and counter-organisation. It was not that their candidates were radical—curiously, they were often the opposite—it was that they represented the ambitions, for the moment, of the Irish mob.

It may not have been coldly reasonable to believe that these Irish menaced the future development of a civilised British society in Australia, but it is easy to understand why the question arose. Similarly, the constant emphasis on their numbers within the immigrant intake explains why some colonists concluded that they constituted a grave threat to the dominance of the English and Scots. Hostility was sharpened by the observation of the incompetence of some Irish migrants when faced by colonial status situations, and by resentment that public money should be spent on what were judged poor returns, and to help Britain to 'shovel our paupers' or rid itself of its troublesome Irish. And the whole anti-Irish farrago steamed with frustration and resentment generated by a hard look at the facts: it was the Irish or nobody. As the *Herald* in one of its clearer moods saw, the colony had the choice of ruin through lack of labour, or putting up with papists from Ireland: the colony's realists lumped this, but they did not like it and they continued to say so, for many years to come, often and offensively. The facts were all there: Ireland was part of the United Kingdom and no realistic or consistent way existed of excluding the Irish; the 'best', most suitable, immigrants from the colonies' viewpoint were those least likely to apply, to wish to leave Britain. But the vision of an ideal Anglo-Saxon Protestant Australia was powerful indeed, and each boatload of Irish was further reminder that this dream was receding, that the mixture was being further diluted.

The basic fact about Irish immigration was that it was unwelcome. A variation and reinforcement of the Irish convict image, this bestowed on Irish immigrants a power to generate fear, which made them formidable. The attribution to the Irish of the ability to swamp and overwhelm the existing majority culture had the momentum of a self-fulfilling prophecy: the hysteria of Lang produced a movement towards what he feared. It gave the Irish not so much a program as some indications of what might be possible to them, and his attack was a goad which firmed their reactions past what they might otherwise have sought. Above all attacks of the type of Lang's united the Irish to a remarkable degree and drove them together towards the kind of unity he believed—erroneously—they already possessed. Moreover, such attacks swung liberal colonial opinion into Irish defence, effecting an anti-Tory alliance (albeit occasional and weak) which helped Irish integration if only by neutralising elements which might otherwise (for example, for religious reasons) have been hostile. Overall, the effect of anti-Irish tirades was to isolate and discredit those who made them, and to undermine the edifice of such bias by exposing it to ridicule and contempt as un-Australian bigotry and extremism. Paradoxically, the operation of a colonial revulsion against such hysteria gradually brought the Irish toward the territory of what was real and acceptably Australian.

But this was gradual indeed, and far in the future. Controversy continued, particularly in regard to Irish female assisted immigrants. The Colonial Office rationale was that these would both correct the sexual imbalance in the colonies and provide domestic servants. The colonial response was that in both respects, the Irish females (about half the total) were highly unsatisfactory. They came from rural backgrounds and lacked education, knowledge, and the know-how needed for service in the homes of the aspiring Australian bourgeoisie—cooking, house management, dealing with visitors and so on. Father Patrick Dunne's story, to entertain his shipboard companions in September 1863, of the Irish servant in Melbourne, sent out for a message but unable to remember the location of her house of employment so as to return to it (Dunne found her another job) was testimony to the problem from a sympathetic source: employers themselves were unused to servants, often ignorant themselves, and excessively demanding. Besides, these Irish girls were often independent to the point of insolence, showed a crude preference for the rough and vulgar side of colonial life, and in general behaved without the decorum and respectability employers would have liked. As well, with domestic salaries at least twice what they were in Britain, they had money to ape their betters, and Irish servant girls promenading the streets in vulgar ostentation was a constant irritant to those who thought the lower orders should know and keep their place.

But much worse, these women were seen as menacing the future of Anglo-Saxon society. This feeling, long latent, welled up in reaction to the sending to Australia of 4175 orphan girls between 1848 and 1850: 2253 to New South Wales, 1255 to Port Phillip, 606 to Adelaide. At first, the criticism came from within Ireland. The *Nation* saw it as one of the most diabolical British schemes since Cromwell's day. The *Tipperary Vindicator* saw it as a variant on the white slave traffic: others too saw it as a device to get wives for depraved 'bushmen and savages'. However highly colonists might think of themselves, and the Irish as inferior immigrants, the Irish press saw Australian society as nothing yet rid of the 'contaminating residuum' of criminals with which it had been founded: it was vehemently opposed to helpless and pure Irish orphan girls being transported to this distant cesspool.

As to the girls themselves, they wanted to go, and those who left in 1848 were promptly employed on arrival at good wages. And at first they were welcome. Well, more or less welcome. The first ship arrived in October 1848 with a highly undesirable Belfast element, 56 girls a local committee found violent and disorderly, pilferers, and grossly profane of language. (When this was conveyed back to the Irish Poor Law Commissioners, they responded that bad language was the natural manner of expression of Belfast factory girls and ought not be construed as indicating immorality)—but they took more care with future selections. But by 1850 colonial criticism had become so intense as to force the termination of the scheme. It had made little impact on the Irish problem: 104 000 children under the age of fifteen were still in Irish workhouses when the last orphan ship sailed in April 1850.

Colonial commentators were simply not interested in the scheme's charitable or humanitarian dimension. J.D. Lang had gained converts to his argument that it was a papist plot to subvert Australian society by ensnaring Protestants (or more likely, irreligious bushmen) into 'mixed marriages'. Then there was their physical quality. The Melbourne *Argus*, long hostile to these 'hordes of useless and lawless savages', saw a future menace to the stock of Victoria in their 'squat stunted figures, thick waists and clumsy

A French sketch of Irish girls arriving in Australia in 1866 suggests affluence and respectability despite the jig being danced by an unkempt welcomer on the far right
from Voyage Autour Du Monde par le Comte de Beauvoir Paris 1878 National Library of Australia

Some female Irish realities in the Ireland of 1899: Mrs Ferry and her children,
Tempo. Co. Fermanagh
Ulster Museum: Langham Collection

ankles'. Other (Protestant) Irishwomen were pleasant to behold: not this lot, 'coarse, useless creatures' from Ireland's benighted south. The *Argus* exhausted its stock of anti-Irish clichés on 24 January 1850 in characterising them as 'a set of ignorant creatures whose whole knowledge of household duties barely reaches to distinguishing the inside from the outside of a potato, and whose chief employment hitherto, has consisted of some such intellectual occupation as occasionally trotting across a bog to fetch back a runaway pig'. This was a masterly conflation of the then (and now) standard insults—dirt, stupidity, potatoes; bogs and pigs.

Not surprisingly, such comments provoked vigorous Irish Australian defence. The Melbourne St Patrick's Society took the position that welcoming the Irish emigrant was merely an aspect of extending justice to Ireland, giving the willing and the destitute an opportunity to emigrate to a country needing them. (It could hardly be expected that the Irish here would echo their compatriots' assertions in Ireland itself, that it was all a fiendish English plot to depopulate Ireland and degrade Irish girls by exporting them to consort with the 'contaminating residuum' of convictism.) The problem with the St Patrick's Society stance was that by 1850 the colony's economy had absorbed all it could for some time: the Widow Gearin informed Lady Monteagle in August 1855 that in Melbourne hundreds of young girls were unemployed.

Controversy over the character of Irish female immigrants continued throughout the 1850s. The most intense exchange was that triggered by remarks made by the New South Wales immigration agent, Captain Hutchinson Browne, regarding 150 Irish pauper women who arrived from the Cork Poor Law Union in 1854, comments which fitted into a general climate of questioning of their intelligence and moral character. This led eventually, in 1857, to Irish organisations petitioning the Legislative Assembly in criticism of Browne and in defence of Irish women—which led on to the setting up of a Select Committee on Irish Female Immigration whose proceedings kept the pot of denigration and reactive outrage boiling into 1858 in its attempts to hear and satisfy all sides. Protracted controversy of this kind could only have one outcome—a continuing reflection on the quality and capacity of Irish women. For ten years from 1848 the public had been treated to allegations that these women were 'useless trollops' (the *Argus*'s phrase)—incompetent, lazy, coarse—and repeated denials merely reinforced that image. And the critics of the Irish had carried their point in stopping the orphan immigration scheme, a signal victory for small-minded bigotry against the demands of generosity and human need. Overall such critics had engineered a climate of caution and restriction—and an atmosphere habitually anti-Irish.

Yet the case of South Australia presents a happier picture. Sure, the first such orphans aroused little joy. They were short and ugly. Instead of being, as promised, Protestants from the North, half were Catholics. But South Australia prided itself on its liberal and philanthropic outlook, so it bore this and smiled; its disposition was to take the view that females were necessary to colonial social health, and that Lang's canard that these were cunning papist marriage emissaries was rubbish. Yet there can be no doubt that the primitive and even loose lifestyles of some of these Irish girls tested South Australian tolerance to its limits. On the voyage out, some had been lazy to the degree of habitually preferring cooking and drinking utensils to the neglect of the lavatory accommodation: similar practices on arrival aroused particular odium. Half the prostitutes in Adelaide in 1851 were Irish orphans. Yet, in the early 1850s, the severe labour shortage meant happy absorption. Even in the mid 1850s, when there was an invasion of single Irish women

(4002 in 1854–55) well beyond the capacity of Adelaide to absorb, the colony as a whole rose to the challenge: assisted by the Catholic clergy this flood was dispersed into country areas. Lest it be assumed that the South Australian immigrant experience was entirely one of sweetness and light, the negative reaction in this process came less from the community (though that was prone to be patronising in its good works: the Irish would become good English citizens) than from the immigrants themselves, some of whom had idyllic dreams of a colonial existence well stocked with prospective husbands, good jobs and high wages. They found themselves shunted out of the city, away from friends, into places, jobs and wages they did not like: however theoretically superior this may have been to an Irish alternative, it fell far short of excessive expectations and was resented accordingly.

Perhaps it is natural that, given the many years of unceasing abuse and contempt in regard to their human quality, the Irish should increasingly claim the opposite—superiority. By the late 1850s, Father Patrick Dunne was demanding that the government provide separate Catholic emigrant ships, explaining to Cardinal Cullen on 15 February 1859:

> Only think My Lord of pure, innocent, Irish country girls being placed in the closest contact, such as sleeping in the same berth, with English protestants of the lowest class and some of them selected from the streets of London, think of them being thus placed under the care of a protestant Doctor & Captain all perhaps combining to destroy their faith and morals.

The English government's refusal of Dunne's demand he took as sectarian persecution. Archbishop Goold in Melbourne had an even more diabolical interpretation of English policy. In 1858 he was of the opinion that emigration agents, who were Protestants, were, with the aid of parsons in Ireland, deliberately choosing the worst Catholics as emigrants, with the object of discrediting Catholic Irish emigration to Australia. This left Goold in the curious position of implicitly accepting that such Irish immigrants were of poor quality and low character, in order to confirm his thesis of English plot. Actually, there was a little more to this than the villainous English. Goold reckoned that any scheme organised in Ireland by his enemy Father Patrick Dunne must be bad. Goold argued that any money collected in Australia for Irish Relief should be used for the benefit of the many, not confined to bringing a few lucky immigrants to Australia. It was a respectable argument, but it sprang, not from Goold's benignity, but from his fear that such as would be sent would come as his enemies. Wisely he kept both his theories and his fears to himself, and left the ground clear for the overwhelmingly popular Irish Catholic assertion of the superiority of Irish Catholic faith and morals, the inverse of the denigration habitually accorded the Irish immigrant by the public mind by the 1850s.

This denigration was, in part, an old and imported habit of anti-Irish mind, but what real basis in fact did it have in the Australian colonies? What justification was there for fear or antagonism? Statistically, none: between 1828 and 1861, the Catholic proportion of the New South Wales population remained almost constant, while its Irish-born component was shrinking rapidly. The hostility, sometimes verging on hysteria, which greeted Irish migrants, related not to proportion, but to simple increase in their numbers, to their concentration of arrival in some years, and to their tendency to concentrate in the lower areas of employment, labouring and domestic service—plus, of course, their visibility, their habits, and the fact that many were being helped to come by public money. That they were such a high proportion of assisted migrants was a constant public irritant—nearly 40 percent in New South Wales for the period 1856–60. But this rose to three-quarters for some years in the sixties, for instance, 3275 Irish of 4633 assisted migrants in 1863, 2041

Further reality: Mrs Ferris, her daughter and perhaps grandchildren, Tempo, Co.
Fermanagh, 1899
Ulster Museum: Langham Collection

of 2717 in 1865. This proportion dropped sharply in the seventies and eighties when less than 30 percent was normal. But the concentrations of the fifties and sixties—at public expense—were a sure recipe for protest, particularly as such Irish incursions altered, or were expected to alter, the character of districts into which they moved. In May 1844 Dr Hunter, Trinity College botanist, visited Newcastle, then with a population of about 1500, Protestant miners from Wales and Cornwall: the few Catholics had not a church, but only a room. However, many Irish female servants were being imported, and 'these will form the nucleus of a future Roman Communion no doubt'.

And these Irish were so obvious. There was the brogue, that distinctive Irish accent, immediately recognisable, often trumpeted out (they were great talkers and loud laughers) readily open to mockery and contempt, and often used loudly enough in boisterous situations to attract attention. That this was noticed, and stored away in judgemental minds, is evident in F.C. Kendall's recollections of the poet John Farrell in 1905. Unlike the 'crude and aggressive' brogue of William Bede Dalley (a parental legacy in Dalley's Australian-born case) Farrell's brogue 'dissolved in a cheery sort of intonation that won a stranger's heart to John right away': Farrell's brogue was also a legacy, for he had been born in South America. Such was the attractive or repellent power of second-hand brogues. Add to this a certain carelessness or bravura of dress (the Irish seemed to have no colour sense and to contrive to look scruffy and unkempt even in their best) and the whole impact was—'Irish!' In Adelaide in 1845 Irishwomen were noted as distinctive, without the usual bonnets, and cloaks over their heads instead. Voyaging to Australia in 1885, J.A. Froude saw an Irishman in the unmistakable national costume, the coat-seams gaping, the trousers in holes at the knees, the battered hat, the humorous glimmering in the eyes': with the Irish their expression, their aura, was somehow part of the 'national costume'. And they

The poet John Farrell, Single Tax enthusiast and author of 'How He Died' (1883)

were everywhere. Their employment gave them a heavy presence in the streets, among street-sellers, cart-drivers, labourers, layabouts, servants on errands, cooks shopping for mistresses—it seemed that the Irish owned the street life of city and town. Nor did they keep their rows to themselves or suffer insult quietly. Norah Cahill charged Judith Hyder, in court, with calling her, from her verandah, a 'bloody Irish Immigrant Bugger', a casual obscenity which must have been uttered far more frequently than its appearance in court records suggests. Nor did Orange and Green always internalise their tensions. In Maitland in the 1840s the Campbell and Foran families were well known for their frequent feuds, expressed in abuse and assaults, beginning it seems at the Catholic burial ground, when John Foran repeatedly called William Campbell 'a north of Ireland paleface bugger'. The homosexual obscenity was particularly relished by the Irish as an insult, representing as it did to them the utter depths of depravity. Generally, their centrality to city low-life is suggested by the name of one of Sydney's tattle sheets of the 1840s, *Paddy Kelly's Budget*, and by the frustrated rage of the labour-starved pastoralist Samuel Browning in 1847: 'Myriads of those people have got obstinately located in all the filthy courts and lanes of Sydney ...' Another hostile appraisal of the Sydney Irish, published in Britain in 1850, had them central to the whole inner workings of city life: '... the Irish do not like going into the interior; they like to hold down together like cattle, where they can squat down and gossip together about all the ins and outs of the neighbourhood, and have their priests and chapel in sight.' They used their positions as servants and messengers to inform themselves of everything planned or arranged, and pretended to be poor while they amassed wealth:

> they know nearly all the affairs of their employers and can give every information at the Catholic headquarters. The greater part of the shops is now Maloneys and Callaghans ... They generally go meanly clad, and will accept any of charity, though earning good wages, and live two or three families in a house, and calling themselves the poor Irish; they soon save money, and then commence for themselves, to level down those who have assisted to pay their passage out: I know of several who are now at work for these, their former servants.

A generation later Melbourne had a similar reputation, with Sergeant Dalton, that 'kindly, good-natured giant' from Kilkenny, being [one of the sources] credited with the invention of the word 'larrikin'—'larkin' or perhaps 'Larry-kin', or even the Gaelic word 'loorikan', half-man, half-elf. Everywhere, but particularly in the street scene, the Irish were different, and often acted larger than life. Little wonder they attracted attention.

The accusation that they were all shiftless unstable paupers was baseless. Some were skilled, though colonial expectations were unrealistic given the youth and rural background of many Irish migrants. Perhaps half came in family groups, though 'with relations'—brothers and sisters, cousins—might be a more accurate terms—the Irish seldom nominated their parents to join them. Many came from the same county. Some ships brought emigrants from the same locality or town: in 1840 the *Crusader* brought 300 Irish emigrants, 127 from Elphin, Co. Roscommon, 58 others from the surrounding district. The significance of these concentrations, and of Irish emigrant localities generally, awaits research analysis. Generalisations or localised observations applicable to the Irish population may not apply to emigrant areas or population segments. The fact that parts of rural Ireland were ablaze with violence and outrage from the 1790s to the 1840s certainly accounts for some of the transportees to Australia, but were free immigrants from those areas affected? Historical research has identified a lack of deference towards social superiors in the Ireland of the 1820s, something in sharp contrast with the situation in England: it is tempting to see this, imported, as an Irish basis for the egalitarianism so noted by observers of the Australian scene. But such transferences—together with Irish rebelliousness, lawlessness, and flamboyant behaviour—are as yet attractive imponderables awaiting test.

Much more can be said on the matter of skills. The commonplace truths about Irish immigrants can be found documented in the report of the Parliamentary Select Committee which investigated the condition of the Sydney working class in 1860—a high Irish component, an Irish migrant unwillingness to move on from city to country, and a remarkable high percentage (around half) of persons of Irish descent among convicted juvenile prostitutes and vagrants. As to Victoria, of the Irishmen who came in the fifties and sixties, 89 percent were unskilled. Yet for all that superior colonial persons publicly decried the alleged low quality of such immigrants, questions abound as what 'quality' meant, and whether in fact the colonies got more or less what they needed from Ireland—labouring men, domestic women—and in fact the best available in those categories. Even more basically, was the colonial avalanche of abuse and lamentation at the quality of these people an accurate appraisal of them? Occasionally a sober, good word for the Irish shines out in the torrent of extravagant denigration. In October 1840, the *Colonist* found the Irish 'a tractable, laborious and generous people'. In 1847 Sir Thomas Mitchell, the Surveyor-General, said they were 'the best and most hardworking' of his employees. But then he was a Celt, Scottish, and perhaps they worked best for their own or near relations. Perhaps they performed best when not subjected to hostility, contempt, and constant alienating denigration.

The consistent ambivalence—indeed contradiction—in Irish public attitudes to emigration makes their interpretation difficult, but judgements favourable to Australian emigration are evident from 1850. On 22 March 1850 the Dublin *Freeman's Journal* in an editorial entitled 'Government Emigration—No Irish need apply' took up the matter of what it claimed was discrimination operative in the selection of emigrants to Australia. It claimed that, deprived of Australian opportunities, emigrants were being forced to go to the United States or Canada, as a result of which many died tragically—at sea, or because of the harsh conditions in North America. (By 1857 Irish American migration had become such a prey to fraud, deception, and exploitation as to merit the description of the Archbishop of New York as 'a system of plundering migrants'; though he conceded that the victims were silly and credulous, such innocence was a fact of Irish migration.) The *Freeman*'s 1850 comparison indicates that the far superior conditions enjoyed by Irish emigrants to Australia were known and appreciated in Ireland itself at an early stage. This is an Irish perception which removes the mystery of the choice of distant Australia; in some cases at least, America must have been a second choice of disappointed applicants.

The same Irish view of Australia as a superior destination can be detected as the century wore on. Certainly the main image is that of distance, of being remote: in the 1850s in Killarney, the parents of Henry Bournes Higgins had a house whose garret seemed so remote from the rest of the dwelling that it was called 'Australia'. This distance acquired an exotic dimension in Irish popular fiction, in a way similar to English: Australia became a romantic solvent, a source of convenient legacies, mysterious strangers, and disposal of awkward characters, a device for resolving the plots of novels. (Occasionally it all came true: the *Irish Times* of 10 April 1905 records the return of a Hobart cab driver, who had fled Ireland as a sailor after a family dispute, now returned as heir to a baronetcy and estates.) But it was a solvent peculiarly benign—and Irish. When Gavan Duffy returned on a visit

The street Irish typified: S.T. Gill's 'Ease without Opulence' captures the stereotype of the city Irish
Mitchell Library

to Ireland in 1865 he found a general Irish belief that a majority in Australia, or at least a very powerful minority, were Irish Catholics. He tried to correct this impression, explaining that it was a happy place because Catholics and Protestants had learnt to live in harmony. But in 1880 he was confronted again with the same assumption, that the Irish were a majority in Australia: the idea seemed impossible to shift.

Irish immigrants already in Australia fed back to Ireland all sorts of impressions and advice, but one theme is common to all: only hard workers would succeed. This advice favoured skills, but much more important was what it advised against. In 1852–53 Joseph Beale repeatedly told his wife in Ireland to make it known that only those who were accustomed to labour should come to Australia, that young sons of gentlemen were unsuitable and that far too many came out unfitted, 'too highly educated for the work to be done'. From Adelaide in 1848 Bishop Francis Murphy had conveyed to the Bishop in Monaghan virtually the same advice: 'Young men looking for situations as clerks in offices have no business here; we are always overstocked with persons of this kind. Carpenters and masons are in great demand . . . Shoemakers, tailors, blacksmiths, in fact all mechanics are in great demand.' So they were, but so was manual labour, and throughout the century this is what Ireland provided, without apology, and in response to colonial demand. However high-flown and superior might be some colonial attitudes to the unskilled on arrival, there was on the other side of the world ample encouragement that they should come, even to direct stress on the need for the unskilled. Throughout the 1880s the Australian scene was glowingly depicted in Ireland, even to the extent of advice not to go to the United States or South America. Even late into 1891, in the face of colonial depression, both daily and weekly *Freeman's Journal* were still reporting demand for emigrants to Australia, especially female servants and unskilled labour, not least because it, and the semi-skilled, was what Ireland could readily supply. That it could and did do so was for Australia a valuable economic fact, but that did not prevent it becoming the subject of smear and sneer. (That the Irish atmosphere was changing was evident by the late 1890s. In 1897 the Queensland emigration agent visited Ireland but got little co-operation: the press would not publicise emigration, nor would the clergy encourage it.)

And it was, nonetheless, a matter of Irish economic unbalance and snobbish social attitudes which came under Irish Australian criticism. Advice against sending out over-educated clerks had particular application to such Irish parents who believed that their own reasonable affluence should enable their sons to avoid any manual work, regarded as demeaning. The Jesuit Fr Michael Phelan, writing in the *Irish Ecclesiastical Record* in 1893, suggested three reasons why Irish success in Australia had been less than it should have been. One was their gregarious habits, which kept them in the city when they might have been pioneering up country, another was drink, not so much in itself, as because 'English evangels and non-conformists make temperance their sole virtue' and had schooled society into rejection of any association with liquor, but a third was ignorance of a trade or the mechanical arts. Phelan upbraided Ireland for stupid prejudice and suicidal pride in sneering at tailors and carpenters and thus depriving the young of skills that would be of the utmost value to them as emigrants.

Phelan also drew attention to 'the lingering ghost of an old idea', that colonial society was primitive and inferior. For all that some of the Australian colonists thought the Irish inferior, some Irish were convinced of the opposite. The convict image lingered—and was revived by the Fenians transported to Western Australia in 1868. John Casey's articles in the Dublin *Irishman* 1868–71 depicted the colony as a cesspool of every kind of vice and immorality, peopled by dissipated cutthroats, immigrants initially simple and pure corrupted in a few months, assisted immigrants dragooned, herded, virtual prisoners, exploited and coerced, servant girls duped and dishonoured—the materials of Victorian melodrama. It seems likely that his purple prose merely added to the air of mystery and romance Australia had already acquired from convicts and gold.

What are the pedestrian facts: what Irish chose Australia? The young, of both sexes equally, with little capital or experience. They came by process of chain migration, assisted by various government and private schemes. At first, and mostly, they came from the South West and the Ulster border areas. When government assistance fell away, from the late 1880s, the real costs of the long passage forced a swing to those in more prosperous areas of the East and Ulster. And they came to Australia in wide distribution, but heaviest around the towns. In the cities Irish women tended to stay, not merely for social preference, but because these were the locations of their employment in domestic service.

Such is a bald sketch of processes which were to evolve in great human variety for half a century or more from the 1840s. To step back again to locate the beginnings of such dynamics, while the Australian public mind of the late 1840s was arriving at paltry and cosily critical conclusions about the character of Irish female immigrants, the great disaster of the Irish Famine had largely passed Australia by, its terrible human dynamic heading for America, only a few ripples reaching these shores. Relatively few Irish emigrated to Australia as a direct consequence of the Famine, although this did not stop local Irish later claiming it to add to the 1798 rebellion as a repository of Australian Irish tradition. Those Irish who did come were, like the Quaker Joseph Beale, not refugees, but men carefully choosing a land of new hope. Beale's case allows illustration of some typical features of Irish migration to Australia. A woollen merchant and miller in Mountmellick, Co. Leix, Beale was ruined by the Famine collapse of trade and demand. Not yet destitute but fearing he could become so, he sold all he could and came to Melbourne (second-class) in 1852, aged fifty. For the time being he left his wife and younger children in Ireland, but the move he saw as being in their interests: his duty was not only to feed and clothe his eight children, but to assure their futures, and Australia would provide 'a chance for our children not known in Ireland'. Ireland was 'wretched and will be wretched', a land without hope. (Among many of the emigrants ran the conviction that Ireland could never be changed, whereas Australia was a land being made, in process.) Australia, about which Beale had read a great deal, had a reputation for offering opportunity and success, had a dry warm climate, an excellent market for labour and—of particular interest to Beale—a flourishing wool industry. Australia's climatic advantages were a constant immigrant theme echoed to the degree of tedium—'how would I bare [sic] it at home where there is so much frost and snow?' asked William Martin in Roma, Queensland, in 1873: he was afraid he had lost the notion of going home, even for a visit. Beale's view was that the very climate bred optimism. Australia meant hard work, but plenty of it—he had various jobs, storekeeper, bookkeeper—and work was not considered degrading, as it was in Ireland. And there was the extra dimension of the gold rushes, which his sons joined. But most of all, after the staid inertia of Ireland, there was action, colour, noise, bustle (it was more rough and raucous than he had expected) heat, strange sights, new demands, 'in many respects, nearly the antipodes of Ireland ...'. Antipodes was not merely geographic jargon: it was a reversal to opposites in the whole climate of life.

The spectacular increase in Irish migration to Australia (and New Zealand) that occurred in the 1850s and 1860s was related to the gold rushes, particularly in Victoria. But whatever their stimulus and attractive power, the gold rushes were essentially a passing phase in the more basic processes of Irish settlement. In its earliest forms, this was marked by the desire and effort to acquire farming land, the tendency to concentrate in certain areas, and the practice of encouraging by letter and remittance of money, friends and relations to join them in Australia. These characteristics, evident in New South Wales by the 1820s, spread elsewhere. The heavy initial concentration of Irish settlers south-west of Sydney, and around the northern Maitland–Hunter River area, became themselves bases for Irish movement into adjacent areas as pioneering expansion opened the squatting age in the forties and fifties. These movements absorbed and generated further Irish immigration. Most marked was the movement south-west from Sydney into the Goulburn and Yass areas and eventually into Northern Victoria, and also down the south coast. In Victoria similar concentrations of Irish developed, though for different economic reasons, around Geelong, in the mixed-farming districts around Kilmore, north of Melbourne, and in the western districts, particularly inland from Belfast (now Port Fairy) and Warrnambool.

To pursue this point, still at the level of generality, it is evident that a major—if not the main—force moving Irish migration to Australia was personal relationships, the Irish already in Australia, beginning with the convict period, encouraging friends and relations to join them and either paying for their passages or sponsoring them for government assistance. A superficial glance at the fact that 85 percent of the Irish who came to Victoria in the fifties and sixties were single might suggest lonely exiles, but very many of these were brothers and sisters, cousins, relations, friends—and usually also met by such on arrival. They then tended to settle close to such Irish as they knew, were often employed by them, and frequently married within the group. Many carried those nineteenth-century travellers' aids, letters of introduction, tickets of favoured entry to networks of known and trusted persons. Even such as arrived relatively alone usually found familiar company. That great friend of Irish immigrant girls in the thirties and forties, the Englishwoman Caroline Chisholm, fostered such Irish concentrations simply because she found it easiest to place Irish servant girls in the homes of the Irish settlers of south-western New South Wales, where they were much in demand, not only as domestics, but as future wives. She also found that the Irish had an instinctive sympathy for each others' shortcomings and previous misdemeanours: 'there are a great number of Irish there [in Australia] who are doing extremely well who formerly got into what is called A Little Bit of Trouble; and they think that their own countrywomen will understand them best.'

This process of Irish aggregation has been detailed by Errol Lea-Scarlett for the 1840s in the small town of Bungendore in New South Wales.

> Bungendore quickly became a very Irish place ... John Dwyer's arrival began the steady flow of families related to his father, the Wicklow chieftain ... Soon Sheehans and Byrnes, Doyles and Donoghoes—all part of the Dwyer connection—were in the district, revering almost as a patriarch John Dwyer ... Rubbing shoulders with the Wicklow men were smaller groups of Tipperary folk associated with Thomas Shanahan who bought 'The Briars' at Molonglo, and not far away from them were other Irish workmen consciously collected on Carwoola by William and Thomas Rutledge.

The ease and self-confidence of the Irish in this general area of concentration is evident in an anecdote of a few years later:

> An Englishman who arrived in 1859 on the Shumack's property at Canberra, remarked one morning, 'Well, Joe, as I came across the lane I met that Irish savage that lives over

there—how is it that they let these Irish savages come here. They should be kept out'. Joseph laughingly replied that he himself was Irish and so were many of their mutual acquaintances. The Englishman got the shock of his life when he found that the Irish were respectable members of the community, because in England the Irish were decried and looked upon as the lowest form of humanity.

The basic individual economics of this process were detailed in William Kelly's *Life in Victoria*, in relation to the growth of Kilmore in the 1850s, in a description both archetypal and somewhat idealised:

> the Irish emigrant almost regards himself as the trustee of his family and connexions; born poor and inured to hardship, he deems it sacrilege to use his superabundant earnings in selfish enjoyment while those he loves and respects may be steeped in poverty and distress, and confined in his knowledge of banking to the name of that which 'he once ran upon' he initiates his thrift by making his lodgement in the heel of his stocking; and when that begins to 'make a decent appearance', he casts about for a respectable countryman through whose agency he can at one relieve himself of a burden of uneasiness, and contribute to that of his far-distant friends.

The effects and implications of these very common practices were much more complex than their simple generous appearance might suggest. That 'respectable countryman' who would act as banker and agent was very often the Catholic priest, and the widespread immigrant use of the clergy in those roles gave the priesthood crucial economic and social functions which tied them intimately into the ordinary family lives of their people. Through the structures of an immigration system operating in this way, the priesthood was often involved in the basic processes of community growth, a central position of great power and influence carrying over to all other community matters.

Kelly's picture is of the Irish emigrant dedicated to personal sacrifice for the good of others. Some of these self-denying peasant immigrants were never to lose the habit of poverty, when any justification for it had passed: perhaps it was less any process Kelly details than ancient peasant traits of caution and frugality. Whatever it was, stories abound, especially in rural settings—for instance, around Binalong in New South Wales—not so much of misers, but of guardians of money kept beyond plan or reason. Wealthy, but retaining the appearance and style of poverty (frugal with candle or kerosene, last to have electricity connected), spurning possessions or conveniences, not knowing how to use their hoarded assets, these Irish left their money to wild and spendthrift children. Or, dying childless, paralysed by the very size of their holdings, they let their money revert to the coffers of a state whose taxation they had resented and resisted all their lives. Such stories are too frequent to dismiss as eccentricities.

Nor does Kelly's emigrant portrait reveal anything of the less flattering variety of Irish family situations. Remittances were sent home both to assist remaining family, and to enable others to emigrate. The Monteagle correspondence in 1850 sugggests diverse motivations at work. John Culhane, who already had a son and a daughter in Melbourne, begged Lord and Lady Monteagle to send another of his daughters there: '. . . we there parents never had a hungarey or a poor Day in Ireland since they went through your Charitable good feelings to that good colony.' Selfless Mary McGrath told the Monteagles that she wanted to come to Australia so that she could earn more to support her parents at home—or, at least, that is what she said. Just how much money was sent home to parents from Australia remains problematical. The emigration commissioners noted in 1854 that large remittances had begun to arrive from Australia, but indications suggest that it was substantially less—obviously in amount, but also proportionately—than that sent from America. The reason is not a lesser Australian Irish generosity but a reflection of the higher economic position in Ireland occupied by the parents of the Australian Irish: they were less likely to need, less dependent on, emigrant remittances. This meant that such Australian remittances were more likely to be applied to further passages than absorbed in mere Irish survival by those at home. Indeed it is significant to see, in periods of strong Australian attractive power, that American remittances were applied to purchase Australian passages. So, in the years of major Australian gold rush, American remittances to Ireland (running at a total of well over £1 million a year at that time) were used by some families to finance sons to the diggings in Victoria. It may be assumed that the same practice operated in the disturbed years of the American Civil War: by that time Irish families were used to international dispersal and some were so widely scattered as to make chain family migration possible virtually worldwide.

Again Kelly's Kilmore immigrant is an idealised case. Not all Irish families turned with enthusiasm to the assistance of their own. In Queensland in 1873, William Martin had risen to be overseer of Tyrconnell Downs station. He had come to Australia with his older brother John, but they had fallen out. William had been more successful in the colony, and John resented this—and his younger brother's advice; it was a common source of family tension and rifts. Moreover William refused to bring out his sister: her education, her writing and spelling, seemed to him inadequate to colonial demands. Nor would he bring out another older brother, until he was satisfied that his brother's wife was 'an educated woman'. Then again, perhaps he would bring the whole incompetent lot out and 'let them shift for themselves . . . as I had to do'.

The Irish themselves made much of their devotion to chain migration, lauding it as evidence of generosity, family loyalty and so on. The general community did not see it in that light. At worst they saw it as people they did not want introducing more of the same, but even at best it was deemed to reflect little credit on the Irish: they were in the forefront of exploiting government assistance schemes in an age when the acceptance of state assistance was seen as evidence of weakness, inferiority, lack of self-reliance and initiative. It was irrelevant that governments had set up such schemes of necessity. It was simply that those who availed themselves thereof incurred an automatic stigma.

Nor should Irish trumpeting of immigrant generosity be accepted without noting its limitations. Some were too mean to help relatives out; they usually argued from the ground that some immigrants disliked Australia and blamed those who brought them. The Monteagle correspondence in particular reveals naked greed, selfishness and the desire to restrict the spoils of immigration to close relatives only. The wider colonial scene shows the same, that many of the Irish already in Australia resented and opposed further immigration which might erode their position. They preferred to aim their exclusion at the Chinese, but their principles were general. The Victorian Land Convention of 1857, whose aim was restricted immigration, had an Irish president, Moses Wilson Gray, who had come to Victoria with Gavan Duffy, and the huge number of Irish who joined it was widely noted.

The initial Irish population concentrations reflected an Irish gravitation towards rural areas and pursuits. In Victoria, for instance, the Irish-born and Catholic population of the towns and cities were, to the end of the century, below the average for the colony. As late as 1877 an Irish settler told the Queensland parliament: 'Our clear aim is a peasant proprietary in the Irish tradition.' Perhaps it was, at least for him. Yet the Irish gravitation to the land may be less than some inherent tendency and more a phase of circumstance, and a function of the development of the Australian economy. In early colonial Australia the land was the chief source of ready wealth (trading required capital) and in any case was available as grants, or as squatting areas (and later, of course, as selections)—at any rate, relatively freely. (Later, when the local economic environment fostered readily available wage labour, the Irish came to see this as better than farming.) Such was the initial pattern of the early emancipists, who often had very large families—commonly ten to fifteen children—which led to more intensive concentration as large initial holdings were divided, or adjacent land acquired. Other Irish provided services within these farming areas: in south-west New South Wales they virtually monopolised the coach service and innkeeping, and of course this too provided immigrant employment. This was a society strongly influenced by the patriarchism of a few dominant and often wealthy personalities, though few could rival the great Ryan domain at Galong, with nearly a quarter of a million acres by the 1840s. Why so few? There is more to this than the obvious economic answers. In a vacant land, when the answer to the question of how to build an empire was, take it, did many Irish have the ruthless gall, the hubris, to take as lords by right what offered to the greedy hand? Few could rise to that challenge: they had been accustomed to the subordinate side of the ruling relationship. Even in the city situation there was Irish paternalism: the New South Wales solicitor-general J.H. Plunkett, himself indebted to the patronage of Daniel O'Connell, frequently extended his patronage and help to Irish families who needed his assistance. Especially in its rural form, the Irish world of early New South Wales was a hierarchical and clannish one, handing on its customs, and even its brogue to succeeding native-born generations. And as with all Irish rules, immediate exceptions come to mind. Whereas the Irish kings of southern New South Wales established local hegemony, the Lawless brothers from Cork, Clement and Paul, used their Queensland empire as base for an aristocratic lifestyle in Ireland. Arriving in the Hunter district in

Irish small business: a cartage firm in the Cooma (NSW) area in the 1880s

1840, they moved with their cattle into pioneering Queensland in the 1850s, amassing runs of nearly 300 square miles. Sharing the commonly held Irish view that colonial women were inferior, they both returned to Ireland to marry, and thereafter commuted between Ireland and Australia, and died in Ireland. Although descendants remained in Queensland, these were lives whose focus and meaning lay elsewhere.

The grand rural life, with its patriarchs and retainers, was to continue, and indeed proliferate, in much more modest terms, but from 1850 it was reduced to merely a facet of a much wider and more populous Irish Australian experience: the discovery of gold changed Australia's Irish reputation from that of prison to El Dorado and created a melting pot which vastly accelerated the process of Irish assimilation.

Goldfields life suited the Irish. They contributed much to its colour, and to the romantic legendry that it generated. One reason for this was simple numbers. In his *The Gold Finder in Australia*, first published in 1853, John Sherer, surveying the composition of the goldfield's crowd, observed that 'many of these were the offspring of the teeming soil of Ireland, which seems to throw off its population with the same degree of prolific spontaneity that it shoots forth the riches of its vegetation'. (The coincidence of the 1867 census with the gold rush to the west coast of New Zealand revealed that the gold-rush areas had double the average proportion for New Zealand Irish. It is a reasonable assumption to conclude that Australia's goldfields were the same.) Irish music was an integral part of the goldfields' scene: hotels, the centres of digger sociability, blazoned forth their Irishness with names like Brian Boru, Harp of Erin and Shamrock.

And the Irish had more of their share of the flamboyant personalities on the fields. Many of the Irish gold diggers were restless fortune-hunters and adventurers who had descended on Australia because it was the next sensation, the new flavour of the month. George O'Reilly was 'heartily sick of New York where a young chap without money has but a poor prospect of making a future'. He came to Australia in 1853 to 'become a Croesus', found Melbourne 'the most awful place', failed in Bendigo, and by March 1854 was writing home to Ireland from Peru where he had heard (in Bendigo) of new diggings. It was a standard story. In 1852 the San Francisco census showed that almost half of the city's sizeable Irish population had arrived from Australia. Not that there was any necessarily one-way traffic. John Birmingham had stayed on in New Zealand, after the gold rushes there, working casually on the roads, but he found, so he told his mother in November 1870, that there was an immigrant inflow of 'all poor Miserable Scotch coming out to their Scotch friends so that no Irish need apply . . .': he soon headed back to a more congenial Australia. But this was in the sober aftermath of gold fever. The frenetic, obsessive, atmosphere of high rush fever is well reflected in John Danaher's letter of 1 January 1852 back to his mother, brothers and sisters—he was one of Lord Monteagle's lucky emigrants, a Melbourne police constable on six shillings a day: 'lose no time to come to the goldfields there will be gold had here for ages to come let all friends and neighbours come as soon as possible'. He was ecstatic about his own situation: 'my pay is now two hundred and forty Pounds per year . . . I can wear Gold Seals to my watch and Silver guards two, and Gold Rings . . .'

But at the more ordinary daily level of the gold-rush years, the Irish thrived in the interplay of excitement and disappointment—and the occasional win. It was a gambling game they enjoyed, the mixture of reliance on work and luck, appreciated as much for its style, its independence and freedom, as much as for its potential big rewards. Irishmen flowered in the easy informality of goldfields life. They were at one with its lack of pretension, with its ignoring and dissolving of the old social order and class barriers, with its disintegration of the previously ordained hierarchies. And they were accepted, more than tolerated, actually valued for being themselves. This process is evident in Sherer's remarks. He could poke standard fun at 'the simple, stupid, potato-like face of Biddy Carroll' in the orthodox anti-Irish tradition, but in light-hearted good part, for he was also grateful for 'the mirth-loving Irishman, ever easing his labour by joke and repartee'. For the first time, the goldfields drew attention to the Irishman's unique human qualities as positive and valuable: he was a source of amusement, of colour, of entertainment, in the harsh, uncertain, tense world of the pursuit of gold. The Irish were funny in themselves—stage Irishmen seem to have abounded on the goldfields—but they also deliberately created fun. They sang. They were good to be with. And this was deeply appreciated in goldfields society. It lightened the load, lifted the spirit, eased the heart.

There was another, more specific, way in which the goldfields Irish captured attention—and respect. Within the goldfield situations the Irish were prominent in just those eruptions of turbulence which attracted most widespread notice. The most spectacular and important of these was at the Eureka stockade at the Ballarat digging in December 1854 when 863 diggers ('Quite half of them were Irishmen,' a witness told the Gold Fields Commission) took up arms against the Victorian government. The immediate issue was the collection of prospectors' licence fees, but this was a culmination of official blundering and harassment: the general cause was democracy against hierarchy. Twenty-two diggers and six soldiers were killed in the resulting engagement. Thirteen men (six of them Irish, including the most prominent leader) were tried for treason before a Protestant Irish judge, Sir Redmond Barry. Their acquittal by a sympathetic jury symbolises an Australian acceptance of an Irish rebellious stand and disposition.

Eureka merits closer attention, for it entered not only Irish, but general Australian democratic mythology as a prime generator of Australian liberties. It was, the popular treatments held, a 'revolution': before it men were treated like serfs, but Peter Lalor and his co-insurgents showed the people the power they possessed.

So entered national democratic legendry, an occasion that exhibits much that was typically 'Irish'. That it did so points to the centrality of Irish initiatives in that myth-making process, not so much in their having any necessary monopoly of bellicose oratory, or aggressive posturing, but in their lending to these things a distinctive flavour and emphasis. Men of any nation might derive from the principles of Chartism, or socialism, or the simple dictates of natural justice, the urge and determination to rebel, but who would add to this what was, as noted by John Lynch, one of the Eureka participants, a fierce competition for immortality and the belief that they would attain it? Which they did. Such was a feature of much Irish behaviour: bids for notice, violent in bushranging, pacific in exploration. And who would add to the occasion poetry which carried both listeners and declaimer away? So Timothy Hayes, popular chairman of meetings, no fighter, a man of peace, easy, humorous, a natural leader, surrendered to the momentum of protest in such a way as to increase it, with defiance inflated to noble resolve, by encapsulation in some stirring quotation from the revolutionary Irish poets. 'Are you ready to die?' he asked his spellbound digger audience. Pause. Then solemnly:

> On the field our doom is sealed
> To conquer or be slaves;
> The sun shall see our country free
> Or set upon our graves.

Powerful stuff. And Hayes looked the part, large, commanding, vital, big in presence.

The importance of the Irish element at Eureka has been a matter for historical debate, asserted by C.H. Currey, denied by James Murtagh. That such an element existed is beyond dispute, with its vanguard of tough 'Tipperary boys', its Irish revolutionary tradition embodied in Peter Lalor, brother of James Fintan Lalor, intellectual of Ireland's 1848, and its publicist Irish nationalist journalist, John Manning of the *Ballarat Times*. Currey's contention is that the dominant physical influence was the 'Tipperary boys' and that the decisive practical tradition, despite those other legacies of unrest, English Chartism and the European revolutions of 1848, was that of the history of Ireland. Without denying this mixture, the Irish case has substantial support. The password for entry into the diggers' stockade was 'Vinegar Hill' the location of the last battle of the 1798 rebellion in Ireland and also of the 1804 convict rising in New South Wales. It was led by Peter Lalor who, whatever his later very constitutional career (MLC, MLA, twice a minister, speaker of the Victorian parliament 1880–87), came from a famous nationalist family, and was earlier eloquent on the wrongs of Ireland and the use of physical force. Perhaps a reluctant revolutionary, he was one nevertheless if no alternatives remained. Rafael Carboni described him as an 'earnest, well-meaning, no-two-ways non-John-Bullised Irishman'. Compelling too is the evidence of aggressive Irish clannishness, the local hill held by 'Tipperary boys' who expelled all others and acquired the reputation of being 'the fixed headquarters of Young Ireland'. Marvellously telling also is the virtually symbolic use of pikes, those traditional instruments of Irish rural insurrection, simply, as John Lynch testifies, 'out of deference to an antique sentiment, it having done some execution at Vinegar Hill and New Ross [in 1798]'. As a modern weapon the pike was useless, but its construction for the theatre of the occasion (by a German blacksmith) 'out of deference to an antique sentiment' was a gesture as Irish as proclaiming the grandiose poetry.

Seen in its Irish context, Eureka was an historical re-enactment of an Irish rebellion fifty years earlier, just as necessary, just as incompetent, just as doomed, just as confused as to objectives or ideology—and just as much a mixture of the glorious, the farcical, and the stupid. And just as divisive. William Craig states in his *Adventures on the Australian Goldfields* that on hearing that 'Vinegar Hill' was the password, and thus an *Irish* rebellion implied, many non-Irish diggers withdrew from the movement.

Eureka was Irish in the same way as so much of Australian history was Irish. For many of its participants, it related Irish history—Irish attitudes, impulses, and individuals—to key situations in the Australian scene. There that history encountered, and often activated, other forces at play, other interests, other understandings, bringing all to bear to produce what has all the marks of the classic Irish historical situation: the dramatic, inspired failure which by virtue of its force as a gesture had a radical effect on changing the atmosphere of the times. But just how uncomprehending of the Irish dimension in such Australian social dynamics might be the non-Irish, is illustrated by the longstanding failure to understand the role and motivation of Peter Lalor. In 1948 the then Labor government's decision to name an electorate after him called forth denunciation of him as a class traitor: as director of a goldmine at Clunes he had supported the introduction of Chinese strike-breakers. Everybody had it—and Lalor—wrong. He did not *become*, in Lynch's words, a 'smug Tory' after Eureka: he had always been one, if that is the correct term for adherence to hierarchical and aristocratic principles. And he had explained this to the Victorian parliament in 1856: 'Honourable members accused him of deserting [the diggers]. The truth was he never belonged to them: they were a class which he always despised.' Despised is a strong word, which should make unmistakable the strength of Lalor's stratified view of society, of his belief in the natural paternal rule of the landed aristocracy, of his confidence in the appropriateness of his own right to rule. A Trinity graduate, trained as an engineer, his father an MP, his family one of the seven septs of Leix, Lalor was no democrat. His leadership at Eureka was not that of a man thrust up from below, but of a descent from above; an individualist, a man strongly moved by principles of justice, Lalor probably saw his role as a duty of his superior position and attainments. That he should be so historically misconstrued speaks volumes for the exclusive dominance of the Irish stereotype in its identification with democracy—it had no room for people of Lalor's type. That Lalor, vestige of the old Irish aristocracy, should have been a digger at Ballarat says much for the solvent effect of emigration and gold rushes, the whole Australian scene, on the social structures of the old world. Despite what Lalor was, and thought, the mythology of Eureka served the causes of republicanism and democracy, coerced by the populist mainstream of Irish-Australian traditions.

The gold-rush element in Irish Australian immigration was quickly dissipated or absorbed, moving on to other rushes, to land settlement, or other employment. But it formed a much wider base than hitherto for the main continuing influx, that from the South West of Ireland, Munster generally: this was overwhelmingly the source of Irish-Australian immigration from the 1840s to the 1880s, the period of the greatest number of arrivals. The decline and end of the assisted passage scheme meant a sharp constriction in the numbers from Munster, and in the 1880s the balance in a diminishing inflow swung toward immigrants from Leinster, especially around Dublin. By 1907 until the war, that weight of numbers had moved north, to the Ulster counties.

But Irish strands other than those of the Munster Catholic majority had always been significant in Australia. Ulster Protestants did not flavour Australian life to the extent they did in New Zealand, but their impact was, nevertheless, substantial and important. And the fact that those charged with treason at Eureka appeared before the Irish judge, Redmond Barry (the same as was to sentence Ned Kelly), exemplifies the presence of a prominent and influential Irish element at the centre of the Australian establishment: if the Irish were at the bottom of the pyramid, there were also other Irish at the top; but between, of course, was a great gulf in education, social background, sophistication, and, usually, religion. These establishment Irish, or Anglo-Irish, were so integral to the colonial process, so much at the heart of the dominant structures of society, that the historical process has tended to take them for granted and be blind to their Irishness—a variation on the historical fate of those other less obvious Irish, the Ulster Protestants.

Such neglect is not hard to explain. Since 1921, the then partition of Ireland into the six counties of Northern Ireland (often loosely called 'Ulster') and the twenty-six counties of what is now the Republic of Ireland, has dominated the understanding of things Irish, and imposed on the imagination geographical and political divisions that did not exist before 1921. It has been a temptation—and a frequent fault—to read back into the past the present fact of partition, and the present existence of Northern Ireland. In fact, comprehension of the Irish in the nineteenth century is best related to very local place, and social class. To the educated mind of the early nineteenth century, 'Irish' meant Anglo-Irish gentry; the common, ordinary, Irish populace, the peasantry, that element which existed as a servile background of hewers of wood and drawers of water, simply had no significant existence; it was a sub-stratum of non-persons. So, in the mind of pre-gold-rush Melbourne, 'the Irish' were the local representatives of the Anglo-Irish ascendancy, an Irish cousinage of gentlemen whose lineage, connections, wealth and social position—all imported from the British Isles—were granted superiority in Melbourne's infant society. This soon changed, but it was not only the solvent effects of the gold rush, burgeoning egalitarianism, and the immigrant flood of 'mere Irish' that revolutionised the Australian scene (though it is important to note that the struggle of such Irish was not only against an adverse image, but against the tendency to concede them no existence at all). It was no less important for the Australian outcome that Ireland itself experienced a rapid process of social change and image adjustment in which the once shadowy and subordinate background of servant nonentities and unpersoned peasants, whose presence was on a par with the scenery generally, edged the gentry offstage into eventual irrelevance, and out of possession (both in fact and in impression) of a place called Ireland. Throughout the nineteenth century, in both Ireland and Australia, the Catholic Gaelic Irish took out a monopoly on the concept and image of Irishness, obscuring the true complexity of the multiple and various Irish contributions to national life and character. Obviously this process was largely impelled by politics; it was an aspect of the redefinition of nationalism that accompanied the move towards Irish independence, but it was more complex than that: it suited the Anglo-Irish to moved towards the Anglo side of their duality and the Ulster Protestants to move to the Protestant side of theirs. But whatever the responsibility, by the end of the century Irish meant, to all intents and purposes, Catholic: in popular consciousness those other Irish had vanished quite away.

But exist they did, and powerfully so. The Anglo-Irish are a neglected but crucial factor in the colonising process, most evident in Victoria between 1850 and 1880, but there from the beginning, and important too in New South Wales and Tasmania before 1850. To define these Anglo-Irish, the terms must be broad and flexible: English-speaking and usually but not always of English descent; not always of Anglican religion, sometimes Presbyterian, often Methodist, even Catholic. Some had adopted Protestantism to get a university education at Trinity College, and then reverted to Catholicism, and there were some of Irish heritage who had intermarried with the English, and those of Norman origin whose lineage went back to the conquest of 1176. In fact religion was less a distinguishing mark than class, and they were hardly one group as several, a compound, with significant divisions between landlords, professional men, the military and navy, administrators and bureaucrats, and with significantly various motivations. The landlords—pastoralists in Australia—such as Talbot of Malahide in Tasmania, or the Irish cousinage in Port Phillip, sought to carve out and possess quiet estates, the lesser gentry and professional men sought creative employment, the public servants and administrators sought to run efficiently this corner of a liberal Empire. In all these endeavours there was a strong material element, but their motives were more complex and less selfish than that: many of them merit that now outmoded adjective—high-minded. They were, the best of them, in the words of Mahaffy, the provost of the Trinity College in which so many of them were educated, 'heroic, splendid mongrels', a mixed breed in decline and increasingly alien in their own Ireland, where they were seen as an English garrison, yet feeling themselves Irish and indeed formed by distinctive and unique Irish attitudes and experience. They were the stuff of the imperial frontier; they saw colonising as heroic work. Gentlemen by training and inclination, their loyalty was to the idea of civilised liberal Empire and to the whole spectrum of notions known to the nineteenth century as 'progress'. And so their contribution to Australia was to be their concern for education, for religious freedom, and for responsible government independent of strong and intrusive metropolitan directives. Far from wishing to re-create Ireland, they were anxious to ensure that its mistakes were not repeated. Their own experience as colonists there had been bitter, and they saw themselves as victims of Tory reaction and blundering.

Australia was their chance to realise frustrated Irish ambitions. The Anglo-Irish were central to every proposal of liberal reform: anti-transportation, the introduction of the Irish National Education system (with its bid to end the sectarianism they deplored), the setting up of universities (those bastions of enlightened liberalism), the moves against the closed society of the colonial exclusives (moves headed by that paragon of Anglo-Irish liberal achievement, Governor Sir Richard Bourke), the implementation of that key practical aspect of nineteenth-century progress, the construction of railways (Thomas Higinbothom was Victoria's railway engineer, 1860–75), and, of course, land reform, that bane of Irish life and politics, though here of course the Anglo-Irish exhibited their divisions—the great landowners among them had views and interests very different from those of the professional-class city reformers. And they were also in the vanguard of the pursuit of law and order, not simply because of their practical involvement as lawyers and judges, but as a salient article of their faith in a structured peaceful society as the cradle of civilisation and human values. Perhaps the epitome of these men of ability, principle and ideals was George Higinbothom, dubbed by Alfred Deakin 'of Australian Liberals, the noblest nature and most refined', described by the historian Geoffrey Serle as 'a saint-like man of extraordinary sincerity, rectitude and unworldliness'. Dying in office as Victoria's chief justice in 1892, he had been a radical in his parliamentary career from 1861, a man of strong democratic instinct, a hater of faction, a supporter in his age and eminence of the 1890 strike. The inscription on his grave caught his temper and distilled his impact: 'The memory of the just is blessed.'

Another facet of this fascinating Anglo-Irish mixture of radical and conservative is evident in the most distinguished of the University of Melbourne's founding professors, W.E. Hearn, whose chair presumed acquaintance with a fair section of all knowledge— Professor of Modern History and Literature, Political Economy and Logic. Despite these demands he found time to draw up the 1862 Land Act for Duffy. The same belief in ideals lay behind their prominence in public office, a reflection not merely of their ambitions and abilities, but of their public spirit, and sense of public responsibility. And they were to be found everywhere in the imperial enterprise, often together: the first premier of South Australia, Sir Robert Torrens, had taken his degree at Trinity College Dublin at the same time as his governor, Sir Robert MacDonnell. Some members of the 'Imperial class' of soldiers, officials, and administrators, who conducted the day-to-day work of the British Empire on the spot, worldwide, were birds of passage, stationed in Australia as one stage in a career. Some of these—Sir Richard Bourke, governor of New South Wales 1831–1838, exemplified this element at its liberal best—made decisive contributions in their time. Others were permanent acquisitions, like, for instance, Captain Edward Denny Day, an Anglo-Irish army officer who resigned from the Indian Army in 1834 at the age of thirty-three—the move from India to Australia was a common traffic in those days and among such official classes. Day became police magistrate at Maitland from 1836 to 1869, typical of Anglo-Irish presence in this middling rank of official service. Seen from the Irish end, the Galweys of Doon, Co. Clare, may be taken as typical. Of four children, the heir stayed in Ireland: by mid-century one was a tea-planter in Calcutta, one was in New

Zealand, and the other was in South Australia. These were families that had connections everywhere in the British world—soldiers, administrators, men of commerce, engineers.

This was the public, most frequently encountered, face of the Anglo-Irish presence. But it also had an aristocratic dimension, the exclusive 'Irish cousinage' of Port Phillip, a group of colonists from the Irish ascendancy, linked by blood, marriage, friendship and upbringing, mostly squatters. A genuine ascendancy in the 1830s, replaced in the leadership of society in the 1840s by men of commerce, overwhelmed by the social upheaval of the gold discoveries, but resilient enough to survive in quiet and withdrawn obscurity, this ascendancy judged itself superior to much of the English society it found in the colonies. Its attitude to Melbourne's first Anglican bishop, Charles Perry, when he arrived in 1848, was patronising: no doubt he was an excellent man, but he had no real talent. And he offended the ascendancy notion of what religion should be: it could not abide enthusiasm or undiscerning anti-Catholicism. The Anglo-Irish objected to Catholicism not on doctrinal grounds, but rather because it seemed undemocratic, and a threat to good social organisation: they were tolerant of Catholic gentlemen and regarded the increasingly anti-Catholic complexion of the colonial Church of England in the late 1840s as vulgar and unfortunate. (It was not only the Anglo-Irish who felt this superiority. Coming to Australia in 1838, the Kerry Catholic gentleman Michael Finn was conscious of background, education and attainments superior to those of the common English: 'What an illiterate body the lower English are. Give me the "alien" Irish.') The foundation of the Melbourne St Patrick's Society of Australia Felix in June 1842 owed much to the tolerant atmosphere created by the Anglo-Irish, though membership of the society drew rather from an upper middle-class than from this gentry. Thus the first president was Dr John Patterson from Strabane, a naval surgeon attracted to Australia by prospects of land grant. He converted to Catholicism in 1843, but was an Anglican at the time of the society's formation. And the ecumenical point is made by the religious persuasions of the initial committee: nine Episcopalians, five Presbyterians, five Catholics. The prerequisite for admission was Irish birth; the aims were the promotion of Irish and Australian patriotism; it was non-denominational and non-political. And its fate encapsulates that of other endeavours of the Anglo-Irish: Father Geoghehan held a High Mass for the society on 17 March 1843, thus beginning its drift into the Catholic camp and the shedding of its non-Catholic members.

The aristocratic stance of the Port Phillip Anglo-Irish is probably at its most confident in Charles Griffith, a man conscious of the mediocrity and claustrophobia of early Melbourne society, of its boredom, materialism, crudity and general inferiority to the elegant polished world of the Dublin he left. In his circle, which stretched to the Talbots in Tasmania, the word 'colonial' signified the second-rate, the inferior, the ungentlemanly: a decent game of cricket was not to be had; drunkenness was the 'colonial vice' (although many 'gentlemen' fell prey to it). Another facet of the eighteenth-century Irish ascendancy world was strikingly exemplified in Samuel Pratt Winter, fastidious dandy, splendid in bearing (he was six feet four), agnostic, with a fine library and a taste for the arts, contemptuous of the philistinism of the colony, yet with a down-to-earth realism and flair for choosing the right managers that eventually made his property, Murndal, in the western districts of Victoria, both beautiful and prosperous.

Such Anglo-Irish gentlemen were wealthy and accomplished. They shot—in the colonial tradition—and also played the flute—in the style of the old world. They read widely, often cultivated eccentricities, and related to the Australian colonies with their own brand of zeal and affection. They judged that, for all their crudity, monotony, and lack of polite society, the colonies offered the great gifts of freedom and prosperity. They shrank from the raucous and grasping life of an increasingly marvellous Melbourne, but their hold on the tone and style of 'good' society remained as a set of criteria. These Anglo-Irish regarded their education and social position not merely as personal assets and privileges, but as responsibilities; they felt obliged to set standards and objectives appropriate to the civilised life. If common, vulgar society was to ignore their sedate and withdrawn proclamations from their aristocratic enclaves, of proper values and modes of behaviour, it was enough that such proclamations should merely exist.

This is the scarcely visible but deeply sensed hierarchical context into which fitted the very visible next layer of Anglo-Irish Australia, the men of affairs. This element, particularly concentrated in Victoria, was mainly composed of graduates of Trinity College Dublin, then the premier of British universities, liberal and innovative. They came to Australia because of 'a superfluity of ingenious and educated men' in the United Kingdom, particularly at the bar, and the group grew as the first arrivals wrote back encouragement to their friends to come. Soon, from the 1850s, Anglo-Irish professional classes of lawyers, doctors, engineers, journalists, educated men of enterprise, were taking a lead in all aspects of the Victorian professional and cultural scene, generating intellectual life, founding diverse organisations and institutions—the Agricultural Society, the Royal Society, the university, hospitals. They sought openings for talent, the satisfaction of ambition, wealth, power through politics, but also to enrich colonial life through the use of their cultivated talents and professional abilities. They encountered no problems of assimilation. Their qualifications, social graces, Protestantism, and relatively conservative politics assured them of a welcome in the upper levels of Victorian life in the period of rapid colonial growth from 1850 to the 1890s. But they tended to be absorbed by their own success: their various initiatives and liberal causes soon became accepted as colonial orthodoxy, indeed as conservative positions, while their versatile capacities allowed them to adapt in such ways as to merge with their new environment, though increasingly on its right wing. By the 1890s their power was in decline. They were, as a group, no longer being reinforced from Ireland, and the increasingly democratic and radical—not to say rough and crude—temper of colonial life and politics was rendering their patrician conservatism, as well as their gentility and cultivation, less relevant and central in public affairs. A dynamic pragmatism gradually took over such affairs, pushing aside such cultivated gentlemen and the civilised values they espoused.

Yet the passing dominance of the Anglo-Irish in Victoria had its legacy in a subtle and expansive flavouring of public life and in a heritage which had real dimensions of the genteel. Its features of public spirit can be seen in the lives of many of Victoria's public notables—Barry, the Higinbothams, a Catholic version in Gavan Duffy—but less regarded if no less important aspects of Anglo-Irish influence were illustrated in the lives of those who were not men of affairs, but rather, landed gentry in the new colonial mould. Such was Samuel Pratt Winter and the Anglo-Irish group he knew, particularly the Cookes, the family into which his sister Arabella married.

Coming to Van Dieman's Land from Agher, Co. Meath, in 1833 Winter, at eighteen, joined the Bryan brothers as an estate manager, by invitation. These brothers were middle-class Irish who had been attracted to Tasmania by the 1822 scheme to encourage middle-class immigration—the promise of free land and assigned convict labour—something not offered by the competing attractions of America. Various published accounts, including W.C. Wentworth's, gave the impression that little skill or capital was needed to establish oneself in the Australian colonies and by 1820 there was already a group of Anglo-Irish ascendancy families established in Tasmania—the Talbots of Malahide, the Fenton, Minett and Faulkner families. All these had had the £500 minimum capital necessary to qualify for the land grant scheme, aimed at the creation of a respectable entrepreneurial class, but in the case of the Bryans, barely so. The Bryans were very much men on the make, with great ambitions and claims, for instance, to have been one of the great families of Ireland. Their impatience and arrogance led beyond their establishment of a (convict) tenantry in the Irish manner, to prolonged conflict with Governor Arthur, via the flouting of regulations, bending the law, and stock aggregation by cattle-duffing. Their whole stance and style was a kind of early Tasmanian Wild West. Their new manager, young Winter, was an orphan. As a gentleman's son he had few prospects in Ireland, indeed a deteriorating future, but he could claim an advance on his deceased father's modest estate. The impulse behind this was not to establish the means to pursue a permanent new life in the colonies, but to conduct what amounted to a brief speculative venture. The assumption that all immigrants intended to stay does not hold good for Winter or those like him. Their aim was to use a small amount of Irish money in order to make a large amount of colonial money, and having done so, to return to Ireland as soon as possible to live the life of a gentleman. (This is, in fact, precisely what William Bryan did.) Their horizons were Irish and their attitudes basically contemptuous of colonial life—remote, rough, and of convict derivation, to be endured while necessary. Such gentleman speculators tended to remain on their properties as little as possible, hire managers, live in the city, and treat pastoralism as simply the way they (or rather, their employees for them) made sufficient for living in genteel style.

Samuel Winter was attracted to the new lands being opened up in the 1830s north of Portland in Victoria, where, as a squatter, he consolidated holdings near Hamilton. His idea at the time was to make a colonial fortune on which to live in Ireland. But a long visit to Ireland 1841–43 gave him serious pause. He found, not what he had expected, but an unhappy, uneasy place, his own class under threat and in decline, and, after ten years' absence, his own family circle eroded not only by death, but by emigration—he was not the only one to seek his fortune elsewhere than Ireland. Returning to Australia, his vision of Ireland was soon clouded even more by news of the Great Famine of 1845–48: for years both newspapers and family correspondence carried details of death, privation, and economic collapse, all on a staggering scale. The family advised him not to return. He did, in 1851, but this time for a visit which confirmed his decision to commit his future to the colony.

This was not simply a negative decision against return to Ireland. It was a commitment to recreating, around his property at Murndal, the civilisation of the eighteenth-century Irish ascendancy in its best aspects, establishing a landed colonial gentry which would be paternalistic, responsible, cultivated and civilised, attracting, and on good terms with, its Irish Catholic employees: it was to be the Anglo-Irish dream, pure and realised.

Central to this re-creation was the erection in 1858 of a 'big house', a dominating residence, in appropriate grounds at the centre of a village-like station community: the general setting was a parklike environment. The whole scheme was both anachronistic and utopian. By the time of its construction, its model in ascendancy Ireland was disintegrating under nationalist threat and the failure of its traditional moral confidence. Winter saw as much in 1867 when he visited Ireland again, deploring 'the old artificial Society where people were selfish and unwilling to sympathise with people in real distress'. He himself had no doubts about the necessity for Murndal to be an economically viable unit in an Australian pastoral world, but he combined this practicality with a vision of social reality so romantic as to be theatrical. His personal appearance and style proclaimed the same polarities. What was to be thought of the successful pioneering gentleman squatter who appeared in the streets of Melbourne in the guise of an eccentric eighteenth-century Irish nobleman—a man of twenty-five, six feet four in height, accompanied by a black boy in livery, two giant white Pyrenean mountain dogs, and a squad of various retainers?—and this as normal practice.

More wondrous still (and confounding for those who hold that Australia imparted instant egalitarianism) in Winter's efforts, from the 1850s, to deliberately re-create an eighteenth-century Anglo-Irish world at Murndal, its traditional lower orders were anxious to fill their allotted servile role. The station diary of December 1856 records that when a shipload of immigrants was met at Portland wharf by competing employers, eager, in a tight labour market to engage them, 'all the Irish Emigrants wanted to go with Mr Winter because he had a very tall hat', which they took as a clear sign that he belonged to the 'quality'. Whatever its sartorial or social bias, it was a wise choice, for although he was opposed to unions, he always paid significantly more than the prevailing wages and his labour turnover was relatively slight. Winter preferred Irish labour, recruiting a manservant and labourers when he was in Ireland in 1842, and choosing an excellent Irish Catholic manager for his property.

Predictably, Winter was conservative in politics and totally opposed to the aggressively democratic (and anti-squatter) temper that entered Victorian politics with the gold rushes: if there was any possibility of Victoria becoming eighteenth-century Ireland this spelt its end. He simply found democracy incomprehensible, a personal mind-set that put out of question any consideration of leading that democracy or relating to it successfully. He was not greedy or irresponsible, playing no part in the unprincipled squatter manipulations which confronted the selectors of the 1860s, but he was quite capable of defending his gains in a hostile world opposed to his hierarchical and subordinating view. Such opposition ruled out his wider ambitions of an old Irish world born again, and compelled him to withdraw to the narrow limits of his own aristocratic property and persona.

Winter's is one of the historical scenarios that might have been, had gold not revolutionised Victoria. However odious its paternalism might seem to the democratic disposition, it is vastly preferable to the other face also exhibited by ascendancy Ireland in Australia—and that also within the Winter family circle. Samuel's brothers Trevor and George joined him in 1837 and 1838. Trevor became an amiable but incompetent alcoholic. George, the eldest brother—and very conscious of that—was an arrogant and aggressive squireen, an unscrupulous opportunist, almost a caricature of the superior, ill-tempered, impatient blunderer of ascendancy fiction. He quarrelled with neighbours and storekeepers, and unlike Samuel, who got on well with the Aborigines, clashed with them violently. He was contemptuous of those he regarded as inferior, blustering with those who differed with him; he lacked integrity in money matters and was little interested in his property save to exploit it. His style eventually cost him any future, for his farm labour left him, unwilling to accept the tyranny of an Irish squireen when ample employment could be had elsewhere. Quarrelling with Samuel, George left for Fiji, hoping for docile labour there.

The fruits of Samuel's enterprise endure still, but the sour taste of George's failure is also written less discernibly in the past, woven into imponderables of impressions and reactions now dead. Nor is ascendancy Ireland simply disposed of by adverting to its obvious and direct Australian manifestations. It—and its twists, frustrations, and darkening chaos—reverberated in the minds of those who had lived in and with it, or saw it as some kind of measure or model: sometimes Australia intensified such pressures. Anglo-Irish dominance of Victoria's legal profession attests to successful adaptation. But as with the Winters, there is another side. The barrister Gerald Supple who came to Australia in 1857 had been associated with the 1848 rising and the *Nation*. A member of the Victorian Assembly, he became so angered by the anti-Irish nationalism of the *Age* that in May 1870 he attempted to shoot the editor in La Trobe Street. Whether by accident or because he was almost blind, he wounded the editor but killed a bystander, resulting in his imprisonment as insane. It is hardly sufficient on the basis of two Melbourne cases to suggest that Irish solicitors were addicted to street assassinations, but in 1882 the solicitor P.A.C. O'Farrell attempted to shoot Archbishop Goold: it may be safe to propose that the migration of professional men placed some under immense nervous strain to which they occasionally capitulated. It was not only the Irish peasant world which was beset by stress and tension, but the world that existed above it. Indeed, that Anglo-Irish world of aristocrats, gentry and professional classes was shaking at its foundations and slowly crumbling, under threat from below, and from atrophy and uncertainty within. The Australian legacy of that flight from the reality of impending collapse cannot be measured simply in terms of the accolades attracted by sunny Australian success. Behind those façades was often emptiness, nothing as confidently or absurdly Irish as Winter's attempted resurrection of a corner of ascendancy Ireland. In *Australia's Debt to Irish Nation-builders* P.S. Cleary indulged his own dreamworld inclinations, counting brave Irish natives in Australian high places—'We have counted a hundred and thirty seven in the lists of Cabinet ministers . . .'—and so on; but then dashing such fancies with 'It would be absurd to claim that all these people were exceptionally good citizens, or that they displayed affection for Irish ideals'. Absurd indeed. Gavan Duffy had made the same vital point forty years earlier: '. . . but they were Celts whose forefathers had broken with the traditions and creed of the island'.

Or tried to break: it was often not so easy. Added to these would-be reprobates were the more central and traditional Anglo-Irish. True, some were hollow men, eviscerated by the society they had left. Yet many were Irish of that different kind, colonial *and* cultivated, not distinctively Irish in any nationalist sense, but in the sense of sharing an Irish place and civilisation, different members of the one family—whose members might dispute their exact relationship. Their Irishness was so subtle, so central to what seemed naturally colonial, so much an anglicised variant, so civilised and superior, as to escape the categorisation its refinement eludes.

A further distinctive strand of Irish migration to Australia was that of Protestants from Ulster, an element fluctuating between 10 and 20 percent of the Irish total. Their Protestantism allowed them to merge more readily into colonial life, but many exhibited characteristics identical with those from the more southern Irish counties—a gravitation to rural areas, a tendency to group together, remarkable mobility—a strong consciousness of being Irish. As a body they were more skilled, and many arrived with modest means, some even with considerable assets. They tended towards the trades and skilled employment generally, while a significant number were sufficiently wealthy to establish themselves easily in the new farming areas or in city commercial life. Very wealthy Ulstermen, such as the Wilson family, or Sir Samuel McCaughey, built land and commercial empires whose enterprise and prosperity invite comparison with those of their Scots cousins.

The bulk of Ulster Protestant immigrants, coming to Australia particularly in the 1880s, and through to 1914, had little patience with divisive Irish politics or sectarian animus. Their considerable preserved correspondence back to Ireland shows them to have been conscious of their distinctive variety of Irishness, of the values of family, respectability, and hard work: they seem to have lacked that wilder and 'poetic' dimension of some of their Catholic compatriots, and also—in large part—lacked such religious intensity and commitment. Nor did they lend themselves to the spectacular: they sought a quiet decent life, integrating rapidly into all aspects of the Australian colonial scene. Given that Ulster Protestant immigrants were more likely to be men (whereas 50 percent of southern Irish were women, only 40 percent of Irish from the North were women, largely because there was work available for women in the Northern linen industry) these immigrants were more likely to intermarry with other groups in the colony, including Irish Catholic women; their correspondence is full of encounters which they retail as contradicting prejudice or questioning old assumptions. These Ulster immigrants seem to have been exposed more quickly, or at least more effectively to the solvent effects of the colony as melting pot, but the process itself had less resilient or 'foreign' material on which to work. Many Irish Catholics carried their name like a distinguishing brand—O'Brien, Hennessy, Murphy, the examples are legion— which invited an instant distancing reaction of categorisation—and the corresponding counter-response of aggression. But many Ulster people did not carry this flag of liability and division, and possessed names which offered neutral disguise. A list of Co. Cavan people married in Victorian churches 1855–70 features, for instance in the 'Ps' and the 'Rs', Porter, Powell, Pratt, Robinson, Rogers, and similar innocuous names. Others were assumed to be Scottish, as was the Northern Irish accent to the untutored ear.

Nor did such Irish group together to the extent the Catholic Irish did: they possessed neither the positive inclination, nor were they exposed to the same degree of isolating pressure. Certainly there were areas of significant Irish Protestant concentration in Australia, but nothing, for instance, like the Ulster group settlements in New Zealand in the 1870s and 1880s, where about 2000 Ulster immigrants were settled, in part through canvassing among Irish Orange Lodges. The Australian Ulster pattern was typified by the loose groupings of parts of Gippsland in the 1880s where the cohesive factor was acquaintance (rather than friendship) and accidental factors—the same group of immigrants seeking available land about the same time: there was no conscious or deliberate wish to form an Irish Protestant community.

The nearest Australia came to this was in the Kiama area, about seventy miles south of Sydney, where Irish Protestants particularly from counties Tyrone and Fermanagh concentrated from the 1840s and indeed from the 1820s: some of them were absentee landlords who introduced relatives and friends as tenants. In the Kiama Church of England 1856–75, 45 percent of brides were Irish, 50 percent of grooms, mostly from the Ulster counties. The area sprouted Orange Lodges: there were nine in the 1880s. Even now on a casual observation the region is physically reminiscent of parts of Ireland of a kind different from those Irish echoes visible in the winter mists in southern New South Wales. In the 1860s the parallels were much stronger. Dominant Orange settlers had graced the landscape with names which expressed their stance—'Loyal Valley'. The subordinate Irish

Catholic farm labourers (curiously, the area attracted both sides of the Irish religious divide) responded with threatening letters to landlords of the kind commonplace in rural Ireland. In the period of hysteria associated with the 1868 attempt to assassinate the Duke of Edinburgh in Sydney, there were occasional (unsuccessful) attempts to shoot Protestant farmers, and prominent Orangemen went around armed, even in Kiama itself. But all this was most unusual, as was the district itself. Its dairy-farming economy entailed much closer and intensive settlement than was the Australian rural norm. Its hilly coastal character had a feel of Ireland in general, but Ulster in particular, and its geology lent itself to another Irish manifestation, the loose stone fence, noted in 1869 and still in evidence. Above all, its population was mixed Irish; Catholic, and Protestant of a military evangelical kind, Presbyterian and Methodist, just the constituents to revive old antagonisms and conflicts. Nor did this Irish concentration evaporate: Kiama, Shoalhaven, Gerringong, had up to double the State average of Irish in the 1891 census. Yet very little violence occurred. Why? One reason was the relative weakness of the Orange Lodge movement, but that in turn was a reflection of the Australian environment, whose temper was such that extremists were unpopular; and the considerable number of Irish-born clergy within Protestant denominations, who had Orange leanings, found their enthusiasms—or fanaticisms—unshared in congregations themselves minorities.

The first Sydney Orange Lodge was formed in April 1845 by Richard McGuffin, a bootmaker from Newry. By 1848 there were 5–7000 Orangemen in nine Orange Lodges, this very modest growth being assisted by the *Sentinel* newspaper (1842–48), and vehemently opposed by Irish Catholics who scheduled hurling matches for the 12 July (the date of the commemoration of the victory of William of Orange at the Battle of the Boyne in 1690): their brandishing of hurling sticks was designed to intimidate any prospective Orange marchers. But it was in Melbourne that the first violence occurred. The first Melbourne lodge was formed in 1843, and the celebration of the Twelfth in 1846 led to a riot in which shots were fired and some people wounded. As attorney-general, J.H. Plunket responded with legislation (appropriately based on an Irish Act of 1832) prohibiting party processions or other meetings celebrating or commemorating anniversaries connected with religious or political differences calculated to provoke antagonism. This legislation was hardly necessary, in that colonial opinion generally was hostile to such divisive demonstrations and neither was the populace inclined to make them. The social climate was liberal, and the immigration experience tended to work against old world divisions of all kinds. This was even more so in the gold-rush period, adding as it did enormous mobility to other forces of social flux. Leading Orangemen joined the rushes and the movement did not revive until the 1860s: in 1864 it was reorganised from Ireland.

This meant that it was in place to make the appropriate loyal responses on the occasion of Australia's first royal visit in 1867–68. The first of these affirmations of loyalty was hardly promising. In November 1867 a transparency portraying King William crossing the Boyne, displayed in front of the Protestant Hall in Melbourne, was stoned by Irish Catholics. The Protestants responded with a volley of rifle-fire into the crowd: a boy of eleven died of wounds. The Sydney Orangemen lacked both the equipment and the stomach to proceed. They were short of banners, flags and drums, and very uncertain of their reception in the streets. The assassination attempt of March 1868 changed this situation radically—for a relatively brief time.

Up to this, Orange Lodges had not been strong in Australia not only because of the low proportion of Irish Protestants, but because there seemed no need for them: Irish Catholics had little power and Australian society did not operate in ways comparable to the old world. True, a few congenital extremists felt threatened by the very openness and freedom of Australian affairs, but their fears seemed absurd until March 1868 raised the spectre of Irish rebellion. Then, briefly, the Orange movement came into its own: this is what it existed to deal with, and its notoriety, as both Irish and sectarian, dropped away. In the apparent crisis of that time, it was not just the tendency of the extreme to attract the middle, but operative also was the clarity and simplicity of the Orange definition of loyalty —ultra-British, ultra-Protestant, ready-made positions at hand to feed the needs of that insecure phase in the evolution of Australian identity. On March 1868 an Irish Catholic and alleged Fenian, Henry James O'Farrell, attempted to kill the Duke of Edinburgh in Sydney: by the end of the year, the Orange movement had doubled its membership to 2000. In 1869 there were 2500 in 28 lodges, in 1876 19 000 in 130 lodges, and a peak was reached with 25 000 members in 1882, in New South Wales alone.

But in this prodigious expansion the Orange movement had changed its character: it was no longer Irish. It was its anti-Catholicism which made it attractive to its new members from 1868. Certainly anti-Catholicism was preoccupied with Ireland, because the Catholic Irish embodied, it was believed, all that was wrong with Catholicism—sedition, super-stition, laziness, being priest-ridden and so on. Those who joined the lodges in the 1870s, from the lower middle class, and the respectable working class, those with a shaky stake in the social order, felt menaced by Irish Catholicism. They were evangelical Protestants and their invasion of the lodges saw the burying of Irish roots and the construction of edifices of extreme Protestantism, with emphasis not on Ireland, but on temperance and fellowship. The early Orange Lodges had met in pubs: it is tempting to date their change in character away from imported Irish institutions from the time they changed their preferred beverage at meetings from alcohol to tea.

It is also tempting to suggest that in Australia it was, in a curious way, the swing away from the lodge's Irish roots that was most divisive. The depiction in verse by Victor Daley of 'The Glorious Twelfth at Jindabyne' suggests the celebration in the countryside of a ritualised faction fight between Irishmen of differing traditions, Orange and Green, who enjoy the occasion hugely and regard it as part of a common tradition which outsiders must respect. But a less colourful measure is available, the national origin of key Orangemen. Even by the 1860s, the English and Australian-born were taking up the cause. By the 1870s the movement was even denying its Ulster origins, preferring to stress its English aspects. It was also moving up the social scale: the lower-class Irish were giving way to an English and Australian middle class. By the 1880s less than one-third of the Grand Council members in New South Wales were Irish, a trend that can be seen at its end point in Victoria in 1981 when only about 10 percent of the Victorian lodge were Irish, and very few of the rest had Irish ancestry.

In fact this is not an unusual colonial situation. In Canada where the lodge was much stronger, it also early lost its Irish character in favour of a local Protestant one. The garrison mentality of Orange Lodge Ireland was not an appealing one in the Australian situation. Gavan Duffy contended, on his arrival in Australia in 1856, that Ulstermen were trying to reconstruct in the colonies the same type of domination over the southerner that they enjoyed in Ireland. It is doubtful if Duffy himself would have made this claim later. In 1856 Orange numbers made it absurd. Later, when it became powerful, the character of the movement had changed to that of a Protestant defence association. Later again, in the 1880s and 1890s, when the Twelfth of July celebrations were frequently the occasion for

An Orange Rally in Sydney in the 1880s. Insets: N.J. Mackenzie, Rev C.B. Madgwick,
W. Robson, J. Wheeler (circle)

riots, both those very riots and the vigour with which they were deplored signalled a potent
colonial disposition hostile, in its different ways, to Orangeism. As a general public stance,
aversion to things Irish did not merely extend to Irish Catholics, but very much included—
indeed even more powerfully—Orangeism, seen as divisive, bigoted, narrow, as all things
inimical to the tolerance of the new world, and as representative of the needless stupidity of
the old. It was troublemaking, organised. Moreover its devotees were seen as alienated
and dissatisfied colonists, and often from the 1870s also as wowsers, importing old-world
attitudes and antagonisms Australia could well do without. Only at periods of British
patriotic intensity (hysteria might be more accurate) did Orangeism exercise any significant

public influence, in 1868, and during the First World War—and then only because it was the obvious reply to its opposite Irish tendency. Both Irish extremes had, in their abrasions in Australia, the effect of discrediting each other, generating similar measures of impatience and detestation, and an overwhelming colonial wish to see a plague on all Irish houses.

The most influential Irish immigrant group was the smallest, the Catholic clergy and religious. To claim this for the Catholics should not be to ignore the numbers and importance of Irish ministers in the non-Catholic churches of the colonies. Many Anglican clergymen were Irish, particularly in New South Wales, and that well into the twentieth century, and many of these were the mainstays of local Orange Lodges, or at least prominent in voicing and supporting anti-Catholic positions—the strong evangelical and anti-Catholic flavour of the Sydney Anglican diocese may be traced, at least in part, to the Irish element. The Venerable W.H. Browne was a Tasmanian example, Trinity College–educated, highly evangelical. There was also a significant contingent of Irish ministers in the Presbyterian Church, particularly in Queensland, but these were regarded by colonials as 'second best', evidencing a 'coarser development of Christianity'. Notwithstanding local preference, these Irish were often all that offered, and congregations accepted them and their shortcomings in refinement without protest. Nevertheless, this often created a sense of (usually unspoken) distance between congregation and minister, particularly in regard to what might be appropriate to say and do in the colonial community—some ministers had a tendency to pursue extreme Irish positions which embarrassed their congregations, or which expressed divisive inclinations the people did not share. The colonial Methodist Church also had strong Irish elements, indeed by the 1860s had more than enough immigrant ministers, the local conference passing a resolution aimed at discouraging such arrivals, there being sufficient local recruits. The problem was that the superfluity of ingenious and educated men that produced a professional class for Victoria also applied to the clergy of Ireland—indeed the British Isles generally. But not only was the colonial demand in religious categories far less, but those offering tended to be the least able, those who had failed to gain appointments at home.

This also had its truth in the Catholic Church. There were frequent complaints about the crudity, greed and incompetence of some of the Irish clergy, but they were the exception; the rule was dedication and prodigies of missionary energy. About 2000 Catholic priests came to Australia in the nineteenth century. Nearly all were Irish, and increasingly from the 1860s, and virtually entirely from the 1880s to the 1930s, they exercised a dominating monopoly within the Australian Catholic Church. Within and without, for they also led the Irish Catholic community in its encounter with the world. The mass of Irish Catholic immigrants lacked the capacities and resources to produce leaders from their own ranks. This made them particularly open to the dominance and leadership of their clergy, a characteristic which largely saved them from the political tribalism and clannishness of the American Irish, but placed them in hazard of becoming perpetual altarboys.

What was remarkable and striking about the Irish priesthood in Australia was its forceful style. To whatever degree it was asserted—as mild paternalism or tyrannical autocracy—the dynamic was consistent. Its procedures were those of seeking firm control of all church matters (very broadly construed) and of pursuing policies of constant clerical visibility. By contrast with Italian clergy—or English—the Irish priests were self-confident and assertive, apologising to no man for their existence, far more likely to fight than

17th MARCH

Faugh a Ballagh

MARK FOY

IS OFF FOR A

HOLIDAY

In honor of
Ireland's Illustrious Saint

MARK FOY'S GREEN RIBBONS
ARE FREE TO-DAY

'Faugh a Ballagh' was pressed into commercial use with a caricature Irishman in Mark Foy's advertisement in the St Patrick Day Sports Programme, Sydney 17 March 1902

compromise or defer. This aggression was, from the accession of Cardinal Cullen as archbishop of Dublin in 1850, part of the temper of the Irish Church, but its Australian application sprang from the conviction that the job of such priests was not merely to minister, but to redeem. Theirs was a war against indifference, neglect, sin, heresy, sensuality and seculardom—all Satan's myriad allies—an Australian holy war to recapture the wilderness. Finding little faith or pious practice, they sought to re-create these things, an imperative which infused their whole social impact: they were active, urgent, men in God's hurry. The effect of such exuberant, belligerent styles in leadership is incalculable, but it was patently a major conditioning factor in the social stance of the Irish Catholic community.

Even in the basic immigration process, the priesthood was heavily involved in the machinery of chain migration and in the multifarious detail of the process of population transfer—money, letters, references, jobs, advice—but none in such a major and spectacular fashion as Bishop James Quinn of Brisbane (he called himself O'Quinn to celebrate the O'Connell centenary in 1877).

Queensland had already, in 1862, attracted favourable notice in Ireland as a place for emigration: a paper to the Royal Dublin Society had stressed its prospects, particularly for those willing to rough it. Soon after he had arrived in Brisbane in 1861, Quinn had truculently (and unfairly) complained to the Queensland government that its immigration policies discriminated against the Irish. He proposed that the government assist a scheme of his own, established in 1862 as the Queensland Immigration Society. The government declined, but agreed to co-operate where possible. Quinn had been casting himself in Ireland (with the aid of his brother Matthew, soon to become bishop of Bathurst) as friend of the forlorn Irish, and Father Patrick Dunne, then resident in Tullamore, Co. Offaly, had approached him with the idea of sponsoring emigration as a measure to relieve famine in that area—the American Civil War had constricted the Atlantic outlet. Quinn responded less, it might seem, to relieve distress, than to build up the Irish population of his Queensland Catholic empire, which critics were already dubbing 'Quinnsland'. His scheme was financed by land orders issued to every migrant by the Queensland government—and by contributions from the migrants themselves. Given this requirement, it is hardly surprising that few of these emigrants were paupers, but rather, as the Irish papers of the day described them, from the comfortable farming classes, 'superior . . . to those who leave for New York'. Indeed Quinn's character and ambitions were such that it is unlikely that he wished the indigent sought out as potential citizens for his territories. So was further confirmed, by episcopal selection, the upmarket character of Australia's Irish immigrants. And wherever a comparison was made that distinction continued to be observed: in the researches of the Irish Folklore Commission into emigration in the 1880s from the parish of Grange in Co. Tipperary, it was the farmers and their sons who went to Australia; the labouring men went to America.

But episcopal sponsorship did not ensure trouble-free worldly operation. The scheme was a success in that it transported about 4000 people, but its administration was inefficient and negligent. The voyage of the inaptly named *Erin-Go-Bragh* forced the government to frame regulations which put the society out of business: that voyage took six months, and fifty-one immigrants died en route. With and without Quinn, Queensland remained a magnet for the Irish as they followed pastoral expansion and gold discoveries, or simply got off the ships in northern ports as these were on some routes first points of Australian call and they were bored with the voyage. By 1865 an Ipswich steam locomotive carried the

Gaelic name 'Faugh-an-ballagh' (Get out of my way or else be run over), a tag which assumed some appreciative readership.

So the Irish clergy managed the Catholic Church, but although their leadership was powerful and real, it did not amount to exclusive possession: they occupied their role in some tension with a laity not always docile, and with expectations of their clergy not always harmoniously met. The close relationship between Catholic clergy and laity was very real, but its existence was less because that laity was subordinate or priest-ridden than because there was a real accord in aims, objectives, and spirit. At times, for very different reasons, they reached compatible conclusions.

The clergy's influence was supplemented, particularly as a Catholic school system was built from the 1870s and 1880s, by that of religious teaching orders from Ireland, so that the entire religious formation of many Australian Catholics, from childhood to adulthood, came, at least theoretically, under intense Irish influence. Typical of such dynamics, profound yet elusive and unquantifiable was the role of the 'Penny Catechism', adopted for Australia in 1885, based on the Maynooth Irish model, in the building of the Australian Catholic mind for the subsequent half-century.

The Irish clergy and religious were a group with continuity and great power, continually reinforced from Ireland, having control of education and the complex resources of the Church, resources of authority, opinion-making, decision-taking, and money, resources which also gave it control of the Irish-Australian press. Those newspapers which were simply Irish in a national sense were ephemeral. Take the unashamedly Irish *Irishman*, edited in Victoria by Michael O'Reilly, former editor of the no less unashamed, and more long-lived *Banner of Belfast*. The longest the *Irishman* was able to deny the hegemony of the Irish-Catholic connection was November 1872–March 1873; it then expired. Those which enjoyed continuity, such as the Melbourne *Advocate* from 1868, and the Adelaide *Southern Cross*, were those with clerical approval, content and involvement, and financial backing. The *Freeman's Journal* illustrates the same point in a different way. Founded in 1850 with clerical support and approval, its swing from the 1860s away from that position eventually led to clerics' founding its main competitor, the *Catholic Press* in 1895. This not only reflected the dominance of the clergy in the Australian Catholic intelligentsia, but their possession of the structures and machinery of organisation and finance.

The rapid growth of the Catholic education system from the 1880s is commonly construed as witness to religious loyalty and solidarity—or to the exercise of clerical power. Its implications are much more complex. It marks the breakdown of the pioneering colonial religious mixture. Up to the 1880s, particularly in country areas, there had been a good deal of practical ecumenism: religious division was, in part, a by-product of growth and sophistication. Catholic education was also testimony to the aspirations of the Munster Irish to social betterment, to their determination that their children would, through education, rise higher than themselves. Yet the making of Catholic education into an Irish tribal cause compelled an involvement in and commitment to education well beyond that which might otherwise have resulted, for the Irish migrant was hardly interested in education for its own sake.

Nor would it be correct to see the remarkable growth of large and imposing Catholic buildings, churches, schools, hospitals, as entirely religiously motivated. Such buildings also proclaimed the public presence of Irish Catholics and, of course, their increasing prosperity. The matter of public 'visibility' was very important to Irish Catholics: these

A proud photograph, sent back to Ireland. St Patrick's Cathedral, Melbourne, in process of construction, 1871
Public Record Office of Northern Ireland

nobodies could in concert demonstrate that they were citizens of no mean city—noble Romans. And if there were critics of the grandiose, and of the Church absorbing so much Catholic wealth (and it did—the costs to the Catholic community were enormous) the poorest Irish Catholic could be at one with his priest in the reply: these buildings trumpeted in stone the importance, the value, of The Word—and those who followed It—in the one, true, holy Catholic, apostolic—and Irish—Church. And make sure, the sacrifice was not in vain, the money not wasted: the non-catholic community was impressed. One case will serve the point. Confronted by the convent, the first brick building in a township which itself had not existed thirteen years before, the Cooktown *Courier* in 1889 gasped 'stupendous'. The word was curiously apposite: it recognised the prodigies of faith, hope, and charity behind that grand bricks and mortar, yet prefigured its less flattering linguistic relation—stupid. Not stupid in its day: imposing affirmation then. But now? Perhaps immigrant vanity, perhaps ambition to impress. The triumphal edifices of the Irish Church in its new Australian world were eventually to ring hollow, their long cool corridors no longer populated other than by ghosts of ambitions past and of immigrant pride satisfied, now serving in other capacities, museums (as in Cooktown), police academies, private homes. Yet to ponder too much on the end of all vanities, the emptiness of gargantuan folly, is to miss the practical peasant cunning of these constructions: they served their immediate purpose—they unified, they affirmed, they impressed, they signalled arrival, and that in force.

The large buildings (the cathedrals, two still unfinished, testify to competition with both England and the Middle Ages) are at the apogee of the constructional impulse. More modestly, but splendid on local scale, each town had its Catholic church, school and convent. Distant hostile critics, brimful of liberal orthodoxy, might see that as dividing a community. Perhaps in theory it did, but in practice it located it, gave it identity and pride, a sense of place and permanence. Local church and school gave the Catholic community a physical stake in a town, compelling integration and commitment by virtue of the character of that very enterprise, by the actual and intangible debts it occasioned to local councils, banks, builders and so on. The Catholic community was drawn together by its real estate and the money owed on it, and drawn into the wider community as well, for these ventures depended on the goodwill, co-operation and trust of non-Catholics: the bankers, whose support was vital, were seldom Irish Catholics.

Irish Catholics were also drawn together and civilised by the social effects of their religion, which did much for the gentling of Australian society, making the environment less harsh and lonely. In small pioneering societies Irish Catholicism introduced and promoted a whole range of refining processes associated with popular civilisation—singing, various activities of beautification such as flower arrangement, popular religious art such as paintings, statuary, stained glass. With this went the enhancement of various aspects of polite society, Sunday best, ritual, standards of dignity and ordered and restrained behaviour. While Irish Catholicism held no monopoly of such socioreligious promotions it was in the forefront of their Australian spread.

And it is here that the character of Ireland bears noting in relation to its Australian legacy. The Irish attitude to the visual, and to matters of art and taste, reflected a poor

Humbler religious structures: church, school and convent, Orbost, Victoria

economy and a persecuted religion, the one without surplus, the other hidden, on the run, both incapable of generating their own natural decoration. Hence the borrowing from the Italianate, a matter not only of the influence of the authority centre of the Catholic religion, but of the admiration of the poor for sumptuous show. From cardinal archbishop to lowliest people, the Irish preference was for the grandiose, the overblown, the garish—the opulent as the seeming opposite of the meanness, deprivation, and grey ordinariness from which they had sprung, and in which many still lived. The rich best must be given to God, and to things and persons religious, and thus standards for taste, beauty, must be the opposite of plain, for that meant poor. Hence the startling contrast between an austere religion of poverty and its acquired and engrafted popular artistic culture—show, tinsel, mawkish Mediterranean sentiment. The real Ireland wore an ancient stone face. It looked out stubbornly from a pagan past, with hard eyes, its natural ornamentation layers of convoluted spirals and knotwork interlacing, true symbols of subtlety, cunning and complexity, with impeccable logic and beauty of their own.

That was disguised by the public Catholic face. But it was not only that that drew communities apart. The very growth of small pioneering societies worked naturally against early ecumenism. Growth in size and numbers meant growth in complexity and diversity, the introduction of diverse and eventually divisive organisations and institutions, the construction of physical expressions of old divisions and ideological forces which separated and distinguished various local groups, and linked them, as communications improved, to similar communities elsewhere. It was common then, and now, to blame the Irish for the development of community polarisations, but the process of growth itself entailed an inevitable end to the old local co-operative and ecumenical spirit, and brought increasing power to the traditional external agencies of impersonal social control—distant and faceless authorities of church and state, political parties, benefit societies, fissiparous organisations of all kinds. These drew old communities of place apart into differing fragments which fitted into larger wholes elsewhere, or overall. For the Irish, their Catholic Church took on that function, but as effect, not cause, of linkage to a wider world. And, of course, sectarianism revived. But the earlier pioneering ecumenism was never quite forgotten, and remained to soften the edges of animus, imported and home-grown.

So it was that for the bulk of the Catholic Irish their church in Australia was not only the road to salvation, it was their social centre, their defiant profession of separate identity, their claim to recognition and status, and their avenue to self-esteem—in *this* world: it was a classic immigrant church. Its increasingly intransigent and triumphalist tone from the 1880s, its eagerness to enter sectarian battle, reflects the aggressive self-confidence of a self-made community rising rapidly in the world, no longer willing to accept any inferior role. This temper was fed by the remarkable success of the Catholic education system. The refusal, from the 1860s, to accept the state's secular education proposals, was a symbolic protest, but also a test—of will, capacity, resources. Could these lowest of the low, bog Irish, build their own separate system? Indeed they could. If it meant a sacrificial financial drain, it proved they had such resource. If it called for organisational ability, dedicated teachers, tenacity, perseverance, aggressive practical religious faith—yes, they had those things too, all that was needed. Small wonder Catholic education was an enormous source of Irish pride.

The thorough Irishing of Australian Catholicism bears the marks of deliberate contrivance by clerics, beginning with Father John McEncroe, who arrived in 1832. Despite the Irish birth or derivation of Australia's Catholics, many forces were working against Irishness in religion. One was the English Benedictine hierarchy in Sydney, but the strongest was a feeling among many of the laity that anything too Irish or too Catholic would offend the Protestant English majority, and thus hinder their own social acceptance and advancement. There is ample evidence that contradicts the Irish clerical assertion, made loudly from the 1850s, that the Australian laity, being Irish, wanted an Irish episcopacy and clergy. Indeed the balance of evidence indicates that the drive towards banishment of the Benedictines (ousted finally in 1883) and the substitution of an Irish clerical authority—Irish clerical imperialism—is related not to the existence of vigorous and widespread Irish piety, but to the reverse, widespread apathy and indifference. To use the words of Bishop Murray of Maitland in 1870, it was in order 'to root out of this land that fatal indifference to religion which is the curse of this country' that Irish clergy and bishops set out to impose on Australia an imitation of Irish religious culture. The basic proposition was, and it was still being proclaimed vigorously by Archbishop Mannix in the 1920s, that to cultivate an Irish atmosphere was to cultivate true religion.

Irish nationalism was another matter. In Ireland, Irish nationalism was often in tension or conflict with the Church. In Britain's colonies it was no asset and often a liability in the Church's relationship with its environment. To maintain a balance where Catholics would be Irish for religious purposes and British-Australian for political and social purposes was a feat beyond the capacity (and sometimes the inclinations) of most clerics, and certainly beyond the comprehension or ready tolerance of many in the general Australian community. The Irish subculture in Australia was a phenomenon imposed by the clergy from above, rather than a natural growth from below. By that time the Irish-born proportion of Australia's population had begun a rapid decline; by the 1880s the actual number of Irish was declining, and the proportions, radically so—from 16.2 percent in Victoria in 1861 to 10.6 percent in 1881, from 15.6 percent to 9.2 percent in New South Wales across the same period. Yet the period when the Irish-Australian subculture flourishes comes much later, from the 1880s to the 1930s: it was substantially of clerical manufacture, a contrivance which went with the grain of an immigrant people, and their children, naturally so predisposed.

The Irish clerical campaign to gain control of the Australian Catholic Church reached its most aggressively strident in the 1850s and sixties, linking Catholicism with Irishness, and provoking public hostility to both. This hostility stemmed first from the gradually developing pressure of Irish Catholics towards improving their religious and socioeconomic position. However, such pressure was diffused, and related to the success of individuals, not expressed in any unanimous or concerted action in the public sphere: the lack of political agreement or solidarity among Irish Catholics in Australia was apparent from the first elections in New South Wales in 1843. However, this did not prevent hostile critics maintaining that the Irish were an organised and clerically disciplined pressure group, subversive of the public good. It is not difficult to find Irish clerical wishful thinking on such matters. On 11 January 1862 Bishop Quinn in Brisbane wrote to Father Geogheghan who was then in charge of the Melbourne diocese suggesting a scenario which would resolve the problems of Catholic education: 'It might be that while O'Shanassy and Duffy are in power in Victoria, a system favourable to our views would be sanctioned there, and afterwards adopted by other colonies.' Simple. Easy. These Irish bishops often dreamt that electorates might behave like bishoprics—do what they were told. Irish Australian politicians were never under such illusions.

Speaking to the electors of Mudgee in January 1872, Henry Parkes, one of Australia's most prominent politicians, made the case against the Irish immigrant:

> I protest against Irishmen coming here and bringing their national grievances to disturb this land of ours ... to distract the working of our political institutions, by acting together in separate organised masses, not entering into the reason of our politics, nor judging public questions on their merits, but blindly obeying the dictation of others as ignorant as themselves ... Until Irishmen learn to be Australian colonists—until they learn to tolerate free discussion—until they understand the uses of liberty, they must not be surprised if people regard their presence as something not very desirable ... I object to seven Irishmen coming here to every three Englishmen. I object altogether to any class of men coming here, to set themselves in motion to extinguish freedom of speech and to impede the work of our free institutions. (A voice: You old baboon!) Those few gentlemen in the crowd should be the last men in the world to talk about baboons...

To Parkes, the Irish were still 'jabbering baboons'. But by 1872 the baboons were answering back.

Were they a disruptive, alien, priest-ridden tribe, arriving in excessive numbers? No. Statistically, Irish immigration was not disproportionate, but Parkes was obsessed by the belief that it was. He had raised the matter in October 1869 in opposing an assisted immigration bill. It was J.D. Lang all over again. 'He had no desire that his adopted country, the birth place of his children, should be converted into a province of the Pope in Rome ...' And he pointed out that of the 20 000 assisted immigrants in the period 1860–67, 15 000 were Irish and 12 800 of these Catholics (so much for the assumption that *all* Irish were Catholics): Parkes' conclusion was that the logic of the continuation of such figures was an Irish Catholic takeover—an absurd conclusion as by this time immigration was a minor demographic influence compared to natural increase. But then (as now) immigration was the obvious population factor in the public eye; and an ideal ground on which to fight back at his Irish Catholic enemies. In 1868 Parkes was the subject of Irish Catholic attack over his education policies and his handling of the 1868 Fenian scare. He lashed back, partly from political instinct and habit, partly because he saw Irish Catholics as committed to principles and beliefs he believed impeded true progress, partly because he saw them as disruptive troublemakers making it more difficult to achieve his idea of social harmony.

Parkes had a selfish point: the Irish would certainly try to make his life difficult and did not see the world as he did. But what of his serious and basic questioning of their Australian social and political role?

The Irish did not act in political concert, but (and this was crucial in sustaining the public impression that they did) some Irish activists believed and demanded loudly that they should. These doctrinaire Irish grouped around the Sydney *Freeman's Journal* founded by Archdeacon McEncroe in 1850. Their central conviction was that the O'Connell model of disciplined Irish Catholic unity, allied with the forces of religion, pursuing a policy of aggressive confrontation of any opposition, was the only appropriate political exemplar for Irish Catholics in Australia. But the *Freeman's Journal* was constantly bemoaning the fact that Irish Catholics would not act thus. Local issues and personalities, and economic interests, counted much more in the politics of Australia's Irish Catholics than their being Irish or Catholic. However, the Irish doctrinaires were forever proclaiming themselves, a small minority, to be *the* Irish in Australia. Sometimes this had a coercive effect on Irish moderates, arousing them, through guilt rather than desire, to support more aggressive or more Irish policies. And always the clamour of the doctrinaires served to convince those disposed to think ill of the Irish that they were correct in doing so.

And was it true, as Parkes claimed in 1872, that Irishmen had not learnt to be Australian colonists? True, some found integration easier than others, but very few found it impossible: few returned to Ireland. And true, in the 1850s and sixties some rural Irish in Neil Coghlan's words 'built farms and communities that seemed oddly out of place in the Victorian landscape ... and bespoke an ethos radically different from the one which dominated the colony of Victoria'. But so what? They formed no ghettoes nor set themselves apart: they opted in to the diversity of colonial life. It is significant that when immigrant Irishmen set up social organisation proclaiming their nationality—St Patrick's Societies, Hibernian Associations, Celtic Clubs—membership was never large, nor exclusive in any abnormal way. Such immigrant organisations, and they were neither many nor powerful, were merely another aspect of the diverse and home-country-oriented colonial social activity of that time.

CHAPTER
FOUR

SETTLERS &
UNSETTLERS

When did an immigrant become a settler? The question is neither trivial nor absurd, for while it admits of no ready or general answer, its asking draws attention to the variety, uncertainty, and state of flux prevalent among the Irish in nineteenth-century Australia. The trite answer might be—when the immigrant decided to settle, to commit his or her future to Australia. In some cases this was the decided intention before leaving Ireland, in others long delayed, in still others, never made: some immigrants drifted into the actualities of settlement—mortgages, marriage, children, property—hardly realising it. And even those might not always dictate an Australian future. Michael Skehan of Bridgetown, Co. Clare, went to Melbourne about 1840. He returned in 1853, with his wife and five children—plus £10 000 and a large quantity of gold nuggets: he bought a farm near Scariff. Few had Skehan's luck, but many dreamt of it—and lived Australian lives based on the assumption that if they struck it rich (and not only in gold) they would return to Ireland. The vicinities of goldfields were littered with 'settlers' whose dynamic as fortune-seekers had at last run out and who had lapsed (they told themselves, temporarily) into various other employments. And then there were those many Irish who stayed in Australia—and wished to do so—but never 'settled'. They were constantly on the move, from place to place, job to job: indeed, that was Australia's attraction to them; its economy and geography made the itinerant life possible. The comparative youth of so many Irish immigrants made them more naturally footloose, reluctant to 'settle down', at least too soon—whatever that might mean; they wanted to have 'a look around' first. Some judged Irish unsettlement an aspect of national character, a facet of the wildness and instability commonly attributed to the Irish. Everybody indulged in explanatory analysis of Irish character, including the Irish themselves: that most charitable of Englishmen, Archbishop Polding, made a representative summation (privately) in 1868: 'Thoughtless, inconsistent, ungrateful, yet detecting ingratitude, impulsive—one day is, with them, in contradiction with another.' Without subscribing to Polding's comment as a law of national behaviour, such inconsistencies can be detected in much of the immigrant scene—and, of course, not only Irish: much deemed Irish was merely generally human, or at least, immigrant human. Just to add to the diversity, there were also those who very much wanted to settle but found it impossible. Writing from Melbourne to a relation in Mullingar on 6 September 1875, Thomas Smyth spelt out his disillusionment: 'Education + gentility out here = poverty'. He returned home: 'The reason for my leaving Australia was a severe illness brought about by disappointment.' The majority could not afford the luxury of a severe home-inducing illness and endured their disappointments as best they could where they were. But this did not necessarily mean that they were 'settled'. Is an immigrant ever settled, ever totally without regrets, or free of wishes to return, ever totally removed from a former self?

This question, with its answers as multitudinous as the immigrants themselves, is the uncertain substratum on which rests the story of the settlement process. That process has to be taken largely—as the immigrants took it themselves—at face value. Many, indebted to relatives or friends for passage money, saw its repayment as a first concern and charge in the colony, closely followed by a wish to provide cash or gifts for those left at home, or at least the need to be able to report some success. Their early days in the colonies were dominated by these considerations, which in practice dictated an immediate search for available employment, a process which could quickly lead to absorption in the colonial scene. But that scene was one of constant flux, even before the gold rushes introduced the atmosphere and expectations of lottery. For a long time—a steady stream until 1853, not ending in Western Australia until 1868—Australia had convict as well as free immigrants. This was a curious internal ambiguity that reverberated within Irish Australia in particular, given the Irish convict stream's political rebel dimension, supplemented as it was in 1848 and 1867. This dimension blurred the distinction that for the non-Irish seemed vital, between criminals and settlers, but in any case the distinction was always under threat as convicts were set free. More than others the Irish were subject to experiencing an unsettlement of traditional social roles. This was no simple egalitarian levelling (though that was part of the process) but a whole range of mobilities, up and down the socioeconomic scale, and between religions and thus cultural localities. Australia offered the Irish social mobility of a kind and degree they had not experienced. This mobility often also entailed a change of religion. Presbyterians often upgraded to the Church of England. Irish Catholic women frequently married outside their church not merely in search of social advancement, but simply in order to marry at all. The process then is not a simple one of settlement, although sometimes that occurred in straightforward ways, but one of participation in flux and change, integration and disintegration, alienation, interaction, acceptance.

That being said, one basic fact of demography determined their Australian social role: it was not so much how they felt or thought that conditioned the future, but how they were distributed—and that was, remarkably evenly across a vast continent. Irish concentrations were few and minor. Their geographic dispersion across the totality of the country conditioned their political role and the whole range of their community attitudes. Had they been heavily concentrated in particular areas, as they were in some cities in the United States or some farming localities in Canada—or bluntly, had they dominated particular electorates—it is likely that they could and would have compelled attention to their presence and grievances (Catholic education is an obvious case) much more effectively. But while the Irish Catholic minority in Australia was large, its effective power was small. Had it been fewer in numbers, but grouped effectively in relation to the electoral arrangements, it might have insisted on its wishes: it is not the size of a minority which counts politically, but how it relates to the existing political system. Of course, the outcome of an Australian situation of concentrated Catholic Irishry is an imponderable. Perhaps it would have compelled swift resolution—or even initial avoidance—of its complaints, but perhaps it might have exacerbated hostilities and tensions beyond what in fact they were.

Yet it is tempting to see, from an Irish viewpoint, the actual situation as negative, unhealthy, and unproductive. Here was a very sizeable and distinctive minority, under frequent criticism and attack, trapped by a political system which permanently excluded it from power, frustrating it unless it abandoned what made it different, and denying the genuineness of its particular claims. The nature and proportions of this minority ensured that it would continue to attract hostility, indeed deep suspicion and fear, but it lacked the opportunity to prove itself innocent—or guilty: it was obliged to remain in the category of a low-level social infection, causing irritation and disquiet, but never being cured. Save by time—for it is one of the theses of this book that it was the condition of constant abrasion between minority and majority that gradually changed both, to their mutual improvement and the creation, by way of compromise, of a tolerant Australian character. Besides, it might be contended that this relative powerlessness had positive benefits, compelling the Australian Irish to come to terms with their total community situation rather than indulging in pressure group politics and system manipulation in the manner of their American brethren. So it was entirely appropriate and healthy that the Irish should not form the Labor Party, merely come to vote for it; and join it on such terms as that it moulded them, rather than they it. Said Maurice Blackburn to Nettie Palmer in 1936, 'A man here is a worker first and a Catholic second'. Irish third. Perhaps these are all benefits, but they had consequences, if not costs.

One was loss, or at least diminution, of identity and what went with it—pride, values. To accept the system, however it might adjust or concede, was to accept the system: the Labor Party was not an expression of Irishness, but of the economic position of most Australian Irish. The difference is both unimportant and vast, and the example merely the most obvious. Loss and gain—the human condition, but for the immigrant, the new settler, a dichotomy most marked, and particularly marked for the evenly distributed, widely dispersed, Australian Irish.

And that spacious geography also relates to the matter of clerical power and influence. There was no concentrated stimulus, no impelling machinery of opportunity and compulsion, to generate and foster natural lay leadership among the Irish. They fell in line with the only leadership that existed, that of the Catholic Church. Only the clergy had the permanence, status, independence, resources and organisational structures to function effectively in circumstances inimical to lay leadership. But the clerical was a leadership which, whatever its advantages, virtues, and inescapability, was at a tangent to the lay situation. It was not controlled by the lay Irish, it was structurally irrelevant to their political strength or lack of it (and thus irresponsible in at least the neutral sense) and, most importantly, (despite Protestant mythology regarding Catholic unity) its objectives were its own, not necessarily expressive of lay interests, or in accord with them. Moreover it was not, particularly at its lower levels, always leadership of quality: it was often composed of the least distinguished products of Irish seminaries; it was at times crude, ignorant, and arrogant.

At best, it was confidently sure it knew what was best for the laity. The Irish dispersion in Australia was a natural interaction between personal preferences and a rural economy, but it received ample encouragement from a clergy schooled in dire American examples: the cities corrupted morality and destroyed religion. This was coupled logically with an anxiety (not always consistently applied or pursued) to get Catholics absorbed into the general community. Cardinal Moran was the most eloquent expounder of this as abstract theory, but its most practical exemplar was, from the 1860s to 1917, Bishop Robert Dunne in Queensland, who worked against anything resembling an Irish ghetto, or even local Irish cliques—and with a consistency beyond that of most Irish bishops, he was also opposed to too strict a policy on mixed marriages.

Dominant clerical leadership had a direct impact on the social disposition of the mass of the Irish in Australia. It conditioned them away from a disruptive role towards support of the social order—and a wish to rise within it. Conservative leadership from above was fairly

The poor Irish or the Irish poor. The stereotype photographed in Connemara
Ulster Museum, Welsh Collection

easy to sustain with Irish lower orders that were not radical or visionary, but backward-looking in their hatreds, the resentment of deposed kings (no foolery this—in his *Realities of Irish Life* published in 1868 W. Stewart Trench reports his amazement at coming across a map published in 1846 purporting to show land possessed by Irish chieftains from the eleventh to the seventeenth century). Running through, and frequently paralysing all kinds of Irish Catholic worldly endeavour, was a deep sense of social and economic loss: they had been robbed and cheated over centuries. And Trench also made clear that the peasantry saw emigration in that light: however much better off they might be in a new land, they were being dispossessed, driven from what was rightly theirs, from time immemorial, to some unknown place across the sea. Whatever the dictates of common sense, or of a taste for adventure, however a deprived past might galvanise individuals to regain in Australia what their forebears had lost in Ireland, that past threw its shadow into moods and dispositions less than productive. That these did not come to dominate the social stance of the Australian Irish—this resentful brooding over a proud past, this continuum of dreams—is largely to the credit of a clergy forever pragmatic, active, building, forever in the lead in relating their fellow countrymen to success in the colonial world. To those who saw the Irish immigrant flood as a mass of undifferentiated pig-in-the-parlour peasants, such inferiors should be properly grateful—and respectful of their betters—for their marvellous chance to better their condition. Some were, and wrote servile letters to landlords and ships' captains in gratitude for their translation. But some saw themselves as exiled kings who had no call to be grateful for banishment, and what they got in their new homes they felt was less than what they deserved, short of any just entitlement. At its positive best, the glow of the vanished kingdoms that preceded their peasantry could induce pride, confidence. They would give no man best, refuse to accept any subservient role, rebel against its attempted extortion: the Irish colonial was the free man again, denying the bonds of his immediate history.

Nevertheless, this high-flying was a new and unaccustomed role, fraught with profound dangers for the inexperienced: the failure rate was to be high, as were to be the number of distortions in the attempts to live it. Indeed it was to be more of a deep impulse, an echo from a past before experience, than a previous part to be resumed. In January 1902 a contributor to the *Austral Light* (DeC. O'D. from Briagolong) revealed, almost as a throwaway, both the elements of this fundamental juxtaposition of identities and the continuing sense of tension between them: 'Altho' I am only a selector, I am the scion of an old Irish family, who claim descent from Carabry Cincait.' The phraseology was sufficiently close to the stock language of farce to be instantly converted into a joke if that was a listener's expectation of such an observation: like so much in the uneasy environs of Irish pride and identity, such claims—and their implicit references to disharmonies between glorious thens and humble nows—were fitted with escape routes and subterranean hideaways. If the listener thought these pretensions to greatness were silly, the Irish shared the joke. But not in their hearts. Or in their church. That practical and democratic institution, that environment where grandeur stood tall, the Irish Catholic Church, provided an atmosphere where all these prodigious secret identities might live, thrive, and be at peace.

For the Irish were indeed blessed; they were the poor in spirit, and theirs was the kingdom of heaven. Within Irish Catholicism was an impulse that gloried in poverty, rejoiced in low status: it came from above, this belief in an ennobling indigence, held at remove by a middle-class clergy. And it was ambivalent: poverty was a kind of martyrdom and holy, but get busy and improve yourself. Bishop James Quinn conveys the flavour marvellously well writing to Archbishop Kirby in Rome in 1872: 'the poor Irish are a wonderful race!' Did he mean poor in sense of destitute? Yes, but more than that. Poor also in the sense of deprived, put upon, suffering, piteous; poor in the context of 'poor old Ireland' that constant cliché of clerical correspondence, loaded with affection, resentment, forbearance, fortitude. And readily translated into the Australian idiom. The idealisation of poverty and faithful resignation to God's will are readily secularised into the egalitarianism and fatalism of battlers, those laconic Australian peasants.

The opposite valuation also applied. In 1906 Rev. P. Hickey of Cowra, New South Wales, published a tedious Irish-Australian novel *Innisfail or Distant Days in Tipperary*. It preached that 'in the higher walks of life it is rare to find a Catholic, except a slimy creature who has sold his soul . . .'. This was a constant principle of judgement: a Catholic in 'the higher walks' was presumed 'slimy' until proved otherwise: Hickey's novel expressed one aspect of the Irish Catholic distrust of wealth. In part this was a justifying prejudice against what was not possessed. The facts were that Irish Catholics were 20–25 percent of Australia's population, but were only 5–10 percent of the wealthy. In part this reflects the economic situation of Ireland itself, where the wealth was held by the non-Gaelic, and was underdeveloped anyhow. Certainly much of Australia's wealth was imported and inherited, but convicts other than the Irish enjoyed—and took advantage of—the opportunities for enterprise offered by the early Australian economy. Why not the Irish? Why so few like Thomas Dalton, the Sydney merchant who left £347 000 on his death in 1900? There were, of course, some: the Toohey brewing dynasty; at the end of the century, those who formed the City Mutual Life Association in Sydney in 1891; Mark Foy—though his father was French. There were some contractors: Michael Fleming, who built several hundred of Surry Hills' less desirable residences; the railway contractor John Walsh, whose daughter married into the Meagher family, merchants in Bathurst and Temora; the Melbourne millionaire property owner, Thomas Monaghan, who lived in Erindale, St Kilda. The list, even were it to be made exhaustive, is neither long nor spectacular. Why this relatively small and quiet enterprise?

The answers are various, and open to contrasting appraisals. Irish resources were at first small, and subject to demands which limited aggregation—financing further immigrants, sustaining families in Ireland, and the support of their religion, particularly church building and schools. Such factors were not unremarked at the time. In 1859 Gavan Duffy charged the Church in the colonies with caring more for self-perpetuatian than for the accommodation and advancement within the community of colonial-born Catholics. (He did not add that there was a contemptuous or at best paternal streak in the Irish church which regarded colonials as inferior.) Irish society encouraged caution and stifled enterprise: its whole climate suggested that wealth was for others and that security and modest property were sufficient goals; it offered little experience or expertise in large financial arrangements.

Add to this the flight from worry, noted earlier in the preference for labouring rather than land. What was the fate of those Ulster Protestant Irish who so often gravitated to small business or modest commerce? Malcolmson Capper in Melbourne, writing in May 1874, made it clear to his brother John back in Belfast: 'A great number of men out here worry themselves to death with business, men become prematurely old.' His comment was occasioned by an acquaintance from Belfast so pressured (he feared his family would starve) that he thought 'his head was going astray'. Within a year his own shirt manufacturing business had failed and his cousin Samuel's drug and medicine importing firm was heading toward collapse. Malcolmson was to die aged forty at Euroa in 1885, Samuel to survive a gamut of commercial ventures into the Victoria of the twentieth century, their experiences testament to the hazards of small business: let those chary of lives of tension and worry beware. All this is true. But it is also true that with the Irish, as a generality, their identity was not linked to measures of wealth or the values of acquisitive capitalism: they did not need aggregations of money or property to prove who they were. (A good thing too, as the most potentially explosive ethnic issues and divisions in Australia—those separating Irish Catholics from other citizens—were considerably damped by lack of any sizeable Irish wealth component. Good also in that lack of capital meant that the Irish tended to go to established areas, there to mix with previous comers. They lacked the resources to carve out their own separate—and potentially alienating—domains.) It was not so much that the Irish heeded, by grinding necessity, the biblical rhetoric—What doth it profit a man ...?—but that their historical experience and cultural structures gave them souls with a sense of self divorced from possessions. History had made them pilgrims and the pilgrim travelled light.

And he was glad of what protection he might find along the way. These poor Irish, marooned in strange and sometimes hostile parts, were grateful for being taken care of, happy that the clergy should represent them, be their respectable public face. Owen O'Neill explained to his brothers in 1909: '... the only curse here is the Orangeman or Mason. We have got a good Protector here in Archbishop Carr or Dean Phelan as the[y] are able to show up those people in there [sic] true light...' Life was a battle. Churchmen cast as protectors and champions was an enduring (and revealing) theme in Irish Australian experience: the church that could command and organise many small men could make them a power in the land, the equal of wealth, large without the loneliness of riches. Their pastors developed that enduring habit of referring to their flocks as Irish working-class, a concept which constrained the initial commonality well past its natural end.

Certainly, in these new settlers, common, shared attitudes emerged. For the Irish Catholic, more than other migrants, emigration was a rebirth, a chance to realise an ideal life free from the trammels built into Irish facts and Irish history in their particular regard: for a romantic imaginative people, addicted to the folk poetry of the dispossessed, it was an opportunity to recapture (in real fact, invent) that which had been lost.

This strange, complex process is evident in the Finn family, whose Australian fortunes and misfortunes from 1838, in Hartley and Portland, and a variety of places elsewhere, have been portrayed by S.M. Ingham. Their stories are fit subject for generalising comment, indeed meditation.

First, the successful John Grant at Hartley and places west. Transported from Tipperary in 1811 for attempted murder, emancipated in 1820, at his death in 1866 he owned about 10 000 acres with thousands more under lease. Small and self-educated, shrewd, with thrift, energy, and foresight, he had another face—harsh and severe, given to black moods, a hard master. Was it that when men of no property became rich, they shrank, becoming indrawn, obsessive, mean? Grant lacked ostentation, but he also lacked flair and flamboyance—the black, hard Irishman seems a recognisable type. He can be found again fifty years later in Western Australia in Daniel Connor, another story of convict rags to colonial riches. His stylised obituary in 1898 read, self-reliant, independent, and thrifty. For those whose mortgages he foreclosed and for the subjects of his real estate deals, the kindest rewording of such tributes might be shrewd, sharp, and unscrupulous.

The Finn brothers, Michael, Patrick, John, Thomas, also represent recognisable types. Free, educated, superior, they follow a usual pattern: they avoid the cities, seek employment, save, buy country stores, then land, become local identities, take up various jobs, even professions, present ordinary colonial immigrant stories.

Not quite: the superficial facts mask a deeper history. The extrovert Thomas Finn (1813–95) at Portland acted out to an extreme the ambitions and fantasies that ran below the surface lives of so many middling Irish: he went mad after his bankruptcy in 1872, his disintegration symbolised by his crumbling, once gracious mansion, Oak Park, eventually left derelict.

The fate of Thomas Finn typifies to exaggeration several central characteristics of the middling Irish immigrant. It is misleading to say they were poor judges of land, though their selections were often of inferior quality: it was not quality that governed their choice, but size, expanse. So, while the poor Irish fell by the constriction of their vision (100 acres seemed vast), the middling Irish fell by the largeness of theirs. Too often they bought extensive tracts of marginal land, just because it was land, and cheap, and their pride was built on quantity, size: too often they became lords of the desert, kings in worthless scrub. And often too the entrepreneurial Irish fell victim, as did Thomas Finn, to an expansive lifestyle. To the dangers of inexperience and chancey judgement, they added an ingredient which made a recipe for disaster—prodigal generosity. They gave loans at no interest, gave money to unreliable friends and relations, were free and imprudent with credit they could not afford, pursued paths of extravagance when thrift was needed and were careless when caution was called for. Such Irish had a boom mentality and they perished by it. Unlike the Scots, they were not 'canny', and the lack destroyed them. It was not so much that they were gamblers—though some were very much that and the racecourses were full of them—as that they were men with big ideas seeing in the colonies their chance to cut a fine figure and break away from mean Irish lives. It was just these high-stepping qualities that made such Irish extremely vulnerable to the vagaries and fluctuations of the colonial economy, which often operated on a knife-edge balance: they lived in that area of risk where the least measure of bad luck, accident, or bad season would transform teetering prosperity into total disaster. These Irish fell victim to their own characters. They started, by hard work and enterprise, on upward colonial paths towards success and substance, but before they were settled into the domains of protected affluence they overreached themselves, to be cut down by failure and bankruptcy. The standard picture of the Irish lower orders gradually pulling themselves up by their own dirty bootlaces, leaves out the constant recruitment from above. Many Irish initially on the way up fell back into the labouring class through failure on the land: some fell to depths they had not known before. There were very few second chances: the land was now shut, occupied by their creditors and that ilk. The only way up again for those who fell was to educate their children for the professions.

Over the whole Irish Australian encounter with the land looms the mental tyranny of the Irish 'big house', most dangerous and seductive of colonial bewitchments. Status and repute mattered more to the Irish than wealth—commendable priorities perhaps, but open to curious perversions. At the lower level this might be seen in those of the poor who did not attend church because they lacked money for the collection, or worse, because they had no 'respectable' clothes. In 1867, the Portland priest complained, though not without sympathy, of 'many poor people absenting themselves from Mass, through shame at having their poverty exposed . . .'. At the higher level, the aspirations of the ambitious were to acquire a big house, a large and imposing mansion which would be the district centre of expansive, warm-hearted, generous living, dominating its local scene. Even without the house, the top of the upwardly mobile Irish aped what they could of its style and trappings—playing cricket (the big house game), riding, forming turf clubs: in the colonial context the ubiquitous horse had cultural pretensions and functions beyond mere transport.

The Anglo-Irish had stamped on the Irish landscape and lifestyle the phenomenon of the big house, creating a visible standard for reference and envy, imposing on the Irish mind, as it viewed these imposing structures from outside and below, a symbol and concrete objective that permeated the imagination. Whereas in England the manor was not a conceivable destination for the labourers, in Ireland, the atmosphere and attitudes were very different. There the middle orders in particular did not look up to the big house in any distancing deferential way; it was the accommodation of the usurping English garrison, and in their minds' eye the Irish could see themselves there as rightful occupants. Ambitious immigrants brought their grandiose desires from Ireland to an Australia in which they saw the chance to translate fantasy into reality. It was a mentality that often led them astray. In Ireland itself—though these would-be imitators seldom understood this—the big house in a culture in decline was often allied with extravagance, recklessness and improvidence, and in some cases, sheer laziness. Thomas Finn was not lazy, but it was the logic of his desperate, accelerating war with debt that he should go mad and that his big house should be vandalised and fall into ruin. Others in similar predicaments kept their reason though not their property.

These phantasms are only one of the aspects of Irish settlement that make it no straightforward humdrum geographic dispersal. The tendency towards concentration itself was no simple process. It waxed and waned: these Irish concentrations tended to dwindle and disperse rather than stabilise after initial growth. The earlier Irish, particularly those given land grants, or those who had become squatters, tended to stay put and to employ their fellow countrymen as labour: this had inbuilt continuity and permanence as long as family succession could be maintained. But the era of free land grants and easy squatting was brief and early and the day of selection was a much harder regime. Besides, the era of the gold rushes, which begins in the 1850s and hardly ends by the 1890s, is associated with a new phase in Irish immigrant attitudes, in which gold is a first priority and mobility the primary characteristic.

Yet both before and during this phase of change, those Irish who did settle in sufficient numbers to give an area an 'Irish' character, present contrasting Irish models. To describe with the staid term 'regional concentration' the Irish presence in south-west New South Wales is to diminish the reality to jargon. Here was the flamboyant creating of grouped and related family empires, adjacent and interlocking, the new dominions of the Ancient Kings of Inis Ailge, resurrected in New South Wales by the Ryans, the Corcorans, the Dwyers, and lesser lords. Here were Irish counties, whose coherence was certainly geographic and economic but whose stimulus was that of the Irish heart and mind. King of Galong Castle aptly describes Ned Ryan, his home not the Anglo-Irish big house, but in the style of the functional Gaelic culture that preceded it. His squatting acres were appropriate to an Irish kingdom, reputed in family imagination to be 100 000 square miles, a tract the size of Ireland. His personal style, gruff, quick-tempered, and his lavish hospitality fitted the lordly image, as did his patriarchal persuasion of many labourers from

Tipperary to join him. His son, John Nagle Ryan, sustained the tradition: 'Everything was on a scale of barbaric grandeur not elsewhere to be enjoyed.' Barbaric grandeur—the phrase captures the flavour of these rough kings in their primitive vigorous courts.

And primitive they were. Mary Durack tells of the Durack daughter Margaret Bennet (married to an Englishman), who died at the family property in Queensland in 1864. A horde of Irish mourners, laden with food and drink, and noisy with loud prayers and extravagant sympathy, descended on the Duracks, determined to make the most of what of necessity, in the hot climate, must be a brief occasion. Her distracted husband recoiled from this invasion with English revulsion, pleading that these 'barbarians' be sent away: if these were 'barbarians' responded Grandfather Durack, then so was the deceased. James T. Ryan recalled in his *Reminiscences* the Irish gatherings of the forties and fifties, when the weddings, wakes and christenings of local clans were all district occasions, lasting three days and nights, the young courting, the old talking and drinking, the talking, even the courting, in Gaelic. The singing, dancing, and story-telling on these occasions was part self-generated, but part professional, in the Irish tradition. The brothers Patrick and Daniel O'Rourke at Windsor brought in two fiddlers, Blind Tommy and Blind Loftus, well known for their performances at district race-meetings, with supporting tambourine player: Blind Loftus, with ugly face and a supply of hideous grimaces, had a splendid voice and wide repertoire of Irish dances which acted as stimulus to general participation. Such occasions lingered longest in the empire of the Ryans, where family connections formed a political network as well. John Nagle Ryan bequeathed his electorate to Tom Slattery: even as late as the 1890s the Boorowa locals swore 'by the hole in their coat' that no one dare show their face in Boorowa against him. And in Ryan's kingdom, into the eighties and nineties, feasting at wakes would go on all night, a social occasion for the district: mourners smoked clay pipes for the deceased soul; a cup of water was left out in case he or other holy souls was thirsty. Australian-born locals cultivated an Irish brogue and swore in Gaelic. It was all a giant performance, lived out in reality.

The style and flavour of Victoria's early Irish concentrations were very different, deriving as they did from a variant (however mild and beneficent) of the Irish landlord–tenant relationship.

In the early 1840s two enterprising Protestant Irishmen based in Sydney, William Rutledge from Cavan and James Atkinson of Armagh, set out to acquire land grants in what is now Victoria, with the idea of establishing themselves as substantial landlords, leasing out small plots to Irish immigrants. In 1843 Atkinson secured 5120 acres (at £1 an acre) of the Port Fairy Special Survey, on which he laid out a town named Belfast. Earlier, in 1841, William Rutledge had taken up another special survey at Kilmore, dividing the land into small farms for potato-growing and even setting aside land for a Catholic church: he understood the needs of his prospective settlers. In the same year, he also joined a 'Syndicate of Irish Gentry' in Sydney—testimony to the kind of venture capitalism then operating in regard to new land—with the objective of purchasing a special survey in Gippsland. This did not proceed, and in 1843 Rutledge came to Port Fairy, together with three brothers, a cousin, his brother-in-law, and their wives. In 1844 he agreed with Atkinson to undertake the management of the new town, Belfast, and of letting the town and country allotments, paying Atkinson various sums. Later, Atkinson began to sell or lease his lands to others, including the tenants he had introduced, but he came under increasing criticism for selfishness and, as owner of the town, as an extortioner, unwilling to sell at reasonable prices. He, and after him his son, were pilloried as absentee landlords in the classic Irish rackrenting and inhuman tradition, until 1885 when a local syndicate bought for £54 000 all the remaining Atkinson land. Partly in order to mark the break with this unsavoury reputation, the town's name was changed to Port Fairy in 1887, though the shire remained Belfast. This, or other inconveniently contrary facts, did not deter J.F. Hogan in 1887 from citing 'Belfast' as 'the only example to be found in Australia of a large town belonging entirely to one man, and he an absentee landlord, living in Ireland and drawing a princely revenue . . .'. In fact, from 1847 Atkinson was always willing to sell, but the tenants were not willing to buy, not only from lack of finance, but because of caution and cussedness. But the story of Atkinson's reputation, false or true, makes very clear that the Australian Irish would not suffer any reappearance of the iniquities attributed to landlordism in Ireland.

Unless there were other factors: it is remarkable that Rutledge—'Terrible Billy' the Hentys called him—did not suffer the same fate, despite the fact that his enterprises seem more in the classic pattern of Irish landlordism than Atkinson's. The reasons seem clear: Rutledge was no absentee, his rentals were within the tenants' capacity to pay, and he lived in the spectacular grand style, a law unto himself, which the Irish tenantry so admired—or at least respected as proper. Living in Belfast, Rutledge became its 'King', or more exactly, its squire. He became member of parliament for the district, showing marvellous contempt for the opinions of his tenants by denouncing the Duffy Land Act of 1862 as 'seditious' and free land selection as 'rebellious'. He settled his own farming survey, centring on Killarney village, with Irish settlers brought from Sydney. They were tenants, and no Australian nonsense: he sold no land to them until 1862 and they lived in Killarney, which he owned. He had started his farming with wheat, but when rust attacked it he changed to potatoes, soon achieving for the district practically an Australian monopoly. But with potatoes Rutledge doubled the rent (to £6 an acre) and imposed the Irish con-acre leasing system. Such were the tenants' profits, there was no objection: landlordism within this region of the Australian economy was very different from its Irish imposition. And anyhow, Rutledge's enterprises dominated Belfast and its surrounding district. His company even issued its own currency, with notes accepted throughout Australia, until the whole empire crashed in bankruptcy in 1862—in all a bravura high-risk performance, kept moving by that dash and self-confidence that itself repels challenge. But there was challenge: in 1855, Michael O'Reilly established the *Banner of Belfast*, a fiercely Irish journal which kept local affairs disturbed by injecting contentious matters from Ireland, and championing the small man against the big.

But even as early as this, the potential of Irish issues to disrupt local tranquillity—or to shoulder aside local concerns—was being diminished by that factor affecting Irish concentrations everywhere in Australia—dilution by the non-Irish. Rutledge's initial tenant community seems to have been brought out from Ireland at his own expense; according to Gavan Duffy they were evicted Irish tenants. However the initial Irish influx of the 1840s changed to an English bias by the 1850s. The 1857 census of the Belfast Road district reveals that this very 'Irish' area was only partly so—under one-third: 1031 Irish, 854 English, 687 Scots, 879 Victorian-born. Furthermore, these Irish themselves did not necessarily stay, or at least their children did not. Many migrated to the Colac district when estates there were opened for subdivision in the 1890s and early 1900s: Irish farmers in Australia were always willing to believe that other land must be better than what they had, and to act on that assumption.

In its heyday as a centre of Irishness from the 1850s to the 1870s, Killarney's story was that of tenant farming under Rutledge: the survey was unavailable as freehold until 1876. Moreover the potato-farming which was to be the economic and social image generated by the area to harmonise in the public mind with its Irishness, was a later construct. The region was founded on wheat and remained so until 1864, the year of the rust and the start of the swing to potatoes. At first the Irish tenant farmers were wheat farmers, with 150–200 acres rented for fourteen years, producing $1\frac{1}{2}$–2 bushels per acre. Drainage and clearing were the responsibility of the tenants. However the soil was six feet fertile black, and according to the contemporary James Bonwick, Rutledge was 'a kind and considerate landlord' who 'furnished his tenants with seeds, provisions and implements and has since made the fortunes of many'.

Rutledge's role in enabling this prosperity was perhaps not quite so positive: it was the gold rushes which made the district the chief grain-growing district of Victoria by 1856, and the quality of the soil which made it difficult to mismanage. Gavan Duffy's comment when he visited Killarney in that year (his local host had made £1500 from his wheat crop) was that he had found 'rude, careless plenty': productivity and demand meant that Irish carelessness could be indulged until it learnt better. And one economic thing fed another. The huge market created by the gold rushes made small farming profitable, particularly in adjacent Victorian districts. In turn gold helped to finance that farming: many Irish made enough in the goldfields to buy land at Koroit, near Killarney. And they hired the Irish immigrants—mainly Irish agricultural labourers and domestic servants—who kept arriving at Portland. These new arrivals were often friends or relations. The *Chance*, arriving in Belfast in September 1857, typifies the migrant situation. Of thirty-eight single Irish agricultural labourers, fourteen joined relatives and twelve met friends: of sixteen families, four joined relatives, three friends. About 15 percent were Protestant. But perhaps the most remarkable statistic is that for literacy—only 21 percent were illiterate, a figure remarkable for 1857. The contemptuous stereotype of the 'thick Mick' does not apply: the fact that Ireland exported agricultural labourers is not a reflection on the quality of Australia's Irish migrant intake; it is a comment on the condition of Ireland's economy.

Yet the capacity of the Irish as 'cockatoo farmers' came under fair question. Bonwick observed: 'An Irish farmer thinks no practice equal to that pursued by his forefathers at home', and he found laziness, unmade roads, no crop rotation, and general inefficiency, offset in terms of productivity by the excellence of soil and climate. Imported customs seemed oddly out of place: threshers got 8s a day—and four glasses of grog. Some farmers reverted to Irish subletting of parts of their farms. As late as 1880 English visitors complained of rude cabins, dirt, and pigs. The whole area was in need of the efforts of the Agricultural Society whose first show in 1854 did much to raise standards. But how much conservatism and inefficiency were general to the whole farming community rather than specific to its Irish elements is impossible to determine. Despite the heavy admixture of English, Scots, and Australian-born, the Killarney area was 'Irish' in the public eye and all its characteristics attributed to that nation.

As to the influx of Irish agricultural labourers, many had no wish to remain such—an ambition that also goes against the unflattering stereotype. A year's work was usually enough to save for a small property, which they would rent from large landowners or buy when subdivisions took place. William Crowe was such a case of highly successful enterprise. He emigrated from Clare in 1855 when he was eighteen. After various jobs he had enough to buy one of the original Koroit town lots. He bought more with the profits from that, sold his potatoes at the Stawell diggings—and bought more Koroit land with the

The Irish agricultural labourer in reality. Francis ('Pincher') Owens turf-cutting at Tempo, Co. Fermanagh, 1899
Ulster Museum: Langham Collection

profit. He was mayor of Koroit six times, had thirteen children, and lived until he was ninety-four. That such a pioneer should die as recently as 1931 shrinks the dimensions of the past to proper perspective.

For all that the wheat rust, appearing in 1864, brought temporary disaster; the outcome of the swing to potatoes, which was the district's reaction to it, was closer Irish concentration and even higher prosperity. A twelve-acre farm was considered large for the new crop. Estates continued to become available as the old wheat farms were broken up. One of the largest in the district was not subdivided until 1888, when it was leased on the Irish con-acre system at an annual auction. Rutledge's own estates were broken up upon his death in 1876, by which time an Irish farming stratification was clearly evident in the Killarney–Koroit area. A few larger farmers owned over 100 acres. Most owned ten acres or less. And some farm labourers rented one or two acres. By the 1880s these farmers had diversified into pigs and dairy herds and land prices had increased to around £60 an acre. Prosperity was the rule, poverty the exception: probate figures of that time show estates from £250 to a not untypical £2500 for Terence Clancy.

The area had a reputation for being intensely 'Irish', but Irish-Australian is far more exact, for Ireland itself could not match the affluence which permitted the local lifestyle, nor pose the unique demands of the colonial scene. The ubiquitous hotels, for instance, served a variety of colonial needs. They housed dances, concerts, public meetings and land auctions, their ballrooms often being the only meeting places in townships. Their attractions for Irish Catholics are obvious beyond the society of drink. Their acquisition required little capital, their operation little skill; their lifestyle was independent and congenial, their management and labour could be made a family affair, and they were a negotiable asset that might be left to widows in an age when men tended to marry younger women. Their proliferation in areas such as Koroit reflects their social importance in situations where a large number of men were single: their basic function as boarding houses is often overlooked by those of a later age making exclusively alcoholic assumptions—as is the fact that the hotel industry was one of the few in which the Irish could operate without the competition of hard-driving, thrifty, nonconformists. The same might be said of horseracing. The races were massive social occasions in the districts centring on Warrnambool, Belfast and Koroit. In 1879 the St Patrick's Day races attracted an attendance of around 1000 people, more than half the population. What is remarkable is not merely the size of the crowd, but, in contrast to Ireland, the disposable resources it suggests.

The contrast with Ireland, however, was more fundamental. Visiting Koroit in 1884 the Melbourne columnist the Vagabond observed: 'Pigs and potatoes are here, but the spirit of the people has undergone a change. The peasant farmer does not touch his hat to me, or address me as "your honour"'. Indeed he did not, but it is a moot point whether the Australian circumstances generated this or whether they let deep, repressed Irish impulses surface. Writing to his father on 29 October 1876 'On the Road with my Cattle' in the Richmond River district of northern New South Wales, his writing paper on his knee, in front of the camp fire, William Martin looked forward, if his station venture was successful, to an income of 'fully 1,500 pounds per year in two years from now. So then if I live so long I can take a run home to rights. I said when leaving home I would never come back unless I was in a position to do without work so I hope to be that soon'. This was a common enough immigrant dream and ambition. Then suddenly, out of that stream of clichéd imaginings, bursts the deeper impetus behind that ambition, the life-incident of

The Irish hotel as outpost of civilisation. The Rock of Cashel near Stanthorpe, Queensland 1872–3
Oxley Library, Brisbane

humiliation, the imposition on him of the arrogance of mere ownership which had haunted Martin's consciousness since: 'Once before I left home Edward Black and I was riding in the cart close to Drumadoone when we met Mr McGildowney and he ordered us both to get out and walk not to ride in his cart and on his mare but to walk. That has ran in my mind from that [day] to this and [I] often thought it strange but always of the notion that he might ride some one day in my cart or car.'

Here is not so much rancour as the impulse to independent equality. Martin had written in an earlier letter: 'home was never a country like this the poore man has a chance in this country to better himself if he only minds himself and keeps steady.' This was a theme to which he kept returning: 'a man that has to work hard at home may as well come and work hard in this country as he will get double the wages ...' John Birmingham, also in northern New South Wales, but writing in the eighties, expressed his egalitarianism with more resentment and edge: 'aney young man has no business to worke for farmer in Ireland let the poor creatures do it themselves young man let you go to the Imigration office & there pay 2 pounds & you get a passage to Australia where you will perhaps become you own master in a very short time altho it has taken me some time to do it but I cept going about too much ...' 'Going about too much' was the usual Irish migrant pattern, but John eventually settled down in the Richmond district. He urged his brother to join him: there was no rent to pay, the soil was fertile, and he would not be under any 'old Irish farmers controle'. The importance he himself placed on such independence was primary and

Digging potatoes in Ireland itself. Tom Carland and his father, 1 October 1899,
Tempo, Co. Fermanagh
Ulster Museum: Langham Collection

decisive. He hoped to see 'poor Ireland' again, 'but to work for a farmer I would not. I would have as good a chance of flying'. Nor was this sense of independence, and determination to retain it, the preserve of the lower orders. Independence was in the air and Anne Higgins, wife of a Methodist clergyman and mother of Henry Bournes Higgins, felt it immediately when she arrived in Melbourne in 1870. 'Everything is superior here, *save religion*. People here who come from Ireland all ask lovingly after 'the old country' but could not bear to live there. Every one says the same ... This is a splendid country: all agree in this. They say they would not return for *anything*. You feel *independent* here.' Even in those areas where authority and hierarchy were part of the structure of ancient institutions—the Catholic Church—they came under vigorous question: from the 1840s to the 1860s the internal history of that church is one of lay struggle against clerical authority and of egalitarianism intruding on sacred areas. That droll fellow Fr Farrelly of Kilmore named his horse 'The Bishop', a joke which, in the circumstances of Archbishop Goold's savage claims to authority, expressed the spirit of mild insolence ever present as a subtle undercurrent in Irish Australia.

Unwillingness to defer without question to authority seems linked with that 'going about too much' characteristic of Irish immigrants: there was the unacceptable tyranny of people, but there was also the tyranny of place, of this or that job, of settling down. By the 1860s some Irish were drifting off the land, but more importantly newcomers were increasingly not going on. Perhaps it was the unsettlement associated with gold, and certainly many Irish continued to seek land, but it became notable that newcomers were staying in the cities or moving around the countryside from job to job. It was not, as has been suggested in regard to the much more marked expression of this phenomenon in America, that the Irish peasant was not equipped to pioneer: ample numbers of them had demonstrated that they were, in earlier situations much more adverse than mid-century. Even the harshest critic of Irish migrants, John Dunmore Lang, had no doubt that the matter was one of choice, not capacity, when he complained to the New South Wales parliament in 1867 that 'a large number of them came to seek employment in the police, or as wardens, or turnkeys of gaols, and other subordinate and menial occupations, instead of going to cultivate the waste lands of the territory'. Some reasons for this have been suggested earlier: simple determination not to return to the situations they were in, or had seen in Ireland, either in terms of the worries of ownership, or the constrictions it would place on freedom and mobility. Again, this is readily understandable in terms of the youth of most migrants, a factor overlooked by staid parliamentarians and bishops but recognised by the observation by the Dublin *Nation* of 12 May 1883 that the settled Australian Irish (it instanced Sir John O'Shanassy, just dead, aged sixty-five) could not speak with authority on recent migrant dispositions. ('Young Australia indeed,' O'Shanassy had sniffed when defeated for parliament in that year; 'time enough for young Australia to speak in twenty years' time'.) It seems that it was the older, less recent immigrants that sought land. Not only were they the ones with some colonial experience, who had had time to accumulate a little capital, but they had worked out some of their restlessness. To blame the opportunities of Australia, or the processes of migration for this unsettlement may be to reverse the true causation: was it that they needed time to recover from the profound depression induced by life in Ireland? The Quaker Irishman Joseph Beale, writing from Melbourne in 1853, vowed that the best 2000 sovereigns ever minted would not induce him or his boys to return to the 'misery of mind' they had suffered in Ireland: they could not ever again 'endure the damps and colds of Ireland *inwardly* or *outwardly*'. There is migrant testimony enough to aversion to the Irish climate, but few had the perception or at least the command of words and concepts to delineate that inner Irish chill that sapped energy, paralysed initiative and reduced life to gloom and shadow.

Even those Irish who had not shared that mental climate did not comprehend it, or the reactions of those at last liberated from its miasma. In the 1860s Bishop Quinn had settled a solid nucleus of small Irish farmers on Queensland's Darling Downs. His vision was Quinnsland, happy Irish Catholic land of settled, prosperous, religious farmers living in harmony with their neighbours. His successor, Robert Dunne, was even more of a rural dreamer: as bishop of Toowoomba in the 1870s he often read out to his congregation, after the Sunday gospel, details from the Government Gazette of land available for selection. By the time Dunne succeeded Quinn in 1882, many of Quinn's initial Irish immigrant farmers (and many non-Irish besides) had been defeated by debt, drought, flood, wheat rust, lack of skill or experience, stupidity and laziness—the usual catalogue of farmers' foes. The small farmers were particularly vulnerable and were frequently absorbed by the large who had greater resources against disaster and who could effect economies of scale—though even size was no sure guarantee of survival. Dunne was blind to these brutal economics, in part because his own parish of Toowoomba was a prosperous exception to the harsh Queensland rule. His constant complaints about the flight from the land mirror the fate of the small Irish farmer; even those who stayed on the land were sinking to become casual labour for local squatters. In 1883 he reported: 'Very few immigrants who, within the last five years have landed in Australia, rarely aimed at taking up land. Their idea is to get a job on the railway, a beat as a policeman, or a billet under Government.' It was Dunne who was behind the exhortation to Catholics in the Australian Bishops' Plenary Council of 1885 that they 'strive to secure for themselves a just share in the public lands, otherwise ... their children must necessarily be shearers or farm labourers, wandering from shed to shed, and from harvest to harvest ... Why then do so many of you leave them no heritage but that of daily toil?' (And so it was unto the next and urban generations. By 1906 it was a common sneer that the ambition of every Irish Catholic parent for a son was the three 'p's'—priest, publican, or policeman.) All Dunne saw in this desertion of rural bliss was shame and shortsightedness; he was too kind a man to develop contempt for his shiftless flock, but that was a step other clergy were capable of taking. Not only did Toowoomba's plea-santness insulate him from the sterner realities of elsewhere in Queensland, but as an Irish townsman, a bourgeois, he had no grasp of the pressures in Ireland which produced immigrants hostile to the whole idea of saddling themselves with land. Nor did he consider the damning fact that the experience of small farming in Queensland had created a reservoir of disillusioned Irish advice from ex-farmers, sour sustenance for the immigrant grapevine: there were plenty to warn would-be farmers off. It was Dunne's conviction—central to a continuing tradition of Australian Irish Catholic rural utopianism—that the farmer lived 'nearer God, nearer heaven'. The farmer's actual experience seemed to him, in those grey hot plains of the west, nearer hell. Whatever the eternal resemblances, such farming demanded qualities of sainthood—or foolhardiness—unlikely to be in general abundance: the wonder is that so many persevered, or even tried and failed. Perhaps it is not to be wondered at. The land in Ireland had many shortcomings as a school in agriculture, but its tuition in matters of character, expectation, privation, fortitude, would have been hard to equal as a basis for the desperate contests with the land (and with the self) that pioneering involved.

Nor were the cooler climes of contemporary Victoria any more salubrious for the small farmer. Nor New South Wales, nor South Australia; everywhere the small farmer, often Irish, lost out to the large, almost invariably not Irish. The least unsuccessful area was Queensland where, against the facts of Australian economic life, Dunne's crusade for the small man on the land was not without impact.

Victoria? Was this not the state of the Duffy Land Act? Charles Gavan Duffy, 1848 rebel, editor of the *Nation*, had arrived in Melbourne in 1856 to be greeted as royalty by the Irish: they subscribed £5000 to buy him house and land to meet the parliamentary property qualification on his arrival. Taking up the cause of the small landholder, Duffy, as minister in the O'Shanassy government, introduced a Land Act in 1862. This proclaimed ten million acres as agricultural areas. Any person could select a block between 40 and 640 acres for £1 an acre, part payable on selection, the rest over eight years: the selector was obliged to cultivate a tenth or make improvements (house, fences) to retain tenure. One-quarter of the money raised was to be used to finance more immigration.

Duffy's intentions were excellent, but the outcome was a fiasco. Yet such a judgement is too harsh, for despite its inadequacies and abuse, the land selection machinery of the sixties and seventies allowed many colonists an eventual chance of independence and self-advancement. Still, it has been estimated that only a hundred bona fide selectors had benefited from Duffy's Act by the time it was replaced in 1865—but its loopholes had been mercilessly exploited by the rich, greedy and unscrupulous. The magnitude of the failure of the Act to provide what Duffy intended, good cheap land for the small settler, was heightened by Duffy's own inflated claims and rhetoric, and by the climate of anticipation in Ireland that preceded it. The *Cork Examiner* of 27 January 1862 expressed general Irish euphoria when it observed that all Irishmen took a keen interest in the affairs of Victoria, that Duffy was a grand man, that it was the desire of many emigrants to own land, that Duffy's Land Act was calculated to ensure precisely this, and that a full tide of emigration to Victoria would be a consequence. This message, or variants on it, was soon Irish orthodoxy. Later in the same year the *Galway Vindicator* trumpeted forth that Victoria offered the greatest opportunities in the world, that its land laws were liberal and that all classes had access to political power. So Duffy's land legislation entered (and still exists in) Irish folk mythology as the land charter of the pauper Irish—which it was, save for its actual implementation. Even by the time the Duffy Act had patently failed, and was about to be replaced, good intentions were enough in an Irish climate so starved of them. When Duffy returned to Ireland on a visit in 1865, speakers at his receptions lauded his legislative achievement, particularly on the ground that 'the merest instalment' of what he had done in Victoria would have settled the land question in Ireland and installed happiness and contentment in Irish homes. Not surprisingly Duffy did not rise to complicate the matter with Australian facts, but one implicit contradiction did not escape the hostile *Irish Times*: while lamenting the flow of emigration from Ireland, Duffy was not beyond hinting that they would be better off in Australia.

It is impossible to gauge the extent to which the vision of a Victorian small-farming paradise opened up by a beneficent Duffy permeated the Irish emigrant mind, but it was certainly the orthodoxy of the 1860s in Ireland. Duffy's role was only one of the stimuli to the Australian land dream in Ireland: his legislation coincided with Bishop Quinn's colonisation scheme in Queensland, and with that extraordinary amalgam of glamour, endurance, hubris and tragedy, the Burke and Wills expedition, itself stimulated by the gift of an Irishman, Ambrose Kyte, 'an Irish lad attained to opulence' as Hogan described Kyte's rags-to-riches progression. While Duffy's efforts purified the ideal of land ownership

in Australia, Quinn's propagandists, notably Father Dunne, pushed Queensland as a tropical paradise and the 'Land of Promise', to be peopled not by ordinary mortals, but by superior persons: said Dunne in the *Cork Examiner* in September 1863, 'our people are not like the ordinary run of emigrant . . . no, the objects of this undertaking is of a far higher order. Our people are to be the founders of a great nation . . .'. And meanwhile, the *Examiner*'s occasional correspondent in Melbourne was engaged in similar rhetoric, promoting the image of the Irish as a pioneer people, closely connecting this with the idea of the resourceful, heroic, and adventurous Irishman personified in Robert O'Hara Burke, cavalier extraordinary, spurred on by national pride and largeness of spirit, characteristics every Irishman was assumed to possess. Briefly Burke became an Irish hero of mythical proportions, symbol of Irish vigour in Australia, the embodiment of the spirit which was 'opening up continents for the sons and daughters of Ireland, far away from the grasp of the rack-renting landlord, the griping agent and the selfish middleman'. It was not to be far away enough to avoid these and other enemies, but for a long moment in the early 1860s emigration to Australia was not a depletion of Ireland's strength, not a danger to its faith, not a threat to dignity, but entry to the land of hope. But Burke was symbol of more than Irish dash and bravery: his fate presaged a host of smaller, less glorious failures among that pioneer people. Their lesser tragedies and ordinary reversals would not merit the notice conferred on the romantic archetype of their pedestrian endeavours. 'Ireland, glorious old Ireland, draw on your mantle of mourning—you have lost one of your bravest, your most heroic, sons.' So intoned the *Cork Examiner* in January 1862. 'Indomitable, persevering, chivalric, Burke, is dead from starvation'.

The mistakes and misapprehensions central to Irish expectations of Australian land were by no means all associated with Duffy's role: some of them pre-dated him. Writing in April 1848 from Adelaide, Bishop Francis Murphy informed the Bishop in Monaghan: 'If any person purchases 80 acres of land, it is an estate for himself and his children; and his children's children.' Perhaps this was true in 1848, of some parts of South Australia, but applied generally in an undifferentiated way, as comments about Australia tended to be in Ireland, it was most misleading. But such acreages kept cropping up in contemporary success stories. In *Life in Victoria* in 1858, William Kelly gives a case of 'one of that poor spalpeen class who [in Ireland] rented an acre of land and mud cabin, and went over to reap the harvest in order to make up the rent', but now owned sixty acres in 'the suburbs' of Kilmore, and a plot in the town on which he had built a house from the profits of his farm. But Kelly's details did not include what were likely other facts—that the land had been acquired very cheaply and was of exceptional fertility, that the gold rushes had created an agricultural boom which would pass, and that the man concerned probably worked in the town as well as having a farm, common practice in such areas. Kelly was also among those who promoted the image of the intense 'Irishness' of various Victorian areas, in his case, Kilmore: 'it gave the idea that Tubbercurry, or Balleroclare, was rafted over holus-bolus from the Emerald Isle, so completely and intensely Irish was the entire population in appearance, in accent, and in the peculiarly Milesian style of huckstering arrangement in which the shops were set out . . .'

Kelly was not the only one to comment on the Irishness of Kilmore: in 1853, John Bond, an English immigrant on a walking tour, called it 'a small Irish village'. Yet it was Irish in a comparative Australian sense, not an absolute one. In 1861 it had 940 Irish-born, but the total population was 2897. According to the *Argus* in 1859, electorally Kilmore belonged to Sir John O'Shanassy 'body and soul', but O'Shanassy relied too long on his claims as Irishman. Kilmore rejected him in 1874 when his conservatism, his landowning, and his failure to fight secular education—immediate, local, Australian issues—tipped the balance against tradition and sentiment and clan loyalty.

Kelly's remarks also indicate that the Irish left behind the worst aspects of Irish agriculture: in Ireland they had neither the means nor the incentive to improve; in Australia they had both and the outcome was a much superior situation. Such was the reportage of Kilmore, and the same might have emanated from other intensely Irish areas, particularly in Victoria, where the generalisation that the Irish did not import their material culture applies least. Take the Bungaree–Dunnstown area just out of Ballarat, with its economy of potato growing, and its reputation, into the 1940s, of being 'Tipperary Gully', 'wild Irishman country', a celebrity generated by the thousands of diggers (giving the word a local twist) who came to lift the crop: 'The land of the shpud and the blarney' as the ballad put it. And celebrated in verse and song was Bungaree, its 'savages', its heroes, and its customs—the sport of Tug-o-War between local families using permanent cleats behind the Shamrock Hotel, Tommy Corrigan, the Western District steeplechase rider, killed in the Grand National at Caulfield in 1894, O'Tufty the fighter, Patrick O'Day, the 'King of Bungaree', the Bungaree cocky, archetypal in his meanness—a procession of local identities, pugnacious, colourful, and vigorously Irish. The same can be found in Queensland variants, a horsey, crude society, Father Horan intervening in a near riot at the St Patrick's Day races at Warwick, restoring order by felling one of the horses with an enormous blow from his shillelagh.

This was the Irish Australia of image and mythology, true enough within its limits: it is salutary to note what was not noted by promoters of this tiny facet of Irish Australia, that the legends and the tales of small-farming wealth spring from the geography of potato-growing. That economy, in Bungaree, Kilmore, Koroit or Killarney allowed small acreages and close society to marry in happy prosperity.

Such was not the Irish Australian norm, or the opportunities of the Irish who formed a concentration in north-eastern Victoria in the 1860s and 1870s. It was not, or not only, legislation that was to blame for their failure. They took up selections seldom above one hundred acres; large by Irish standards, large by Bungaree standards, but desperately, calamitously small for their location and infertility, and for the amount of clearing necessary to establish a productive area. There was nothing especially Irish in such mistakes: Scots settlers made the same errors. Only the native-born had the experience to select the 320-acre upper limit available under the 1865 Act, and to have sufficient saved to develop their property to productive capacity and to subsist during the time it took to do so. In general the Irish in Australia did not choose their land as carefully and sensibly as did the Canadian Irish—the obvious comparative example. They took pot luck and often lost. Why the adverse contrast? It seems unlikely that the greater proportion of a canny Scots-Irish Protestant element among the Canadian Irish is a factor: Scots-Irish (and Scots) seem just as capable of the same Australian mistakes. What is most distinct about the Australian situation is Duffy. Or to narrow the geography down to make an internal Australian point, it was Victoria that was distinctive. By the 1860s, its Irish atmosphere was more confident, more secure, more central to the general system of public and political life, than was the Irish presence in any other colony. In part this was a legacy of the gold-rush period, in part a spin-off of the centrality of the Anglo-Irish to the Victorian enterprise, in part due to the impact of O'Shanassy and Duffy on the public mind: no other State had Irishmen of comparable power and stature. This aura of Irish eminence was to cling to Victoria, but it was to be damaged and diminished, and that colony brought back into sectarian line, by the education controversies, and by what was to happen to Duffy in the seventies. A mythology had grown around Duffy, extending back to Ireland itself, that he was the saviour of the immigrant Irish peasant: he would see to it that the parliament would provide for such deserving persons, make land available, give them protection. No one thought that their champion would let them down. Nor did he. He too was ignorant—and he too was banished from power by Ireland's age-old enemies, sectarianism and rapacity. When, into the sixties and seventies the illusory paradise of free selection collapsed for so many Irish into nightmare, they did not turn against Duffy but included him in their paradigm of martyrdom. His fall, after the brief premiership of 1871–72, was another element of proof that the poor Irish were being exploited and excluded again, as always, by the thieving and cheating landlords, the gombeen men, the unscrupulous establishment.

They had a point, in that a system of land selection intended to advance the small settler had been perverted and manipulated to serve the interests of squatters, who in turn employed the police to protect those interests. But the extreme rural poverty, anger and frustration which was the context of the famous Kelly outbreak in north-eastern Victoria has internal dimensions attributable to Duffy. He was the centre and foundation on which were based illusory hopes of an arcadia for the Irish in Victoria: the more extravagant the hopes, the more confident the expectations, the more bitter the disillusionment. The selectors encountered drought, fire, flood and disease, but most of all they were defeated by failure to select viable farming units. This situation was peculiarly embittering, a form of slow economic drowning, a protracted exposure to all the humiliations of failure while struggling desperately for survival, and hoping for rescue; having led them into this morass, Duffy himself lost his grip on power in 1872, cut down for being Irish. What hope was there now?

Such was the background to the saga of Ned Kelly, bushranger, the long feud between a wild Irish settler clan in north-eastern Victoria and a harassing police force itself largely Irish: smouldering through the 1870s, it erupted into open violence, robbery, death and permanent Australian legendry in 1878, to close as fact, but by no means as legend, with the hanging of Ned Kelly for wilful murder on 11 November 1880: 'Such is life,' he is reputed to have said, the noose around his throat.

The atmosphere of the Kelly outbreak is Irish, its grievances and conditions local: the Irish were not alone in their rural poverty and frustration, and support, active and passive, came from an economic group and an alienated region rather than a nation. Persecuted, indomitable Ireland was for Ned Kelly a symbol of his—and his own people's—plight. Its cause generated in him an echo of common feeling in oppression; it took him out of himself to share in some elevating inchoate way, the fate of that inspiring, familiar nation; he sought dignity in the posture of claiming to embody the protest of a whole people; he yearned to sublimate the criminal into the defender of a noble cause. And so this shabby criminal became more than himself, much more, and enduringly so into permanence.

The process of identifying with Ireland as a symbol of local grievances and predicaments writ large was to become a major dimension of social conflict in Australia in the period 1916–21, but it had been a subterranean continuum since the beginning, surfacing in 1804, 1854 and so on. In Ned Kelly's case it was only one aspect of his stance, but an entirely natural one, given his family, upbringing and cultural location: he was Australian Irish from a deprived locality and a persecuted tradition, and Irish history was the natural contextual language in which he couched, paraded, and dignified his very Australian bushranging exploits and rough criminality. In playing to the audience he sensed as increasingly fascinated by his actions, the Celtic rebel role was particularly advantageous, for it harmonised with his name (and Kelly's mere name was the first attractive signal to gain public attention) and he was shrewd enough to see the parallels between the beleaguered, oppressed, and betrayed Ireland of his family lore and the wellsprings of frustration, bitterness and hate that poisoned the narrow Victoria that he knew. The historical debate about what was Irish and what Australian in Kelly's stand and motivation (in fact the one fed the other) has tended to obscure one remarkable feature of his knowledge of Irish history—that it existed at all. That it existed in an applied Australian version that suited Kelly's circumstances, temperament and purposes is even more startling, and does much to explain the Kelly legend, then and now. Kelly's Jerilderie letter of 10 February 1879, intended for newspaper publication as a manifesto and apologia from an outlaw on the run, testifies by implication to the existence of a hidden Ireland whose language this was, a bitter tribe of outcasts buried with their pride and resentment in isolation from the rest of Australian life, their poverty crushing them below the surface, passing their hatred and alienation, their sense of being cheated and degraded, down to their children, their lone voice that of the outlaw son. Who would have heard their cry of rage and desperate fury but for Ned Kelly? In page after page of the Jerilderie letter it spills out in explanation, self-justification, excuse, abuse, and colourful indulgence: the police are 'big, ugly, fat-necked, wombat-headed, big-bellied, magpie-legged, narrow-hipped, splay-footed sons of Irish bailiffs or English landlords'. Kelly works up the image of the hateful policeman until he is the centrepiece of a quasi-poetic torrent of popular Irish history and mythology adapted with an Australian dimension to spew out venom and self-pity and defiance woven into a fabric of Irish Australian victimisation:

> A Policeman . . . is a traitor to his country, ancestors and religion, as they were all Catholics before the Saxons and Cranmore yoke held sway. Since then they were persecuted, massacred, thrown into martyrdom and tortured beyond the ideas of the present generation.
> What would people say if they saw a strapping big lump of an Irishman shepherding sheep for fifteen bob a week or tailing turkeys in Tallarook ranges for a smile from Julia, or even begging his tucker? They would say he ought to be ashamed of himself and tar and feather him. But he would be a king to a policeman who for a lazy loafing cowardly bilit left the ash corner, deserted the shamrock, the emblem of true wit and beauty to serve under a flag and nation that has destroyed massacred and murdered their forefathers by the greatest of tortures as rolling them down a hill in spiked barrels pulling their toe and finger nails and on the wheel and every torture imaginable. More was transported to Van Diemens Land to pine their young lives away in starvation and misery among tyrants worse than the promised hell itself. All of true blood, bone and beauty, not murdered on their own soil, or had fled to America or other countries to bloom again another day were doomed to Port McQuarie Toweringabbie Norfolk Island or Emu plains and in those places of tyranny and condemnation many a blooming Irishman rather than subdue to the Saxon yoke were flogged to death and bravely died in servile chains but true to the shamrock and a credit to Paddy Land.

So ranted Ned, in that blend of white-core fantasy and felt history that gave his crusade against the way things were a mythical dimension—even purged his violence and evil of their corruption, for they were patently, on his own flaring declaration, innocent (or

Ned Kelly, man and myth. Kelly as a prisoner in 1878. The myth of the Kelly gang, nonchalantly keeping at bay a vast army of terrified police armed with artillery
National Library of Australia

innocent enough) of hypocrisy or what was venal. Kelly's was evil on the grand scale, trapped and desperate, provoked, nothing mean or trivial about it; a story of persecution, escape, action, death, and lesser tribulations which grasped the attention not only of those who could identify with it as ordinary mortals, but of heroes, poets and artists. Kelly, in some strange way, transcended himself, evoking in dreamers and intellectuals not only curiosity, but ambivalent benevolence, and a sense of mystery at the strength and meaning of their own instinctive response. *I am Ned Kelly*, John Malony titled his recent study of the outlaw. To what were they responding? To heroism? Violence? The fate-ridden totality of the whole drama? The answers get easier the further down the artistic scale. But they are still not easy. Lurking and festering in the mind of the son of an obscure ex-convict settler was a demonic Irish-Australian world. Goaded, it burst out, lashed back at its tormentors. Its escape into violent action was greeted by too much satisfaction, tolerance, interest, not to prove that this was an impulse shared by others.

So Kelly had elements of the universal, but when the Melbourne *Age* saw all this as an Irish phenomenon it had a point of truth beyond mere expression of its hostility. Here was a dimly realised echoing antipodean variant of the Irish land war, an episode of agrarian outrage. Here also was a dimension additional to that of the ordinary criminal and dramatic, the element in the Kelly affair which consisted of keeping down the flash Irish: the name itself was provocation enough to those who felt such suppression to be a public duty. The Irish were upstarts in the colonies and should therefore be put down, shown their place—at the bottom; which is why they attracted the support or goodwill of others at the bottom, Irish or not. The Kelly gang, to whom Ireland was a symbol and a language of social interpretation, themselves became a symbol, of defiance, cheek, of the cynical rejection of authority, victimisation, much else—generally, the fate of the man at the bottom. To be 'as game as Ned Kelly' was commendation indeed, but the Irish Catholic world from which he came offered the ultimate accolade, the great absolution for all his sins. It is the favoured bushranging word of 'John O'Brien', spokesman for the repute of that region. Ned was 'daring'.

So were other bushrangers, among whom the Irish were prominent. But Kelly was unique, a bridge figure between the Irish and the Australian, an ancestral paradigm—for what? Anything. Everything. The Irish bushrangers were much simpler. Bushranging was, after all, a logical consequence of, even a necessity following—escape. And escape was the obsession of the earliest Irish, those determined walkers to China. For those with more choice, it was light work promising high returns. It offered adventure and the prospect of fame. To progress beyond these simple motivations into complex areas of social banditry and sublimated (?) socioeconomic protest, may be to complicate what is certainly various, but probably straightforward: only Kelly country defies artless explanation. It would seem no accident that the ballads of bushranging celebrate *Bold* Jack Donohue and the *Wild Colonial Boy* (Jack Doolan—or Donovan, or Duggan, or whatever—was his name). Robert O'Hara Burke was able to legitimise this impulse into exploration, nor was it without significance that he was a police officer. Was not Burke a lawful version, seventy years later, of the Bathurst 'Ribbonmen', green ribbon in their hats, or of 'Riley, the captain of the Hunter River banditti, vaunting that he should be long spoken of (whatever his fate might be) in fear by his enemies, and in admiration by his friends'?—this from Peter Cunningham's *Two Years in New South Wales*. And this from the mythical Irish hero Cuchulainn, over the entrance to Patrick Pearse's Rathfarnham school in 1908: 'I care not if my life have only the span of a night and a day if my deeds be spoken of by the men of

Ireland.' Questionable and dangerous as national generalisations may be, many Irish seem dazzled by the prospect of fame. In early Australia, the only fame accessible to such Irish who came there lay in bolting, so that by 1830 the bushranger might alternatively be called a croppy. This kind of fame went together with failure: it was doom-laden and its celebration was inevitably linked with wry comment on the human condition and affirmations of popular stoic virtues; the failure motif in Australian history has its roots here. Nor is it the pursuit of full-blown heroism, or its commemoration hero-worship: the bushrangers are very limited paragons, embodying limited qualities of narrow applicability—courage, endurance, and the like, of particular meaning to the ordinary pioneer. The bushrangers filled the role of Australian Everyman, the ballads that grew up around them a ritual chant of consolation and defiance in a world harsh, unjust, and ruled by others.

The actual facts were hardly relevant to such constructs. Bold Jack Donohue, convicted in Dublin in 1825, convict runaway, shot as a bushranger on 1 September 1830, is all legend—'no hero in any sense' commented 'John O'Brien', of this small, colourless man. But immortalised in balladry, the only access the nameless might have to history, the only way they might rise up to affirm—vicariously, through their symbol—who they were; not nobody, somebody, me, Bold Jack, the singer and the song merged in the bid for History. The ballad seeks to evoke not pity (as in the transportation ballads) but solidarity, fellow feeling. Bold Jack was both actuality and symbol. He was one of those active heroes around which ancient Irish history revolved, and he was symbol of resistance to constituted authority. His mere existence, or indeed belief in his existence, was enough to provide a focal point for the generation of legends necessary to sustain the life of the nameless soul. As the scribe of the Book of Leinster chided his more gullible readers in the twelfth century (the warning was superfluous in that cultural tradition) 'Do not credit the details of the story or fantasy. Some things in it are devilish lies. And some poetical figments. Some seem possible. And others not. Some are for the enjoyment of idiots.' The enjoyment of idiots indeed. The ballad fantasies of bushranging are in this category—tales told to please uncomplicated minds, tales so true that it does not matter whether they are true or not, tales which tell more of the storyteller and of shared dreams and emotion than they do of the names that people them.

What does bushranging tell of the Irish? That they were overrepresented among lawbreakers, that they were violent? Hardly. Certainly the Irish were among bushranging's big names and those that have attracted the fame of balladry—Donohue, Doolan, Henry Power, Captain Moonlite (Andrew George Scott). In the same romantic tradition is Matthew Brady, best known of Tasmanian bushrangers, handsome, glamorous, defiant, offering an outrageous counter-reward, in April 1825, of twenty gallons of rum for delivery to him—Brady—of the person of the Governor, Sir George Arthur. Glamorous too is the Tasmanian career of Martin Cash, reprieved after murder, repentant and reformed, to die a free man, pardoned, at sixty-nine.

But the statistics tell a much less Irish story: bushranging is an area where the Irish genius for colourful behaviour has stolen the stage. Analysis of the birthplaces of Australia's most prominent hundred bushrangers 1789–1901 indicates that twenty-two were Irish, hardly a disproportionate number. Twenty-nine were English-born, thirty Australian. Of the Australians, some—obviously the Kelly gang for instance—were of Irish descent: fifteen of the thirty Australians were Catholics, a suggestive indicator—but then, several of those of Irish birth were Protestants. As to the glorification of violence, the bushranger ballads suggest that violence was marginal to popular interest. What these songs express is respect for, admiration of, those who could survive and act decisively and independently against overwhelming odds. To those who knew the bush, sheer survival in it was achievement enough, but to do so while on the run from the law—portrayed as a nemesis common to the human condition—deserved some kind of immortality: these deeds needed to be spoken of by men and the sons of men. Like the Irish poetry of the dispossessed in the seventeenth and eighteenth centuries, this primitive, unlovely Australian balladry reflected and evoked a mood and a passion the common people thought vital to preserve.

In part, that mood was hostile to the police—a truism of Australian historical attitudes, often attributed to convict origins, but sitting none too well, it might seem, with the strongly Irish complexion of Australian colonial police forces. Just how Irish is evident in figures for the New South Wales police. In 1851–62, 61.4 percent were Irish-born, in 1865, 66.7 percent. In 1872, of a force of 803, 479 (nearly 60 percent) were Irish. By 1901, this had dropped to 16.2 percent (351 Irish in 2172), and by 1914, to 8 percent (210 of 2626). But all these proportions were away above the Irish proportion of the population. In Victoria the situation was even more Irish: in 1874, of 1060 police, 81.7 percent were Irish-born. Not only had a high proportion of Australian police recruits previous experience in the Royal Irish Constabulary, but various elements in Australian police force legislation and regulations were based directly on Irish models. The stereotype of the policeman was a man with a uniform, a brogue, and a big free thirst.

But what kind of brogue? As much the Ulster Scots Irish variety. The assumption that Australian policemen were Catholic Irish (an image probably fed by an American stereotype spillover) is only partly correct. Irish Protestants were disproportionately very strong in the police—perhaps half the Irish element, and that in the higher, decision-making, ranks. Whereas the Catholic Irish tended to take police employment temporarily—indeed sought it out as secure and light work, unskilled employment with pay above the unskilled (some joined for adventure)—they tended to move on fairly quickly to other jobs. The Irish career officers tended to be Protestants. This split in the Irish composition of the police force is vital to understanding its operation and popular reputation: its odium stemmed only in part from a convict heritage; given its derivation from the Royal Irish Constabulary and its significant continuing recruitment from it, and given its Ulster Protestant orientation at career levels and positions of policy and leadership, it was inevitable that many Irish Catholics would hold it in low regard—and see joining it as a form of treachery. Further-more, the continuing role of the police in Ireland, in assisting evictions and the like, welded their Australian image to that of the tyrants—landlords, squatters, the possessing classes.

In contrast to Victoria, and Kelly, the Irish settlement of South Australia seems small and humdrum indeed. Yet Robert Torrens, that major figure in South Australian colonisation, was born in Cork, educated at Trinity College Dublin, and in his 1847 essay *Self Supporting Colonies. Ireland Saved without Cost to the Imperial Treasury* indulged his visions of New Erins and New Dublins in the colonies. It was not to be. The initial settlement was of Wakefield plan and attracted affluent nonconformists and the Irish proportion in the colony remained always low—10 percent in 1861, not quite 8 percent in 1871. Such Irish who came were attracted by the promise of high wages for labourers and an eventual chance to own land, but they could hardly have welcomed the patronising tone of emigrant handbooks which

promised that South Australian life would tame the wild Irishman and end their improvidence. But tame them it did. Its St Patrick's Society, founded in 1849, was full of
Anglicans, and it listened to a Torrens inaugural in which he sounded the themes of the
future: 'They had buried all recollections of former contentions. They would twine the
orange lily and the evergreen shamrock into one immortal wreath.' The Irish community
had sufficient resources and sense of separateness to found a newspaper in May 1869, the
Irish Harp and Farmers Herald, later the *Southern Cross*, a name change which itself makes
the point that the South Australian was the most irenic of Irish Australian publications.
This newspaper joined a growing number of Irish Australian journals: the Sydney *Freeman's
Journal* had then been in existence for nearly twenty years, but the Melbourne *Advocate* was
new though it had been preceded by the *Catholic Tribune* in 1853 and the *Victorian*
1862–64, edited by Daniel Deniehy. The *Advocate* was founded in 1868. Queensland
waited another ten years for its Irish voice, the *Australian* of 1878, with its title also a bid
for local acceptance (it carried a crest with a kangaroo and emu, and the motto 'Advance
Australia Fair'): The Brisbane *Age* of 1892 had similar integrationist pretensions. These
newspapers gave the local Irish a voice and a sense of commonality, linking them with
people of like mind and culture, and bringing them much closer to Ireland itself, not only
in terms of providing information, but in generating a feeling of being involved in Irish
affairs as they developed. This closer and more active perspective on Ireland did not have
only simple and straightforward effects. In some Irish Australians it roused or consolidated
Irish consciousness, but these were a minority. In most, a more intimate acquaintance with
Irish affairs was an education in how different Australia was from Ireland and a stimulus to
work out their own distinctive identity. Moreover, while such newspapers gave the Irish a
voice this did not mean that the general community would welcome what they wanted to
say: the function of the Irish-Australian press became one of testing and delineating the
boundaries of tolerable accommodation between Irish Catholics and others. In hostile eyes,
the very existence of the *Irish Harp* testified to separatism and faction, confirmed by the
Harp's efforts to foster Irish Catholic political unity. The Adelaide *Register* denounced the
formation in 1871 of an Orange Association in South Australia as indicative of faction, but
from the Orange viewpoint the *Harp* was no less so. But of all Irish Australian papers under
this stock criticism, the *Harp* was most insistent—and justified—in its denials. It was loyal
to Ireland and the Queen. It did not favour trade unions: they were divisive because social
harmony was a function of reciprocal responsibility based on mutual goodwill between
employer and employee—a pleasant theory. The future might have proved the *Irish Harp* a
benign reflection of integrated South Australian Irishness had not the divisive issue of
Catholic education come to dominate the affairs of the Irish Catholic community, sub-
suming that Irishness into a combative Catholic grievance. True, it was that Catholicism
that sustained papers such as the *Harp*—in its later form—and thus enabled Irishness to
retain its voice, as a facet of that continuing Irish Catholic identity. Whether that survival,
as a partly artificial construct, was a socially healthy thing is a debatable point: propping up
cultures beyond their natural vitality and span seems close to arrogating the powers of
God—but, of course, it was done by men of God.

Even at its founding, in 1869, the *Irish Harp* had an antiquated look: the *Irish
Harp*—and *Farmers Advocate*. No, this was fair for South Australia at this time: the
township of Clare speaks its origins and the dispersion of the Irish in farming areas. But
within a decade, the then and future movement of the Australian Irish had been discerned
gloomily by Bishop Dunne in Queensland. He was afraid that new Irish immigrants, and

those already deserting Australian land, would gravitate to 'the unwholesome lanes and purlieus of the bloated Australian cities.' In so far as the attractive power of the land was concerned, his fear was well based. Even work on other people's land was particularly scarce for the kind of Irish Dunne had in mind as desirable colonists. When the *Austral Light* complained in 1906 that squatters' advertisements for help excluded married couples with children ('no family' 'no encumbrances') that practice had been long in train. But Dunne's point can readily be confirmed for the 1870s, in that reputedly most lush of rural Irish colonies, Victoria. It has been noted of those who made up the Kelly gang in the 1870s, that, although they were eligible to select land, none did: they relied on seasonal work and casual jobs. Certainly, the fate of the Kelly gang was unique, and their earlier encounters with the law hardly fostered settled pursuits, but the question still remains: was their drift away from the paths of land selection exceptional, or part of an increasing Irish-Australian pattern? The latter, prompted for Irish-Australian sons by direct experience of the poverty of their parents' selections, but that poverty was for all to see and to draw their own conclusions for their own lives.

Dunne's fear that the Irish would capitulate to the attractive power of the cities was misplaced, or at least, exaggerated and too soon. In fact the cities were, as he said, 'bloated', and could not readily provide what the Irish most wanted—ample, unskilled work. The remote places of Queensland still had great attraction for the Irish, so long as the prospect of gold lasted, which it did from the late 1860s to the mid-eighties. In the Charters Towers Catholic Church, between 1872 and 1885, 65 percent of marriages were of the Irish-born; not that marriages were the dominant mode in that frontier town—de facto relationships were. It was said that many Irish came to Queensland because its towns were first ports of call for ships from Plymouth and by that stage they were totally bored and determined to get off. The motivation of most Irish was nothing as mindless and haphazard as that: they came for gold and went wherever they hoped it was, or provided labour for deep mining. When the gold ran out, there was silver, or tin, or whatever offered beneath the earth. And if there was no mining, then there were the railways. Queensland was an environment so intensely Irish as to sprout in its primitive mining towns early and vigorous branches of the Irish Land League and Irish Famine Relief organisation.

No, Dunne was wrong to think that the Irish would not farm because they were under the spell of the cities. Those who would not farm were often natural nomads, many of them seized with a gold-rush mentality. Farming wealth was not only too uncertain, too worrisome; worst of all it was too dull, too slow. Failing gold, railways would do, and Queensland could supply ample of this variety of nomadic construction work in the 1880s. Not that all Irish stuck permanently to such work: as the lines progressed they shed Irish ex-navvies as they went. From the railway camps the Irish found their way to the inland towns, not only as labourers, but as suppliers of goods and services. The proportion of Catholics in the 1881 census points to what was happening to the Irish—26 percent in Brisbane, but 30 percent in Charleville and Toowoomba, 40 percent in Dalby. Visiting a railway camp at Roma, all Dunne's worst fears about the degradation of the noble Irish seemed realised: here were 5–6000 of the roughest navvies in Australia, and they were drunken, quarrelsome—and irreligious.

But the Irish held no monopoly of Australian railway work, and where they did it was often in spite of employer preference. In the early days of railway building in northern New South Wales, the 1850s and 1860s, English railway workers far outnumbered Irish or

Some family contrasts. Above, Ireland: Joseph Shannon and his children in the turf bog, Tempo, Co. Fermanagh, October 1899 Below, Australia: Seven of the nine Hartigan children of Yass, NSW about 1888; Patrick (John O'Brien of 'Around the Boree Log') is on the far right
Ulster Museum: Langham Collection. Fr F. Mecham, Sydney

Scots. Certainly the Irish were renowned for their great strength and endurance as labourers—they built the British and American railroads—but other aspects of their overseas reputation had also reached Australia, so that English labourers were preferred: they were believed to be more reliable and to need less supervision. Overseas stories suggested that Irish drinking habits delayed contracts as did the fights—indeed riots—that seemed to be so frequently associated with an Irish presence. Given the high cost of labour in Australia, contractors preferred the less troublesome English. But, as in matters of immigration, preference was often irrelevant: as with so many other areas of hard, dirty and remote labour, the Irish were the ones who applied, were willing to do the job. In 1891, the young John Monash, then an engineer, commented on the navvies he encountered on the construction of Melbourne railways and bridges: 'It is a mistake however to suppose that any ragamuffin can turn navvy. He must be a physical giant and his endurance of continuous hard labor must be almost beyond civilised conception . . . Nine out of ten are raw ignorant Irishmen, strong and muscular, intemperate, improvident, unclean to look upon, and with not a thought beyond the day, and the very narrowest possible horizon.' Monash added some insights into their gipsy lifestyle. The navvy often had his own horse and dray, to do the carting (rubbish or fill) associated with his job. On this travelled the whole household, often a wife and five children. They seemed to sense work from afar, appearing from nowhere exactly when needed, but equally liable to suddenly vanish, to move on restlessly out of sheer caprice.

Those who did not marry. The Misses Julian, Bogolong Homestead, near Bookham, NSW, in the Yass area, December 1913

This kind of Irish labourer was in fact a member of a special caste, and his nomad existence was his chosen form of settlement, likely to have such permanence as health, circumstances and the economy would lend to it. Others were by no means content with labouring or with the limitations they had brought from Ireland. In May 1909, Owen O'Neill told his younger brother that he was in Melbourne 'qualifying for an engineer on the trams ... I thought I would learn something besides farming. You must understand that we Irishmen know how to do nothing only use a pick and shovel, no matter what you go in for you have got to serve your time ...'. O'Neill's letter is full of a sharp awareness of a new, complex, and unfamiliar economy, in which the rural Irishman often found himself disadvantaged to the point of perplexity and confusion: he told his brother, 'The Kangroo is another native [bird]. I have not seen one, I think it is also called the Emu ...' Owen O'Neill resented an Ireland which had not prepared him for his new life, he detested the Irishman's menial and worker image, the Stage Irishman syndrome made him angry, and he was bitterly sensitive to his own ignorance. Did he escape from the world of Irish pick and shovel? With such sentiments and determination, it is likely that he did. But many Irish were well content with their physical endowments and their lowly station: if navvying was not available they would turn to what was—farmwork, shearing, timber-cutting.

So did the selectors: Bishop Dunne's moral hierarchy of labour with small farming at the top and city labouring at the bottom simply did not fit the Australian situation. Sharp divisions of function did not exist, as labourers worked to save for a selection and as selectors took labouring jobs, sometimes for months in order to survive, or pay for improvements—and as all these plans and intentions went wrong, had to be changed, postponed, abandoned, as human affairs and economies dictated. Nor did the pioneering have a stop which might allow stability of the kind Dunne craved for, to blossom and grow idyllic. The land grants to the emancipists of the convict period gave way to sale and selection, systematised and increased dramatically with the Selection Acts of the 1860s, continuing on indefinitely as new land was opened up or big estates divided. Nor did each phase of land release simply cater for that period's new migrants. The Irish settlers of South Gippsland when it was opened up in the 1880s were in part fairly new immigrants, but perhaps equally they came from other parts of the country, internal migrants from, for instance, Ballarat. Some of these were looking for their first land, but some—bitten, they would openly acknowledge, by the land-selecting bug—were what amounted to small-time gamblers in land, leaving their old property to 'go back to its Mother' (Nature) in search of something new and better. What would Dunne have thought of these itinerant farmers (contradiction in his terms) leaving ruin in their wake in seeking to better themselves, or pursue mere novelty? With the arrogance of love, Dunne claimed to know the mind of God on this matter: 'God never meant the Irish Catholic to be the wanderer that he is over the face of the earth,' said Dunne through the 1885 Plenary Council of bishops. It was a narrow view of God's intentions, to which an Irish St Augustine might have retorted 'Our hearts are restless till they rest in Thee'. The instincts of the devout told them that their country of permanence was not Ireland, or Australia, but Heaven, and they were travelling people until that destination. What of those less touched by holiness, less in tune with the spirit within? Too complex to sort out, but suspiciously like a sophisticated form of rural vagrancy. Sometimes these wanderers found their better country, sometimes they were killed by the trees they cleared, or drowned in local creeks, sometimes they stayed because they lacked the will or the circumstances to move on to that next selection, which would certainly be more fertile, rich, salubrious and happy. But invariably these selectors became the local labour battalions supplementing the main forces that opened up their localities with road, bridges, railways, dams. As in all else in pioneering Australia, traditional demarcations were blurred.

Even by the 1870s all Australian states evidence decline in Irish born population, not only in proportion, but in actual numbers. Victoria is a clear example: 100 468 in 1871, 86 733 in 1881, and the Irish-born proportion had been dropping since the very early days of Victorian settlement—16.7 percent in 1854, but only 7.5 percent in 1891. As Oliver MacDonagh has remarked in relation to 1851–91, 'To treat the Irish element in our period as strictly synonymous with those inhabitants actually born in Ireland would be most misleading . . . we are concerned almost exclusively with new or first generation Australians in whom identification with country of origin or extraction was extremely powerful'. This identification seems most powerful in Victoria, that most 'Irish' of Australian colonies, but in addition to the question of why this should be so, there is the very complex problem of the nature and extent of that identification with Ireland—or some vision of Ireland, or some group or cause deemed 'Irish'. This book generally is about such problems and it would be absurd to do more at this juncture than to note their appearance as significant procedural difficulties from the 1870s—and to suggest that the crude equation of Irish and Catholic, traditionally adopted to cope with (and often to implicitly denigrate) such allegiances is to transform a partial correlation into a pseudo-explanation.

J.F. Hogan's *The Irish in Australia* published in 1887, shows no methodological rigour, but sound practical instincts. He uses the terms 'Irish' and 'Irish-Australian' interchangeably: both can indicate either Irish or Australian birth. When he uses 'Irish-Australian' to describe a person of Irish birth, it denotes those who have made some prominent contribution to Australian life in such a way as to identify themselves with it, say in politics, or commerce, or exploration. The more usual use of the term is, perhaps, the reverse; a person of Australian birth who makes some kind of an identification with Ireland, usually through descent. In either case, one conclusion is clear: an Irish-Australian was a person with some degree of dual allegiance, identifying him or herself with both Ireland and Australia—or Australia and Ireland—making some kind of personal balance between the demands of the two identities and attempting to blend them when and where possible. If 'the Irish in Australia' be understood to mean those who made a complete identification with Ireland, to the exclusion of their Australian environment, this was a very tiny group. Used to label that very much larger sector of Australia's population whose origins were Irish, at whatever remove, and whose culture and loyalties were partly or sometimes Irish, the Irish in Australia are notable for their very substantial and decisive Australianism: the balance of their allegiance was decidedly Australian, but that did not mean it ceased to be Irish. Indeed, in such times within Australia when British loyalties were being stressed, for such 'Irish', their Irish and Australian allegiances tended to coalesce, each tending to determine the definition of the other.

The 1870s is an appropriate decade in which to note the appearance of such complexities and shifts in the composition of Irish Australia, and, perhaps a suitable point at which to insist again on the generality, elusiveness, and imprecision of the whole concept. But it is not to suggest that those of Irish birth were ceasing to dominate Irish Australia from that time. Two O'Connors will make the point: Daniel, born 1844, arrived Sydney 1854, ardent nationalist, parliamentarian 1877–91, died 1914; J.G., born 1839, arrived Sydney 1841, printer, a key figure in a procession of Irish organisations, died 1913. Throughout the nineteenth century, and into this, the public and organisational face of Irish Australia was that of the Irish-born. They were the immigrants of the 1840s and later, whose Australian activities had brought them prominence and established them as leaders in the Irish community. Simply by effluction of time and usual social processes they remained dominant throughout the rest of the century, a position they reinforced through their preference in patronage for new arrivals from Ireland above the local-born. This strong Irish-born bias was replicated to the point of almost total monopoly within the Catholic Church. The public presence of Irish Australia, its image, its organisations, its spokesmen and media, remained under the control of the Irish-born long after they had dwindled to a small minority of those for whom they claimed to speak.

That being so, it is peculiarly difficult to disinter the reality of Irish Australia at, say, the end of the nineteenth century. The major sources contain a whole set of constricting and misleading biases: they reflect the views of not only an older generation, but an Irish-born one, and are thoroughly sanitised by their intimate connection with the Catholic Church. This makes for far more difficulties than are usually inherent in appraising that institution central to the production of the Irish Australian in the usual sense—marriage.

That there were differences here between the Irish-born and their Australian children is clearly evident. When T.A. Coghlan came to report on the birthrate in New South Wales in 1903, he found contrasts in relation to marriage and childbearing between the Irish-born and their children. Their children married earlier, and had fewer children—signs of differing values and outlook, and of movement towards an Australian norm. How far did such children see themselves as local copies of 'The Irish Mother' lauded in the *Austral Light* of July 1909: 'I do not think one can find in the whole world a class of people who pray with such ardent faith as the mothers of Ireland.' Such antiseptic saintly ideals tended to exist mainly in the minds and sentiments of their clerical promoters rather than represent any widespread sociological reality. Was John O'Brien's 'Little Irish Mother' of south western New South Wales very much the exception, rather than the rule? In a broad statistical sense she was obviously exceptional, in that the weight of Irish female concentration was always urban, not rural. She was exceptional too in that the stalwart pioneering Irish Catholic woman was, obviously, a feature of a pioneering situation, a phase in Australian history which was transitory, not permanent: the frontier moved on. And she was exceptional also in her faith, piety, and family influence: in 1909 a priest informed the Australasian Catholic Congress that many outback Catholic women were 'ignorant of their faith and totally incapable of either influencing a careless husband or instructing careless children'. Yet some, perhaps many, were indeed exceptional. Stripped of its cloying sentimentality, given the tough realism that comes with harsh encounters with life and land, the figure had reality enough in good women whose lives were an active prayer beyond the favoured forms and rituals of their day. They sought, knew, and promoted goodness, in no way 'little': the dismissive diminutive has undervalued generations of achievement of Irish mothering, given actual and diverse forms in remembered history, such as that of the female Duracks—fierce forms, such as Sarah Tully, with her forceful, almost terrible vitality, as well as varieties softer but no less formidable. The mother was especially important when sons married late or stayed close, when she organised the domestic economy of poultry and milking, and when she appeared in the form of 'Reverend Mother', the principal of the local school, administrator, financier, diplomat, organiser, manipulator, civiliser, teacher, powerful local figure, woman of God.

What was the Irish marriage norm? The stereotypes are contradictory—late marriages, lots of kids. The reality was much more complex and in the process of rapid change. The Great Famine of 1845–49 wrought fundamental changes in both economy and mentality, and particularly, a revolution in attitudes to marriage: where before it had been early, widespread, and lightly embarked upon, it became late, restricted, and most cautiously viewed. This revolution was the immediate background to most Irish immigrants. Overwhelmingly they were young and single and thus those most directly affected by that change in the Irish mental climate; indeed their very emigration itself was a product of economic changes such as the consolidation of small holdings and a swing to livestock which made small farming and marriage no longer possible for them. This Irish background, in which marriage had suddenly come to be regarded with extreme caution, continued to exercise a powerful influence, at least initially, on immigrants to Australia. So did the continuing Irish view—still present at the very end of the century—that colonial women were inferior: this was a protraction of the image generated by convict society but it was frequently reinforced by reports from immigrants, usually those on the fringes of frontier society. Thus William Martin, writing to his father in Ballycastle, Co. Antrim, in December 1873, from Tyrconnell Downs near Roma, was totally opposed to his sisters or female relations coming to join him.

> This is a bad country for girls unless the[y] be very wise and steady. Woman is very scerse and the inducements for girls going rong in this Country is something frightfull, in fact the[re] are one third of the women that is in the Bush leaves their husbands and goes with other men for the reason than woman is so scerse that men actually worships them and the[y] be come so vain that the[y] are almost sure to go to the bad. [sic]

Martin also illustrates several other factors impinging on the colonial marriage situation. Like many immigrants, he already had an Irish sweetheart, but she no longer wrote to him, or replied to his letters. Eventually he was reduced to asking his sister in Ireland if his sweetheart had 'picked up a fresh lover'. Obviously he was upset and his ego hurt: he was too proud to write again. On top of this, his parents took to badgering him to marry an Irish girl he did not know. Her photo showed her handsome, but, like other immigrants, he now had some colonial questions to answer that would not have occurred in Ireland: was she educated, could she write a good letter, was she acceptable in good company? He reminded his parents that he had changed since he left home. Still, respect for the authority and wishes of parents remained strong: 'However if she writes me and that I like her style of writing . . . I might make some promise . . .' Pushed further by his parents in matrimonial matters—they pointedly informed him of the marriage of an eligible local girl he knew—William spelt out bluntly a number of governing principles general to Irish migrants: 'making money occupies my mind more than thinking of women', 'Women is easily had at any time when you have the wherewith', and 'when a man sees as much of the world as I have, he will be very carefull about Matrimonial affairs and look well before he enters into it'.

All these considerations worked towards later marriages, as did the general disruption of life emigration entailed, the high mobility of migrants, their heavy presence in remote isolated situations in groups of single men, and the continuing belief, hope, or illusion among some migrants that they were in Australia temporarily and when they had made their fortune they would return to Ireland to settle down.

Against all this were other Australian circumstances and pressures encouraging marriage. In Ireland a family, and particularly a large family was an encumbrance, a liability and a worry. Late marriages and emigration were responses to economic pressures and facts impossible to ignore. But in Australia big families were regarded as an essential adjunct to successful colonial rural life: they were a pleasure in that they provided a ready-made social group, and an economic asset, sometimes an utter necessity, providing labour where it was scarce and expensive. The family farm was a basic unit of the rural economy, and as *Around the Boree Log* shows, capable of generating and sustaining a lively and satisfying culture of its own. Research has shown that in areas of strong Irish family representation—north-central Victoria, 1864–99—Irish family farming is not radically different from that conducted by any other nationality: kin networks were of great advantage to all. Though not radically different, it was arguably more intense, fostered as the Irish family was by its links with traditional Irish society and the vigorously pro-family stance of the Catholic Church. In two superb books Mary Durack has immortalised the growth of an Irish family in an Irish-Australian, and then an Australian, dynasty. Its values were strict codes of family loyalty, with its governing poles of decency and disgrace. Its snobbery was the idea of 'good stock', 'coming from a good family', as measure for marriage. Its vices were faction and envy. Certainly the intensity of family feeling in immigrant correspondence is striking, perhaps heightened by the situation in which it was the young and single rather than whole families that emigrated: to leave parents perhaps strengthened the bonds. In a sense Australia reversed or retarded, for Irish immigrants, the 'modernisation' trends evident in post-Famine Ireland, creating that illusion (or was it genuine anachronism?) of Irish Australia being more Irish than Ireland which struck some observers (such as Dr Kevin Izod O'Doherty) and some wishful thinkers (such as the *Freeman's Journal*). The ideal Irish family, rural, humble, large, pious, reasonably prosperous, happy, stable, such as is depicted in *Around the Boree Log*, was simply not a possibility in post-Famine Ireland in which land was being consolidated into pasture and in which the dominant demographic facts were celibacy, late marriage and emigration. The large and vigorous Irish family reappeared in Australia. But truncated in reverse, without grandparents and some of the usual range of senior relatives. And by no means as submissive to age as the Irish model: Irish sons and daughters in Australia did not defer to parents automatically, as would have been the tendency in Ireland; they were seen as distant, ignorant of Australian conditions, and often misinformed by rumour or prejudice. For all that the move to Australia might have revitalised the Irish model family, it in fact loosened its authority structures and introduced into it strands of democracy and pragmatism unknown in the old culture.

Above all, one great fact disposed the emigrant Irish to marry, and contradicts the myth of repressive sexuality that surrounds the Irish. That fact was the decision to emigrate itself. The choices facing the young people of later nineteenth-century Ireland were, to marry late, remain celibate—or emigrate. Usually (but not always) unspoken, but everywhere understood in Ireland, the choice of emigration went with the decision, or at least the disposition, to marry. The very constituency of the emigrant group demonstrates this: not family groups, but individuals. In 1877–90, the period of peak migration, 77 percent were single, 12 percent married, the rest children. On a calculation of the continuing vitality of the impetus to emigrate, Irish sexuality was in a very healthy state indeed. And the Australian statistics confirm this. Few Irish women remained celibate in Australia if they had the opportunity to marry. If they could not find husbands of their own race and religion they married otherwise. Figures from all periods and places illustrate this. About half the Irish Catholic females who married in Victoria in the 1850s married outside the Catholic Church. In Victoria 1855–60, while 80 percent of Irish men married Irish wives, only 48 percent of Irish women acquired Irish husbands. In the parish of Croydon, New South Wales, between 1924 and 1962 there were 498 marriages: one-third (172) were mixed—interfaith—and in 80 percent of these the Catholic was the woman. Against the dictates of their religion, and outside their own racial group, many Irish Catholic women chose marriage, despite what that might mean in terms of breaches with church, family, friends, the whole of their former society. For these women—and there were very many—marriage was a greater good than preserving relations with kith or religion. The likely socially solvent effects of this phenomenon should be noted, however beyond calculation: it drew Irish Catholics into the community, and, whatever the religious regulations and racial preferences, tended to erode cultural isolationism.

Outside their group—and down: Irish women tended to marry beneath their social scale. For them, marriage was not an opportunity for improving their social status: to marry at their own level, or up, usually meant marrying outside their religion or group. The colonial situation told against Irish women in that they heavily outnumbered Irish men, in the cities. Irish men tended to have inferior occupations. Faced with the prospects of an intolerable drop in status and living standards, or simply unable to relate to prospective partners within their own religious and cultural group, many Irish and Irish-Australian women never married, especially those better off. This was not a matter of preference, but of cold circumstance: for Irish women, marriage itself remained a highly desirable state. There was more to this than simply that of being the female norm of the time. It was what many emigrants had left Ireland expecting: for female emigrants a central aspect of the great adventure was its romantic aspect; they would meet a rich and handsome lover. To fail to marry was to admit the death of that dream, to concede major personal failure, and to admit the possibility of having made a major tactical mistake: remaining in Ireland might have led to marriage, or at least a less lonely and distressful spinsterhood.

For Irish men, the considerations mentioned earlier applied. They would marry when they had enough money, if they decided to stay in Australia, when they felt like settling down—and so on. But a major factor inhibiting marriage was shame. Many Irish men were painfully aware of their low status and of their inability to offer a woman much better than poverty and drudgery: pride silenced many a proposal. And many determined they would not marry until they had sufficient wealth to keep a wife and family in the superior style they wished. The outcome was substantial age differentials between husbands and wives in the Irish community: a husband might be twenty years or more his wife's senior. This in turn led to one of those curious social compensations and enrichments characteristic of Irish-Australian society. In the hotel trade, so central to the Irish-Australian experience, the death of an older husband frequently led to the licensee being an active widow of impeccable respectability. Her social role often became that of matriarch, confessor to the community, dispensing advice to those who sought it. The archetypal figure of Mrs O'Hara who ran the Brian Boru was a feature of the Irish life of many a country town, respected and sought out particularly by single men who needed a sympathetic female ear, thought to be experienced and independent. Such a worldly yet respectable widow embodied functions of great antiquity and practical utility, an ancient institution of grandmotherly recourse reborn in colonial circumstances virtually devoid of grandmothers and the benefits of their social roles in the lives of the unmarried. These widows—or the wife of mine host—commanded motherly resources: the hotel dining room provided meals to men often denied nutritious cooking otherwise, the bathrooms provided cleanliness, the bar provided contacts for employment, friendship and entertainment, the parlour provided a newspaper, some quiet, the occasional meeting place for organisations. Above all, the Mrs O'Haras provided that female dimension to which the Irish were used, met that need they felt to include the female perception and to value its unique encounter with the world. Among the many absurd libels foisted on the Irish by those incapable of understanding them is (it is a fairly recent construct) that they dismissed and subjugated women. On the contrary, that was something they found in Australia. On his arrival in 1882, Phil Mahony was astonished by the dominance of masculinity, at least in Melbourne: '. . . business is done by men in this country. I firmly believe there are not one hundred young women in the whole of Melbourne storekeeping.'

Linked with this is the mythology that surrounds Irish sexual attitudes. Crucial to understanding these, and the evolution of their mythology, is an appreciation of the coercive power of the mores of the Evangelical Protestant puritanism that grew to dominate Victorian Britain. These became peculiarly powerful in Ireland, and even more so in Ireland's British colonies—peculiarly powerful for three main reasons. The Irish had no comprehension of the convenient English double-standard practice in regard to morality which affirmed the highest theoretical public standards but tolerated private moral anarchy. The Irish conceived of themselves as being in a situation of competition with the Protestant English: they had to prove themselves superior in virtue, in the English game of morals and respectability. And all this became an aspect of the crusade from 1850 by the Irish Catholic Church for greater control over Irish society: imposition of the new moral stringency became a test of the Church's power and standing in the community.

Such studies as throw light on pre-Famine sexuality in Ireland (and there are several of great competence) show a traditional society healthily non-repressive, demonstrating a balance between respect for sexuality and a lack of sexual prurience: the degree of marital fidelity was quite remarkable, as was chastity. The development of a puritanical and repressive Jansenism is a post-Famine phenomenon and associated with the growth in the power of the clergy. To the extent that it was real (as distinct from a paragon promoted by the priesthood) its roots were in two features of the economy and society of post-Famine Ireland—the Famine had taught an inescapable lesson about the consequences of overpopulation, and an Irish middle class aspired to the lifestyle and respectability of its English equivalent. In Australia, before, say, the 1860s, the pre-Famine atmosphere would appear to pervade Irish Catholicism, but one considerably loosened and coarsened by the influence of the convict and colonial pioneering situations: cohabitation was a feature of the colonial scene. Evidence of the appearance of Jansenist rigour and concentration on sexual morality within the Australian Irish Catholic community suggests it was surfacing in the 1890s, coincident with the clear emergence of an Irish-Australian middle class bent on demonstrating their respectability, and a priesthood increasingly determined to raise the status, spiritual and temporal, of their charges. Certainly colonial laxity in sexual matters, as in many others, was a challenge which no zealous reformer—indeed no civilised person—could ignore, but the drive to suppress the sexual went much further than that. How much it was a reaction to English criticism is unclear, but that contempt and snobbery always had a sexual edge. When John Martineau visited Australia in 1869 he published his view that 'the Irish here, as everywhere, multiply much faster than the rest of the population'. In 1881 A.M. Topp claimed that the poorer Irish propagate 'rapidly and recklessly'. It was a familiar refrain, from J.D. Lang to present times: their breeding was disgusting, their numbers a threat. It was the English implication that sex was dirty that pushed a natural Irish reticence, in the minds of a clergy extremely sensitive to English reproof, to extremes of prudery and prurience as a standard mode of dealing with sexual matters. Their own celibacy made a lack of sexual balance a likely area of clerical weakness, and one where a mixture of ignorance, avoidance, and sensitivity could issue in unfortunate pronouncements and produce painful effects among those of goodwill.

How far this went into the minds and hearts of Irish Australia, how seriously the anti-sexual polemic of the clergy was taken, awaits its historian, but on the strength of desultory reminiscences, and such many marriages as appeared happy—and from such crudities as are preserved in lore—the balance greatly favours an outcome determined by nature, common sense, love, and the wider virtues those clergy did know how to teach and live.

Irish settlement in Australia has a rural image—encapsulated in *Around the Boree Log*—of independent and reasonably prosperous farming. The image is justified. It may have been a happy accident that the heaviest wave of Irish migration to Australia arrived at a time of agricultural boom, in the sixties and seventies, thus making their farming viable, but it was nevertheless a fact that by the 1880s nearly half of Victoria's Irish lived outside metropolitan Melbourne, with similar distributions in other colonies. Moreover, while very few unskilled Irish immigrants came into immediate possession of a farm, the fact that so many eventually could do so—not only through luck with gold, but via wage labour—illustrates that openness of the colonial society and economy that so quickly won the allegiance of the Irish. In this they did not differ radically from the fortunes of their English or Scots counterparts. Nor did they have markedly less success or prove themselves less adaptable. In New South Wales, from the foundation of settlement, Irish farmers had assimilated to the farming methods and produce of their fellow farmers—large-scale sheep and wheat acreages. In Victoria they had turned the traditional Irish small acreages, intensive settlement, and potato cultivation to their advantage by supplying the Melbourne market. Later, in the 1880s, they had pushed out into the Wimmera wheat belt, as they had done into north-east Victoria in the 1870s, with as much success as anyone else. Perhaps a little less, as they were more bedevilled than others by lack of capital to clear and stock land. But many, perhaps most of them, made a reasonable living in a middling way, stable and stay-put enough, though occasionally moving on, to provide sons with adequate land or to search for something better. Intertwined with this Irish farming community was another, mobile, much less stable, of casual and seasonal labourers, of various kinds of contractors and agents—fencing, well-drilling—and yet another, the inhabitants of the country towns, pub-owners, railwaymen, government officials, and jobs long forgotten: in 1876 the grandiose firm of Denis O'Brien, Flynn and Co. purveyed water in Goulburn at ninepence a cask. The local Catholic church tended to link them all, but so did their economy and spirit: few wealthy, most with a touch of the gambler, mobile, sociable, averse to anything too dull, like staying put, or the iron of the soul necessary to making big money.

But if half lived in the country, obviously half lived in cities and, from the 1880s, the proportions gradually changed, to reflect the urban drift. Yet to say that many of the Irish stayed in, or drifted to, the cities is misleading, if interpreted in an American, English or European context. Australian cities lacked the legacy of walls. The old cities wanted to be worlds apart, fortified islands in a hostile countryside with their own distinctive culture: they bequeathed this sense of separation, this inturned focus, to their modern successors. In contrast, Australian cities were dispersed in themselves, and looked outwards. Their structure blurred the distinction between town and country and it was often where this blurring process was most evident—the periphery—that the Irish preferred to live. The same preference, for the space of the country allied with the society of the city, is reflected in the strong Irish presence in many country towns.

In relation to Sydney itself, the first 'Irishtown'—named after the local concentration of Irish—had been in what is now the Bankstown area, at first farming and timber-milling land made easily accessible to Sydney by being on the Liverpool Road. In the 1850s another 'Irishtown'—Presbyterian—had grown north of the harbour in what is now Turramurra. As with the Catholic variety, the nucleus came from a few settlers who attracted others of that faith and culture. Of these the most prominent was Samuel King from Donegal who, from 1853, developed several extensive orchards in the area. Farming, timber-getting, orchards—these were not city pursuits, but were related closely to a city market. The growth of Sydney city itself, and its associated suburbs, accelerated from the 1860s—in 1861, 95 789; 1881, 224 939; 1901, 480 976—the population multiplied by five times in forty years. Irish concentrations developed, in the city itself, particularly in Surry Hills, Redfern, Waterloo, Paddington, but also in the more salubrious suburbs of Hunters Hill, Randwick and Woollahra, reflecting the high proportion of Irish among the house-and-garden servants of the rich. The concentration of inner-city Irish reflected their overrepresentation in unskilled occupations and their need to live close to their places of work—docks, railways, industry as it grew. In such mean suburbs as Surry Hills could be heard the strains of what Ruth Park has immortalised as *The Harp in the South*; Australian Irish families, 'hard working, hard drinking, and as carefree as the day was long'—or so the folk-lore had it: the reality was often less cheerful.

Melbourne offered a similar scene. J.F. Hogan observed in 1887 that 'north and west Melbourne, from their proximity to the central terminus of the Victorian railway system, where many hundreds of Irishmen are regularly employed as porters, guards, pointsmen, engine-drivers, etc., have necessarily a larger Celtic population than south or east Melbourne'. This particular example also illustrates the tendency of Irish workers to seek government employment rather than with private employers. Not only was this the case with labourers, but also with clerical workers: the Irish regarded government employment as offering greater security and more protection from prejudice.

It has been contended that the Australian Irish subculture or 'heritage' is less the product of a rural situation than the creation of an industrial or urban life. Not surprisingly such suggestions tend to emanate from those whose origins and familiarities are in such urban Irish areas, while the proponents of the rural thesis have country links and origins. It is hardly an evasion to respond by further suggesting that both are variants on similar themes, especially when the 'urban' thesis, as advanced by Chris McConville, argues that Australian 'Irishness' was less a heritage of any quintessential 'Irishness' than the creation of in-teraction between the Irish and their urban environment, a composite of suburban, Labor, church, class, work and sport loyalties, with a national flavour: that variety of interaction with elements both the same and different is also part of the (varieties of) Irish rural scenes. The moment one suggests in reply that the Irish rural element were better integrated, more flourishing as individuals, less likely to join Irish organisations, on easier terms with their neighbours, the exceptions leap to mind, such comparison becomes questionable, and the whole idea of such an inquiry becomes absurd: what does integration mean? Is it not compatible with the preservation of 'Irishness'?

The urban argument has particular power in that its living champions are vocal and numerous, mainly in Melbourne, and that the evidence to support it is tangible and concentrated. Indeed nothing was more important to this urban Irishry than a shared and demarked separate territory. And nowhere is it better exemplified than in Richmond, inner suburb of Melbourne, 'Struggletown' Janet McCalman calls it. Around the name and place of Richmond, the shared and sacred symbols of the local variant of Irish Australia were grouped, bidding in their vigour, stridency, and clannishness to claim monopoly of the image. The municipal council, a Labor Party branch, a football club (Australian Rules) which in 1920 had seventeen Irish Australians among 37 players, a Catholic church, a common work (and unemployment) pattern, fierce friendships, tolerance of hard drinking and larrikinism—all these things were conditioned by Irishness, flavoured by it, but still remained their Australian selves. Or, to reverse the flow of the process of interaction, support for, loyalty to, the cause of Ireland and the Catholic religion drew on the structures of suburb, workplace, economic position, sport—the whole spectrum of the Irish Catholic position in Australian life—rather than on any deep informed belief in the cause of Ireland or philosophic commitment to Catholic doctrine. Ireland and the Catholic Church were, in a real sense, automatic tribal loyalties; they were, in their epic dimensions and grandeur, part of a defence mechanism against the diminishing drudgery of work and the humbling constrictions of low status, and they were one dimension of a set of commitments and organisational expressions which integrated individuals into the local community, which in turn was woven into the wider community. Nor were Ireland and Catholicism necessarily the most important loyalties. This urban subculture was one in which church and clergy were a part, but not always a determining focus. Its Irish life was both separate from and involved with, other city dwellers, other slum tenants, other Labor Party members, other neighbours. They married each other, but not always; helped each other, but also others, non-Irish, in the same working-class boat. To say that the Irish were proud of the way in which they related to the whole community is to simplify their reaction to charges that they formed ghettoes, or were isolationist, or divisive: they were part of a totality, they belonged to their locality and it belonged to them, they had their place and their lives, of which Irish heritage and Catholicism were but one dimension. To question this integration was to touch a sensitive Irish nerve because it reduced such Irish Australians to being Irish, it deprived them of an integral aspect of their identity they knew themselves to possess. When Anthony Trollope recorded in *Australia and New Zealand* (1873) that he had been told that there was an 'Irish quarter' in Melbourne, J.F. Hogan responded to it as a contemptuous libel, denying it hotly: 'the Irish in Melbourne are not to be found herding together, like the Chinese ... in each of the municipal districts there is a strong contingent of independent Irish ratepayers, men with a stake in the country, freeholders qualified to vote, and good citizens in every respect. Of course, some suburbs will be more representatively Irish than others.' This last may sound like an equivocation, but recent research confirms the Hogan appraisal and contradicts Trollope. Hogan pointed to the grouping of the Irish in north and west Melbourne, but the reasons are not those of the ghetto: in both Melbourne and Sydney the Irish were compelled, by the economics of time and money, to live near where they worked—the railway and waterfront. In those very areas of highest Irish concentration, research proves that the Irish were mixed with the rest of the population. Even in streets blazoning forth Irish allegiance—St Patricks Lane, Shamrock Alley—there was no Irish monopoly, or endeavour to create one: neighbours were fellow workers, English, Scots, Australian, not fellow nationals. Celtic labels (Tara seems the most popular) were restricted to houses: the affirmation of Irishness was personal rather than of the group. The sociability of the Australian Irish was not of a kind assuaged only by each other, but by anyone: their gregariousness and need for conversation were satisfied by street living, by neighbourliness. These urban Irish also displayed another feature foreign to the ghetto: they were intensely mobile. They moved house and job often, not only within the city, but from town to country, and vice versa. Far from being the stagnancy of a ghetto, the dominant ethos of the urban Irish seems to have been a restless state of flux.

This too describes the female face of that character. A salient characteristic of Irish female immigration into Australia was that it was employed before marriage in domestic service. There were some middle-class women immigrants, mainly Protestant, employed as companions and governesses. Mrs Blanshard of the London-based Female Middle Class Emigration Society spent 1874–80 in Ireland recruiting 'useful, companionable women, but not what is known as "fine ladies" or too highly accomplished governesses'. But the demand for these was relatively small, and just as the colonies offered little opportunity for 'gentlemen' without capital or willingness to tackle rough labouring work, 'ladies' with genteel accomplishments found it extremely difficult to find appropriate paid work. Many Irishwomen were trained as needleworkers but that was a skill in little colonial demand. Crudely, even for those who felt this to be beneath them, the economy dictated domestic service or nothing, until the development of, for example, the clothing industry, later in the century. In 1857 more than a third of Catholic marriages in New South Wales were celebrated in St Mary's Cathedral, Sydney. Of 316 brides in that year, 259 were Irish-born; 237 of these (over 90 percent) had been in domestic service. The growth of cities, and of wealth, maintained demand, particularly as this was employment prone to attrition by marriage. By the 1880s, the Irish domestic servant had become a standard subject for caricature and for hostile comment, as being incompetent, lazy, devoted to Irish causes, and saucy besides. Certainly some of this criticism was natural to the existence of servants as such: they are, as a class, likely to be found wanting by those they serve. Moreover, those who employed them in Australia were often deficient in their own attitudes or instructions: unused to servants, and without skills in management, they had unreal or unreasonable expectations. In some cases they harboured prejudices which created negative standards of measurement: '. . . my housekeeper is Irish but honest and good for all that . . .', so G.W. Rusden, the historian, informed W.H. Lecky in 1893. Rusden, like many in the employing class, was vehemently opposed to Home Rule, and the Irish politics of servants was a constant irritant and source of distrust. But the caustic diatribe of Richard Twopenny was a classic Australian appraisal of the Irish domestic—Bridget, Biddy as counterpart to Pat, Paddy. In *Town Life in Australia* (1883) he labelled Irish servants liars and dirty, perhaps less impertinent than colonials, but stupid; Biddy was stupid, and, with no experience except hovels, likely to stare in astonishment 'to find you don't keep a pig on your drawing room sofa'. However exaggerated, such comment held elements of truth in regard to ignorant and inexperienced country girls called on to fill a supporting role in Australia's imitation of polite society. Even their initial appearance told against them. J.V. Gorman told the Commission on Emigration in 1858 that 'when those girls arrive in this country they have heavy shoes and thick woollen stockings, and all that sort of thing' and 'require a little management and kindness'. They seldom got it, for as soon as they shed their plebeian footware they were accused of wasting their excessive wages (£20–40 in contrast to an Irish £2–4) on finery: in 1850 an Irish servant was brought before a magistrate because she insisted on working at the washtub in 'patent leather pumps'. There was no pleasing mistresses even if Irish girls, as a witness assured an 1860 inquiry, were 'tractable, cheerful, and desire to do what is right'. 'I believe many have never been shown how to do it,' he remarked: the girls were supposed to know. They were also supposed to know the elements of child care in a climate very different from the one they had left: 'infants of eighteen months are exposed to the sun and allowed to eat anything that comes in the way' a witness told the same inquiry into the condition of the Sydney working class. (Another witness had an easy solution to the parallel problem of the Australian inexperience of Irish farm labourers: Hon. R. Fitzgerald remarked 'they do not know how to use a short spade, but then they want very little teaching'.) Nevertheless, Hogan's defence wisely concentrated on their character rather than their competence: he echoes the affirmations of their 'proverbial chastity', expatiated on their generosity to church, parents, and Irish

WAGES AND PATRIOTISM.

MRS. LENNOX HILL: "WHAT, WANT YOUR WAGES RAISED, BRIDGET? I AM PAYING YOU VERY WELL NOW, I THINK?"
BRIDGET: "YIS, MUM; BUT WE'RE GOING TO DOUBLE OUR CONTHRIBU-TIONS TO THE CAUSE OF OULD OIRELAND, MUM!"

The politics of Irish servants' wage demands
Bulletin 10 August 1889

causes, and defended their dressing well in public—a practice their critics denounced as ostentation and tasteless extravagance. Their generosity raises questions not easily answered. Was it because of later marriages that they had capacity to give? Or because their expectations of worldly goods and comforts was less? Or that pressures from church and Irish community were intense? Or simply that they were, by nature and inclination, generous?

What of Irish competence generally? And the climate of prejudice as it affected employment? The Irish push towards government jobs was not a simple urge to avoid discrimination and ensure fair promotion. For some the motivation was the direct contrary: they carried over to Australia an Irish conception of government appointments as being an aspect of political patronage, as being within the gift of ministers particularly, but politicians generally. Probably this was also fed by presumptions of an American situation, in which the bureaucracy was highly politicised: the non-political character of the Australian bureaucracy was unfamiliar to the Irish. Thus both O'Shanassy and Duffy were importuned for jobs over the period of their various ministries from the 1850s to the 1870s: hostile stories circulated, about the Irishman who had a suburban postal round but could not read the addresses on the mail—and so on, predictably. O'Shanassy and Duffy did increase Irish appointments, but not beyond a reasonable reflection of population proportion, a claim very quickly tested—and supported—by inquiries instigated by those who resented any Irish Catholic preferment at all. Similar allegations of public-service packing by Catholics abounded in New South Wales, quietened, but of course not ended, by an inquiry in 1902: 23 percent were Catholics. Nevertheless, various devices existed to allow patronage to operate, and adept politicians used them: mendicants and the politically deserving who had neither qualification or ability could be assigned 'temporary' appointments which by-passed the entry examination system, or they could be rewarded with rapid promotion. But this was increasingly unnecessary as Irish Catholics—and their children—moved into the twentieth century. Diligent pupils of Catholic schools—the Christian Brothers were renowned for their success in ensuring this—easily mastered competitive examinations.

The Irish Catholic preference for the public service had its positive elements—security, protection from prejudice—but to some extent these made virtues of necessity: where else was there to go? Irish Catholics lacked skills, and they found them very difficult to acquire in any branch of the employment system, and that was then most branches, controlled by apprenticeship, or dependent on the decision of a single employer. Appraising this situation in 1893, the Irish priest Michael Phelan believed it must be remedied in Ireland itself, before the emigrant left. 'Tradesmen in the higher branches get wages almost beyond belief. A good tailor-cutter earns from five to seven pounds a week.' All trades enjoyed ample leisure. And there was no social stigma in trades: 'Socially, a tradesman is highly respected, and invariably addressed as "Mr".' But Ireland was unlikely to adjust its economy and job-training to the needs of emigrants. They were confronted by an Australian employment system in which it was, in private employment, overwhelmingly the non-Irish who governed the intake. Even if these were innocent of anti-Irish prejudice, they would naturally favour those they knew, people like themselves.

But there was prejudice, and there was discrimination. The adjunct to employment advertisements—'No Irish Need Apply'—was sufficiently common by the 1860s to prompt a ballad critical of this practice. F.R. Phillip's *No Irish Need Apply* was published, words and music, in the *Australian Journal* of 5 December 1868 and was available from principal music sellers at three shillings. Its message was that the Irish were hospitable, loyal, had made up the armies that had fought Britain's wars, were poets, lawyers and statesmen, and that harmony between Shamrock, Rose and Thistle was the country's strength. Ballads were consolation for the aggrieved, not instigators of social change. Some employers, such as Frederick Cato, the Sydney grocer, made little secret that they would not employ Irish; indeed he boasted of it. Others were known or quietly assumed to have similar policies and the Irish knew enough not to apply. Writing of the earlier twentieth century, Arthur Calwell remarked that it was very difficult for a boy who went to a Catholic school to secure a permanent position in a bank or commercial life. Some firms would employ Irish, but never promote them. The Victorian railways were Catholic. It was said that an Orange Lodge clique dominated the Melbourne tramways in the 1890s. This domination may have been apocryphal, or it may have been loose enough to permit employment of Irish Protestants who were not members, but as soon as its alleged existence became part of Melbourne employment lore, it became self-policing: Catholic Irish simply did not apply. Obviously, the effect of such rumours was to bring about exactly what was claimed to be true: those allegedly not wanted stayed away, and left the field to those who allegedly were—whether or not discrimination existed in intent. Moreover, in such an employment atmosphere, hiring, firing and promotion were open to continuous sectarian or racial interpretations, and incompetent, lazy, or dishonest employees were always willing to suggest such discrimination as being behind their termination. The area is shadowy and uncertain, full of assumptions and undocumented assertion, but the general drift is clear: the Irish believed they were discriminated against, and to some extent they were.

How complex is the task of arriving at a reasonable evaluation of such matters is suggested by a defence of the Irish mounted by a Melbourne Englishman in 1863. James Smith saw antagonism to the Irish as destructive of the harmony that should mark Australian society, and as simple injustice. Accordingly he gave 'A Lecture on the Irish Character from an Englishman's point of view'. He declaimed: 'The nature of an Irishman is essentially emotional . . . His heart is sooner touched than his head.' He was patriotic, imaginative, poetic, sentimental, brave—indeed impetuous—hospitable. He suffered from an excess of his virtues: generosity led to waste and excess; conviviality led to drunkenness. Family loyalty was paramount with them, and the chastity of their women was without compare. They had prodigious wit and humour. Smith supplied the usual lists of famous Irishmen (heavily Protestant) and suggested that the failings and faults of Irish character were the natural result of the treatment which the people of Ireland had endured at the hands of the English—an interpretation popular with the Irish but hardly likely to impress others.

As with so many treatments of the Irish character, Smith sought to divert his audience, and ensure an atmosphere of good humour, by telling funny or whimsical stories. There was laughter—at the silly Irish. The larding of praise for the Irish with reference to their droll behaviour or sayings had an effect very different from that intended, the fostering of kindly tolerance and simple enjoyment: it proved that the Irish could not be taken seriously. For non-Irish listeners, humour of this kind elicited contempt; seriousness could be equated only with solemnity. The light-hearted Irish were, by definition, a joke. If they were also melancholy, as Smith also said, this was sentimental self-indulgence. And if they were also—Smith claimed this, too—religious, devotional, then that was another minus, given the inferior quality of their preposterous religion.

Smith's praise for the Irish character as emotional, imaginative, humorous, fun-loving, warm, religious, patriotic, together with his conclusion that England had treated Ireland badly—'there is injustice to be atoned for'—and that his countrymen were prejudiced against the Irish, were all views which would have confirmed rather than decreased antagonism. The 'qualities' of character he listed were precisely those that critics of the Irish held in suspicion and contempt. They preferred and admired what they believed were their own qualities—rational, practical, reserved, respectable, serious, the very opposite of Irish characteristics. Nor were they prepared to concede that the Irish had been treated badly by the English: such qualities as Smith had paraded were obviously childish, immature, and the English had been dutifully trying to get them to grow up for centuries. As for 'prejudices', these were sensible, well-based, justified opinions. As for discrimination, who on earth would want an emotional, imaginative, fun-loving employee? No: the work of the world called for rational, practical, serious persons, and to prefer them above lazy Irish clowns was sound business sense, and the only possible economics. So hummed the minds of those non-Irish who listened to Smith. Apologias such as his, which pointed up the Irish stereotype, but contended it was good, merely confirmed that stereotype in the minds of those who were sure it was bad, and strengthened their belief that the Irish should not be encouraged to move above their natural station in the labouring and servile classes.

Quite evidently, the nineteenth-century Irish in both city and country were in no position to produce an elite, or even leaders. It would require several generations of education and upward mobility before the descendants of this group were properly represented in all sectors of society. And besides, the existence of a clerical leadership which took a wide view of its social role discouraged the emergence of lay leadership. However, the very fact that the Irish element tended to be grouped heavily at the bottom of the socioeconomic scale, especially in the cities, was of great importance. This element related itself naturally to the trade union movement as it emerged in the seventies and eighties and to labour political parties as they were formed in the nineties: the Irish thus came to exercise a very powerful influence on Australian politics and society through the labour movement. (Given the Catholic dominance of the labour image, the Ulster Protestant labour element bears noting, for example, in the person of Thomas Glassey, born in Armagh 1844, trade union promoter in England, and first labour member of the Queensland parliament 1888–1901: Ulster skills, and sense of righteous justice, found trades unionism of natural relevance. An earlier example was the radical merchant Henry McDermott, who sought, in the 1840s, to give Sydney operatives and labourers some sense of their worth and rights as workers.) But this influence was slow in developing and was never particularly distinctive in any Irish or even Catholic sense. This was for two major reasons. The Irish element active within the labour movement was an element of Irish descent rather than birth, and its activity was for labour not for Irish reasons: that is, it was concerned with matters stemming from its socioeconomic position in Australia, not with Irish issues. And second, the labour movement, with secularist roots and non-sectarian intentions, was strongly resistant to Catholic pressures and demands. The movement became the avenue for the political and organising abilities of those of Irish descent and working-class position, but not for the aims, ambitions and values that derived from any Irish culture.

Yet the basic reason for the failure of any distinctive, militant Irish leadership to emerge in nineteenth-century Australia seems very simple. The Irish as a whole did not want it. They could identify happily enough with an Australian situation sufficiently open to allow

Irish migrants to assimilate into it with success since about 1810. To offset what resistance
to them existed in Australian society were considerations of necessity. The Irish in
Australia were much further from their homeland than those in America. There could be
small hope of any eventual return. They were committed to Australia and had to make the
best of it. Their attitudes towards affairs in Ireland and towards that portion of their
identity they regarded as Irish were profoundly influenced by their Australian political
environment. Whereas the Irishman in the United States was in a republic which existed as
a consequence of successful rebellion against Britain, Australia (and New Zealand) were
contented parts of the British Empire, reliant on that empire for defence and status and
self-image and cultural orientation. In this loyalist colonial community Irishmen lived as a
minority, and to a very large extent they accepted its dominant ethos and attitudes, though
not necessarily uncritical of Britain's treatment of Ireland.

The simple consequences of an Irish minority needing to adjust to the pressures of an
overwhelmingly British colony is probably sufficient explanation of itself to explain the
relatively temperate character and quick assimilation of the Australian Irish. Perhaps not
quite sufficient. The increasing importance of the education question from the 1860s, to its
dominance of Catholic affairs from the 1880s had a radically diminishing effect on all other
concerns of the Irish Catholic community. Everything was subordinated to this issue: there
was little time, money, or energy for anything else. Invariably the affairs of Irish
organisations deferred to this or that Catholic education occasion as members of such
organisations—and often chairman clerics—were involved in their Catholic capacities. And
however confrontationalist and divisive the century-long Catholic education campaign
might look at a superficial glance, in fact it welded Irish Catholics into the general

Distilling as child's play. Poteen making in Connemara
Ulster Museum: Welsh collection

Australian community with their constant insistence that they were an integral and equal part of it and that their children must be treated accordingly: the whole rationale of Irish Catholic educational claims rested on their determined assertion that they were Australians, a crucially formative orientation in a group which had, at least theoretically, another, Irish identity available to it. What might have been the character of Irish Australia had the education question, and crusade, not existed, is impossible to say, but that it would have been more vital, stronger, seems reasonable to suggest. Of course, had Catholic education not been at issue, presumably Irish religious teaching orders would not have come to Australia, or in such numbers. Given their usually ascribed role in the cultural formation of Irish Australia, that would pose another imponderable.

Nor is it possible to overlook the importance of the individual policies of Catholic clerics. At the height of the development of Australian Irishry in the eighties and nineties, its outlook was formed and expressed by Cardinal Patrick Francis Moran, Archbishop of Sydney 1884–1911. He held a strong concept of 'the honour of old Ireland', but his policy was one of close identification with Australian life and imperial enterprises. His great influence tends to be masked by the fact that he was encouraging a process which was occurring naturally. (Clerical determination of Irish Catholic attitudes to the community and to Irish affairs is much more obvious when it went against the assimilationist trend: such was the case with Moran's cousin, Bishop Moran in Otago, New Zealand, from 1871 to 1895, and of course later, in Australia, with Archbishop Mannix.)

However numerous and large be the exceptions noted, there is ample evidence to indicate that the general rule was that the Irish in Australia thought their adopted society to be essentially a good one. Their most serious criticisms, of intolerance or inequality or injustice, took as their points of emphasis that such features were departures from the true norm, disfigurements sure to be removed soon. Whatever Irish elements were truculent and uncooperative, whatever the tensions and abrasions between the Irish and the rest of the community, the generalisation that the Irish as a group were 'agin the government' is false. On the contrary, the Irish in Australia identified proudly with the power and prestige of the Empire, which they saw as in the main won by Irish blood and Irish valour: their wish for Ireland was that it be as free as they were in Australia.

Nowhere is this more clearly expressed than in Cardinal Moran's speech of acceptance of the freedom of the city of Dublin, in 1888:

> And whilst the Australians are thus one in heart and one in hand with their brothers of the dear mother country, we are not the less loyal to the empire of which we are proud to form part. In our sympathy with your struggles in the cause of liberty, we are impelled, not by hatred of England, but by love of Ireland. The freedom which we enjoy is the mainstay of the empire's strength; and we desire that Ireland should, to the fullest extent, enjoy the same freedom, without which the empire cannot stand.

In fact this was, by then, traditional Irish Australian rhetoric, and sincerely held. Gavan Duffy had said much the same when he visited Ireland in 1865. So had the popular Irish playwright Dion Boucicault after an Australian visit in 1885. The only place where the Irish were poor, unfree and unappreciated was at home: in Australia they were valuable citizens—and ready to defend the Empire. Moran had already given his sentiments practical expression in his strong support, in 1885, of Australian involvement in the Sudan campaign—itself the special enthusiasm of the then Acting Premier William Bede Dalley, Australian-born son of Irish convict parents. This campaign certainly showed that some few

Irish-Australians were either opposed to or unenthusiastic about Australia's involvement in a British war, but it also showed that by far the greater weight of opinion supported this involvement on the grounds that it strengthened the Empire and gave the colony some international stature. The *Freeman's Journal* claim that the New South Wales contingent to the Sudan was probably as much Irish as Australian seems to reflect this outlook, as well as the fact that the 46 soldiers of Irish birth among the contingent of 769 represents very closely the then Irish-born proportion of the population.

Here was, of course, that attitude that responded with enthusiasm to the Home Rule movement in Ireland, a response that became a comfortable orthodoxy from the 1880s until the 1916 rebellion destroyed it. But central to this imperial orientation was a particular Irish-Australian emphasis evident in Moran's words: 'The imperial flag is the symbol of our strength and unity—of justice, prosperity, and peace. It guards our commerce, protects our industry, and is the aegis of our liberties.' In this view, the Empire was the protective context for the freedom of Irish-Australian elements within a diverse Australian scene. The Australian establishment took a much narrower, monolithic view of empire, equating it with all that was most conservatively English, indeed Tory. Herein lay ample grounds for friction. Overall, the Irish in Australia wished to be included in that colonial society constructed on the British model, but they wanted inclusion as themselves, not as imitation Anglo-Saxons. A colonial society determined to be English did not readily admit members on such conditions, and the insistence that the Irish abandon any element of divergent identity led to tension and conflict.

But far less grand themes than the future character and identity of the Australian colonies were the usual matters at issue between colonial society and its Irish elements. That society in general persisted in taking its image of the Irish not from those who were 'respectable', and who constantly professed imperial and Australian loyalties, but from other, disreputable sources—notably spectacular Irish criminality (elevated to heroic mythology in Ned Kelly) and from the international contemptuous stereotype, the stage Irishman. The portrayal of the Irish in Melbourne *Punch* in the 1880s was that of its London namesake: the Irishman was a roistering drunken ape—unless she was an ugly insolent slattern. This importation of British attitudes was grafted on to the divisions of the colonial situation—sectarianism, the animus associated with the creation of a separate Catholic education system, and the tensions natural in a new and vigorously growing society engaged in a running dispute as to what groups and what values would control it. As the then underdogs, who were also racially and religiously distinct, the Irish presence aroused contempt and disdain—and also indignation and fear. This community reaction was bitterly resented by the respectable Irish, who could be proud of Eureka—Birthplace of Freedom—but could not abide Ned Kelly: J.F. Hogan ignores him entirely; P.S. Cleary mentions, in relation to Father Gibney, who gave 'spiritual aid to the dying sinners', 'a notorious band of outlaws, known as the Kelly gang'. But while the respectable Irish regarded this adverse imagery, linking the Irish to criminality and drunkenness, as unfair, indeed part of a climate of persecution and intolerance, their reasons for thinking it unfair tended to be fluctuating and ambivalent: in some respects their thinking seemed to be that 'unfair' was not untrue, but exaggerated, or explicable, excusable.

An important element in the Irish Catholic drive towards social self-redemption was the campaign against alcoholic drink. Irish clerics and lay leaders worldwide saw this as a major Irish problem and conceded it to be—one of the very few such concessions—a national weakness. In fact, this general admission may have been inordinate, given such recent studies as demonstrate that Irish drinking is less excessive than that of some other national groups, that it was, relatively, moderate and controlled social drinking. What the concession does prove is the sensitivity of Irish leaders to the enormous social pressure generated by those evangelical Protestants who insisted that drink was the ultimate social evil and its suppression the mark of a decent, civilised society. Irish vulnerability to criticism from such sources derived from the fact that their drinking tended to be highly visible—public and noisy, in contrast to the less obvious consumption of the more affluent, in clubs and private homes. Certainly a good deal of ordinary Irish social life was marked by—some would say enlivened by—heavy drinking, though this might be confined, in individuals, to particular celebrations or periods after a time in remote areas, droving, fencing or the like. This occasional overindulgence is perfectly illustrated by Michael Normile in April 1855: 'I did not take much liquor in this country since I came there, that did me no harm, but one day, that was Patrick's day, I drank plenty that day in rememberance to the old shammerick shore.'

There was also in the Irish attitude to drink, complex elements of fun-making and disrespect for authority—including that of the episcopacy. Archbishop Kelly of Sydney was a leading temperance crusader. He told the 1912 St Patrick's Day assemblage: 'Many of you would be prepared to lay down your lives for Ireland, but as a missionary I have always said: Give me the man who will lay down his glass for Ireland (Applause).' 'And give me the man who will fill it up for me again,' a wag is reputed to have whispered. Revenue-thirsty governments were, of course, fair game. From the time of Governor King, illicit stills were being discovered, particularly in Irish areas, such as the MacDonald Valley north of

Pleasure concentrated. The Harp of Erin Hotel, Piper St. Kyneton, Victoria, with tobacconists next door, 1861
La Trobe Collection, State Library, Victoria

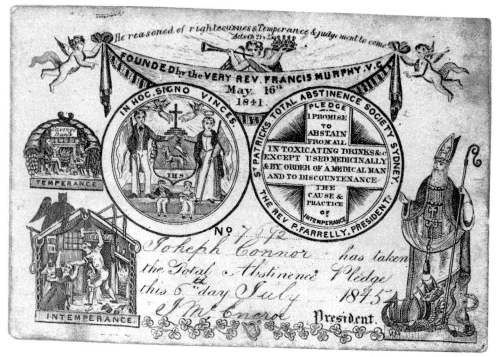

A temperance pledge of the St Patrick's Total Abstinence Society, Sydney, 1845. Signed by Archdeacon McEncroe and numbered 7692, it is in the name of Joseph Connor

Sydney, activity whose motivation and atmosphere is precisely caught by Geoffrey Serle: 'As late as the nineties, "jovial good-natured Irishmen" back of Warrnambool, aided by a "wonderful system of bush telegraphy and espionage", were distilling huge quantities of whisky on Crown land, for fun and from tradition rather than for profit.'

Hotels were centres of life and good humour. The Beehive in Goulburn in the 1860s displayed such claims explicitly in a sign outside:

> In this house we're all alive
> Good liquor makes us funny.
> If you are dry, come and try
> The virtue of our honey.

Drinking and spuds were part of a good-natured Irish image which could always raise a colonial grin—and entertaining banter. Confronted by a serious verse submission by a local produce merchant, Patrick McShane, the Goulburn *Penny Post* rejected it thus:

> Now write us, Pat, some rhymes on spuds—
> Sound, healthy, mealy, Gullen goods—
> Fit to boil or roast or fry,
> And feed a hungry family,
> And we will give the screed insertion,
> Without a whisper of aspersion.

Harmless waggery eddied around the Irish and their preferences in food and drink. Nor was that drink always alcoholic. They were known to consume vast quantities of tea, particularly a cheap green variety called Hyson-skin. It had a pleasant flavour but fell short of the standard required in the dialogue of that familiar Irish novel of 1798, Samuel Lover's *Rory O'More*, published in 1837 and widely read in Irish Australia. Such tea was not known for 'taking a great hold of the second water', and thus was a constant colonial disappointment to frugal and thirsty Irish Australian households. Nor, perhaps, were fulminations against the money squandered on alcohol accurately directed. In the early years of the colony Sir John Jamieson's estate at Emu Plains was let to Irishmen who grew tobacco, then used as a sheep wash as well as for smoking. By the 1840s it was tobacco, not alcohol which was the Irishman's luxury, the indulgence which he—or she—was least willing to forgo, for it was a staple adjunct to the cheapest form of Irish entertainment— talk: talk in all its Irish forms, story-telling, mimicry, gossip, forever floated in a fog of smoke.

Yet, for all the qualifications and explanations, many Irish drank too much for their own and their families' good. A basic reason might reasonably seem to be the low socioeconomic position of the mass of the Irish, in that situation where pressures and circumstances encouraged drinking beyond relaxation, into escape. Some Catholic clerics appeared unable to appreciate such harsh social realities, and their denunciations of alcohol took the high

On the downhill slope. Callaghan's Hotel at Burrinjuck, NSW December 1913

moral line—that excessive drinking was sinful, and that their drinking made the Irish outcasts in 'respectable' society. It did, but they were outcasts to begin with and would remain so whether they drank or not. What is more, many Irish were simply not interested in joining 'respectable' society. Indeed some were vigorously averse to it: consorting with 'wowsers' and temperance advocates in polite society did not represent their ambition. Nor was it, for instance, Cardinal Moran's, himself averse to 'wowsers' and unwilling to merge with Protestant temperance societies.

Irish Catholic temperance societies in fact expressed internal Irish moral energies rather than any response to public pressures. Later in the century the spirit of the temperance movement was summed up in the popular slogan 'Ireland Sober, Ireland Free', but from its beginnings with Father Mathew in the late 1830s, when O'Connell associated himself and his Repeal movement with it, the temperance movement had strong connotations of being an aspect of a bid for total national regeneration, one facet of the political and moral emancipation of a people, an effort to elevate and purify a nation; to that extent, temperance was a symbol of wider achievements of self-mastery, dignity and strength by the Irish. And so it was seen by those clerics who imported the cause into Australia. Beginning with Archdeacon McEncroe (himself a reformed alcoholic) in the 1840s, clergy constantly imported Irish temperance organisations into Australia. In 1842 the St Patrick's Total Abstinence Society assembled 400 people at a temperance tea at Illawara: it reached a Sydney membership of 2400 the following year. In 1847 the Father Mathew Temperance society claimed 1400 members. Such organisations waxed and waned as did the Irish parent bodies. The League of the Cross, the form taken by the movement in Sydney and Melbourne in the 1880s, was typical in its widely fluctuating membership centred on a core of compulsory members—the children of Catholic schools: mothers in particular supported juvenile coercion of this kind. Catholic parish missions often had temperance dimension. Two thousand people took the pledge in St Stephen's Cathedral Brisbane in 1879. The missioner estimated that Catholics spent £10 each per annum on drink. With that they could pay for their education system twice over—there was always a practical dimension to the crusade. That tireless social analyst Archbishop Dunne was convinced that the only thing preventing the Irish from settling down on the land was their drinking habits. He introduced the abstinence pledge for children into the confirmation ceremony in 1882. In 1885 he argued the temperance case at the 1885 Australian Bishops' Plenary Council, claiming that drink was also to blame for that other bar to Irish Catholic acceptance by genteel society—their alleged propensity to violent crime. (But he would admit that drink shared this responsibility with the fact that many Catholic children grew up with little or no education because of ignorant, lazy or selfish parents who failed to send them to school.)

Dunne's strictures in 1885 illustrate one variety of the Irish Catholic response to the unceasing hostile criticism to which that community was subject: while seeking explanations, excuses, and solutions, he implicitly conceded the point; that Irish Catholic groups had more than their share of the drunken, the ignorant, and the criminal. Other Irish in Australia would have none of this, particularly in regard to criminality. Writing in the 1850s on life in Victoria, William Kelly claimed—and also claimed that statistics (which he did not give) bore him out—that the Irish were a very small proportion of loafers or criminals. He found this a logical outcome of the contrast between Ireland and Australia: conditions in Ireland were so impoverished and degraded that any Australian occupation was seized on eagerly, with gratitude and dedication. But there was another way of interpreting the effect of Irish conditions on the people. In 1870, writing on why Ireland was poor and discontented, Gavan Duffy argued that the Famine was to blame for Irish demoralisation: it had killed the temperance movement and converted a tender, brave and pious stock into a new race of beggars, poor, mutilated, debased. One could hardly expect such a new race to be instantly redeemed on exposure to Australia. As has been seen, the Irish contributed at least their proportionate share, and a bit more, to the annals of that most spectacular avenue of Australian crime, bushranging. But at levels of criminality less open to excuse and hero-worship, the Irish contributed far more than their share. Herbert Moran has a comment which links such levels and puts such Irish behaviour in context: 'Restlessness, the habit of discontent, a belief in the heroism of lawlessness afflicted many to their own misfortune'. When the first national breakdown of crime statistics was released in Victoria in 1861, the Irish-born were revealed to have double their population proportion in the prisons of the colony. In 1861, 15.6 percent of the New South Wales population was Irish-born. But in 1859–61, more than a third of convictions at circuit courts for general crime, and more than a quarter of convictions at quarter sessions, were of Irish men. In 1871, 118 prisoners were in New South Wales gaols convicted of armed robbery. Of these twenty-one were Irish-born and sixty-nine were Catholics, that strong indicator of Irish descent. In Victoria, of those forty-eight men executed 1865–79, eighteen were Irish born. Of those arrested in 1879, the Irish-born were more than half. Small wonder the Irish reputation for violence and crime. The classic Australasian confrontation of that reputation was made in 1909 by Rev. Dr H.W. Cleary, editor of the New Zealand *Tablet*. In a widely circulated book *An Impeached Nation being a Study of Irish Outrages*, whose statistical references were confined to Ireland itself, he contended that Irish crime was, first, greatly exaggerated, second, provoked by oppression and misgovernment.

The second of these responses was not available in the colonial situation. Nor was the explanation that would be favoured today—that the Irish occupied that lower stratum of society most open to pressures towards crime and most likely to be apprehended by the police. However true that might have been, it was an explanation which Irish pride and concern for matters of status would not allow. Nor would it concede, as Kelly's roseate picture shows, that the migration process itself commonly induced some degree of trauma, placing on the individual expectations and pressure to succeed, adapt, make decisions, which may have been beyond the capacities of those used to the lesser demands of Irish situations. That most rose to the demands of the occasion is remarkable: that some personalities should collapse or disintegrate or turn to crime under such pressures is hardly surprising.

And collapse they did. The under-care and admission rates of Irish-born into New South Wales mental institutions in 1881 makes this point in a striking and inescapable way. For males, per 10 000 of the population those born in New South Wales rated 2.7 admissions with 15.5 then under care; for the English-born, 14.8 admissions, with 67.2 under care; the Scots, about the same. The Irish-born were almost double the English in their insanity rates: 22.2 admissions, 113.4 of their 10 000 in the population, were under care. The same extraordinary disproportion is reflected in the female rates (NSW 2.2, England 9.5, Ireland 17.1) and in other States. There is no simple explanation of this. Obviously there must be another side to that image of the Irish immigrant which sees him or her the member of a happy and secure family group or with ample support from relatives and friends: some must have been isolated, friendless, unable to cope. Indeed, the families of some Irish deliberately dispatched to Australia relatives with mental problems, to relieve themselves of that burden. (The same was so of physical illness, although here the motivation was often humane rather than callous: a long sea voyage was reputedly therapeutic for, for example, tuberculosis. But it may be presumed, in the absence of research findings, that the disease and hospitalisation rates of the Irish in nineteenth-century Australia were higher, given an Irish background in which nutrition and life and work experiences in childhood and adolescence would have been adverse.) Sympathetic professionals at the time tended to blame the Irish background for the excessive mental problems of the Irish—famine, the tyranny of landlords, estate clearances, fundamental disruption of traditional economies and lifestyles. They might have added, poverty in Australia, for the Irish again occupied just that class most exposed to the strains of bare survival. In fact it is often impossible to disentangle mental illness and poverty. Asylums themselves tended to be pauper institutions because the poor were the least capable of supporting their sick. It seems needless to document the poverty of the Australian Irish, but when it sank to utter destitution it became a charge on the charity or taxes of the public and thus a demonstrable, quantifiable thing. For instance, in 1888 the Destitute Board of South Australia admitted 157 persons; 56 were Irish, over a third, in a colony in which their proportion was less than a sixth. This was in fact an improvement. The figures for Poor Relief in 1856 show the Irish as nearly a half of recipients: 7116 in the week ended 8 January.

In all the casualty areas of Australian society, the Irish were prominent to the extent of at least double their proportion of the total population. In a society whose tendency was to regard poverty itself as a crime, and which was ill-disposed towards state expenditure and the taxation necessary to sustain it, the negative image of the Irish was constantly reinforced by their continuing presence in those areas. The annual reports of government departments—police, prisons, asylums—and of charitable organisations, gave frequent reminders to the successful and the industrious and thrifty that here were these indigent, incapacitated, parasitic and inferior Irish being maintained at their, the taxpayers', the property-owners' expense. It was outrageous that such should be so: to prejudice from many sources was added resentment that they should have to pay for such people.

To make a defence against such a multitude of charges, given their substance and character, was virtually impossible, save by invoking some variant of the consolations of the beatitudes, the sermon on the mount—Blessed are the poor in spirit, for theirs is the kingdom of heaven; Blessed are the meek, for they shall possess the land. This was precisely the response of Irish clerics in Australia: the construction of a counter-image of the utmost nobility and promise. This reached its most extravagant in the declaration by Cardinal Moran to the second Australasian Catholic Congress of 1904 that 'the sons and daughters of Ireland are, beyond all question, the most enlightened, the most progressive, the most virtuous people of Christendom at the present day'. A large claim, but Moran was by no means alone in that conviction: it was a commonplace in Irish Catholic Australia by that time, in various forms and degrees. Writing from Dublin in April 1858 to the Sydney *Freeman's Journal*, Dr Kevin Izod O'Doherty, one of those transported to Australia for his part in the 1848 revolution, described Australia as 'my true home': 'there only, in all my travels, have I been able to meet with the true Catholic spirit, sturdy and independent, as it ought to be. Here we are overburdened and weighed down with the influence of Protestant imperialism and Protestant gold.' In a curious inversion of the Irish model, many Irish, particularly enthusiasts, idealists and dreamers, felt stifled and constricted in Ireland—and free in Australia. Thus the virtues of the Isle of Saints and Scholars were conferred on Irish Australia by descent and by the relative freedom of its political circumstances. Monsignor Maurice O'Reilly C.M. explained to the 1911 New South Wales Catholic Educational Conference: 'It was true that their children were not Irish—they were Australians—but everything that was best and noblest in Australia was Irish.' Celebration of the enlighten-ment, progressiveness and virtue of the Irish in Australia became a constant theme among those of the Irish and Catholic camps who appraised that community.

This very high self-regard may appear excessive, even ludicrous, when seen by itself in a later age, conditioned by cynicism and an untroubled willingness, even among descendants, to see their forebears as poor, ignorant, splay, surly, and intolerant: such is the poise and confidence engendered by achievement and acceptance. But in its time, this trumpeting of Irish virtue was a counterpoint to a tune of hatred and contempt no less absurd and disharmonious. What was the truth? In 1939 Dr Herbert Moran published *Viewless Winds*, depicting Irish Catholics in New South Wales in the 1890s as 'a breed apart, firebranded like travelling stock in a strange country', referring to ignorant Irish priests 'constantly belching forth a windy hatred', to drunkenness among priests and people, to inferior schooling: the wealthy (Papal) Countess Freehill attempted to buy up the whole edition for destruction. Herbert Moran's dark view was one way of perceiving the reality: but was the bottle half-full or half-empty? And, if indeed they were, who had made them 'a breed apart'; who had 'firebranded' them; why was the country 'strange'? There were two ways of interpreting such postulated processes—they had left on their own accord, or they had been driven out of the society of which they were members.

Yet the Herbert Moran thesis of apartness is suspect, partial, one side of the ambivalence: the whole drift of Irish Australia was to attempt to identify with its Australian environment. Sometimes this falters, is frustrated, repelled, and there was animus, hostility, and a sense of difference, but the impetus is consistently in that assimilatory direction, as every indicator shows—its organisations, its culture, its education system, even its celebration of St Patrick's Day.

Before the 1880s such Irish organisations as were formed were nearly all ephemeral, usually associated with the collection of funds for some immediate Irish purpose, such as famine relief, or religious projects such as church-building. Some had the simple social aim of gathering Irishmen, as a viable group, for convivial purposes or mere society. Their stimulus and rationale seem to have been the positive ones of drawing on common background and interests rather than the negative one of response to exclusion, actual or imagined, by the rest of society: many members of such Irish organisations also belonged to others in the general community; they were *also* Irish. None of these earlier organisations made much enduring impact on the Irish, let alone the general community: they served their immediate purposes and then lapsed. Their memberships were small, and of the same people: J.G. O'Connor in Sydney and Morgan Jageurs in Melbourne personally sustained virtually all Irish organisations in those cities during their active lifetimes. For O'Connor this began in the 1850s and continued until the 1890s. For Jageurs the concentration of his contribution to Irish organisations founded in Melbourne was from the 1880s. As well as political organisations—the Irish Land League, the Irish National League and the United Irish League—he was a founder of the Celtic Club, and of various cultural activities, particularly the Melbourne Irish Pipers Club, for whose continued existence he was personally responsible. Besides, as a monumental mason by employment, he took a keen

J.G. O'Connor in later life

interest in Celtic art forms as they became a feature of the Gaelic revival in Ireland. It was Jageurs who was mainly responsible for introducing a feature which came into vogue in the more affluent sections of Australian Catholic cemeteries from the 1880s, the traditional ancient Celtic cross.

It is difficult to imagine Irish life in Sydney without O'Connor or in Melbourne without Jageurs. They possess one curious personal feature in common. Both were Irish-born. O'Connor came to Australia with his parents in 1841 when he was two. Jageurs arrived with his parents in 1865 when he was three. It is hard to avoid the suggestion that the Irish enthusiasms of both men have something to do with questions of personal experience and identity. Neither returned to visit Ireland. For both, Ireland must have lain just beyond the first horizons of a developing consciousness, refracted through the eyes of parents, the stuff of dream landscapes where the real, the remembered and the recounted all blend.

Whatever it reflected of the needs and character of such organisers, what Irish activity there was in Australia depended in very large degree on the enthusiasm and activity of a few people. None of these were radicals in Ireland's causes and very few had any prominence in society at large: they had no intention of attracting attention as extremists and they lacked the position to reach the community with any moderate message. The result was that they had negligible influence, and that even among the Australian Irish. The multipicity of Irish-Australian organisations disguises a remarkable degree of common membership, particularly at the office-holding level. The mass of the Australian Irish would not join such organisations.

And this was despite the fact that most such organisations made nothing more than the most vague and general acknowledgements of Ireland's nationalist causes. Up to the 1880s Irish organisations with any specific political objectives—support of repeal, the Land League—were particularly small. The Australian obstacles to Irish societies were numerous and large. There was the size of the country, the dispersion of the Irish, the power of the church, the hostility of the community. And there was diversity to the degree of factionalism. Most Irish societies in Australia found that they could go little beyond preserving some witness to Irish origins, which in practice usually meant helping to celebrate St Patrick's Day. Anything much more was likely to be criticised by the general—and Irish-Australian—community as divisive, irrelevant, inappropriate, or whatever other hostile or distancing description came to mind. Indeed the only sure way to avoid offending or alienating some element or other in the diverse and strongly assimilationist scene of Australian Irishry was to do little or nothing. And this, until the 1880s, was exactly what Irish-Australian organisations did.

The largest flourishing 'Irish' organisation in Australia was (and is) the Hibernian Australasian Catholic Benefit Society, originating in Victoria in 1871 and spreading rapidly throughout Australia and New Zealand in the 1880s. It was a friendly society whose objectives were to provide relief to members in sickness or accident situations and to pay for funeral expenses through an insurance scheme. As such it was not in an Irish organisational tradition, but an English, which had been imported into Australia in such forms as Oddfellows and Rechabites: one of the reasons why the Catholic Church supported the Hibernian Society was to attract Catholics away from other benefit societies which were believed to have a secret or masonic dimension. The need among Irish Catholics for such an organisation had first been recognised in the Irish-Australian Catholic Benefit Society established in Melbourne in 1865. This spread to other Victorian towns, but by 1870 the total Victorian membership was less than 750. To some extent this reflected the smallness of the Irish-Australian group who needed it and who had founded such organisations, that is, ambitious younger men from the upper working, and lower middle classes, with modest means, who made virtues of thrift and respectability. The Irishness of this benefit society movement was, in a sense, accidental: its purpose was to provide some financial security for a low income group particularly vulnerable to sickness or accident, people who happened to be Irish or of Irish origin. In its early 1860s forms its declared objects were 'to cherish the memory of Ireland; to promote the moral, social and intellectual improvement of its members, and the Celtic-Victorian race'. By the time the society had stabilised into its permanent form in the 1880s this had consolidated into a reminder to each candidate for admission, of the meaning of the symbols on his scarf (which, from Federation, included the Australian coat-of-arms): 'The Harp of Erin denotes by its position the undying love entertained by the Society for the "Island of Saints", from whence the great majority of us received our faith'; and an injunction to members: 'With fond recollection ever "cherish the memory of Ireland", condoling in her sufferings, rejoicing in her prosperity and happiness, and impressing on the minds of the rising generation a love for the noble and devoted race from which they have sprung.' Here was no Irish nationalist program, but the declaration of a sentimental disposition, and one strongly religion-oriented at that.

This may be taken as a fair reflection of the extent and nature of the Irishness of the Australian Irish at the end of the century, but it also reflects the power and influence of the Church. From 1880, the year of the society's foundation in New South Wales, it began to expand at a rapid rate, in keeping with economic growth and upward Catholic mobility: the demand for the society's insurance provisions was accelerating. It was not only the Hibernians who met this, but the Irish National Foresters introduced direct from Ireland, and the long established (1845) Australian Holy Catholic Guild: that the guild had its own life, deriving from the Benedictine phase of Australian Catholic history, is evident in its refusal, in 1890, to merge with the Hibernians. This Hibernian expansion offered both an opportunity and a challenge to the Catholic church authorities. The opportunity was that it brought together significant numbers of Catholic men who could thus be conveniently assembled for spiritual purposes: the society rapidly took on a religious sodality dimension and became both a school of morality and a parish organisational structure. The challenge it offered was that its membership was divided and disputatious in keeping with the divisions of Irish Australia itself and that the public airing of factional clashes seemed unedifying to church authority anxious to present Irish Catholicism's best face. The divisions were predictable; between elite and commoners, and between those who wanted involvement in Irish politics and those who did not. The battleground was the possession of the St Patrick's Day celebrations. Through the 1860s that celebration had been virtually the preserve of the Irish-Australian elite whose social policies were strongly integrationist and whose commemoration had been by way of a formal dinner. Hibernian lower-class elements had entered their alternative celebration into the St Patrick's Day lists in 1873 with a picnic, which co-existed with the dinner until 1883, when the elite changed their opposition to the inclusion of Irish nationalism into promotion of it, meanwhile beginning a permeation of the Hibernian Society so as to enhance its respectability and prestige: the Sydney Hibernian Society in fact split over the issue of whether the 1885 St Patrick's Day celebrations were to be non-political or a celebration of the Home Rule cause. But the elite gradually increased their control of the Hibernian Society making it easy for Cardinal Moran to take charge of the St Patrick's Day celebrations from 1895, exercising full control from 1896.

Obviously, as they were drawn into the orbit of the church, these benefit societies, notably the Hibernians, took on other functions. Their meetings provided a meeting place for Irish Catholics and a forum for the Irish clergy who were so prominent at their gatherings. However, the fact that the Hibernian Society, which alone—the Catholic Church apart—had any extensive contact with the colonial Irish, was no seedbed of Irish nationalism, is of the greatest significance. In one sense its membership was large: 24 710 in Australia and New Zealand in 1905. Yet in relation to its potential membership it was small, and failed to live up to the expectations of its enthusiasts. Yet again it did contain many prominent Irish Catholics, indeed most of those who could be deemed to be so. And they had ample opportunity to take, had they wished, an assertive and influential Irish nationalist role. The fact is, the Hibernian Society remained a benefit society with increa-

St Patrick's Day activities in Sydney 1884, as seen by Hop of the Bulletin

Hibernian Society delegates doing their part in digging the site of the Federal capital in Canberra 1912
Hibernian Society, Sydney

sing dimensions of a religious confraternity. Even as a benefit society it had no Irish or Catholic function: it could bring no business to Irish Catholic doctors or chemists because at the time of its formation there were virtually none and by the time there were, patterns were set. The Hibernian Society did have an Irish national function, in that it was regarded —and properly so, given its membership and geographic extent—as substantially reflecting Irish opinion in Australia. Significantly, it rarely took any initiative in nationalist matters. Its main functions in regard to Irish nationalist activity were to pass generally sympathetic resolutions, provide moderate counsel and influence, and act as an organisational structure through which such people as Home Rule emissaries might be received and welcomed, spread their message and make appeals.

The absence of any strong, widespread political motivation is also evident in the Melbourne Celtic Club, the next oldest Irish organisation still surviving. Formed in 1887 as the Celtic Home Rule Club it was, and still is, a social centre open to those of Celtic descent regardless of religion. True, at its formation, its most enthusiastic members tended to be Home Rule sympathisers, but this was a characteristic of their personal opinions, not the reason for the club's existence or at least for its growth from the original seventy members to 400 within a year. Similar was the Sydney Shamrock Club, which seems to have been formed to give aid to newly arrived migrants. That the leaders of this club should support Parnell after the split, and venerate the grave of Michael Dwyer, the 1798 hero, then in the Devonshire Street cemetery, proclaimed a militancy unusual in Australia. And its short history is comment on the shallowness of such radical roots. More to the point in illustrating the temper of nineteenth-century Irish Australia was the formation in 1898 of the Queensland Irish Association, founded by the respectable and the successful, graced early with a library (which emphasised its collection of *Australian* books), having its own premises, and with a membership of judges and politicians: it was, and continues to be today, one of the faces of the Queensland establishment.

The larger Australian Irish societies were moderate, cautious, and respectable, and strongly Australian in terms of reference. Their Irish orientations were general, cultural, and past-directed. Before 1915, the smaller ones had lives usually in reverse ratio to the radicalism or contemporary relevance of their position: the more extreme, the smaller their size and the briefer their existence. With one spectacular exception. There is a case for arguing that the most 'Irish' society in continuous existence in Australia is the Loyal Orange Lodge, various branches and forms of which have existed since the 1840s. In 1858 William Kelly made the contrast between those two 'importations from the old country', the Melbourne St Patrick's Society and the Orange Lodge:

> But while the disciples of St Patrick allowed their religious and political zeal to subside into the more genial emotions of good neighbourhood and brotherly love, the proteges of Dutch William 'move their wrath to keep it warm', never permitting a festival to pass over without the usual dinner . . . while the toast of 'The Pope in the Pillory of hell, and the devil pelting priests at him', is drunk with yelling honours, evangelical clergymen joining most boisterously in the demonstration.

Kelly's point was valid for its time, but it was made before that change in the composition of the Orange Lodge movement which occurred in the 1870s and which took it away from its Irish origins into the control of English, Scots and Australian anti-Catholics. Still, the case has its force: the most long-lived of Irish organisations in Australia is that which was dedicated to opposition to the entry of Irish Catholics into positions of power and influence in Australia, and which sought to prevent their integration and assimilation. The longevity of the Orange Lodge movement is also testimony to a residuum of distrust, suspicion, and suspension of full acceptance, that still stains the Australian imagination so far as Irish and Catholics are concerned.

Organisations? Overwhelmingly Australia-oriented. Culture? The same—even when the Australian situation was one of vacuum. Irish visitors in early Australia were highly critical of the mindless tedium of the colonial scene. Dr George Hill Adams, from Antrim, a ship's doctor, visited his sister in the Grampians area of Victoria in 1848–9. He complained: 'there is nothing almost in any of the settlers' heads but some half dozen things, to wit sheep, wool, bullocks, drays, servants, horses, and occasionally a little about tallow and boiling down and huts and such like. That is the eternal, never ceasing lingo, day and night, summer and winter. It becomes horribly boring, and you can rarely get anyone to talk even for a few minutes on any other possible subject whatever. They shirk it immediately . . .' Dr Harvey, later Professor of Botany at Trinity College Dublin, visited Western Australia in 1854. He told his sister: 'I think this place would be perfect as a residence if there were better soil, more frequent intercourse with Europe & *something to do*! Idleness is the complaint of most of the residents.' Perhaps of those residents the doctor encountered socially, but most Irish immigrants were not in a position to suffer the luxuries of idleness and boredom. Those who would have liked to have read could find little time for it: 'We have no time to read, business occupies us every moment', Joseph Beale told his wife in July 1853; one had to use every moment to 'get on'. Those many in labouring jobs enjoyed such (and as much) leisure as they could contrive, and found it far from tedious. The climate encouraged outdoor activity—walks, picnics, sitting in the sun, various sports.

Yet the question remains, what happened to the old Irish culture in Australia? The question has been raised, and answered earlier, but it obtrudes again in relation to the Gaelic revival movement at the end of the century. The Gaelic culture which the earlier

Irish immigrants had brought to Australia had been in decline and was of no practical relevance or utility in the new environment. Its predominantly oral character was a major disadvantage in Australia. It needed society to live, but convict authorities regarded it as subversive, and with the growth and dispersion of colonial society it lacked any concentrated location. The solitary Irishman, as selector or prospector, sought company in newspapers, certainly often those sent from Ireland: all were in English. And the Australian Irish lived under a giant if distant cultural shadow, that of Irish America with its popular energies—particularly in song-writing—so powerful as to dominate the whole image of the Irish migrant, and express, with polished blandness, his or her standard emotional reactions. It was not so much perhaps that the Australian Irish lacked sufficient nostalgic cultural energy to manufacture their own brand of Irish-oriented sentimentality, as that they had no need: the Americans had already done the job at the popular level, and at a level more genteel there were the drawing-room ballads of Thomas Moore. Moore's melodies—Irish, refined, accessible, easily performed, and very beautiful—were ideally suited to Australia's conditions of an Irish bid for respectability in an English setting: it is no surprise that there is a statue of Moore in Ballarat.

But all roads of explanation or rationalisation terminate in the same unavoidable conclusion: the Australian Irish did not wish to retain their cultural traditions, which were casualties to their dominant assimilatory urge. This was again demonstrated by the Australian reception of that movement in Irish culture variously called the Irish Renaissance, or the Celtic revival which began in the 1880s. What its champions in Ireland regarded as its basic ingredient at the popular level—the Irish language—was virtually unknown in Australia by the 1880s. A tiny group of enthusiasts attempted to revive Gaelic in Melbourne in 1879. These seem to have been the same people who sought to revive the old Irish game of handball the previous year, and who re-launched in 1885 the much more popular (and dangerous) game of hurling. In Sydney, Ryan's Hotel in George Street was a centre of Irish culture in the 1890s: there, even card games were conducted in Gaelic. It was the home of Eugene J. Ryan, Sydney's most enthusiastic student and teacher of Gaelic. Tipperary-born, he spoke and wrote in Gaelic, but he died, aged forty-two, in 1903. Even when he was alive, Gaelic folkways in Sydney had been little more than a vestigial curiosity, save for what remained of the wake, and that had been very much subdued and sanitised by the Church.

The fact was that the Gaelic revival as it developed in Ireland from the 1880s established little if any contact with such of the Australian Irish—and that meant most—as were below the reach of an intellectual and literary movement: the popular aspects of the movement in Ireland, in politics and sport, had no appeal in Australia because they sought to displace commitments long and firmly made, to Home Rule, and to well-established games. Moreover, even in Ireland itself the Catholic Church was divided and ambivalent about aspects of the movement, particularly the language. In Australia, the Church, as arbiter of all things Irish, could see no advantage in the language, rather that it was divisive in an English-speaking community. In Australia, the Gaelic revival found a response only in those very few with both higher education and Irish enthusiasms and loyalties. Without serious inaccuracy this might be narrowed down to two men in Melbourne: Morgan Jageurs, that infant immigrant, and Dr Nicholas O'Donnell, who was Australian-born, in 1863, of Irish parents. Jageurs' interests were musical and those of a craftsman. The Irish pipe band was a major involvement outside his monumental mason's business, and there, probably relying on the models in Henry O'Neill's 1857 book of Irish sculptured crosses, he introduced an Irish funerary revolution. O'Donnell's interests were much more intellectual. By the early 1900s he had become Australia's foremost Gaelic scholar, a distinction for which he had very few competitors. His mastery was real. O'Donnell developed an interest and expertise sufficient to form a professional friendship with Douglas Hyde, among the greatest of Gaelic scholars and activists: O'Donnell provided Hyde with a transcript of the late Middle Irish text Hyde published as 'The Adventures of Leithin' in *Legends of Saints and Sinners*. O'Donnell also conducted a column in Gaelic in the Melbourne *Advocate*, which had obtained in the early 1900s the first set of Gaelic type in Australia.

How many read the column? O'Donnell was not quite alone. The United Irish League of Australia, formed in Sydney on 20 March 1900, with M.C. O'Halloran as president, devoted itself to the 'great national revival in Australia', mainly through offering Irish history and language prizes in Catholic schools—'national purification' it called it. Between 1900 and 1906 it examined nearly 2000 children in Irish history, thirty in the first year, over 400 in the fifth. It also examined 'several' in the language: history in the predictable heroic mould was easy; the language was the hard bit. Efforts to launch an Irish-Ireland monthly newspaper, partly set in Gaelic type, appear to have foundered with one issue of *The Gael*, for October 1906, although 10 000 were printed. (Another *The Gael* appeared in the 1920s, to a much longer existence. It was published by the Sydney Gaelic League, which also sponsored an Irish-language school in the city, Irish music and Irish games. Its membership was largely Irish-born and its political sympathies Irish republican, both characteristics combining to make its appeal minimal.)

Undoubtedly, efforts to generate Australia's own 'Gaelic revival' went against the character of Irish Australia as it had evolved. But *The Gael* itself revealed other reasons why this particular venture was unlikely to succeed: it gave the strong impression that the genuineness of the United Irish League's cultural convictions was open to some question and that its concentration on the revival of Ireland's heritage was in the context of disillusioned reactions to Irish politics following the fall of Parnell. As in Ireland itself, concentration on the glories of Irish culture were something of an escape from sordid Irish politics. All of which was human enough, but it was accompanied in *The Gael*'s case by a strong dose of factionalism and personalised venom, certain to alienate the establishment Irish, and churchmen, and ensure that the league would have difficulty dealing with Catholic schools. *The Gael* was bitterly critical of the 'shandy gaff' Irishmen who were organising the visit of the Irish Home Rule party delegates: 'the whole thing has been manipulated by a clique, and the genuine thousands kept outside the fence.' According to *The Gael* the last hope of Home Rule had died with Parnell, and all that Sydney Home Rulers (F.B. Freehill was mentioned) were doing, was seeking the limelight, behaving like jingoes with their militarism and imperialism (the reference was to the Boer War) and competing with Melbourne. They were 'Dublin Castle hacks' seeking to aggrandise themselves and prevent the exposition of the true Irish national spirit. *The Gael* was aggressively 'Irish Ireland', and fierce in its denunciations of cowards, traitor and shoneens (so was *The Gael* of the 1920s)—that is, the leaders of the Sydney Irish. It was particularly emphatic in its emphasis on an Irish education for the young; more than a full page was given to advertisements for Catholic colleges in Sydney. And it insisted that Home Rule was not a final settlement, merely another form of slavery.

None of this would have been welcome either to those who controlled Irish Australia in 1900, or those who might be regarded as its rank and file: it cut across the drive towards respectability, its emphasis was on Ireland rather than Australia, and it rejected Home

*English faces of Australian Catholicism: John Bede Polding, Archbishop of Sydney 1834−77; and
Roger Bede Vaughan, Archbishop of Sydney 1877−83*

*Miss Kathleen O'Sullivan. Winner of the Gaelic
League Gold Medal (Senior) Sydney 1925*

Dr Nicholas O'Donnell

Rule—virtual sacrilege. Its abusive content and hectoring tone would have confirmed what was already known and feared in the Irish-Australian establishment, that the Parnell affair in Ireland in 1890–91 had lifted the lid off some most disturbing tendencies in Irish affairs. But that these could be controlled easily in Australia, the establishment had no doubt. Indeed the rage of *The Gael* and the United Irish League was a tiny shriek of impotent fury at what had already been done to firmly and decisively distance Irish Australia from Ireland.

The arena of this decisive action was both symbolic and practically important—St Patrick's Day. The instigator of the action was Cardinal Moran. He began his moves on the St Patrick's Day following his arrival in Australia. In 1885 High Mass was celebrated on that day in St Mary's Cathedral; previously it had been at St Patrick's Church Hill. True, the change in venue reflected the change away from an English Benedictine archbishopric in Sydney, but it was also a step towards bringing Ireland's national day in Australia under Moran's personal control and towards giving it the character he wanted it to have. That was definitely not the boozy downmarket festival he had inherited. The centre of the celebrations in the 1880s was a procession through city streets, maintained in Melbourne into the 1920s and thirties, indeed until 1970, but discontinued in Sydney in the mid-nineties. (It has been revived in both cities in recent years.) This procession had a strong tendency to disperse into hotels for the remainder of the day, which is one reason why Cardinal Moran disapproved of it and tried to substitute a major sports meeting which would be a family occasion and have some fitting dignity. Tensions and splits between the various Irish organisations and personalities involved in preparing the celebration made such dignity difficult to achieve, quite apart from what might eventuate on the day itself. And following the Parnell split in Ireland in 1890–91, and the virtual collapse of the Home Rule Party which followed it, these problems became exacerbated. To the bitter question of what

Some of the pupils of St Enda's Gaelic School
(Junior Section) Sydney 1925

faction of the fragmented Irish party should Australian Irishmen support, was tied a difficult practical matter: to what faction should the proceeds of the St Patrick's celebrations be donated? Neither these circumstances nor the continuing internal disputes made for public edification or attentive sensitivity to the Cardinal's preferences.

Accordingly in an action centrally symbolic of what had happened to Australian Irishism in general, from 1896 Cardinal Moran took over control of St Patrick's Day celebrations from lay organisations. He set up his own committee of prominent public lay figures. His intentions were to stress the religious character of the day, a saint's day that is, rather than a national day. He set out to change it into a mass demonstration of Catholicity, and to make it a vehicle for his general aim of Catholic integration into the Australian establishment. And he instantly solved the problem of which faction of the Home Rule Party would be the beneficiary of the funds raised. None. All proceeds would go to Catholic charities. The character of the banquet was altered from what amounted to a Home Rule meeting into a formal Catholic occasion of an elevated social kind, in which the Cardinal would preside over a distinguished gathering of the leaders of state and society, assembled without regard to their religion or racial origin. Moran's efforts to use St Patrick's Day to persuade Australian society to recognise and honour its Irish Catholic element reached their height in his unsuccessful attempts to persuade the New South Wales government to declare it a public holiday. Queen Victoria had granted it in 1902 to acknowledge the great efforts of the Irish Brigade in the Transvaal, but the government ended this in 1903; various country towns honoured the day with informal holidays in response to local Irish Catholic requests (or friendly coercion). The best Moran could do was to make it a holiday for Catholic schools, which it remained until 1967.

The Melbourne celebrations of the early twentieth century were not notably different in character—governors-general in attendance, masses of marching schoolchildren, a procession that amounted to a historical pageant representing the glories of Ireland's past, nothing contentious. Even as late as 1916 the Melbourne St Patrick's Day procession halted outside Federal Parliament House while *God Save the King* was played.

St Patrick's Day, Sydney 1914

Lest one be tempted to wax irate at Moran's 1896 clerical takeover of St Patrick's Day, that move, unprotested, was entirely in keeping with the then mood of Irish Australia. Ireland was history—and hardly relevant at that. The Irish organisations that had up till then organised the celebrations were tiny, factious and inefficient. Yet even the resources of the Church could not save St Patrick's Day. Moran's efforts to revive it as a triumphal Catholic celebration only temporarily arrested the decline. By 1914, the Sydney celebrations were teetering on the verge of collapse: only 4685 of Sydney's 185 000 Catholics attended the 'monster' sports meeting.

This was the norm. There were of course later aberrations—the 1917–22 St Patrick's Day in Melbourne with Dr Mannix as the star and Ireland the cause. But by the end of the century the fundamental realities of Catholic life in Australia were not Irish, but Australian. Australian with an Irish flavour yet, but not a real Irish flavour, an artificial one, a gloss, a veneer, a static badge of difference on a product of basic Australian manufacture. The Catholic school system holds this implicit lesson and the Irish contribution to popular literary culture spells it out: the Irish were assimilators beyond compare, making what was native seem their own.

It has long been a matter of common assumption that Catholic schools were 'Irish' in the character of their cultural influences and formation. Such a conclusion flowed from the pressures of an inimical Australian environment which linked adverse images of 'Catholic' and 'Irish' to their mutual detriment: the linkage generated a defence in the same terms, which stressed and asserted that singled out for attack. The sneer of 'Irish' called forth the boast of it. Added to this more recently have been memoirs whose selective emphasis and eye for the colourful (and commercial) has picked out and exaggerated elements more superficial than profound.

In fact, a hard look at the historical realities (as distinct from the nostalgic inventions) suggests that neither the church nor the school authorities, nor the Irish Catholic population, took much interest in Irish cultural values, nor tried to impart them, except in regard to religion. One clear strand of evidence of this lack, is the occasional (they were greatly discouraged) efforts of Irish culture enthusiasts (or fanatics) to get such Irish culture introduced into the Catholic school system. The campaign of the United Irish League in New South Wales from 1901 was an instance: the league wanted Irish history and language taught in schools and offered prizes to encourage this. Cardinal Moran would not support it, and up to 1905 only twenty-seven of the 350 Catholic schools in New South Wales had participated. In 1904 there were 32 000 children in Catholic schools in New South Wales: the Irish history essay competition of that year attracted ninety entrants. True, 400 sat Irish history examinations in 1905, but this was still a tiny minority. And from a remarkable peak of 6000 members, paying three shillings per annum in 1902, the United Irish League collapsed in 1906. In Melbourne Archbishop Carr did support similar efforts by the Gaelic League but the outcome was no better. In the 1940s, the founder of the Irish National Association, Dr Albert Dryer, was appalled by the total absence of any Irish elements in the tuition of his son by the Christian Brothers at Waverley: his protests to the headmaster were in vain. Little thought is needed to discover why this should be so. The Catholic school system had elected to compete with public schools in public examinations. For this a state syllabus was laid down which Catholic schools were obliged to follow both for purposes of registration and to ensure success in the public examinations toward which they were oriented and by which they measured their achievements. To this the Catholic schools added religious instruction and attendance at Mass and various church occasions, all of which absorbed time. Simply, there was no room in the school day for Irish culture. Nor did the parents want it. Most regarded the study of Ireland as irrelevant in the Australian situation. Indeed they had already acted on this belief themselves: retention of Irish traditions, culture, or language had not been a feature of the behaviour of the Irish-born in Australia. Why should they wish this inflicted on their children?

Did such Irish influences creep in via textbooks? Catholic schools used not only Irish Christian Brothers' books, but Collins Australian Series and a series of readers from the English Catholic publishers Burns and Oates. The Approved Readers for the Catholic Schools of Australia introduced in 1908 were more 'Irish' but not radically so. Leading Catholic colleges, with their emphasis on a 'classical' education, and superior convent education (girls' colleges educated many non-Catholic young ladies) had very little if any Irish elements in either curricula or textbooks. Indeed many of these superior Catholic educational institutions shared that element of snobbery in the social classes to which they belonged, or aspired, which looked down on anything Irish as inferior, grubby and common—attitudes held, and communicated, even by teachers Irish themselves. The thought that Catholic educational institutions may have been anti-Irish, some of them even in intention, has not been entertained let alone investigated. Yet that was the drift of some socially aspirant Catholic education, towards identification with the attitudes and values of an English-oriented great public school system. Nor can the schools of the poor be always cleared of such a charge. The special mission of the Australian Sisters of St Joseph was strongly conditioned by notions and presumptions then current about the station of the poor. These views were unspecific, but their effect was anti-Irish given the Irish representation in the ranks of Australian poverty. It has been suggested that the Josephite rejection of music teaching flowed not only from the spirit of the order, but from views about subjects deemed appropriate in the education of those destined for a future of manual labour or domestic service. The whole atmosphere of such schooling confirmed a status quo in which the Irish were on the bottom. Nor was it innocent of contempt: some teachers of superior Irish station conveyed their disdain and distaste to the offspring of Irish-Australian slums with such intensity as to instil permanent hatred of Ireland and persons Irish.

But surely in matters where there was choice, Australian Catholic schools chose Irish? Louise Mazzaroli, whose research has raised many of the questions adverted to here, in relation to Catholic education, has analysed the programs of Catholic school concerts in New South Wales in the 1890s. 'Irish' items were a very small proportion of total programs, and such items were predominantly the polite and innocuous Anglo-Irish ones, or American sentimentalia. She has pointed out that memory, as usual, selects and highlights the unusual, the different, in the recollection of participants. In this case, the Irish elements stayed in the mind while the usual and the ordinary—in the case of poetry English and Australian items, in the case of songs and music the same, plus European compositions—are forgotten. What was unusual was that Catholic schools added to the standard Australian concert fare, a dash, but only a dash, of Irish.

As to why, no doubt the initial decisions had elements of sentiment, defiance, the determination to be a little different, the aim of pleasing the Irish bishops and clergy who attended such concerts, but soon it was a matter of habit, routine, the way Catholic schools were, a tinge of green to distinguish them from the red, white and blue.

It was just a little cheeky indulgence, but in important matters, such as sport, individualism of any Irish kind was not permitted. In fact sport is also an area in which the

The Surry Hills Hurling team, 1925. Dan Minogue, future M.P. for West Sydney (1949–69) is seated third from the right

principle, Australianise or perish applied. It is a popular belief that Australian Rules football was derived from Gaelic football. The case can be argued from the striking similarities between the two games in both general character and specific rules, and from circumstantial evidence. The documented presence in Australia of that other major Irish game, hurling, from the 1840s suggests that it is likely that the Irish brought their variety of football as well: Irish hurlers were said to have played the first game of football in Melbourne on 12 October 1843. Earlier in that year, on St Patrick's Day, the first reference to football being played in South Australia—in the *Southern Australian*—spelt out the Gaelic origins of the players, if it leaves to probability the Irish nature of the game: 'A few of the colonists from the Emerald Isle intend this day enjoying themselves in honour of the Saint with a game of football.' The fanatical popularity of the game in 'Irish' areas of Melbourne and the Victorian country might imply a similar conclusion of derivation—and adaptation. Hurling was not adapted and while its Australian existence has been historically fairly continuous its support has been narrow, confined in the main to recent Irish-born immigrants. These seemed to enjoy the tendency of matches, in the period before official rules were introduced in the 1880s, to degenerate into free-for-alls, and to be the natural recruits for teams which tended to grow around particular hotels. The five hurling clubs that existed in Sydney 1898–1900 were based at hotels, and competitions often had incentives which were alcoholic. (An 1885 championship carried the prize of a case of champagne and a case of poteen whiskey, donated by William Walsh of the Miner's Arms Hotel, Haymarket.) Nevertheless the sport could attract large crowds and respectable patronage: in 1904 Cardinal Moran was among 3000 spectators at an interstate match. Hurling's problems related to the characteristics of its players—recent immigrants. Constantly on the move, following employment or in search of variety, they provided no stable basis for either teams or organisation, and the vagaries of such movements and the unpredictability of recruitment via immigration gave the game an erratic and fluctuating history. Football absorbed the Australian ethos in important respects. In October 1894 the *Ballarat Star* reported the Wallace versus Dunnstown match. The public stake was £20 in a time of severe depression: the side bets are not reported. But no less important than its offering the opportunity to gamble was that football offered the chance both to join the general community and compete with it. Irish-Australian tribal teams both assimilated with the rest of the community and contested with it, as a microcosm of Irish Australia itself. Athletics and boxing narrowed this down to individual contests, but the principles at issue were the same—and the money at stake much greater. At the Easter meeting at Botany in 1884 the Irish champion Tom Malone, racing over 120 yards, created a record of 11.5 seconds which stood for over fifty years: such meetings could attract 10 000 people and see wagers total £40 000, a huge sum in those times.

Enthusiasts for specifically Irish games were not numerous in Australia, but they were energetic and saw that the only way to ensure a future for such sports was to gain their acceptance by Catholic schools. Their efforts to achieve this failed, save for the introduction of handball, an area where they did achieve some success: it became, perhaps, the main informal, playground sport of Catholic schools, at least in New South Wales, from the late nineteenth century to the 1940s. Irish campaigners for hurling and Gaelic football made virtually no headway in Catholic schools against those English games, cricket and Rugby football. The reason is abundantly clear: those games were the avenue through which the Catholic schools related to the rest of the Australian sporting community. To drop them in preference for Irish games, would be to opt for the ghetto, to isolate such schools from the mainstream of Australian life, to abandon efforts to compete and win against the world. No Australian Catholic school, or its parents, or church, would countenance that.

What then is Irish about these schools? From whence does their reputation for being Irish derive? In part, from the atmosphere of association of the state-aid issue with the persecution of Ireland and the Irish. From their staffs and religion. That is true in fact, but the inferences drawn from it are questionable and highlight the power of religious propaganda machines. The idea that Irish religious teachers, priests, nuns, brothers, were a very important cultural influence was constantly touted by all facets of the Catholic media from episcopal foundation-stone layers down. Australian Catholicism's debt to Ireland was an axiomatic principle of life, repeated, embroidered, insisted upon by clerical authorities with a vested interest in maintaining that authority by fostering an attitude of subservient gratitude and humble acquiescence.

Such Irish teachers had come to benighted Australia out of dedicated self-sacrifice: it was right and proper (and also necessary) that their achievements be celebrated as successful: they must have imparted their Irish religion and culture to their pupils.

But did they? And in the case of their culture, did they seek to? The celebration of the Irish contribution to Catholic education is a feature of Australian Catholic life from the 1880s on. But Irish influence dates from much earlier. About half the teachers in Catholic schools under the Denominational system since the 1830s had taught under the National system in Ireland. To quote the 1858 figures, of ninety such Catholic teachers, at least seventy-two were Irish-born. Yet no one suggests the Denominational system was

THE LATE MR. EUGENE J. RYAN.

Mr. Eugene John Ryan, one of the best-known Irishmen in Sydney, and especially well known in connection with the University College, Regent-street, died last week at the age of 41. Mr. Ryan took a prominent part in the '98 memorial movement, and was one of the most enthusiastic students of Irish history and the Gaelic language in Sydney, being himself a fluent speaker and ready writer in the ancient Irish tongue. He was on several occasions asked to stand for Parliament, but always declined the honour, although probably there was no more popular man in the old Phillip Electorate. His home, "Ryan's Hotel," 20 George-street West, has for years past been a rendezvous for Irish Nationalists now resident in Sydney. The interment took place on Sunday in Waverley Cemetery. The chief mourners were:—Mrs. Ryan (widow of deceased), Rev. Brother Bernard Ryan (brother), Sister Rosarii, Mr. J. G. O'Connor (Newcastle), Mrs. Harrington (cousin), X. T. Dwyer, Mr. and Mrs. P. Ryan, P. Costello, Mrs. W. Ryan, Mrs. Phillips, Mr. and Mrs. J. English, Miss A. M'Grath (cousin), Misses Ryan (three), Superintendent Larkin, Inspectors Boyd and Broderick. Among others present were:—Dr. M'Carthy, Messrs. E. W. O'Sullivan, John Woods, J. M'Laughlin, John J. Hayes, James A. ...yes, Frank M'Kenna, J. F. M'Cabe, M. O'Rior-...Mayor of Alexandria), and W. Armstrong.

Eugene Ryan, teacher of Gaelic

culturally 'Irish'. Perhaps these earlier lay Irish-born teachers may have possessed a different, passive brand of Irishry from religious Irish teachers, who had been raised in the later more aggressive religious and national atmosphere of an Irish revival. Probably true. But the point does draw attention to the possibility that this later, religious, generation of Irish teachers have been credited—or discredited—with more 'Irishness' than they had, by propagandists who exalted 'Irishness' above teaching ability. The good teachers—and many of the religious generation were excellent, and public examinations proved so—taught an Australian syllabus to Australian children in Australian Catholic schools, and, from 1911, celebrated their own Australia Day. The difference was the 'Catholic'. These teachers also taught Catholicism, an Irish angle on it certainly, as this was what they knew. But the most Irish thing they conveyed was themselves. Much can be made of this or little. The general point is that such Irish influences were subtle and hidden and in areas of human and spiritual values. Their pupils were given an Australian education in an Irish Catholic way. Pupils were exposed to an Irish conditioning process which conveyed a dimension of difference, a variant on the common English culture. That this was an individual process, the spillover from the idiosyncratic Irishness of teaching personalities, is evident in that such pupils were not stamped out in some green mould: the capacities to give and to take were as various and as numerous as those involved. Some general suggestions are possible. First, it should not be forgotten that these teachers came from an Ireland itself caught up in an anglicisation process, particularly powerful in the education system, so pronounced and profound as to draw from Padraic Pearse in 1913 the description of 'The Murder Machine', so ruthlessly did it kill Irish culture. To see such teachers as apostles for rampant and aggressive Irish cultural nationalism is to grossly misunderstand the English Ireland of their day—and to underestimate the power of the bourgeois culture of refinement and respectability which headed Ireland's list of British imports. These Irish religious 'teachers' —the term might be broadened to include the priesthood—through their contact with children and adults, infused into Australian Catholic life (and infused is the appropriate word) a variety of qualities; sociability, ease, hardness, grace, humour, certainties, a host of intangibles that imparted an Irish flavour. That this was so important an infusion is due to two factors. These teachers came from an ancient, rich and complex culture to one which was young, poor and starved of the nutrients of a full and civilised life. And they continued to come. As Irish Australia gradually grew away from its aging origins, these teachers continued to arrive, sustaining that dimension of difference. Just when, as the nineteenth century drew to a close, the original Irish were vanishing in Australia, leaving their children with cultural resources primitive, skimpy and thin, the battalions of Irish religious teachers began to grow. From, say, the turn of the century, but particularly from the formation of the Irish Free State in 1921, these battalions had been exposed to an Irish cultural conditioning process in Ireland itself. But not before. Thus the curious time lag in the flourishing of Australia's Irish subculture, a phenomenon accompanying the period of rapid decline of the proportion of those of Irish birth. Said Rev. W.B. Mangan of St Patrick's College, Manly, urging in 1916 the study of Irish history: 'I had never heard or read anything of Irish history worth recollecting...' Nineteenth-century Irish parents had little knowledge of Irish history, and what they got did not come from school: the National school curriculum was Anglo-centric. Thus the formative importance of the more recent teacher imports. Eventually, by the 1930s they had outlived their function, but for a crucial generation or more they had bridged the cultural gap for the Australian Irish, with their confidence, their Catholicism and their colour. They did this with a curious construct which was taken at the time and in retrospect to be 'Irish', but was not. It was a weird Australian translation from the Gaelic, a phantom culture in a way, as its derivation was a land that never was, but its inhabitants were real enough and it served them well enough in their day.

One other Irish educational influence requires mention, though it has escaped even the notice, let alone research attention, of those sensitive to the ideological promotions associated with Irish Catholicism. Dr Alexander Leeper was warden of Trinity College, University of Melbourne, for over forty years, 1876–1918. Through such men and such institutions of higher education, (and indeed also at the level of the non-Catholic private-school system, in which headmasters and other staff were often Anglo-Irish) the values and attitudes of Protestant and Anglo-Irish Ireland passed into the formation of the minds of the leaders of Australian society. In Leeper's case, for nearly half a century and beyond (he died in 1934) he moulded student minds and the public atmosphere towards hostility to Irish Catholicism. Proudly Irish himself, he was born in Dublin in 1848, son of an Anglican clergyman. He had a brilliant career at Trinity College Dublin, then Oxford, coming to Australia in 1875. The influence of Leeper, and those like him, at a crucial stage of colonial development, on the minds of the colonial elite, in breeding suspicion of Catholics and Catholicism, was immense. One of his students was Herbert Brookes, a key figure in the anti-Irish Catholicism of the First World War period. Brookes was Australian-born. His biographer suggests that his bigotry was inherited from his Ulster mother, brought up in Portadown. Perhaps. It would certainly have been nurtured under Leeper at Trinity.

Sixteen Sisters of Mercy from Queensland visiting Rome and Dublin, August 1966

The faces of clerical Irish Australia. Bottom left *Fr P.J. Hartigan ('John O'Brien'), representing sentimental nostalgia;* bottom right, *Dr Pat Tuomey of St Patrick's College Manly and the Irish National Association, representing revolutionary nationalism, with Revs Arthur McHugh P.P. and Frank Hartigan, Narrandera, NSW, 1920*

As one might expect, Irish-Australian newspapers and journals are uncertain reflections of the cultural dispositions of the community they sought to serve: part of their role was to convey what was Irish rather than foster what was Irish-Australian, and many of their contributors were Irish-born, with inbuilt assumptions that what was Australian must be inferior. Yet such journals consistently revealed an Australian awareness and sensitivity that pointed to their main cultural concern—how might the Irish and Australia be reconciled, be blended, brought together in harmony of spirit?

   The verse of 'John O'Brien' (Father P.J. Hartigan) first published in book form in 1921, but appearing in various journals from 1906, is the best, and best known, of Irish Australia's ambivalent affirmations of identity with the Australian experience. (It has a female counterpart in the Queensland verse of Alice Guerin Crist.) The ambivalence is evident in settings and situations which are Australian, but spirit and points of reference which are Irish, even down to Gaelic phrases which are given footnote explanations. The enormous and continuing success of O'Brien's verse springs from its reconciling and amalgamating the two cultures in a kind of easy equipoise, from which contrived balance comes its basic appeal. It succeeds in achieving in popular art what Irish Australians were attempting to do in life. It feels right as verse because it captures a real everyday tension resolved, or at least at peace.

O'Brien is central to the Irish-Australian literary tradition in many ways, and not only in his reconciliation of Ireland and Australia at the level of popular experience. He was a Catholic priest, a member of Irish Catholicism's only educated leisured class. No other Australian priest had such literary success, but many others tried their hand at poetry, even novels, and the literary pages of Irish Catholic newspapers and the *Austral Light* were full of their reviews and essays. This was not necessarily a Catholic clerical characteristic. That most colourful of Melbourne Presbyterian ministers, Derry-born J. Lawrence Rentoul, Professor of Greek and Hebrew at the University of Melbourne, also published poetry. But it was an Irish Catholic characteristic to be constantly concerned with working out some appropriate relationship with the Australian environment. Perhaps this is a distant echo of the influence of that enormously popular and prolific Irish priest novelist of the day, Canon P.A. Sheehan, whose work was a serious effort to relate his characters to the political and social forces in the Ireland of his time. Perhaps it was because these priests came from a verbal tradition, a culture of words. But in practical terms it was because they had the money to buy books and the leisure to read them: their personal libraries prove that the Catholic priesthood was a significant segment of the market not only for Irish books, but Australian.

O'Brien is central too in his contacts with, and affection for, the *Bulletin*. Irish-Australian writing revolved around the *Bulletin* in an orbit sometimes close, often sufficiently distant to avoid the heat of that fiery particle, but always in some relationship to its nationalism and independent spirit. In 1911, Father Hartigan gave the last sacraments to Jack Riley, the original of Banjo Paterson's 'The Man from Snowy River'. On that occasion Riley recovered, but it was a brush with Australian bush mythology that was peculiarly and symbolically appropriate: Irish Australia had strong links with the bush tradition.

And O'Brien is central also in his nostalgic sentimentality, perhaps the dominant and most enduring theme in the Irish-Australian literary tradition. O'Brien's verse has a constant historical dimension. He is writing about a world which has gone, a nobler, better world fading into an Austral-Celtic twilight. In so doing he reflected the literary atmosphere and directions of his time, but he also established a trend which continues: Irish Australia was to have a literature of nostalgia, not a literature of realism or social comment. More recent evocations (Keneally, Buckley, R.D. Fitzgerald, Campion) have been in that backward-looking tradition: the tone has changed from affection to something less, the perceptions have been very much more, but the stance has been the same— sentimental journeys.

But in this O'Brien was merely the most accomplished practitioner: the trend was established with Australian settlement and the ballads of the convict period. Those ballads served various purposes, not least as a substitute for rebellion. The songs *were* the rebellion, as only they were possible in prison circumstances, and they saved the singer from sheer despair and relieved his feelings of frustration: their curses were like delivering a blow. Yet the work of Frank the Poet—Francis MacNamara, best known of the Irish-Australian convict balladeers—makes clear that while the spirit and tone of his work are Irish-protest, the rejection of tyranny—the form is more that of the literary written tradition of the English (or Anglo-Irish) than the oral tradition of the Irish bard he characterised himself to be. The ballad tradition was an early and narrow expression of Irish Australia in which angry or derisory protest was the keynote, but the literary mainstream was that which accorded with the spirit of the mass of free immigration—sentiment.

Here the key figure is Thomas Moore, his importance to the Australian Irish tradition evident in his statue in Ballarat, his poems and melodies the encapsulation of the colonial Irish disposition. Moore's popularity arose from the coincidence of the sentiments he expressed so well in words and music, with the feelings of the colonial Irish—or with what they thought ought to be their feelings. His most frequent themes were loss, parting, distance, memory, absent or dying lovers, lost friends, loneliness, melancholy, death.

> Oft in the stilly night
> Ere Slumber's chain has bound me,
> Fond memory brings the light
> Of other days around me;
> The smiles, the tears,
> Of boyhood years
> The words of love then spoken;
> The eyes that shone,
> Now dimmed and gone,
> The cheerful hearts now broken!

Etcetera. These were classic Victorian emotions, and Moore was only one of the songwriters who expressed them, but he was arguably the best in his class, and he—and his songs—were Irish. His popularity in English drawing rooms, his 'respectability', the charm and accessibility of his settings, were all additional positive features, but the main attraction was what these songs expressed in an emigrant situation. They offered what the cynical might call emotional indulgence, others catharsis: they provided the immigrant with the opportunity to identify with a rush of emotions—sadness, loss, guilt and grief. They brought, in concert situations, the tingle, the prickling, of a shared melancholy, a spasm of that multitudinous common grief that would, on such occasions, swell up to choke the immigrant heart. These were songs that brought both unity of feeling and reconciliation, resignation to the unhappiness of parting: they were a release from profound immigrant tensions. Moreover, the mood and style of these songs were drawing-room, discreet, utterly respectable, fit for polite society, in tune with colonial decorum, harmonious in situations pervaded by the Church. Their Irish nationalism—'The Minstrel Boy to the War hath gone'—is suggestive, muted, noble, generalised; another colonial plus. Moore and his genre satisfied the Australian Irish craving for nostalgia, the need to remember emotionally. For them he was Ireland enough. Moore's sweet distant echoes of a highly romanticised Ireland was all the 'Irish' music that they cared to hear: the beat of colonial busyness and success were much more their tune. The ration of sentiment the Australian Irish allowed themselves was not all that great and it served a healthy psychological purpose: songs and poetry such as Moore's, ritualised homesickness, and, performed in group situations, generated emotional commonality and release in the very process of acknowledging origins.

In similar vein was the reception accorded the popular melodramas of the Irish play-wright Dion Boucicault, particularly *The Colleen Bawn* (1860) and the *The Shaughraun*

Victor Daley, poet

(1874). Boucicault wrote many such plays, variations on the theme of the trials and perils of the noble Irish peasant boy or girl, amid stock Irish rural situations, characters and plots. He toured Australia himself in 1885, with tremendous success: his audiences totalled 30 000: his son (of the same name) spent many years in Australia until his death in 1929. Typical of the Boucicault output was 'Shamus O'Brien, or, The Rebel Chief of '98', a play with sure Australian Irish appeal, which began a run of forty-two performances in Melbourne in 1889 and continued in various theatres until 1901. While such plays exploited sensational techniques, and centred on engaging positive versions of the Stage Irishman, they were built around Irish historical events and carried a pro-Irish political message: they were history melodrama of strong popular potency in evoking emotion and nostalgia.

This romanticism distanced the Irish from a good deal of Australian literature, and generated in Irish Australia a strong preference for dreamy emotionalism in literary content and style. The belief was that literature should inspire, call out the heroic and the good, rather than reflect the real—and Australian writing was held to lack this ennobling note. Lawson's genius was partly conceded, but he had libelled the bushman, had iron in his soul, and his stories were infused with dark pessimism and peopled by low moral types: the Australian had not yet 'found' himself. The Irishman had—in the mystical Celtic temperament from which flowed his superior sensitivity. Though just this was not enough. On Victor Daley's death in 1905 the *Austral Light* remarked that a subtle and dreamy sadness pervaded most of his work, an intangible regret, the weight of pre-existence— phrases that might have applied equally well to much other Irish-Australian verse. But the *Austral Light* denied Daley any greatness. His Bohemian reputation had not been redeemed enough by a deathbed repentance: he lacked seriousness of purpose, energy and direction.

No doubt such shortcomings in minor poets, of whom Irish Australia produced a host— John Farrell, Roderick J. Flanagan, J.B. O'Hara, M. O'Reilly, Roderic Quinn,

Bernard O'Dowd, Bernard McElhill, David McKee Wright, and many more—arose mostly from a paucity of gifts. It is hard to excuse, beyond the limits of laughter, such infelicities as Daley's homage to the labour of washerwomen:

> From birth till we are dying
> You wash our sordid duds,
> O Woman of the Washtub,
> O Sister of the suds!

Or not to agree with Brian Elliot's censure of O'Dowd for 'dressing up his Irish fairies in bowyangs and putting them out to populate the Bush . . .'. Or to feel of Wright that there is 'too much of the "och" and the "sure" and the little pigs that done it'. But this 'blarney Irish' element, this 'quaintly ludicrous incongruity' which Elliot discerned, is explained, though not excused, by conflicting cultural and literary demands to which these writers were exposed. That lesser talents were unable to cope convincingly with this is hardly surprisingly. Their Australian environment insisted on attention and required confrontation to comprehend and get on terms with it, but their Irish background dictated literary modes which emphasised dreams and memories—and claimed spiritual superiority. In *Talks about Poets and Poetry* (1915) Rev. J.J. Malone was one of those many who dilated on 'the peculiar constitution of the Irish mind', radically distinct from the English in its pure, non-materialist, spiritual inlook, and Irish inability to escape Ireland's magic power: 'Whatever ties of citizenship bind her emigrant children to the lands of their adoption, she remains ever the bride of their affections, and they turn to her with a yearning that makes the poetry of exile more wistful and entrancing than that of any other wandering minstrel people.'

It would have required the compulsion of greater genius than any of the minor Irish-Australian versifiers possessed to move beyond the expected framework of commentators who insisted that the softness of Ireland as a memory world was necessary to escape the harshness of Australia. Their achievement was to attend to Australia at all, however stilted and uneasy was the encounter. But the Irish accents had to be figuratively written in: M. O'Reilly did it actually in some of his verse; it was more often done with lashings of anglicised Celtic twilight. Given this uncertainty and ambivalence, this imposition of the divided soul and conflicting criteria of locational relevance, it is not surprising that Irish Australia produced nothing of high literary worth. John Boyle O'Reilly's novel *Moondyne* (1879) is interesting in its postulation of an arcadian Western Australia where an idealised past might be reborn, but more to the taste of Irish Australia were such fripperies as Marion Miller Knowles' *Pretty Nan Hartigan* (1928) or *Pierce O'Grady's Daughter* (1928) with its subtitle 'An Australian Story' but its chapter headings such as 'Come Back to Erin, Mavourneen, Mavourneen' and 'The Fairy Hills of Heart's Desire'. Or worse still, the trilogy of adventures of Mrs Bridget McSweeney, stage Irish inhabitant of Sydney, with twins Pat and Mike, concocted by the Englishman Thomas Edward Spencer and published between 1906 and 1911. Popular materials yes, some excellent journalism—the Irish Australians loved, and had a way with, words—but no real confrontation with Australia as a place and as a life. Their imaginations were burdened with too much Ireland, more fantasy than reality, for that.

Yet, more importantly and with more subtle sway, beyond the narrower confines of Catholic Irish Australia, among those budding Australian literati, who were remote from this clericalism and uninvolved in its close-buttoned culture, the literary renaissance in

Ireland set up intense awe-inspired reverberations. Louis Esson, dedicated to the idea of founding an Australian drama, was at the opening of the Abbey Theatre in Dublin in December 1904. J.M. Synge advised him on creating an authentic Australian drama; he was vastly impressed by W.B. Yeats with whom he stayed overnight; George Moore, G.B. Shaw, Lady Gregory—all these were Esson's acquaintances and idols. Other aspiring Australian cultural nationalists were dazzled by that bright Irish circle, and paid court to them in person on visits to culture's then capitals. Spencer Brodney came, the Palmers too, to be enraptured by literary Dublin and hypnotised by AE. It was hardly surprising that this should be so, given the extraordinary power of that Irish explosion of genius and creativity and its coincidence in objectives and time with the beginnings of a serious search for Australian cultural expression and identity. It was not the Irish content of the renaissance that held Australian relevance, but its ambition and fact as a national literary declamation, its style and concern as an exploration of the ordinary folk, and its impact as a cultural force. Here was Ireland, in unfamiliar Anglo-Irish guise, as inspiration and exemplar in a role central to the evolution of the broader general Australian literary culture.

    Was this exaltation a real and genuine Ireland? Indeed it was, but the curious continuum of spirit between the rarities of its cultivated insights and the living and humble subject matter of its concerns walking the Australian earth, was to pass unheeded, an improbability beyond the bizarre.

C H A P T E R
F I V E

N A T I O N A L I S T S

The expression of Irish nationalism in Australia was never simply an expression of loyalty to Ireland: it was always also a part of the processes of settlement, a mode of testing the Australian environment and of Irish-Australian interaction with it, a way of defining who and where Irish Australians were.

And so, because of that dual and fluctuating function, and because adherence to any form of Irish nationalism was a contentious matter in Australia, it is possible to form contradictory views of its strength: that it was too strong (indeed should not have existed at all), that it was too weak to be of any significance whatever, and the intermediate and activist view, that it was weak but should and could be made powerful. But the weight of the apparent historical evidence must be to exaggerate the importance of Irish allegiances in Australia: both those who saw these as disloyal menace and those who led expressions of Irishness conspired to inflate the extent, depth and power of these things. As an initial balance, a conclusion is necessary as a preface: Irish nationalism, as such, was never strong in Australia: Ireland as a symbol was. Such nationalism was strongly constitutional in main character, closely tied in its appearance to brief moments of Irish crisis, and became powerful in its Australian context only when it coincided with, or could be made to express, local grievances.

The leaders of and spokesmen for the Australian Irish were self-appointed. Like all enthusiasts their expectations were high: their assumption was that they were leading, speaking for, a powerful and united Hibernian community imbued with a deep love of Ireland and vitally interested in Irish affairs. They were not interested in, nor did they believe, constant evidence to the contrary. Brushing aside such disappointments was necessary to their own sense of importance and to sustain the validity of their convictions. Besides, Ireland was not only a national but a holy, religious, cause.

But the actuality was stolidly recalcitrant. Irish immigrants came from a country in which primary loyalties had been to family, then, clan, then town, region, or at widest, county: confirmation of this hierarchy of allegiances keeps cropping up everywhere among Irish immigrants well into the twentieth century, when nationalist ideologies were allegedly widespread. They were, but as an overlay: the old loyalties remained the first instinct. Australia itself did something to change that, by lumping all Irish together as Irish, neither comprehending nor caring about the locational differences of origin so important to the Irish themselves. And of course the translation to Australia mixed and dispersed these local Irish loyalties so that they became much less meaningful: more meaningful in Australia were the distinctions of being 'Irish', from Ireland. Australian pressures had two effects: that of instilling, or encouraging the idea of being 'Irish' as a general identity, and of transferring old habits of loyalty to some manageably small locality to new locations in Australia.

Because of all this, there is a strong case for pausing to question whether this was 'nationalism' at all, since the primary emotions appear to have been sentimental nostalgia, and that much of Irish Australia's sense of identity was focused on the separate assimilation and success of individuals, rather than the assertion of a national group. The reputation of the Australian Irish for strong national loyalties was substantially based on the widespread phenomena of individual Irish colonists bringing out specific and known relatives and friends: was Irish 'nationalism' merely family loyalty misconstrued and writ large? Can nationalism be equated with the narrow individual impulse revealed in so many emigrant letters—I am sad I will never see you, or the old farm, again, sentiments both personal and restricted to particular localities? And what is to be made of the dictum pronounced by the Sydney *Freeman's Journal* as early as December 1856: 'The *nationality* of Ireland consists in, for it is inextricably interwoven with, its *Catholicity*. You cannot separate the one from the other.' For all the extravagance of this claim, and its demonstrable areas of inapplicability, for some Irish it was true.

Australia had another confusing effect, but not on the Irish-born. Those of Irish descent but of Australian birth had no locational loyalties within Ireland: if they were to have Irish loyalties at all—and family and religious pressures often combined to see that they did—these would have to be to Ireland as a whole, as a general concept, as an idea, as a nation, as something distinct from actual experience. The power of this kind of affirmation of Ireland can be seen in the prominence, within the Irish nationalist movement in Australia, of men who had never seen Ireland, or who had come to Australia as infants. Their Irishness was a product of their intimate, immediate culture, and of coercive forces within an Australian culture experienced as unreceptive or hostile, pushing them into a general category 'Irish'. This category was denoted by name, school, religion, family, and so on (even appearance) and its imposition need have nothing to do with Irish birth. Some so categorised embraced the label belligerently, some rejected it, some were indifferent.

Acceptance of the idea of being 'Irish' need not have had any nationalist consequences. Indifference and apathy are, perhaps, universal laws of human behaviour, compounded in this case by factors of distance. Ireland was remote in every way: it was simply too far to sustain any sense of involvement, and that spelt the death of real interest. The only effective action was to send money, and that became a substitute for real caring, and the purchase price of guilt-free Irishness at the Australian remove. There were compelling local factors shrinking Irish organisations. In so far as they were the initiatives of enthusiasts they repelled others who could think of any convenient reason not to join—the organisers were too old, too young, too radical, not radical enough, from Cork, whatever. Involvement with the Catholic Church was another complication: Irish organisations were criticised both for being creatures of the clergy, and also when they espoused, as they often did, non-sectarian principles. A major limiting factor was their social composition, and the colonial impulses and attitudes such organisations implicitly expressed. There was a strong tendency for Irish nationalism in Australia, or at least those organisations most obviously Irish, to be the preserve of the relatively well-to-do. Their membership consisted of skilled or white-collar workers—printers, clerks—and their executives were composed of shop-keepers, hotel owners, men of commerce, prominent community names. They were bastions of respectability, and their atmosphere and spirit was that of affirmation of the achievements and aspirations of the successful Irish: these were people who had the position and freedom to be proud of what they were, and the impulse to celebrate their origins. All this distanced them, and their organisations, from those many Irish who were unskilled

The height of Irish Australian respectability. Sir Patrick Jennings, born Newry Co. Down 1831.
Emigrated to the Victorian goldfields 1852, first Irish Catholic premier of NSW, 1886

workers, who were not successful, and who saw no particular reason to glory in Irishness or take any interest in Ireland. They did not feel at ease with these Irish-Australian worthies, were prone to label them with the standard terms of Irish abuse (shoneen, Castle Catholic) and ascribed to them all kinds of discreditable motives—self-promotion, power-hunger, toadyism and the like. Those at the bottom of the Irish Australian socioeconomic pyramid were often resentful that those few who were affluent and secure at the top should claim to speak the mind of the Irish community to the general public, and tell the Australian Irish themselves what they should, as Irish, think, feel and do. For most Australian Irish, involvement in Irish causes was a luxury they could not afford, and their 'leaders' and 'spokesmen' could make contact with them only at times of extreme Irish emergency, or when Irish affairs took on a role symbolic of Australian Irish situations. So the story of Irish organisations in Australia is only a fragment—although a focal fragment—of the Irish scene. Outside these is a wider informal community of Irish origin to which the organisations bear a fluctuating and uncertain relationship. These organisations are set in an Irish climate generated by a whole range of differing orders of allegiance to Irish origins and Catholic religion: at the remote fringes of this green universe are those to whom the Micks were their team, their instinctive tribe, rather than Irish Catholicism their religion, and to whom Ireland was not so much an allegiance as a badge of difference: it was the reference point of their ultimate identity, the distinction between themselves and others. However vague, critical, and unpredictable, this pro-Irish climate established a wider context of tolerance in which the specifically Irish organisations could exist.

Should such organisations exist? Was acknowledgement of Ireland an asset or a liability to Australian Catholics? Was it an inescapable and honourable fact of birth or heritage that demanded a response, or was it an irrelevance or diversion in a distant and different Australian environment?

The argument that Irish consciousness promoted the vitality of the Catholic religion goes back to the early colonial period, was exemplified in the foundation of the Sydney *Freeman's Journal* in 1850, and hardly dies until Daniel Mannix. The counter-assertion that Irishness disadvantaged Catholics in Australia and damaged good community relations goes back to the Sydney Benedictines in the early colony, but was not restricted to them. Archbishop Robert Dunne in Brisbane from the 1880s was Irish and held precisely that position—play down the Irish, foster the Australian, and relations with Protestants would improve. That presupposed that such an improvement would be a good thing, and also that Protestants would share such neutral Australian ground. Many did not, embracing English attitudes and values no less stridently than Catholics held Irish: the two national positions provoked and confirmed each other. Moreover, some Irish held that Australia was not nearly Irish enough. A 'Voice from Australia' complained in the Dublin *Nation* in January 1883 that one-third of Irish urban dwellers had lost their devotion to Catholicism, and that children turned out to be more 'English' than 'Irish'. To him, it

seems strange that a people so brave and enterprising as the Irish have not established a colony in some part of the world where, like the valiant Dutch Boers, they might save themselves from the contamination of the English race and from the effects of their relentless hostility—where they might maintain their religion and their nationality unimpaired, and afford a refuge and a rallying place for those of their race who are forced by the wicked legislation of a foreign government to leave their dear native land and so live abroad.

Such commentary may seem extreme in an Irish context, but there was ample historical precedent, not only with the Boers, but with seventeenth-century English religious sects in the colonisation of America: it was a logical endpoint of worried lines of Irish thinking common in Australia. Thirty years before, in July 1855, the Sydney *Freeman's Journal* noted, with grave concern, that children born of Irish parents in Australia evinced an extreme dislike for everything Irish. The *Freeman's* position was that all should be Australian, but 'without the ignominious sacrifice of noble principles—without becoming a recreant of his race and a traitor to his blood'. And without (and the implacability is evident) 'without giving the oppressors of the land of his forefathers the sweet delight of feeling that the children have hated all the father loved—that the children have cursed all the father blessed—that the children have despised all the father battled, perchance, bled for'. The prose may be overblown, but the intensity of feeling is real: is the patriot to survive only to face the bitterness of his children corrupted and uncaring? An old question now, it was a new question then, the more alarming for its being unthought of by the legatees of a traditional society. The *Freeman's* believed that the choice in the minds of children was not between things Irish and things Australian, but things English. It laid down: 'there are a few great chapters of Ireland's story which every father is *bound* to teach his Australian child: he is moreover bound to make him learn it.' These glories were: the Celtic Race, the civilisation of Ancient Ireland, the Christian achievement, the Isle of Scholars, and the Irish missionary conversion of Europe. It should be noted that these were not a list of nationalist triumphs in any usual sense: they omitted Brian Boru and a host of other heroics. Nor were they at all recent. Their principle of cohesion is not the claim that Ireland was a nation, but that Ireland was a Christian civilisation and culture. The distinction is of the utmost importance because it reveals what the Irish thought was most under Australian threat, not their assertion that they were a nation, but their sense of themselves as a separate, distinctive, and civilised people. The *Freeman's* fear is best understood in the light of the assumption of that time, shared by Irish of all creeds, that the English and the Scots were 'foreigners': the attitude is not Catholic; the word is that used by the Irish Quaker Joseph Beale en route to Melbourne in 1852, and the English returned the discompliment. A strong sense of separate cultural identity pervaded the Irish, and as Beale and other Irish shipboard chroniclers noted, this pulled them together strongly to exclude English 'foreigners'. Irish Catholic separateness was only one variety of that Irish consciousness of distinct identity, the strongest brand, but nothing untoward in the national dispositions of the day: all Irish held themselves different from the English. And it was this consciousness of distinct and valuable identity which the *Freeman's Journal* feared was being lost by the first Irish-Australian generation, something deeper than nationalism, a sense of Irish self.

Could this sense survive apart from Ireland as a place? A doubtful proposition, particularly if taken into a generation that had never experienced Ireland. But, in any case, it was under profound if well-meaning intimidation within the Irish community itself as the Catholic Church moved in to substitute a religion for a culture, to reduce a culture to the dimensions of a religion. Edmund Finn's Melbourne lecture on St Patrick's Societies, their principles and purpose, in November 1860 was already an anachronism in its strong rejection of any identification by Irish national societies with religion or politics. Finn's claim was that such societies should provide 'neutral ground'. That was not what most Irishmen wanted. An educated, cultivated man, Finn represented a class and style of Irishman already eclipsed in the colonies. He saw St Patrick's Societies as cultural centres, fostering adult education, providing libraries and lectures, supporting charities, setting up benefit societies, assisting immigrants. This dream of organisations which were noble affirmations of Irish commonality surfaced regularly thereafter, but what the Irish in Australia actually wanted were organisations which would identify them with particular causes in Ireland or provide them with the society of people like themselves. Or in which they could pursue local grievances. Or simply factionalise. Within a couple of years of Finn's exposition of his highly theoretical irenic masterplan, Melbourne Irish provided an excellent example of the unreality of such ideal organisations. The Irish Relief Fund set up in August 1862 to aid distress in Ireland's South West was effectively a Catholic body: its assumptions were all exclusive of Protestants. It then split into clerical and non-clerical wings, a division sparked by factions and personality disputes which had nothing to do with Ireland. The 'secular' wing of the fund soon became the rallying ground for critics of the absolutism and financial unaccountability of Archbishop Goold, a Victorian Catholic issue. Indeed the fund organisation was used deliberately for advancing the anti-Goold cause, a development which did not endear its alleged nominal purpose to clerical champions. The potential of such purportedly Irish charitable or political organisations to become in fact vehicles for local Catholic insubordination against clerical authority is a further reason why such organisations were few and weak: cautious clerics distrusted them, aborted their formation when they could, frustrated their growth when they could not. The anti-Irish presumed an Irish clerical–lay nexus in furthering the cause of Ireland: the opposite was the case, since clergy and laity represented competing power centres. Nor was this purely an outgrowth of local Australian circumstances: the experience of the nineteenth-century church in Ireland was of difficulty and conflict with the nationalist movement in its various forms. Many Irish clergy brought to Australia their suspicion of Irish nationalist movements, some being opposed to them as a loyalty competing with religion, others seeing them as necessary or good—if in harmony with the Church. The clerical takeover of the Home Rule form of Irish nationalism in Australia in the 1890s was a logical outcome of the Church's position. Support for Home Rule was constitutional, powerful and popular. It would be impossible to suppress, undesirable to oppose, and in any case unnecessary. The obvious tactic was for the Church to absorb it, and tame it by making it its own.

For Australia, this was nothing new. The precedents go back to the first mass popular constitutional movement of the century, Daniel O'Connell's agitation for repeal of the 1800 Act of Union between England and Ireland. From 1830, Daniel O'Connell, as a leading member of the British parliament, himself took a direct interest in the affairs of the new colony of New South Wales, being critical of the despotic powers of governors, delighted by the appointment of Governor Bourke in 1831, keen to see the distinction between free settlers and emancipists abolished, urging the provision of a freely elected Legislative Council, and generally pressing for free and independent British institutions. Admiring Irish colonists in Australia saw him as the apostle of liberty and social harmony under the British constitution, his program the prototype of their own pursuit of demo-cratic reform within the boundaries of imperial loyalty—to them he represented British politics at its best. However, to conservatives in Australia, as in Britain, he was a disloyal Romish demagogue, who had extorted Catholic Emancipation from the British parliament by the threat of Irish mob rule. That Act enabled the appointment of two of O'Connell's protégés as officials within the New South Wales administration; in 1829 Roger Therry as commissioner of the Court of Requests, and, in 1832, John Hubert Plunkett as attorney-general: O'Connell occasionally supplied emigrants to Australia with letters of introduction to Plunkett. Governor Bourke's liberal policies, implemented by his lieutenants Therry and Plunkett, drew from the conservative Sydney *Herald* in 1835 denunciation of 'the O'Connell tail faction which at present afflicts this colony'.

Whatever of the general reforming spirit O'Connell represented, it was not until Irish Catholics gained an Australian public voice with the foundation of the *Australasian Chronicle* in August 1839 that O'Connell became a specifically influential and divisive symbol in colonial affairs, which not only set Irish Catholics against British Protestants, but divided the Irish among themselves.

A branch of the Repeal Association, the organisation O'Connell had set up in Ireland to support the cause of repeal of the Irish Union, imposed by England in 1800, was formed in Sydney towards the end of 1842. It was never large nor strong, nor were the amounts of money it transmitted to Ireland substantial, but its very existence appears to have been a reaction against the anti-repeal stance of the Scots Catholic editor of the *Chronicle*, W.A. Duncan. Duncan argued that while repeal might be in Irish interests, it was certainly not in Catholic interests, in that it would remove Irish members from the imperial parliament: this would allow Tories and Anglicans to dominate that body in a way detrimental to colonial Catholics. Duncan's attack on repeal, and his distinction between what the Irish saw as indivisible—Irish and Catholic interests—called into play a basic law of Australian Irish life: any criticism provoked an Irish response beyond any real wish for commitment. The Irish response to Duncan was to regret that he had raised the issue of repeal at all in the colony, and determination to support it now that he had, as it would be a betrayal and a disgrace not to.

This had its own logic. The leaders of the Irish Catholic group in New South Wales were all, in the 1830s, pre-Catholic Emancipation men, in that they had been accustomed by their Irish background to the ways of discretion, a low profile reinforced by their convict and emancipist positions in the colony. The heady aggressive atmosphere of O'Connell's Ireland of the thirties and forties took considerable time to appear in Australia, for its surfacing entailed the displacement of old leaders by new, and its dispersion depended on the emergence of new immigrant forces from the forties. The Irish Australian leaders of the early thirties were reasonably affluent emancipists, naturally conservative, with a conservatism strengthened by self-interest: they were self-made prosperous men, opposed to the forces of reforming democracy O'Connell represented, and even more opposed to the mob rule he was alleged to represent. But his championing of repeal was another matter. They would have liked to have forgotten it, or to have supported it privately and with discreet sentiments, but Duncan would not let them. To support it became a matter of identity and pride.

This group owned the *Chronicle*. They ousted Duncan, and Fr John McEncroe, a vigorous admirer of O'Connell, took over the editorship: he admired the way in which O'Connell exemplified the harmonious alliance between Irish nationalism and Irish religion, and that was to be the durable theme of the Australian Irish future. In 1844 O'Connell's trial and imprisonment provoked an Australian Irish outcry. The raw nerves touched were not those of Irish nationalism, but those of status and loyalty, and indignation meetings were essentially occasions for the respectable to protest their loyalty against a colonial press that described O'Connell as a conspirator and repeal as treasonable. Such charges were imported from England but had a local dimension. In 1843 the Port Phillip (Melbourne) district was seeking separation from New South Wales and the election of that year seemed full of rowdy Irish. O'Connell seemed the epitome and model and inspiration for all radical separatist democrats, or crudely, the justifier of mob rule and social disorder, and as such was detested by the colonial establishment.

They need not have been so concerned: some of the local Irish had the same worries. O'Connell's release late in 1844 revealed the factionalism and faintheartedness characteristic of the colonial Irish. The prominent wanted no celebration—it would be provocative and undignified. The lesser Irish would have none of this. A Sydney O'Connell meeting in January 1845 attracted 3000, mostly labouring men. Speeches glorified O'Connell, but the meeting's basic preoccupations were not Irish but local. Speakers expressed resentment of the local Irish elite, who had stayed away, asserted that those 'whose brawny arms by their industry upheld the state' were the real Irish, celebrated their power, and claimed that O'Connell was the friend and protector of the poor. And as to all the optimism of the elite that soon the Irish question would be settled happily, the meeting derided the idea that British policy in Ireland might be improved. This Sydney meeting was a fleeting revelation of the uncompromising and bitter temper of outcast Irish Australia, that hidden proletariat that felt cheated and inclined to be ugly, concerned with local issues and its own grievances but seeing them through Irish eyes, cynically critical of its established leaders lay and clerical.

Those leaders were anxious to avoid any such manifestations in the future. Thereafter it was the image of O'Connell the champion of Catholicism, not O'Connell the poor man's friend that was dominant in the Australian Irish scene. Besides, by this time attention was shifting away from O'Connell's campaigns toward famine relief as Ireland was overtaken by the Great Famine of 1845–48. Here the Church could provide facilities for appeals and collections, a role that helped confirm its central position in the direction of Irish-Australian affairs. So, when news of O'Connell's death reached Australia in September 1847, it was the clergy who took the initiative in arranging tributes, all taking the form of solemn High requiem Masses, plus meetings organised and chaired by leading clergy. A correspondent in the *Chronicle* lamented the failure of the influential Sydney Irish to organise a public meeting of sympathy. He admonished them for ingratitude to the man who had wrung their political rights from the hands of tyrants.

Standard Irish nationalist rhetoric, but did it have meaning in the Australian colonies? There, the O'Connell model became the basis of aggressive Irish Catholic politics. Would O'Connell himself have encouraged this application? He seems to have appreciated the essential differences between the colonial situation and the Irish—no aristocracy, no established church, no historical national question—and to have regarded the system of British government, without these hindrances, as naturally productive of civil and religious freedom. So did his colonial disciples, when they were thinking quietly and normally. The first colonial elections of 1843 were, however, not a promising introduction to the tranquillities and equity of the British system, given the eruption of sectarianism and allegations about 'the Catholic vote'. In the reactive Irish situation, such allegations that there was such a vote, with the assumption that it must have been split, generated a demand among the ultra-Irish that such a vote be mobilised and used. The Sydney *Freeman's Journal*, founded by Archdeacon McEncroe in 1850, insisted that the O'Connell model of a disciplined Irish Catholic unity, in which politics be pursued with the forces of religion together in aggressive confrontation of community, was the only appropriate political exemplar for Irish Catholics in Australia. This message appealed to some of the newer generation of immigrants schooled in O'Connell's Ireland, where it had taken the form of blending belligerent appeals to religion and nationalism so as to create a mass

popular voting unity for the purpose of remedying the grievances of the Catholic majority.
But its very basis was at variance with the realities of Australia. The Catholics were a
minority. Most had no serious practical grievances. Such as they did have were not
specifically Catholic, not Irish . The political concerns of the colony bore little relationship
to those of Ireland; substantial freedom and equality existed, opportunities abounded, and
local issues dominated politics. Catholics of Australian birth did not react to Irish stimuli,
and well-to-do Irish Catholics, even those of Irish birth, acted in conformity with their
personal economic interests.

But the *Freeman's Journal* was founded on the postulate that the affairs of the colony must
be seen in an Irish context of oppression, penal laws and the like, believing itself to be at
war with a phalanx of anti-Irish forces which, when they did not oppose, carped and
sneered. It specialised in editorials and reportage on the woes of Ireland, its first editorial
loaded with phrases that became a predictable stock-in-trade: 'ill-governed', 'unprecedented misery', 'bad laws', 'the caprice and cupidity of a rapacious landlord interest'.
Whatever the accuracy of such clichés in Irish fact, in the remote antipodes they took on
the complexion of indulgent Celtic emotionalism, a national persecution complex. Ireland
seemed, to other than enthusiasts, to induce in its devotees spasms of confused and
irrelevant pomposity. Ah, Ireland, sighed James Garven in a typical gush in March 1869:
'What a deep, deep thought, poetic imaginings, hopes, fears, and aspirations did it stir up
in the breasts of every man . . .' Not so—many were quite unmoved, at least in that way.
And political realities continually contradicted the O'Connellite ideologues. From the
1843 elections onwards, colonial Irish Catholics refused to conform to the imported Irish
model. Their voting could not be directed by either clergy or nationalists: they reacted to
local issues and personalities, prompted by the ordinary range of Australian political
considerations. The Irish Catholic vote was never united, always split. Yet the self-
appointed spokesmen of Irish Catholics, through the *Freeman's Journal*, continued to insist
that this must cease, that the proper way for them to act was in unison, apart from the rest
of the community and against it, so that the serfdom of Ireland would not be duplicated in
New South Wales. Such diatribes confirmed, in the general community, a repellent image
of Irish Catholicism as selfish, obsessive, and perversely at odds with the rest of society.
Irish Catholics in Australia in the 1860s still gave the appearance of acting out a role of
reaction to persecution appropriate to the Ireland of O'Connell, and some were in fact still
doing just that, so influential had been the example of his political style.

The adoption of an O'Connellite stance was, however, not entirely self-generated. It was
encouraged by sectarian hostility and colonial attacks on O'Connell and his policies. John
Dunmore Lang, consistent with his democratic principles, favoured repeal, but he
interpreted the O'Connellite movement as confirming the proposition that 'Roman
Catholics . . . are always a compact and distinct political party whenever they come into
contact with Protestants'. This characteristic was of great menace to Australia, given his
parallel proposition that Protestants would always be divided politically and thus open to
Catholic political dominance. In 1847 Lang made clear that he regarded O'Connell as
operating a Roman Catholic dictatorship in Ireland, and that he believed that this was
threatened in Australia. In the sectarian circumstances of that time, nothing was more
likely to encourage assertive Irish Catholics to embrace O'Connellism than Lang's expression of fear of it.

Given the dominance of O'Connell, the Young Ireland revolution of 1848 made little
Australian impact, despite the eventual banishment to Tasmania of its leaders. True,

O'Connell was then dead, but his reputation was not, and in any case the minor violence of 1848 was hardly notable in the aftermath of the staggering disaster of the Famine. As to its ideological content, Young Ireland's efforts were an Irish dimension of a European movement later dubbed the revolution of the intellectuals. This character estranged it from the Australian Irish, whose 'intellectuals' were very few, and O'Connellite. For the ordinary Irish, O'Connell was the big name, and Young Ireland criticism of him did them, not him, harm; that clash had some later consequences for the colony of Victoria in forming an element in the abrasion between John O'Shanassy, O'Connellite, and Gavan Duffy, Young Irelander. In appraising the importation of Irish nationalism into Australia it is important to realise that at the popular level only the strongest personalities, and the largest and most simple ideas could survive that enormous journey: complexities, refinements, minor figures in the nationalist pantheon tended to get lost somewhere en route, melted away by the equatorial sun. In this reductionist process, popular instinct was usually sure, but it was greatly aided by what could be readily illustrated, reduced to a picture. Their very numbers worked against the Young Irelanders, though the reverberating poetry of their names—Terence Bellew McManus, William Smith O'Brien, Kevin Izod O'Doherty, and so on—helped towards a nationalist litany. But there was no substitute for pictures: they stirred the mind, focused the imagination, and formed a nationalist iconography parallel to that of popular religion. What is more, like the holy pictures, the statuettes, they proclaimed allegiance and identity. Nor are these totems remote in time: people now living can remember grandparents being moved by nationalist effigies into declamations of a melodramatic kind. Mrs Brenda Carroll of Randwick recalls her grandmother, who came to Australia about 1866, standing in front of an enormous portrait she had of Robert Emmet (it would have been about 1910) wailing, 'Oh, my poor country'. But then her grandmother also had a most terrifying picture of Moses receiving the Ten Commandments. Both items were examples of the joint iconography of nineteenth-century Irish Catholicism, tough and terrible, then without the dimensions of lachrymose sentimentality they were later to acquire. The veneration of Emmet into this century, and in pictorial form, makes an important point—the carrying of the Irish nationalist message, in a visual way, paralleled similar simple reminders in religion. In remote bush huts pictorial evocations of the Irish national tradition lived on, garish illustrations torn from books, coloured supplements from nationalist newspapers. The Dublin *Weekly Freeman* of the 1880s catered deliberately for this demand for nationalist wall art, with its large-format colour lift-out cartoons on political themes of the day. Such papers poured out of Ireland, but apparently, far short of the demand. Writing from Maitland, Michael Normile from Derry said he had lent his last home newspaper to sixty people, being eventually compelled to hide it. The next he had, at time of writing, lent to twenty. Such papers were sent sometimes as a substitute for correspondence, often to supplement it with broader local news, ideal lining for bush huts or whatever other rough accommodation their recipients had: this was wallpaper of multiple function—exclusion of draughts, casual reading, decoration, and reminder of identity. And it could be quickly varied with the next layer. Its successor in a less primitive, bourgeois, display was the mantelpiece standing framed picture, commonly in Australia—as both the popularity of the artefact and his fame coincided—of Archbishop Mannix.

The Irish nationalist portrait in Australia obviated the need for words. It was a signal from those who exhibited it to those who viewed it, which let them both know where they were: it, like the holy pictures in a Catholic house, defined the ground on which one stood,

1920·

ALDERMAN MacSWINEY,
Lord Mayor of Cork.

*Some later Irish Australian iconography: Terence MacSwiney, Lord Mayor of Cork, the famous
hunger-striker of 1920 as centrepiece of an ornamented 'holy picture'*

located one, and spared the need for exploratory inquiry or embarrassment. For some Irish, to exhibit such portraits was an aggression, but for most it was a reminder to themselves and a courtesy offered to others: in a mixed society, such pictures said to the casual caller, the visitor, the family itself, here are my sensitivities, my allegiances. O'Connell's was the favoured portrait, not only in representations, simple or ornate, for walls, but painted on shawls, the centrepiece of rosettes, and—supreme Australian example of The Liberator's admission to the ranks of sanctity—in stained glass. In the Catholic church in Boorowa, in southern New South Wales, O'Connell's likeness glows proud, haughtier than the saints who keep him company, uncrowned king of Ireland in an obscure Irish-Australian mansion of the King of Kings.

Holy nationalist pictures—and the stained-glass O'Connell has a fitting medieval peasant simplicity—were the currency of ordinary Irish folk. The better educated wanted, and were capable of sustaining, something more complex and more in touch with contemporary Ireland rather than dead heroes. A Celtic Association was formed in Sydney in 1857, and reformed in 1859, by newer middle-class migrants, those of Lyon's 'Forties Generation'. It was largely cultural in orientation and connected with the Ossianic Society in Dublin, one of the harbingers of the Gaelic revival. Its initiators saw the need to establish good relations with the older generation of Irish-Australian leaders, and to engage the interest and support of the prominent. J.H. Plunkett was president, Daniel Deniehy one of the vice-presidents: both were candidates for West Sydney in the 1859 elections. Its objects were 'to promote and sustain amongst Irishmen and their descendants in Australia, the love of fatherland', and it sought to provide reading rooms and a library, lectures and debates to that end. Discussion of religion was strictly prohibited. A subscription of £1 defined the membership as affluent middle-class. With the Celtic Association J.G. O'Connor, a committee member, began his long association with Irish causes and with printing their materials: O'Connor's capacities in the printing trade were important in facilitating the operation and publicity of Sydney Irish organisations—of which the next appears to have been the Australian-Hibernian Association of 1863. The same group were behind this, this time seeking a direct correspondence link with Ireland itself, in the person of A.M. Sullivan, editor of the *Nation* in Dublin and a leading figure in political Ireland. That contact led on to the formation of the Irish National League, a moderate repeal body associated in Ireland with John Martin of Young Ireland fame: by 1865 this body had strengthened its Australian existence to over 2000 members in several branches. Its novelty lay in its being in support of a movement in Ireland to which it sent funds, rather than an expression of local social impulse. The league's rules prohibited involvement in local political or religious matters, but various of its members moved into the arena of municipal politics, which they saw as providing experience, publicity, and some local patronage, and of course a step to higher political levels. They did not hesitate to use Irish cohesion if they thought an appeal might work: 'Men of Ireland! Vote for Hurley' enjoined an election slogan of November 1866. Local politics, in their areas of residence, was an Australian field the Irish were never to leave.

With these organisations of the late 1850s and early 1860s, the immigrant generation of the 1840s, the young men of O'Connell's Ireland, those who had been tutored in the national consciousness expressed from 1842 in the Dublin *Nation*, took the initiative in Irish Australia. They believed that the earlier Irish in Australia had neglected, indeed betrayed, the national duty, that colonial conservatism needed to be challenged on Irish issues, and that an educated and informed and moderate Irish nationalism was possible and necessary in Australia. Thus their contact with A.M. Sullivan in Dublin, a natural step for devotees of the *Nation*.

Yet by the mid-1860s, when they had scarcely found their feet as Irish Australians, developments in Ireland were rapidly leaving these constitutionalists behind. A constant danger with Irish-Australian initiatives and organisations was the obvious time-lag: no sooner had locals become fully aware of, and determined to support or imitate some Irish development, than the Irish situation changed. In fact the seeds of change had been planted in 1858 with the formation in Ireland of the secret and revolutionary Irish Republican Brotherhood which began to emerge to public attention in Ireland, England and America from 1865. By 1867 this 'Fenian' movement of Irish extremists had amassed a formidable record of terrorist achievements—dynamitings and shootings in England, an extraordinary if abortive invasion of Canada by 800 Fenians, infiltration of the British army, and eventually an insurrection in Ireland in March 1867—which not so much electrified colonial attention as kept it in a constant state of incipient panic: it might happen here, warned the *Herald* in Sydney; Melbourne went on to virtual military alert in March 1868.

But before this had happened local developments had occurred which gave overseas events apparent Australian point. In December 1866, Richard O'Sullivan, younger brother to A.M. Sullivan, became editor of the Sydney *Freeman's Journal*. A fierce Irish nationalist, O'Sullivan's sympathies were with the Fenians, if not with their violent methods. He used their activities to launch his own brand of anti-British assault, stinging, vituperative sallies which soon enraged loyalists to heights of denunciatory fury in which not only O'Sullivan but the whole Irish community were branded Fenians, disloyal Irish revolutionary plotters. O'Sullivan's anti-British tirades were bad enough, but loyalists also had an Irish organisation they could accuse of local plotting, of being a front for Fenianism. In 1866 some Irish community leaders, J.G. O'Connor foremost among them, had set up a State Prisoners' Fund to make local collections to assist the families of Fenian leaders arrested in Ireland. This split the local Irish. The fund's initiators were not sympathetic to Fenianism: they held that there was a duty in charity to act as they did. The Irish National League, however, bowing to a public opinion coming to see anything Irish as Fenian, believed this imprudent and refused to support the fund. The fund organisers condemned this as cowardice, and denounced the league for betraying the Irish cause. It was a deep and enduring rift from which the Irish cause in Australia might be said never to have recovered. Coming so early in the history of such organisations, among such a small group of enthusiasts, involving such basic questions of loyalty, and eliciting such personal charges and recriminations, it was destructive to the extent of inducing paralysis. Particularly in the context of what was about to happen, the effect of the Fenian scare was that Australian Irishism fell apart.

News of Fenian terrorism in England filled the Australian newspapers from November 1867 to January 1868. Those caught were executed—the 'Manchester Martyrs', judicially murdered, said Irish opinion; and also the *Freeman's Journal*. Rumours of Fenian activity were rife in Sydney. Any Irish gathering was suspect: pubs were reputed hotbeds of terrorism. And all this was in the air as the first royal tour, by Prince Alfred, Duke of Edinburgh, got under way in December in Melbourne to a frenzy of colonial patriotism.

On 12 March the Prince, at a picnic at Clontarf on Sydney Harbour, was shot and wounded by Henry James O'Farrell. O'Farrell claimed to be a Fenian. It is most unlikely that he was. Irish-born, he had been brought to Australia as a child of six. Well educated, at one stage he had studied for the priesthood, but at the time of the attempted assassination he was probably insane, as his defence maintained, certainly with a history of illness and instability, of drinking and mental unbalance, of addiction to fantasies. Far from being a dedicated and formidable terrorist, O'Farrell—shorn of the hysteria of the time—seems a sad, disturbed person, a figure of pathos.

He was quickly executed, but his act unleashed an explosion of anti-Irish hate hardly less terrifying and much more sustained than his brief violence: 'Fenian scare' is hardly adequate phraseology to describe the ugly and protracted farce that followed. The Premier, James Martin (closet-Irish himself) made clear his conviction that here was a deliberate and well-

Henry James O'Farrell in Darlinghurst Gaol, 1868
National Library of Australia

organised plot involving an Irish revolutionary organisation. Evidence of this would certainly be found. Despite intensive police efforts, it was not. The Colonial Secretary, Henry Parkes, was even more certain. Parkes claimed to be in daily fear of his life—the police force itself, being Irish, was suspect. He reported to the New South Wales Governor that the main source of the Fenian contagion were 'Americanised Irishmen' coming into Australia from unsettled gold-rush California, together with the new Irish emigration which had taken advantage of the assisted passage system. He told the Governor that it was 'no uncommon thing to hear of persons of this class who openly boast that the time is not far distant when they will possess the government of the country'. And Parkes, caught by the momentum of career possibilities as the unmasker of deeper Irish horrors, was to go even further in unsupported absurdities to make himself the reviled of the Irish at a time and in circumstances which had disastrous effects on the formulation of education policy.

With politicians fanning the flames, public anti-Irish zeal was at white heat. Senior (non-Irish) police wanted to get a gunboat to blow up Irish houses, and to boil down all priests. J.D. Lang maintained that O'Farrell's pre-execution denial of any Fenian connection was a priestly plot. Non-Catholic Irish clergy, such as Reverend Zacariah Barry, felt compelled by their nationality to outdo all others in loyal protestations and expressions of outrage: to him the *Freeman's Journal* was treason protected by the guise of religion. And parliament's zeal in passing an emergency Treason Felony Act, drastically suspending civil rights and prohibiting 'language disrespectful to the sovereign' was supported by police and public in seeking out such wrongdoers. More than fifty persons were so charged. All were drunk, or claimed to be so, at the time of the offences. They were alleged to have said such things as 'there was no more harm in shooting the bloody Prince than a black fellow' (a truism probably lost on the courts of the day), or 'up with the green, the Prince will play hell with us'. Anti-Irish fantasies abounded particularly in relation to gold diggings where the Irish were numerous. All of this, hate-filled, persecuting, ugly as it was, was too much for wags, yahoos and frustrated Irish actors keen to fill their expected roles. At the Marengo Races on St Patrick's Day 1868 a noisy crowd of drunken diggers ended the day dancing on the road, roaring at the terrified townspeople: 'We're bloody Fenians! Come on! We'd soon kill a man as look at him.'

The amusing aspects of the situation were discernible only in retrospect: at the time the air was electric with fear and venom. In 1869 in his *Letters from Australia*, John Martineau reflected the then establishment view of the Irish. He reported that great efforts had been made some years ago to swamp New South Wales with Irish migrants to make it a Catholic colony. There was no chance of this happening now, 'but there is an element of disturbance and lawlessness in their separate and sectarian organisation which in critical times might be dangerous, and is at all times injurious to political morality'. Catholic priests were said to be not very strict about a man's morality or how often or seldom he went to Mass or confessed: all the priest wanted was his money and for him to vote as told. A squatter had told him (Martineau) that the maidservants in his house up country were assessed as high as ten shillings for church subscriptions: it was 'voluntary' but in fact compulsory. These people voted as instructed by ecclesiastical authority, a process beyond state control but with serious political results. The priests preached Fenianism. And there was their hero, Gavan Duffy, a criminal who, on emigrating to Melbourne had been given several thousand pounds, to which he had responded by declaring he would always be a rebel to the backbone. Now he was wealthy, with an ill-deserved pension, and would like to forget his dedication to ceaseless rebellion.

The leaders of the Australian Irish quailed in the face of these blasts of hostile mythology. The older and more established went to earth. Those who remained standing for Irish causes, mixed caution and defiance and fell out among themselves. The St Patrick's Day regatta committee of March 1868 fell apart. Some resigned. Others attacked them for cowardice. Then others walked out in disgust, angry that those who remained should be deemed 'Fenians'. Some attempted to escape charges of disloyalty by branding others as disloyal—the league, the *Freeman's Journal*. The *Freeman's* went quiet, then plucked up its courage and began a counter-attack on Parkes, claiming that the Fenian scare was of his manufacture. The Irish community persisted in tearing itself apart: every sign from the overwhelming majority that they wished to disassociate themselves from disloyalty and sedition was greeted by the minority with charges of treachery to Ireland, cowardice and betrayal of origins.

Perhaps this phase of internecine strife would have been brief had the Fenian issue subsided, but it was protracted and regularly refuelled by the action of the British government in sending Fenian prisoners to Western Australia and releasing groups of them over the following ten years. The initial landing, in January 1868, of the sixty-two Irish political prisoners among the 279 convicts aboard the *Hougoumont*, caused a local Fenian scare and gave Fenianism a direct Australian reference. John Boyle O'Reilly escaped from a road gang in February 1869, eventually reaching America—sensational events. Then from May 1869, the British government decided to pardon and release thirty-four of the Fenian prisoners. It released more in 1871, still others in 1876, and the last in 1878. And in April 1876 the American whaler *Catalpa* had snatched six prisoners from captivity in a highly spectacular rescue which took them to America. All this kept Fenianism before the public eye—and on the conscience of the Australian Irish. It would not go away as a nationalist issue, nor would cease its divisive effects on the local Irish, particularly as, while the British government was prepared to release Fenian prisoners in Western Australia, it would not assist them to leave that colony: the British were happiest with Fenians kept far away, though Fenians at local large might be the stuff of colonial nightmares.

Faced with a situation in which Fenians freed in Western Australia wished to return to Ireland but lacked the means, the *Freeman's Journal* set up a fund to help them do so. Public hostility was predictable. So was that of members of the Irish community who objected that such action was provocative just when community antagonism to the Irish was simmering down. What was surprising was the support for the fund. The wealthy would not give, but £1500 was given by over 4000 subscribers, mainly small men in country areas: they were more concerned to stand up and be Irish than placate community hostility. The Fenian scare had scared some Irish, but others it had firmed into resentment of unjust charges and into determination that when the cock crowed, they would not deny. (As to the numbers of actual 'Fenians', who can say of an oath-bound secret society? In 1857, when the American headquarters reviewed its potential Australasian support, it came up with the fantastical number of 7000, based hopefully on the number of subscribers to the various Fenian assistance funds. But these were not 'Fenians' in any meaningful way and any informed guess at an Australian dimension of actual oath-bound membership might be nearer seven than even seventy, whatever the thousands who evinced some degree of sympathy.)

The voyage of the Fenians thus assisted from Western Australia kept the Irish pot boiling. At first prohibited from landing in terror-stricken Melbourne, they journeyed on to freer Sydney, where O'Sullivan of the *Freeman's Journal* had organised a delicious piece of anti-loyalist provocation—a picnic of welcome at Clontarf, scene of the royal assassination attempt of the previous year. The government threatened to prohibit this, and under Catholic presssure it was cancelled, to O'Sullivan's rage. This time he put his frustration to practical point by departing for California, no doubt in the hope of finding some real Irishmen there. Thereafter the *Freeman's* was much milder. But there were 'real' Irishmen, in O'Sullivan's aggressive sense, in Australia: it was just that they seldom appeared above the respectable surface. There was a glimpse of them during the December 1869 election. At the goldfields town of Araluen in the Braidwood electorate, Irish diggers took over the polling booths in support of the Irishman Michael Kelly, and they excluded any voters who did not meet their approval: Kelly supported public schools and could not be seen as a Catholic candidate, so support for him was racial, not religious. The following day troopers policed the booths, but the diggers controlled the surrounding roads and waylaid and intimidated voters there. As a result the election was declared invalid and a new poll held in October 1870. On that occasion the anti-Irish had organised. A group of 400 was stopped and relieved of revolvers by the police. Otherwise the poll went quietly.

By 1871 the simmering animus had cooled to the degree where it was possible to sublimate it in a sporting encounter. In March 1871 a prize fight was held between Larry Foley, one of the most famous of nineteenth-century Australian pugilists, and Sandy Ross. Foley championed the Green, Ross, who had militant Protestant associations as a meetings bouncer, represented the Orange. The police intervened before a final outcome, but the Green claimed the day, while the Orange—or at least the leadership of an Orange Lodge anxious to emanate respectability—bemoaned this vulgar display. Persistent enthusiasts eventually circumvented the respectable inclinations of their leaders to contrive a re-match in 1875. Foley won, and the moral thereof was variously interpreted. In fact, though the 1870s reverberated with threats and scares centred on the Irish, particularly in relation to 17 March and 12 July, there was very little actual violence. Recollections of Hill End goldfield suggest some ritualised Orange–Green clashes of a kind similar to Irish faction fights. After their 12 July march, Orangemen were wont, it is said, to leave their families at the sports to come into town to drink—and brawl with the Irish Catholics who had also come to town for the occasion. The belligerents would adjourn to their families for tea and resume fighting in the evening. A variety of this colourful country custom is enshrined in Victor Daley's 'The Glorious Twelfth at Jindabyne' first published in 1898, which details such a contrived and friendly fight, with punches pulled, and underpinned by a common Irishness cemented by proximity and intermarriage—diluted too by the unwillingness of Australian-born children, although familiar to the point of boredom with the conflicting Irish legendry and history, to see any meaning in the imported enmities. Such balladry makes real, historical points of consequence. On the level of more polite social contact, in some country districts Orange or Green occasions served ecumenical purposes in places short of people and starved of entertainment. Stylised exchanges of Orange–Green animus could even be a diversion in the wilderness for those involved, if not for observers. 'Tom Collins' (Joseph Furphy) recounts in *Such is Life* (1903): 'Now there was just one man within a hundred miles who knew less of Irish history than Martin, and that man was Moriarty; consequently the two jostled each other as they rushed into that branch of learning where scholars fear to tread – each repeatedly appealing to me for confirmation of his outlandish myths and clumsy fabrications'.

The cities were another matter. And the Irish Fenians, upon release, contained elements both radical and irreconcilable. One of them, John Flood, established a radical newspaper in Sydney, the Irish *Citizen*, which existed briefly in 1871–72: he employed some of his released fellow prisoners. This was far too nationalist for the local Irish. Edward Butler described this extremist element to Parkes as 'an uninfluencial rabble'. They were hardly a rabble, in that their education and attainments were generally superior to those of the Australian Irish they encountered, but they were certainly uninfluential. Why is evident in a letter from one of them, J. Edward Kelly, to O'Donovan Rossa, the Fenian leader. Recalling the 1871 situation in Sydney, Kelly observed: 'Irish nationality stinks in the nostrils of the "respectable" community, but they glory in being Catholic and loyal to their Queen.' He was contemptuous of Sydney's major Irish society, the Hibernians, which he saw as toadying to the English, as weak, Catholic, and not truly Irish. As a Protestant, Kelly found the stifling clericalism and Catholic exclusivity of the Australian Irish offensive and unnational.

Quickly disgusted by the Irish condition in Sydney, Kelly, Flood, Michael Cody, and other released Fenians went mining, first gold, then tin: Flood went north to Queensland. They agreed, together with John King, who had left Ireland voluntarily after the collapse of the Fenian movement, to establish the Irish Republican Brotherhood in Australia, with Sydney as headquarters, but having its main strength in the goldfields in New South Wales and Queensland. This decision had two aspects of practicality; these goldfields were where the released Fenians would be located, and such Irish diggers had always demonstrated a radicalism well beyond that of the city respectables. But against this, the Fenians viewed Australia as a mine, a place for fortune-hunting, and all except Flood and Cody were anxious to leave it behind for the real world, America. Nevertheless, as they were in Australia, they felt some responsibility to leave behind a Fenian organisation which 'can be of some assistance', as Kelly put it to Rossa. The idea was that Australia become part of an international IRB Revolutionary Directory based in America. In practice this reduced itself down to one man, Michael Cody, and soon even that was reduced 'by communication difficulties' to a dead letter.

Perhaps these dedicated Fenian fire-eaters were wise to leave Australia: those who stayed caught the contagion of respectability. Or was it that they discerned they had no quarrel here? John Flood, Jesuit-educated in Ireland, a linguist, with experience in law and in his father's shipping trade, had been head of the IRB in England and Ireland in 1867. In Australia, after prospecting on the Palmer River, he settled in Queensland, first in Cooktown, then in Gympie where he was a successful mining secretary, sharebroker, insurance agent, and proprietor of the *Gympie Miner*. Quiet, reserved, comfortably settled in middle-class respectability, Flood nevertheless remained active in Irish affairs, founding branches of the Irish Land League, and, in 1888, the Queensland Irish Volunteer Corps, commanding the Gympie company. Taxed with wearing the Queen's uniform, Flood replied: 'I was never a disloyalist. If we had the Government in Ireland we have here I would have been wearing the Queen's uniform all my life.' This was a common Australian Irish response to such questions about consistency and about symbols of British imperial rule, but it was not the only local Irish reaction when faced by a question of donning the Queen's colours. Phil Mahony was not a Fenian, but he had 'marched many a mile in procession' for the Manchester Martyrs in the Ireland of 1867. Writing from Footscray in Melbourne in 1887, he too was a great believer in Australian freedom being applied to Ireland, but his reaction to the Queen's colours was very different from Flood's. When he was working for the Melbourne Harbour Trust, the Russian invasion scare resulted in an ultimatum to workers to join the reserve forces or be dismissed: 'I pitched the Queen & all her followers to Hell & left. Of course I was called a dynamitard but what did I care. I was & is still thinking that considering the cruel manner in which poor old Ireland is used no Irishman should be so mean as to assist Queen Victoria in any shape or form . . .' Perhaps Mahony might not have been quite so sure of his ground had he not acquired what he regarded as a better job, by which he meant easier physically—a yardsman counting cattle in the Melbourne cattle market. But his attitude was more in keeping with the popular conception of the Fenian spirit, irreconcilable, uncompromising, defiant, than was Flood's reasoning adjustment to a different environment.

The bold Fenian men soon marched (or rather, sailed) out of Australian history, America-bound. The rescue of six of them, at Easter 1876, by the American whaler, *Catalpa* was an adventure story of splendid dash. Organised from America, costing $25 000, involving preorganisation in Fremantle by spies in disguise, escape in an open boat, a chase at sea by a gunboat, bickering among those rescued, a happy ending in a delirious Boston—this was all too exciting, too heady, for sober Irish-Australian imaginations to absorb: this brilliant escapade dropped out of Australian history, even Australian Irish history, for a century. With the humdrum, Australians could cope, those who had laid down their Fenian banners in Australia. In 1904 a West Australian committee was formed to assist two of the remaining Fenian ex-prisoners: one, aged eighty-two, was in a destitute men's home, the other, aged seventy-six, was living in a tent. Two others were still alive, but did not need such assistance. A national appeal was launched. In total keeping with the Australian reception of Fenianism from its beginning, the appeal never met its target. Further in keeping, William Redmond as emissary of Home Rule met the two old men in 1905: he hailed them as patriots and claimed that their advocacy of physical force was the prelude to the success of Home Rule. John Redmond's son William seemed rather more at home in 1911 when he unveiled, in front of a distinguished gathering, the impressive green granite cross that had been erected over the grave of John Flood.

Fenianism was too strong a meat for the average Irish-Australian stomach. They had come to Australia, convict or free, in peril of the deep, praying for God's protection and mercy, and for His care of their loved ones. The Fenians were made of different, sterner stuff. On their convict ship in 1867 they recited communal prayers, not for deliverance, nor for fortitude in adversity, not indeed for anything personal at all. No, they prayed to the God who was the arbiter of the destinies of nations, to look down on the sufferings of their poor country, to scatter and confound its enemies, and to send help to Ireland, from His holy place.

The Fenians gone, or almost so, by 1873, the locals settled back into their own more cautious affairs. These were not without their tensions. As they had in Melbourne in 1872, the newly formed Hibernians were flexing their muscles in regard to St Patrick's Day; claiming that no one else was interested they said they would take over its organisation. J.G. O'Connor, who was eventually to claim a record forty years as organiser, protested that the usual committee would act. An uneasy tandem resulted, clarified in 1874 into the old committee holding a banquet in the evening and the Hibernians holding a picnic in the day. The future lay with the Hibernians, who represented a more Catholic, and a less socially pretentious initiative. The Irish organisations of the 1860s had not been utterly Catholic preserves, and had combined a degree of openness with a modicum of social climbing: banquets and regattas were genteel-sounding occasions, whereas picnic or sports had a decidedly plebeian ring. From the mid-seventies picnic and sports became the St

St Patrick's Day in the new land: a somewhat unflattering sketch from the 1880s

Patrick's Day thing—Mass in the morning, sports and picnic during the day, drum-beating Irish concert in the evening. These were popular occasions and the Irish elite avoided them.

The celebration of the O'Connell centenary in 1875 could not be avoided, since the Irish internationally were to be involved. But Australian preparations had an air of caution and reluctance. It was an unpropitious time for anything Irish. There was the whole Fenian imbroglio, still bubbling, the aftermath of the royal assassination attempt, the recent collapse of the 1871–72 Victorian government of Charles Gavan Duffy in a storm of anti-Irish and sectarian abuse and controversy, and in every State there was conflict between the governments and the Catholic Church over the nature and control of education. The choice faced by the leaders of the Australian Irish was one between being shamed into celebrations or being shamed out of them.

But the real question, which soon surfaced, was: was O'Connell relevant to Australia at all? And that question was coming from within the Australian Irish community, not only from outside it. Enthusiasts for O'Connell celebrations took the view that these would allow the demonstration of a dual affirmation of nationality, Irish and Australian, what they regarded as the amalgam of their future. But they soon found that they had grossly underestimated the narrowly Australian and virtually anti-Irish balance of that mixture as it had developed in their own community: the effect of the anti-Irish focus of the dissensions of the previous decade had been to convince many Catholics that their Catholicism was burden and liability enough without adding an unnecessary and totally extraneous commitment to Ireland. This was the colonial frame of mind revealed by efforts to organise fitting commemorations. In Brisbane, an initial meeting to arrange an O'Connell centenary celebration passed an amendment not to proceed: 'That it is inexpedient in this dependency, the nation cherishing the memory of many of its illustrious sons, to single out for honour by a public demonstration, one whose fame principally rests on services rendered in particular to the Church in Ireland.' The terms of this amendment made clear that O'Connell was not only deemed an Australian irrelevance, but that his image had shrunk, under clerical patronage, to that of a mere servant of the Irish Catholic Church. A Brisbane celebration was in fact held, at which the main speakers were the 1848 transportee, Kevin Izod O'Doherty, and Bishop James Quinn, but O'Doherty took pains to conciliate those within his own community opposed to the celebration; that is, 'those sons and daughters of Australia who consider that their National sentiment is, as it were, slighted by demonstrations of this kind, believing that they sow the seeds of dissension in our young community. They are jealous of their Australian dignity, which they consider compromised by celebration of men and events which have no direct connection with their native land'. However, Bishop Quinn's enthusiasm was lyrical and unqualified. He 'took back his respected ancestral name' adding thereafter an 'O' to his surname. For O'Quinn, O'Connell's principles were sanctified, for he had possessed the confidence of the Irish hierarchy.

O'Quinn's total commitment to his clericalised version of O'Connell is one of the many illustrations of the gap between an Irish clergy and an Australian laity on matters to do with Ireland. Within the Catholic Church the Irishness of the clergy was indulged with tolerance even affection, by a laity accustomed to this curious behaviour: this generous tolerance and wish to please was often mistaken for enthusiasm and shared feelings by a clergy often less than sensitive to loyalties other than their own. Outside the Church the laity had other criteria by which to judge what was polite: both in Sydney and Melbourne organisers of the O'Connell centenary celebrations made strenuous efforts to avoid alienating the general community or dividing Catholics. Dr Badham of Sydney University was commissioned to write a suitable commemoration cantata (Hail, mighty Orator! hail, wise Defender!). In Sydney, the English Benedictine coadjutor archbishop, Roger Vaughan, was invited to give the celebratory oration, although the organisers might have chosen any one of the several Irish bishops appointed to New South Wales dioceses since 1865. Their choice of the English Vaughan reflected their wish, just as strong in other Australian colonies, to put forward O'Connell not merely as an Irish nationalist, but as a benefactor of mankind—which is precisely what Vaughan did. His treatment of O'Connell's gifts—those of fusing loyalty with liberty—and of England's relationship with Ireland—the inclination to grant freedom and fair play flawed and frustrated by occasional tyrants and bigots—struck just the balance sought by most Irish Australians. And Vaughan emphasised O'Connell's non-Irish concerns—electoral and parliamentary reform, free trade, the emancipation of Jews, anti-slavery, the rights of man generally. O'Shanassy in Melbourne, Sir George Kingston in Adelaide, and speakers in Perth, placed similar stress on O'Connell's services to human freedom.

The celebrations were not a success. Most of the speakers at the celebrations throughout

Australia had either known O'Connell personally, or had, at least, attended his meetings in their youth. The audiences were something of the same narrowly Irish-born complexion. When J.G. O'Connor rose to speak at the Sydney commemoration, he remarked that 'he was sorry to see so few persons around him who could claim Australia as the land of their birth'. W.H. Cooper, the Australian who rose to respond to O'Connor, made a passionate plea for Australian nationalism which implicitly rejected such Irish celebrations as both irrelevant and divisive:

> There was too much faction in this country. There was no pure national sentiment. There was no general instinct of patriotism giving vigour to the national heart ... the capture of Limerick was made a red letter day, but the date of Cook's landing had slipped out of the calendar ... we had no O'Connell here to oppose his divine eloquence and dauntless heart against the wiles of schismatics among us, and therefore it the more behoved every man who wished this country to rise to the status of a great nation to aid in the destruction of these factions ...

The reaction of Catholics to the celebrations was not markedly different from that of the general community—a few in cautious praise, some in condemnation, most apathetic. In Sydney the proceeds from the celebrations were to be devoted to a scholarship at St John's College of the University of Sydney. £1500 was required; only £44 was raised. In Melbourne, O'Connell was to have a statue, costing £3000. That project also fell short of target, though the statue was eventually erected in 1891, not, as was hoped, in some commanding public place, but in the grounds of St Patrick's Catholic Cathedral: the situation symbolised the firm location of O'Connell's image within the official Catholic fold. The celebrations also revealed the great distance in understanding and divergence of temper that separated the Irish in Australia from their homeland. The Irish in Victoria had deputed Charles Gavan Duffy to represent them at the Dublin celebrations, but an audience hostile to Duffy because of his conflicts with O'Connell in the 1840s refused to allow him to be heard. This was painful and bewildering to the colonial Irish. During his Australian career, Duffy had become 'the O'Connell of the South': the divisions, distinctions, and enmities of internal Irish politics had become, to most Irish in the antipodes, both incomprehensible and repellent.

Of course that reaction was that of those who took the time and trouble to look, and in the mid-1870s an even stronger drift in Irish Australia was away from any interest in Ireland at all. Those who marched in the Sydney streets in 1875 to commemorate O'Connell wore green rosettes—and blue for Australia. If they could have maintained that dual personality they would have been happy, but the public and parliamentary protests against their marching, as being in breach of the Party Processions Act, made it clear that many regarded such Irish-Australian personalities as split, not dual, a community disorder which must be treated, suppressed, purged, by a choice—one or the other. If such a choice could have been enforced in the late 1870s most would have relinquished their Irishness readily enough as an irrelevant liability, as sentiment for a land now distanced and made strange to them by the violence of Fenianism: the sentiment of the exile did not sit well in the factious, troubled Ireland of the 1870s; that Ireland was too real, drab, and too petty to command allegiance and affection.

Eighteen seventy-nine to eighty saw that situation change. Just when the affairs of Ireland and those of Australia seemed about to drift permanently apart, events and developments occurred which drew Irish Australians back into Ireland's orbit, allowed them to identify

The archetypal Irish-Australian St Patrick's Day float, with emu and kangaroo. Hibernians in the Maitland NSW showground in the 1930s
Hibernian Society, Sydney

with Ireland's destinies, and reinvalidated the claim to dual Irish-Australian allegiance. This reinvolvement process centred on the Land War and the growing power of the Irish Parliamentary Party in the cause of Home Rule, but its fundamental Australian appeal lay in the ability of these things to capture the imagination, idealism and self-interest of Irish Australia.

Irish Australia's vision of Ireland was of a very particular kind, strongly historical and rigorously idealistic. Essentially it was not an involvement in Ireland's contemporary life, but rather an identification with past glories, particularly its reputation as an island of saints and scholars in the days before the British came. This emphasis was built in to every aspect of Irish Australian culture. As Tobin remarks of such Irish aspects as there were of the Catholic education system: 'Whereas public school children learned that they were heirs to a tradition of invincible English superiority, catholics learned that their forefathers had suffered under the English yoke and while public school children were learning that they lived in a golden age, at the apex of human progress, the children of catholic schools were told that the golden age had been a thousand years ago, when Ireland was at the height of her glory.' This same backwards look was evident in the paraphernalia of St Patrick's Day processions—floats, banners and the like—in the emblems on the embroidered scarves of Hibernians, in pageants and tableaux, (such as that in Melbourne in 1903 to celebrate the centenary of Robert Emmet), in stories and poetry: all were crammed full of round towers, celtic crosses, heroic Irish kings, every trapping of a remote past. It is an emphasis easily explicable. It expressed a desire to avoid, in a British dominion, contentious and divisive contemporary Irish affairs while at the same time asserting the claims of the Irish to civilisation: it was important for the Irish in Australia to assert that despite whatever were the present appearances of inferiority, they came from a rich cultural tradition which had once preserved, in the Dark Ages, the Christian civilisation of Europe. This not only established their past credentials but their present claims to make a contribution to an evolving Australian civilisation. The backward look was common in Ireland itself, but there it had to contend with the pressure of an insistent present which kept breaking through the moods of contemplative romance with rough reality: in distant Australia the Irish past could be more easily maintained. And the impulse to do so was strongly linked with a conception of Ireland as the home of goodness, truth and beauty. Melbourne Irish nationalist, the Australian-born Dr Nicholas O'Donnell, put this well in word and mood when he burst out in 1908: 'I wish my descendants to know and *feel* that though Australians by birth and fealty, they are Irish in blood and have not a drop of English blood in their veins. I wish

St Patrick's Day Adelaide 1915: the girls of the Dominican Convent, Franklin St. in the typical Irish historical context
Adelaide Catholic Archives

them also to be unflinching in their fidelity to the catholic faith. It ought to be part of their nature like their nationality. Because they are Irish they ought to be proud to be catholic, and they ought to be truly catholic because they were Irish.' Non-Catholic Irish in Australia could be no less convinced of this aura of true worth which emanated from things Irish. Justice Henry Bournes Higgins based his then vast (£20 000) bequest to the Royal Irish Academy on his 1927 conviction, as expressed to George Russell, that 'such glimpses as I have had into Celtic literature convince me that it has some unique value—spiritual value'. This sense of the spiritual seemed purer and more intense the farther back one went into the Irish past, which is why the Australian Irish were happiest there, and least happy with those phases in contemporary Irish history where heroism, nobility, ideals, principles, virtue, were buried by violence, factions, mean grubbiness generally, and lack of national direction. So seemed the 1870s. But in 1880 emerged a new glory, the pursuit of Home Rule, the drama of Ireland on world centre stage, powerful and active, with a new hero figure, Parnell.

It was another facet of the Irish-Australian spirit which first responded to things Irish in 1880—generosity to kin. The appearance of famine in the south and west of Ireland seemed to prefigure a disaster as great as that of 1845. By the end of the year Australia had contributed the then staggering sum of £95 000 towards the relief of distress: in ratio to population Australian gifts exceeded all others. Brisbane, with a then population of 20 000, gave £10 000. The tiny mining town of Charters Towers, crammed with Irish diggers, raised £1000. But it was not only the Irish in Australia who gave, but the general community, and the appeal had support at the highest level. Lord Augustus Loftus was the New South Wales chairman: that State sent £25 000. West Australia could not resist blending its generosity with a little self-interested practicality. Its committee hoped that some of the funds would be used to assist migration: Western Australia was desperate for all types of servants, farming and domestic, those unafraid of hard work. (But the appeal chairman's tribute to Irish industry was hardly a model of tact: 'Some of the best servants I ever had were Irishmen who came out as convicts, but few of them did much good—spent the savings of years in the public house.')

The effect of this generosity was immediate and practical: it 'saved the famishing Irish peasants at the most critical moment of the year', declared the Dublin Fund committee. This 'magic shower of gold' from Australia was astonishing. £62 000 had arrived before the Dublin committee knew whom to thank, and the Australian gifts (£94 916) were more than half the total: there was only £26 875 from America.

All this was immensely gratifying to the Australian Irish: they had outshone America, had made a real impact on a situation which threatened starvation, and taken their fellow Australians with them in common cause, a warming achievement after years of dissension. True, the Catholic Church had provided the initial stimulus and basic organisation for much of this massive fund-raising enterprise, but this was because no other widespread organisation existed among the colonial Irish, and in any case the public response was much wider than the confines of that church.

Irish starvation is what attracted initial Australian Irish attention in 1879–80, but this soon widened to the Irish context of Land War and Irish Parliamentary Party activity in which this misery was set. The Land War amounted to a concerted and organised (by the Irish Land League) peasant refusal to pay rents, to which landlords responded with mass evictions: the aim of the increasingly large and powerful Irish Parliamentary Party in the British Parliament, under its new and charismatic leader, Charles Stuart Parnell, was to achieve Home Rule, that is self-government for Ireland within the British Empire. Compassion was the first Australian reaction, the instinctive compulsion to make some open and tangible declaration of where the sympathies of the Australian Irish lay—with Irish suffering, but not necessarily with Irish political aspirations and certainly not with Irish violence. Besides, from the so-called 'New Departure' of 1879, which linked the politicians and the peasants, an alliance between the Irish Parliamentary Party and the Land League, Ireland entered a period of highly dramatic events which aroused continuing international publicity and attention. This was in contrast to the dullness of Australian doings and had both appeal and relevance for the Australian Irish, both high and low. The appeal lay in the way in which Irish affairs had expanded and grown to again fill the heroic mould the Australian Irish expected and needed of them. The relevance was at two levels. The struggle of Irish peasants for land was quick to elicit widespread interest and sympathy among the lower orders of the Australian Irish, not only because so many of them could identify instantly with it, coming from that very peasant class and now farmers in Australia, but because the battlegrounds were painfully familiar. The Land War was being fought most bitterly in the very localities from which they had themselves come. The city workers in Sydney or Melbourne were no less moved. Their origins were the same, and their circumstances encouraged identification with radical protest. At the other end of the Irish-Australian social scale, the Home Rule movement had obvious appeal. It had a constitutional and parliamentary basis, postulated an Ireland which would be an integral and contented part of the British Empire, and offered a cause in which the respectable and successful Irish could achieve their ambition to be public men, cutting big figures in their own Irish world, and participating in the manoeuvres of nations.

Deep interest did not necessarily imply or generate immediate commitment. Acquiring reliable Irish information was a slow, uncertain, and confusing process. Irish-Australian opinion wisely distrusted the Irish news cabled by British agencies to the Australian daily press. It relied more on extracts from Irish papers culled by the Catholic weekly press. But these accounts, arriving by sea-mail, were never less than a month old, often represented a bewildering variety of Irish opinion impossible for distant readers to appraise, and had frequently been overtaken and rendered outdated by subsequent cable news. The natural reaction to this was suspension of judgement indefinitely and caution meanwhile, a disposition which accorded with colonial Irish inclinations generally. So a (unfounded) rumour in 1880 that Parnell might tour the colonies found little favour with the Melbourne *Advocate* which saw this as potentially controversial, offensive to the majority of Australians. In contrast to the Famine Relief Fund of 1880, the Parnell Defence Fund of 1881 (Parnell and other members had been charged under Coercion Acts) met a poor response. Parnellism had connotations of anarchy and influential Irish Australians had no intention of appearing to condone this. For instance, Sir John O'Shanassy, so prominent in the famine relief fund, would have no truck with an Irish movement reputedly violent, anarchic, or destructive of property. Nor would clerics, who, by 1881, were much exercised, following their Irish counterparts, with the question of the morality of the Land War.

So, when the movement to support Parnell broadened in 1881 into a campaign to establish Australian branches of the Land League, the initial support was short on 'leading Irishmen', long on 'men and women of the labouring classes.' Save, that is, for the usual super-Irish enthusiasts: according to Michael Davitt the first branch of the Land League in Australia was formed in Gympie by Rev. Matthew Horan in 1880, a branch which, in October 1882 took the unusual (for Australia) step of criticising the Vatican condemnation

Sydney Irish Australia takes John Walshe for an outing in 1881. In the driving seat Mr McGough and Eugene Ryan, standing from left, Dr O'Donnell, J. Woods, J.G. O'Connor, unknown, and J.W. Walshe

of Land War tactics. And the formation of the Melbourne branch in January 1881 saw the emergence of Joseph Winter, proprietor of the *Advocate*, into prominence as an organiser. The Winter brothers, Samuel and Joseph, were key figures in the Irish world of Melbourne from the 1870s. Like O'Connor in Sydney, they were printers—and editors—and their role in providing facilities to propagandise Irish causes was vital. To this Joseph added basic organisational work as treasurer or secretary for the various appeals and societies of the seventies and eighties. But the division growing in Australia was probably as much one of generation as of class: older migrants had lost touch with Ireland to the degree of finding the Parnell phenomenon and the swing to peasant militancy incomprehensible.

This problem of losing touch with Ireland was about to be remedied in ways which would alter the temper and character of Irish Australia. In August 1881 there arrived in Australia the first in a procession of Irish agitators and politicians who were to explain the Irish situation to Australian audiences, enlist their financial support, and give them a sense of involvement in Irish affairs they had lacked before. This first emissary was John W. Walshe, one of the organisers of the Irishtown meeting of April 1879 which led to the 'New Departure'. There is some doubt whether Walshe, a commercial traveller, came to Australia for his health, or in response to Australian requests for some properly authorised envoy. Certainly J.G. O'Connor had written to Parnell late in 1880 to express approval of his cause, and Parnell had replied courteously. And despite all that was to happen, O'Connor was to retain his admiration for Parnell: to Parnell's 1881 letter he later attached a sprig of shamrock from the dead hero's grave. (But then O'Connor, like so many Australian Irish, treasured all dead or retired Irish patriots: he also kept an ivy leaf from the house of the Fenian chief, James Stephens, picked in 1892. As his biographer noted of him, the watchword of O'Connor's public career was 'Defence not Defiance'. A good man, he was prone to generosity and kindness rather than confrontation: he gave gifts of tobacco, in his cheery parlance 'the chosen leaf of Bard and Chief'.) Whatever the prompting—perhaps the resources evident in the astonishing generosity of the Australian contributions to the 1880 famine fund had registered in Irish political minds—Walshe's objective was to make collections and encourage formation of branches of the Land League. He also established Fanny Parnell's Ladies' Land League in Sydney. It collected nearly £1000. Walshe's two sisters had been associated with the Ladies' League in Ireland: on emigrating to Australia in 1884 they had been welcomed by the Sydney Irish as 'pure souled warm hearted Irish girls', 'accomplished and delicate Patriots', proof that '. . . the same spirit of Patriotism which fires the souls of her men animates the tender bosoms of her women!' Walshe's mission was successful. He often received clerical support, such as that of Bishop Lanigan of Goulburn. So warm was his reception that Walshe decided to stay in Sydney permanently. He married, and eventually owned a hotel. But his activities in Irish nationalist causes gradually fell sad victim to alcohol, and he returned to Ireland to die in obscurity.

Yet his reception held elements of falsity, or at least reserve. His cause met generosity and politeness from the local Irish, but also caution and even resistance. The true mood of the Australian Irish was very distant from that of the Ireland of the Land War. Their

W. J. K. REDMOND, Esq.,

John and William Redmond in Sydney, 1883

The Sydney Reception committee with the Redmond Brothers, 1883. The two Toohey brothers, of brewing fame, are marked with crosses in the back row, the Redmond brothers are sitting, one each side of the bearded J.G. O'Connor, and J.W. Walshe is reclining in front

priorities and loyalties are indicated in the St Patrick's Day Banquet of 1881. The toasts were: 1. the Queen, 2. the Prince of Wales and the rest of the Royal Family, 3. the Governor, 4. the Day we celebrate, 5. the Land we live in, 6. the Parliament of New South Wales; then Ladies, Press, and Chairman. Presumably Ireland got a look in under 4. Of nine musical items, only two were Irish. When some Australian Irish—in Melbourne— roused up enough pluck to address the Irish Land League directly—as they did on the occasion of the centenary of Grattan's 1782 parliament, their action received very hostile public notice, particularly in regard to the use of the word 'despotism' to describe British government in Ireland. Five Irish Australian members of the Victorian Legislative Assembly—John Gavan Duffy, Callaghan, Toohey, Brophy and Longmore—had signed the address, some without reading it too closely—it spoke of the imperial government as 'alien' as well. They should have paid more attention to the caution exhibited by their more eminent colleagues: Sir Bryan O'Loghlan, then premier, would not support Home Rule until after Gladstone's conversion in 1886, and Sir John O'Shanassy always objected to such colonial interference in Britain's affairs. The Grattan address earned its signatories the censure of the whole Legislative Assembly.

This was nothing to the climate of anti-Irish outrage generated by the Phoenix Park murders of May 1882 and sustained until the trial that eventuated in February 1883. On 6 May 1882, Lord Frederick Cavendish, new and conciliatory Chief Secretary for Ireland, and T.H. Burke, Permanent Under-Secretary, were stabbed to death in Phoenix Park, Dublin. The trial of eight accused began in February 1883, the Australian audience for it being poorly informed about Ireland, but agog with shock and horror, and seething with

883

anti-Irish indignation. In January, the brothers John and William Redmond had arrived in Adelaide, to represent the Irish Parliamentary Party and the National Land League. They established an Adelaide branch, moving to Sydney exactly at the time when the Dublin murder trial produced sensational allegations that the party and league were implicated. The *Daily Telegraph* said they were collecting for 'a murder fund': others said it was for a civil-war fund. The press continued throughout in inventive vein, linking the Redmonds with the murder of a Chinese doctor in Armidale, and alleging that Land Leaguers had cut the telegraph cable in Malaya to intercept news which would damage the Redmonds' Australia visit. Henry Parkes proposed that they be expelled. Public halls were closed to them: they resorted to tents. Hotels refused accommodation—a ban easily circumvented in a city of Irish hotel-owners. Or perhaps not so easily, given the Redmonds' then reputation. They stayed in the hotel of Thomas Curran, later to be briefly Irish member of parliament for South Sligo, retiring back to Sydney in 1900. John Redmond's recollection goes to the heart of colonial Irish attitudes and divisions: 'I received a chilling reception. All the respectable people who had promised support kept away. The priests would not help me . . . The Irish working men stood by me, and in fact saved the situation. They kept me going until a telegram arrived exculpating the parliamentary party. Then all the Irish gradually came round and ultimately flocked to my meetings.'

This last claim is only partly true, and gravely oversimplifies the outcome. Certainly John Redmond won over many of the colonial Irish. And certainly he made a point of thanking the Irish 'working population'. (The press accused the Redmonds of being parasites on the half crowns of the poor.) Although he was then young—twenty-six—and unknown, he had much that had commended him in the Australian situation—membership of the House of Commons, a good education, an impeccable family background and great platform ability. He also had an Irish reputation for moderation, the main reason for his choice as envoy to Australia by the Parliamentary Party above the extremist Thomas Brennan, who was one of the most violent leaders of the Land League, and who had asked to go. There had also been an American nomination for the role of emissary to the Australian Irish infidels: Australia had at last been discovered—or at least, her financial resources.

John Redmond was an excellent choice, but his personal attributes could not disperse the violent reputation of the movement he represented. Nor could his most strenuous efforts, nor flair for encouraging others. Hugh Mahon, who had been imprisoned with Parnell in 1881–82, had arrived in Sydney in 1882. He had helped Walshe in Land League formation earlier in the year. At Redmond's suggestion he dashed off a booklet, *The Land League*, to counteract Australian press prejudice: that indefatigible and convenient printer J.G. O'Connor printed it. In some areas Redmond's visit occasioned enormous enthusiasm, particularly in the country districts of southern New South Wales: at Temora he was met by a cavalcade of about 1000 men on horseback. But his visit also attracted the active hostility of anti-Irish elements. Sydney mounted an anti-Redmond public meeting, which rung with charges of sedition and disloyalty and sent its resolutions to the British Colonial Office. (The baselessness of such hysteria is evident from the considerable correspondence on the Redmond visit between the governor of New South Wales, Lord Loftus, and the Colonial Office, which passed it on to Gladstone, the Prime Minister:.Loftus reported that Redmond's later lectures were lucid, moderate and loyal.) Redmond's Melbourne reception was, if anything even more hostile, the denial of public-hall facilities being so widespread as to prompt the Melbourne Irish to set about building their own Hibernian Hall. The *Age* and the *Argus* were implacably hostile, and summarily contemptuous. Worse still, the respectable Irish ran for cover. Sir Bryan O'Loghlen, a former premier and family friend of the Redmonds, declined to be present at the meeting: John Redmond vowed he would never forgive him. William Redmond told J.G. O'Connor, 'Such a row you never saw. Young Duffy turned up ultimately and spoke—*goaded* into it by my remarks.' Young Duffy was Frank Gavan Duffy, afraid of the damage his association with the Redmonds might do his law practice. He spoke on their platform, but suggested that it was not unreasonable that Australians should deprecate the introduction of Ireland's problems: this pleased nobody. Henry Bournes Higgins was also on the platform: a man of principle who believed in Home Rule, he felt he must bear the cost of witness to his beliefs. Higgins was subsequently blackballed for the Melbourne Club, but in the long run his identification with the Redmonds probably helped his political career in that it gained him Irish Catholic votes he might otherwise have lost as a Protestant.

But others did pay. At Orange, James Dalton, Patrick Burke and Michael Casey, prominent Irishmen, were removed from the commission of the peace for having signed 'a disloyal and seditious address of welcome' to Redmond. Association with the visit was thought to have lost several Irish municipal councillors their seats and three years later was still being cited as an anti-Irish electoral factor. And of course the visit left a legacy of recriminations and accusations of personal cowardice and national betrayal against the more successful Irish who had avoided commitment to Redmond's cause. Their endeavours to distance themselves availed not at all with a press such as the *Age* and *Argus* which branded the Redmonds extremist agitators and Home Rule as dangerous and impossible: all Irish were tarred with the same brush whatever their protestations. And this press could always find ammunition that suited its guns. One of Redmond's contemporary biographers adverts to the source of what was a major problem for Irish Australia. From Australia the Redmond brothers went on to America. 'While they were in Australia the danger was to avoid being too disloyal: in America the danger was to avoid being too loyal!' The joke was lost on the Australian Irish as local papers reprinted what the Redmonds were saying in America; citing in defence of the Redmonds what they had said in Australia was only too likely to be gleefully checkmated by what they had said in America.

The Redmonds were aware of this problem, and their own personal temper and style were more at one with the Australian Irish atmosphere than the American, something they demonstrated in an unique and unarguable fashion. They both married into the Dalton family. The Dalton brothers were among the wealthiest Irishmen in New South Wales, James having substantial pastoral interests at Orange, Thomas owning a large Sydney import firm. In September 1883 John Redmond married the brothers' half-sister, Johanna, at North Sydney. Later, William married James' daughter, Eleanor. But lest the story seem too idyllic, an incident the day before John's wedding bears noting, as one of those human dimensions of history apparently otherwise edifying. Neither Thomas Curran, at whose hotel (Pfhalert's) the Redmonds were staying, nor J.G. O'Connor, approved of John's marriage: O'Connor confronted him with the charge that he was a mere adventurer who had come to Australia to get himself a wife and a fortune. A fracas followed in which Curran knocked down William Redmond, and then ordered the brothers ('scrubbers' he called them) off his premises. But it was Curran's local reputation that suffered most from his incident: the Redmonds' marriages cemented a set of relationships between the brothers and Australia that endured for their lifetimes.

The immediate purposes of the 1883 tour had been realised—to inform the Australian Irish and tap their generosity: the Redmonds' personal involvement in Irish nationalist affairs communicated immediacy to their audiences newspaper reports could not. But the visit also stirred up local problems and questions, generally the question of the place of the Irish in the community, particularly their divisions and degree of commitment to Irish causes. This element of disturbance caused some bitter resentments, evident in the content and tone of Archbishop Goold's comment in a letter back to Ireland: 'I wish the home rule principle were strictly observed. Each one to mind his own business at home . . . Keep your red hot politicians in Ireland where they are much needed.' Goold had troubles enough without the maverick intrusion of the Redmonds. Such visits placed the prominent and successful in a no-win situation. If they attended meetings they were held by Protestant friends and colleagues to be consorting with anarchists and rebels; if not, they were accused by an Irish proletariat of cowardice and treachery. If they attended, but not conspicuously, they risked being singled out publicly and identified, with contempt, by the speakers: the Redmonds had no sympathy with local pressures and a heedless supply of abuse for those Irish who viewed them with caution. The tour demonstrated that active leadership and support would come, not from the wealthy and the prominent, but from the lower middle class: it was they who were prepared to commit themselves, they who had less to lose, they who could mobilise the generosity of the rank and file. That very generosity signified a limitation of commitment, another form of evasion: money was enough. A few leaders of Irish-Australian organisations might be actively antagonistic to English rule in Ireland, but all others wished to evade that issue. To subscribe money to the nationalist cause salved Irish consciences, testified to allegiance, and satisfied sentiment and pride. It purchased a warm glow without too deep a committal.

Nevertheless, the national convention of the Irish National League and all kindred bodies which Redmond advised should be held to consolidate and unify all Irish organisations in Australia and New Zealand attracted intense interest among Irish Australians when it was held in Melbourne in November 1883. However, the occasion, presided over by Dr Kevin Izod O'Doherty, was largely oratorical. O'Doherty's performance exemplified one problem bedevilling Irish (and all other) organisations—State rivalries. Not conceding anything to the spectacular Victorian Irish, with their Duffy and O'Shanassy, he extolled the virtues of Queensland governments: the best government that ever existed in any of the colonies included the Irishmen John Murtagh Macrossan and Patrick O'Sullivan. Yet O'Doherty could hardly be reasonably accused of rabid and aggressive Irish nationalism. Quite the contrary: 'I can confidently aver that, as regards my own countrymen, a year or two of residence under the free Australian sky suffices to make loyal men of those who have been driven here from home with soured and embittered hearts . . . We have furled our old flag, the Irish sunburst, with all its attendant bunkum, for good and all . . .'

But there was no appeasing an Australian press determined to put these Irish down. The delegates spent much time and energy congratulating themselves, warming themselves around the fire of their cause, in the face of unrelenting press and public hostility. The *Sydney Morning Herald* typified the press in its claim that 'an Irish convention in Australia is a mischievous anomaly however considered. Irish Australian it cannot be, because an Irish Australian is a creature of whom we cannot possibly conceive. He is or he is not one of us . . .'. It was beyond the capacity of the outlook embodied in the *Herald* to conceive that 'one of us' appeared to those of Irish sympathy to mean British-Australian as opposed to Irish-Australian: the establishment took its own norms and assumptions as defining the tolerable limits of Australian loyalty. And it made a direct equation between the Irish in Ireland and the Irish in Australia which, though false, explains its attitude. It has been suggested that most of the Australian press attacked the Irish at home in Ireland rather than locally. This was true, but the distinction was of no consequence. The implication in the press was that true Irish behaviour was that revealed in Ireland itself, in violence, and much else of menace, and that this was the danger in Australia. The Irish-Australian position was the reverse; that Ireland itself was a coerced distortion, and the free and pacific Australia saw the true Irish face. At first glance the *Herald*'s rejection of an 'Irish Australian' as inconceivable seems absurd, but it came from a source which was the centre of reception of news from Ireland and America. Translated on its premises and definitions, the *Herald*'s condemnation was of an amalgam of terrorist and Australian. From the *Herald*'s viewpoint, denials of any such violent intentions or tendencies among Irish Australians were in the face of ample evidence of real Irish behaviour in Ireland itself.

This Irish convention over, and the Redmonds gone, Irish activity lapsed. The reason was, as the circumspect Sir Bryan O'Loghlen asked the St Patrick's Day banquet in 1886, what practical measures could the local Irish take? Organisations set up during the Redmond visit were left with little to do other than receive donations. By the end of 1883 nearly £25 000 had been sent back to Ireland, for payment of Irish MPs' salaries, but thereafter donations dropped off sharply. Another law of Irish Australian activity had asserted itself: enthusiasm for Irish causes tended to depart with the delegates themselves. Early in 1886 there was a flurry of congratulatory excitement at the election of Kevin Izod O'Doherty as member for the Irish constituency of Meath, a remarkable testament, it seemed, to Irish colonial importance. He progressed around the Australian coast, en route to take up his seat in the House of Commons, via a series of banquets, picnics, and meetings at which the Irish celebrated this new involvement with the homeland. But when O'Doherty left, again enthusiasm went with him.

It was W.E. Gladstone who revived Ireland's cause in Australia. Acknowledged the greatest English statesman of his day, Gladstone's commitment—indeed religious-type conversion—to Home Rule in 1886 made that cause respectable in Australia. It brought that cause within the limit—if not barely—of the British-Australian outlook: Gladstone's enormous colonial reputation was such that his policies had to be accepted by the colonial establishment as lying within their area of tolerance. Had to be? Well, that was more the anticipation of the colonial Irish than the reality, more the appearance than a transformation of real feeling. Nevertheless how vital was that elder British statesman's blessing is indicated by the fact that 1886–88 represents the high point of the Home Rule movement in Australia: in 1888 Sydney St Patrick's Day celebrations attracted a high point of attendance estimated at 20 000. In 1887 Lord Aberdeen, visiting Australia, conveyed back to Gladstone himself expressions of profound gratitude from the Irish in Australia.

What were they grateful for? Acceptance. The acknowledgement by the paragon of British political morality that their cause was just. Inclusion in the mainstream of British political life. Yet in actual effect, far from settling the issue as the Australian Irish automatically assumed, Gladstone's was a divisive and polarising influence. With him on their side, Australian Home Rulers could not resist the temptation to gloat over the discomfiture of opponents. Local Ulstermen in particular felt at first betrayed, then determined to campaign against Home Rule and to obstruct the colonial Home Rule assistance movement as much as they could. Certainly, in the realm of general colonial opinion, the press and the politicians changed their tune. Their abandonment of hostility probably helped Home Rule fund-raising. But the main effect was that, for the first time in

Sir Thomas Grattan Esmonde, 1889   *John Dillon in October 1889*

Australian history, the Irish felt they stood tall. Gladstone's imprimatur raised their cause to the recognition they craved: British approval was not simply political necessity, it was a response from that area whose approval the Irish, particularly the Irish of the Empire, most desired. But hostility did not disappear: it narrowed and intensified. The leaders of Irish Australia took it for granted that Gladstone's Australian admirers would simply follow him wherever he went. Some did—Parkes, Sir James Robinson, Sir Patrick Jennings, Edmund Barton. G.W. Rusden's letters from Melbourne in 1893–94 to W.H. Lecky in Ireland reflect what also happened. He denied Gladstone 'title to the name English', renamed the G.O.M. (Grand Old Man) of English politics 'Ghastly Old Mischief-monger', and claimed that Home Rule was condemned 'universally' in Australia, 'though of course we have some fools and a few Fenians amongst us'. Candidates for such appellations in both categories did not necessarily support Home Rule or trust Gladstone: for some Irish in Australia it was enough that a British politician should embrace Home Rule to reveal it as the deception and sham it was. The lunatic horizons of some aspects of the Irish-Australian terrain are visible in the paranoic visions that possessed Fr Matthew Horan, president of one of the most active Australian branches of the Irish National League, that of Gympie in Queensland. Horan was convinced that the Vatican was plotting to de-nationalise the Irish in Ireland and Australia. He put it to a league meeting on 8 October 1887 that Gladstone, through his Roman contacts, sought to de-nationalise Ireland, and had obtained a large sum from the British parliament to be employed in expatriating evicted Irish to Australia, and to pay Vatican agencies to de-nationalise the Australian Irish through appointing 'Anglo-foreign' bishops and English nuns, with the object of divesting the Australian Irish of every vestige of national sentiment.

These fairy-tales within the Irish camp were hardly encouraging examples of political perception, but the tales the Home Rulers had more to fear were those emanating from the opposing forces, who not only had local energies but were drawing on help from Britain. In 1886–87, a British pamphlet, *The Irish Question for Australasian Readers*, gained wide circulation. It described the Home Rule party as 'Disruptionist' and 'unscrupulous agitators, who, no matter how mildly they were represented in distant lands, shocked humanity and paralysed national progress at home'. The pamphlet's message, aside from charges of revolution, disloyalty, violence, murder, boycotting and disruption of parliament, was that the Redmonds had fled to Australia to escape arrest, and had lied and misled Australians, sheltering behind 'God Save the Queen'. Opposition to Home Rule had now concentrated in the Orange sector of the colonial community. This was a sector determined, outspoken, and vigorously formidable in its enmity: though its numbers were small, it was powerful, passionately convinced of its rectitude, and had important supporting forces in the British Isles.

From 1886 the sectarian issue, always latent, became inextricably involved with Irish affairs in Australia for the next forty years. Home Rule became very much a Catholic cause in Australia. The Church took up the Irish Tenants Eviction Fund. Parish priests became presidents of local branches of the Irish National League. Church machinery was used to collect and remit funds to Ireland to support the Irish Party. Churchmen, from Cardinal Moran down, took to commenting on and expressing satisfaction with, its achievements. And opposition to Home Rule became an anti-Catholic cause. The issue rapidly tended to be sustained, not so much for itself as for what it symbolised—to Catholics, justice and recognition, to anti-Catholics, Catholic sedition and tyranny. In Australia, Home Rule's connotations became religious more than Irish, as was the case thereafter with every Irish cause. The stable continuing support for Home Rule came from Catholic church dignitaries such as Cardinal Moran who saw in it a cause accepted by the general community as respectable and whose winning would greatly improve the status and prestige of the Catholic element in the Australian population: obviously the emphasis here was not on an Irish political campaign but on the social position of Australia's Catholics. In this regard there was difference of opinion, but Bishop Dunne of Brisbane was in the minority when he remarked that 'much agitation among the Irish in Australia was open to the danger of taking people's minds away from settling themselves in homes in this country, and providing for the independence, bye and bye, of their families. Excessive separate movements would also tend to isolate them among their fellow colonists and perhaps to challenge into existence and foster hostile organisations'. Here, the difference was not one of objectives but of tactics: the Moran line was that achievement of Home Rule would foster Irish Catholic integration in Australia; Dunne's contention was that such movements militated against integration.

Outside the Church, Home Rule tended to be a fluctuating cause, waxing and waning in keeping with Irish events. The defeat of the first Home Rule Bill in 1886 produced great despondency in those confident of Gladstone's success. Papal condemnation of the Plan of Campaign (a scheme of rent-withholding and bargaining with landlords) and of boycotting, led to further dismay and confusion, although a Sydney meeting, like many in Ireland itself, took the view that the Papacy had interfered improperly in Irish politics. However, enthusiasm revived again with the arrival in Australia in March 1889 of three new Irish delegates—John Dillon, almost as legendary a figure as Parnell himself, John Deasy and Sir Thomas Esmonde; once again it was to be demonstrated that Irish politicians alone could vitalise Irish Australia. The tour was to collect funds desperately needed to sustain the Plan of Campaign: its organisers supported evicted tenants in the manner of a strike fund. It was a tremendous success: Dillon raised £35 000 (Davitt says £40 000) at a time when the campaign verged on collapse, enabling the land-and-tenant issue to be kept alive when defeat seemed certain.

This Australian money played a decisive part in the success of the extension of the Land War, and the Dublin *Nation* took to reporting Dillon's triumphs under the heading 'Greater Ireland'. But the Australian Irish were not conscious of this, nor aware of the ferment of differing policies and personalities within the Irish nationalist movement, particularly the tensions between the parliamentary and peasant-populist wings: they entertained a simple impression of undisturbed unity. And their main concern was the reaction of colonial society: Dillon himself testified, on his return to Ireland, that his Australian support sprang from sympathy with the suffering peasants, not from any wish to reorganise the Empire, that is, from any enthusiasm for Home Rule. John Curtain JP put the mood exactly in the Melbourne Irish Australian Convention in September: 'Now I don't believe in this cutting the painter business . . . What we want is moral force, freedom, and fair and equal laws for all. We have married and intermarried, we speak the same language, we are one big family; and all we ask is for a just mother who shall treat all her children alike' (Cheers). Faced with real live Irish politicians, clerics who had embraced Home Rule at a distance became extremely nervous. Archbishop Carr, a man of perception and independent mind, consulted Cardinal Moran on whether or not he should attend the meetings of the 1889 delegates. (In 1892 he explained his view of the loyalty issue: 'no matter what trouble may exist at home . . . when the Irish people get a fair chance they are a loyal people, they are a conservative people, and they are a people who seek to fuse with their neighbours, no matter from what country they come . . .')

The public reaction to Dillon was much more tolerant than it had been to Redmond; the *Herald*, for instance, was favourable. This gave the Australian Irish much more satisfaction than assisting the cause of Ireland, and they indulged their pleasure in ritual ways: 150 ladies on horseback, daughters of Irish settlers, met Dillon at Warwick in Queensland; a massive Sydney welcome was attended by an estimated 40 000; at a picnic at Chowder Bay in Sydney Dillon presented J.G. O'Connor with a gold watch; Dillon was the moving force behind a reorganisation of the Victorian Irish National League from which emerged as leading figure, Dr Nicholas O'Donnell, who had never seen Ireland; local Irish organisations mushroomed to cope with Dillon's visit. The only sour note was the performance of John Deasy. His sensational allegation that his mail had been opened—the implication was that of secret official spying—led to a Royal Commission investigation which implicated the vigilant mother of a young lady to whom Deasy had been paying court: it was not a discovery which added to the dignity of the occasion, and it fuelled predictable contemptuous humour. The Irish were anxious to forget the jokes, but hardly less quick to forget their enthusiasm for Dillon as soon as he left. Irish Australia would respond when evangelised by big Irish names, but at their departure Irish Australia went to earth—or diverted to local concerns. The strength and character of this diversion is remarkably illustrated by the brief history of the John Mandeville Branch of the Irish National League of Newcastle, New South Wales. Formed in November 1888 to assist the Parnell Indemnity Fund, it organised a meeting of 1500 and a collection of £400 for Dillon and the Evicted Tenants Fund. Thereafter the meeting topics reveal its real interests. On 16 September 1889 its meeting was devoted to the London dock labourers' strike, the next meeting discussed 'whether the land question was at the root of the general depression'; then followed, into the next year, discussions and debates on the eight-hour day, single tax, local option, gas versus electricity, worker co-operation, and, of course, the 1890 strike. What of Ireland? The branch president was Father O'Gorman, whose presence was crucial to the prestige and vitality of the league. He told the first annual general meeting: 'the struggle of the Irish . . . was the struggle of labour root and branch and the struggle would be fought out on Australian soil. When the time came for that struggle they would have to look to Ireland for intellectual and moral support.' The local, labour, concerns of the Irish could have hardly been put more bluntly. It was to be the same when Michael Davitt toured the colonies in 1895. He was feted by the Australian trade union movement, and his greatest applause came in relation to his sketches of the rising political figures of the British working class, Keir Hardie and John Burns. The Newcastle Branch of the Irish National League was a society for the discussion of labour questions and local issues, garnished with songs and conviviality. By 1890 usual attendance at meetings was less than a dozen, sometimes half that: by 1891 it was three or four. It suspended itself in 1891, finally destroyed by the Parnell divorce case.

As the concerns of the Newcastle league strikingly demonstrate, the natural drift of the Australian Irish in the 1880s and 1890s was towards interest in the affairs of the then emergent trade union and labour political movements. In this atmosphere the effect of the visits of Irish delegates was anachronistic, taking immigrants back to loyalties they were rapidly forgetting. In the case of the Dillon-led delegation, this effect was protracted by John Deasy's staying behind on a further lecture tour. Six thousand attended an 1889 Boxing Day picnic in his honour. But the pressures to be Irish did not come only from the Irish delegates. Their visits provoked loyalist counter-demonstrations. In September 1889 in Melbourne a man with a revolver attempted to attack Dillon. The Irish delegations provided a recurring stimulus and focal point for anti-Home Rule and anti-Irish Catholic forces. Each delegation had the effect of reviving moribund Irish Unionism and Orange energies within Australia and of providing them with the materials and occasions necessary for them to sustain their sense of outrage and the vigour of their attack. Such attacks in turn firmed the resolve of the Irish Catholic forces to revive their own weakening Irishness and rally around a cause they believed in, though with dwindling enthusiasm.

Australian Irish loyalties were clearly revealed in the reaction to the Parnell divorce case scandal from November 1890. Parnell had been cited as correspondent in the O'Shea divorce. Australian Irish opinion was unanimous in its refusal to believe him guilty: this was another of those monstrous English frame-ups which had dogged Ireland's champion. But he was guilty. Gladstone urged his stepping down as leader of the Irish Party. He would not, and the party split, or rather, disintegrated.

The intense bitterness and sense of betrayal which welled up in Irish Australia against Parnell was prompted not so much by what he had done to wreck the Home Rule cause— that was Ireland's business—but by what he had done to them personally, that is, taken their money and trust, given them a heroic myth to believe in, and then humiliated and degraded them publicly in the eyes of a scoffing colonial society: he had delivered them into the hands of their enemies. Especially among that section of the Irish-Australian community which was hypersensitive to the regard of their fellow citizens, their association with Parnell, whose behaviour was now revealed as morally scandalous and politically selfish and divisive, was felt to be an indignity they would not court again.

The split in the Irish Parliamentary Party threw the Australian Home Rule movement into a confusion additional to its prevailing weakness. Not knowing how to act, whether to

support the Parnell faction or those who opposed him, the Sydney and Melbourne organisations decided to await advice from Dillon, their most recent visitor. Meanwhile they
remained officially neutral, while opposing groups of partisans warred within them. Rural
areas in particular demanded denunciation of Parnell and severance from his faction, a
stance reflecting the clerical domination and aspirations to respectability paramount in
these areas, but also revulsion from the sordidness of the whole affair. Some Irish members
of the city proletariat saw things differently. A small but very vigorous group of Parnell
supporters in Sydney saw him as the revolutionary hero, undermined by English guile and
prudery, betrayed by Irish weakness. Confronted by news from Ireland that both pro- and
anti-Parnell factions intended to send delegates to Australia, both Sydney and Melbourne
branches of the Irish National League made it clear they wanted neither. They feared a local
split. Indeed a Parnell Independent Irish National Club had already sprung up in Sydney.
The Catholic bishops shared this fear, believing the Parnell affair had the potential to
destroy all peace among the Australian laity—surely an exaggeration stemming from
familiarity with the mood in Ireland itself, but indicative of the trepidations of the time.
Cardinal Moran himself breathed the electric air of plot and treachery. He believed that the
leader of the pro-Parnell group in Sydney was not only a Protestant (crime enough) but
probably a spy for the government employed to sow dissension within the Catholic body.
In March 1891 the Australian bishops unanimously decided, in view of the risk of 'serious
disunion in the ranks of our Irish Catholic People in Australia', not to support either of the
rival groups.

This neutrality is worthy of note, given its contrast with the immediate and virtually
unanimous anti-Parnell reaction of the bishops of Ireland itself: it is hard to conceive that
the potentially divisive effects of the Parnell affair were judged more dangerous in Australia
than in Ireland. Perhaps distance counselled caution to the Australian bishops, or they
confused the intensity of the few who took sides in Australia with a more widespread
feeling than in fact existed. In actuality, exaggerated fears of divisive repercussions seems to
have worked to dampen them. The visit of the anti-Parnellite J.R. Cox was not a success.
F.B. Freehill warned that it might create division. It did. Some meetings ended in fisticuffs
and assault charges. Other meetings were cancelled. Various Irish organisations met to
consider what they should do—the Irish National League, the Hibernians, the Shamrock
Club. Cox, who was equipped with modern visual aids, was forced to exhibit his scenes
of Irish evictions privately, despite the fact that Australian Irish opinion was rapidly
hardening in his faction's favour, supporting the Irish clericalist line that Parnellites were
in opposition to church and clergy, destructive of Ireland's good repute, and undermining
the national interest for selfish purposes.

But the strongest feeling was determination that Irish schisms must not be allowed to
damage the Australian situation, and it is in this context that the bishops' statement makes
most sense: they did not wish any involvement whatever in this appalling Irish scandal,
even that of denouncing it. The main Irish organisations in Australia succeeded in preserving formal neutrality until Parnell's convenient death in October 1891 appeared to
resolve the problem. Some did so not without trauma: the Melbourne Celtic Club virtually
fell apart and had to be re-formed. The avoidance of a significant split in Australian
organisations on the Parnell issue testifies to the mild temper of such organisations and to
their priorities. Despite sharp divisions of opinion on the issue, feelings were not intense
enough to produce a split, given that the first Australian consideration was not the principles at stake in Ireland, but the welfare and public image of the Irish Catholic people in

Australia. The main effect was to induce a feeling which called a plague on all Irish houses, Parnell's or otherwise; to generate and reinforce feelings of caution and distrust in relation to Irish politics; and to confirm the strong existing trends towards Irish Australia's identification with Australia. If Ireland had let them down, perhaps Australia would not.

After Parnell's death, Australian Home Rule organisations tended to support the Irish Parliamentary Party faction led by the anti-Parnellite Justin McCarthy. They did this with little enthusiasm and no energy: the Parnell affair had sapped them of any will, and membership, beyond mere organisational survival. Besides, given their habit of idealised interpretation of the intricacies of Irish politics, the colonial Irish were utterly bewildered by the fever of factionalism that now gripped the nationalist movement in Ireland. They assumed Parnell's death would bring unity. Instead, it brought a decade of disruption, and contending Irish political personalities unwilling to shelve self for nation. These disputes disgusted the Australian Irish and engendered a revulsion from any involvement in Irish politics which was never substantially dispelled, even by the emergence of the familiar John Redmond as leader of a reunited party. Ten years was too long a squabble to retain the interest of distant outsiders, and in any case the Australian Irish had pressing local concerns to absorb their interest—serious economic depression, widespread labour disturbances, and the growth of labour political parties. The membership of the Irish Parliamentary Party by three Irish Australians—J.F. Hogan, the journalist author of *The Irish in Australia*, Thomas Curran, the publican, and his son T.B. Curran—gave Irish politics some additional interest but this was hardly more than curiosity value.

Very briefly it seemed as if the second Home Rule Bill might pass the British parliament in 1894. There was some local enthusiasm—various Irish organisations sent cables to Gladstone—but more typical was the reaction of Patrick McMahon Glynn, who had little interest in, or respect for, Irish politics. For him, Ireland was a country of 'patriots, quacks, grandiloquent bombast, real and poetical grievances', in which the leaders were a flatulent lot, their cause unfortunate (a pity it had arisen) and Home Rule likely to be as much a failure as Unionism. On this occasion, more energy was displayed by the Australian opponents of Home Rule than its promoters, and their display was particularly revealing of the way in which that opposition related its stand to its total concepts of social order: much more was at stake than some adjustments to the governance of Ireland. In May 1893 J.C. Nield addressed a Sydney 'By ticket only' meeting: 1 800 were present. It was predictable that he would say that the Bill would 'shake the foundations of the mightiest Empire the world has ever seen and, . . . impair the relations of Australia with the Mother Land'. But then he went on to describe it as the thin edge of anarchy, supported 'by republicans, socialists, and the lawlessly disposed of every type and of every creed' (Applause). Home Rule was the current face of 'the forces of disorder', and it was not being opposed because of the prevailing ignorance, indifference, and, above all, cowardice. Seen thus, Home Rule was an assault on the very basis of British civilisation and its values, a threat to the whole existing social order, backed, of course, by 'the vast, the deep, the dark power of the Church of Rome'. Its real menace could be appreciated only by stalwart and perceptive men of principle and courage, for it disguised the real objective—republicanism, the bringer of chaos, disorder and disruption. Nield's anti-Home Rule audience may have been relatively small compared with the mass of Irish Australia which vaguely approved Home Rule, but it was a phalanx of fanatics to whom an army of undisciplined well-wishers offered no competition at all.

Besides, the war was being fought elsewhere. The Bill died, and Gladstone himself soon after it. The movement in Australia seemed close to joining them. Australian Parnellites launched the weekly *Irish Australian* in October 1894: claiming 3000 subscribers, it survived a year. In 1895 the Catholic businessman D.R. Haugh tried unsuccessfully to launch a paper called *Sydney Irish World*: in November there appeared the new *Catholic Press*, with strong clerical sponsorship. The conjunction spelt out the facts of Irish Catholic life. Even Michael Davitt, who of all Irish politicians had retained most Australian respect (he contributed a column to the Melbourne *Advocate*) and seemed apart from the degrading factionalism of the nationalist movement, could do little to change this. For one thing Davitt, the leader of peasant Ireland, never in awe of bishops, unfailing agitator, had not pleased Cardinal Moran when Moran was Bishop of Ossory in Ireland. Davitt's appearance in Australia in the second half of 1895 did not please him either, as Moran would have preferred that all Irish politicians stayed at home until they put their own house in order. But Moran judged Davitt's reputation to be such as not to permit an outright snub. He received him coolly but used his chairmanship of one of Davitt's Sydney meetings in September to appeal for Irish Party unity. (Davitt later maintained that it was Moran's appeal, together with that of the Archbishop of Toronto, that led to the Irish Race Convention of September 1896 in Dublin—but he did not add that this produced nothing, or that only two Australians attended this: Australian interest was satisfied by appointing Davitt himself as representative.) Davitt's tour temporarily revived enthusiasm, but as is demonstrated in the published account of his visit, *Life and Progress in Australasia*, his own interests were less in expounding the Irish cause than in observing the new society of the colonies: he was particularly interested in the operation of state socialism and prison governance. Or simply, he came to learn, not to teach. His intention had been to give lectures for his own personal benefit, but the calling of an election in Britain led to his also canvassing for funds for the McCarthy Irish Party faction—and eventually for all factions. Davitt found Irish Australia a curious concoction. He was struck by all the constant toasting of the Queen's health, and, on the walls of many of the houses he visited, especially those of Catholic clergy, he noted an odd assemblage of portraits—the Queen, and Gladstone, then Parnell, Dillon and O'Brien—personages he found hard to reconcile as a coherent group. The consistencies lay in the preferences of Irish Australia, not in the actual relationships of the persons portrayed.

From the mid-1890s on, Irish nationalism in Australia came more and more under clerical control, particularly that of Cardinal Moran, a situation increasingly recognised in Ireland itself. This was made possible by the atrophy of the post-Parnell movement, by incidental factors such as J.G. O'Connor's leaving Sydney in 1892 to work in Newcastle, F.B. Freehill leaving for Spain in 1896, and made desirable by Moran's belief, which he shared with bishops in Ireland, that the Parnell period in Ireland, the 1880s, had shown that unless the Church was a major influence on the national movement, or controlled it, that movement would capture the people and lead them astray for its own purposes. Further, it would besmirch the fair name of holy Ireland. Moran's takeover made that movement both more and less Irish—or to be precise, more assertively Irish in appearance, but in an Australian context, less Irish in the degree of relationship to current Irish affairs. So, when he summoned a meeting at St Mary's Presbytery to organise the 1897 St Patrick's Day celebrations, he suggested from the chair that the concert be restricted to Irish music only, a quite new development. Behind this was his conviction that there should be no dilution of the richness of Irish culture, no apologies or compromise in regard to what was

Cardinal Moran, followed by Archbishop Kelly, landing from shipboard, c.1902
Tyrrell's Bookshop

Irish: Australia must swallow the Irish potion neat. And Moran moved to make sure that it was of the highest possible quality. By 1902 the shilling portion of the Hall at the St Patrick's Concert had been curtailed to the point of virtual abolition: the concert became not only respectable, but fashionable. These various moves reflected Moran's conception of Irish Catholics in Australian life. They would be loyal citizens interested—an exact word in this situation—interested in home (that is, Irish) affairs, and proud of their cultural and religious traditions, but avoiding any belligerence or offence and so proving 'that they who love Ireland most are at the same time the best citizens of Australia'. It proved impossible to convince the generality of Australian society of this: Ireland and Australia seemed to most non-Irish to be distinct if not conflicting loyalties. But until his death in 1911, Moran successfully dominated Irish nationalist activity in Australia—placing Australian considerations first. He wanted the colonial Irish to be integrated into Australian society and he saw Home Rule for Ireland as a means to that end. So he supported the Home Rule cause strongly, but generally, refusing to back any Irish faction or to be drawn by any particular Irish policy.

At times, maintaining this position was far from easy. The Davitt visit passed off well enough. But 1895 brought another potential Irish troublemaker to Australia, Edmund Dwyer Gray. Dwyer Gray had visited Australia in 1887 and 1889, but he was both proprietor and editor of the Dublin *Freeman's Journal* during the Parnell affair, at first siding with Parnell, then deserting him, manoeuvres which had not only brought him enemies on both sides, but brought him also in danger of excommunication, and involved him heavily with Archbishop Walsh in Dublin. Fortunately from Moran's viewpoint, he soon moved from Sydney to the periphery of Irish Australian affairs in Tasmania, where he becamed a Labor editor, member of parliament, and, for a few months in 1939, premier.

The celebration of the centenary of the 1798 rebellion raised much more difficulty. Moran would have preferred it to be forgotten. His Irish heroes—St Oliver Plunkett, Cardinal Cullen, a galaxy of Irish saints and martyrs who were invariably churchmen—were not the same heroes as his Irish laity, who celebrated the rebels of 1798, the Young Irelanders of 1848, those whom Cullen had condemned as sources of dissension. Moran did not want these rebels or their traditions resurrected in Australia: he had other plans for creating the best Irish image, and did not perceive the need the laity felt to honour that aspect of their Australian origins. Nor was he happy with the political and religious ecumenism of the celebration's Australian organisers. The first appeal was addressed to 'Irishmen and their descendants, of every shade of Irish Political Belief . . .' and Dr McCarthy, one of the organisers, kept remarking that the lesson of 1798 was the union of Protestant and Catholic.

Besides, despite the prominence of Dr McCarthy, the initiative towards erecting a monument to commemorate 1798—it eventually cost £2000—appears to have come from those lower Irish orders of whom Moran was not fond. The idea originated with the Shamrock Club, formed in 1885 by largely working-class Irishmen as a social club. Beginning in 1886, the club had organised an annual pilgrimage, of about a hundred members, to the grave of Michael Dwyer in the Devonshire Street cemetery. The club itself had closed in 1895, victim of both the Parnell split and the depression—its members were at an economic level vulnerable to recession. The idea of a commemorative monument survived, but to the Cardinal's displeasure.

So, at first, Moran refused to allow the exhumed bodies of Michael Dwyer and his wife, to be taken from the Devonshire Street cemetery to a new monument at Waverley, to lie in

The group gathered to form the committee to organise the Michael Dwyer reburial and the 1798 commemoration, 1898. J.G. O'Connor is seated in the centre, holding his top hat. Dr C.W. McCarthy, committee chairman is next to him, on the right

College St Sydney packed for the Michael Dwyer reburial procession, 1898

the cathedral before reburial. This provoked bitter criticism, to which Moran bowed, even pronouncing a eulogy. It was a politic retreat, since the reburial procession was estimated at 100 000 people and photographs confirm the assemblage as vast: however tepid they might be about Home Rule for distant Ireland, Australian Irish Catholics regarded Dwyer as theirs, and in honouring him they affirmed themselves, who they were, and from whence they had come. Whether Moran liked it or not—and he did not—they would bestir themselves to salute what was rebel Irish. Nor was this Moran's only tactical error. Opposed to the whole idea of commemorating 1798, he described the rebellion publicly as 'a blunder and a crime'. Again there was outrage. So he added a few days later, 'committed by the English government', claiming this had been omitted from the initial report. Eventually, by 1902, Moran had revised his opinion of 1798 to conform to nationalist orthodoxy. He did this by distinguishing between the politically selfish and infidel elements, typified by Wolfe Tone—these should be condemned—and the mass of ordinary Irish who rose up and died at the time—these should be praised. Indeed canonised. 'The great body of the people were genuine Martyrs. Hatred of the Faith was the motive of those who forced them into rebellion & they freely died for their Faith'—so Moran rationalised in 1902. The myth of 1798 was too near the bone of Australian Irishry to be questioned, even by Moran, and he fell into line with the popular conception of events.

Not that his conversion was at all at odds with the general flavour of his time. The widespread idea of Ireland's Spiritual Empire was coterminous with Moran's Australian reign, appearing first, perhaps, with Canon P.A. Sheehan in 1882, best expressed explicitly in Father P.S. Dineen's 1910 article 'The World-wide Empire of the Irish Race: a plea for its organisation'. The *Austral Light* published an Australian version in June 1909, Fr Michael Phelan's 'The Supernatural Destiny of the Irish Race'. 'No! our empire is not of clay or of iron. It is something vastly nobler. It is the conquest of the supernatural, the triumph of the spiritual; hence it is imperishable.' This emotional vision transcended nationalism, but it included it, subsumed, as a subsidiary. The officers and agents of this empire were, of course, priests, its experiences essentially religious ('Ireland has been crucified because she has been true to Christ'), and its destiny beyond any grubby politics. Moran's Irish nationalism was more this brand of imperialism, of which the best earthly exemplar was not so much Ireland, as the British Empire, with its admirable appearances of freedom, constitutionality, and serene law and order. It is significant to note that Moran's attitude to the Boer War was conditioned by his belief that the Boers were anti-religious bigots—and his conviction that the British Empire was an agent of civilisation. But Moran was aware that this was only one way of seeing the issues of the war, and that others in his flock sided with the Boers as a group of small farmers heroically struggling with an oppressive imperial tyranny. He was probably also aware that the Transvaal Irish Brigade, which fought with the Boers against the British, had been organised by an Australian, Arthur Lynch, later to be arrested for treason and sentenced in 1903 to be hanged, but pardoned, an Irish MP, and a supporter of the Allies in the First World War. While few Irish Australians shared Lynch's passionate pro-Boer commitment, many were unhappy with the South African situation, and Australian loyalist critics of Irish Australia's lack of patriotic enthusiasm had basis for their comments. Moran's anti-Boer remarks were made only at the time of the departure of the second Australian contingent. His first reaction shared the circumspect and noncommittal stance maintained by most of the Catholic hierarchy and press throughout, the attitude that Australia should keep out, and that true patriotism rested in staying home to defend one's own country. Those Irish Catholics who supported Britain did so more in terms of not wanting a British defeat, since Australia's defence lot was cast with her, or with the vague idea that a grateful Britain would help Ireland. But the whole business was an embarrassment, best avoided. Australia was the proper measure.

In the Irish Empire in Australia, its priest officers, under the firm direction of their commander-in-chief Cardinal Moran, had wrought much good. In Irish organisations hitherto prone to dispute and faction, the clergy acted as unifiers, pacifiers, and referees, settling such disputes as that which threatened the Hibernian organisation in 1901, giving sound advice, taking Irish matters up into elevated areas of society and government not accessible to lowly Irish plebeians. Law, order—and power: what was the point of fostering noble Irishry if it was condemned to live in subjection?

Moran's dominance of Irish Australia not only meant an exclusive stress on its Catholic religious aspects; it also entailed a marked shift upwards in the class or status basis of active colonial Irishism, away from the lower middle class, towards the more socially prominent and prestigious personalities in Irish Catholic society. These personages tended to regard with some disdain the lower Irish orders who still controlled the remnants of the Home Rule organisations. Cardinal Moran himself illustrates this in his response in 1902 to the proposal, by the United Irish League, that Irish history be made a regular part of the Catholic school curriculum: 'I don't know the president of the United Irish League. Some of the members of the league are not very presentable, and hitherto I have kept entirely aloof from them. I dare say it is much better they would have nothing to say to our schools.' Archbishop Kelly, his successor, took a similar attitude. Moran also took over control of Home Rule fund-raising activities after 1902, using a committee of politicians and professional men well known in the upper levels of Sydney Irish Catholic society—and excluding the United Irish League. He further clericalised Home Rule fund-raising by announcing on St Patrick's Day 1905 a plan, based on episcopal patronage and parochial collections, whereby Australia and New Zealand would undertake to raise £2000 annually for the Irish Parliamentary Party. This scheme failed, not least because there was no machinery set up to implement it, but the old Home Rule organisations found themselves ignored and rendered virtually irrelevant by Moran's initiatives. The Church had become the arbiter of Ireland's destinies in Australia. It was entirely appropriate that when William Redmond published a book describing his prolonged Australian visit in 1905—*Through the New Commonwealth*—it should not only be dedicated fulsomely to Cardinal Moran, but carry his portrait as a frontispiece.

Moran saw Ireland's destinies as being pursued most appropriately at the highest possible levels. In 1903 the Canadian parliament had petitioned the King in support of a just measure of Irish Home Rule. This was the fifth such Canadian parliamentary resolution (the first had been in 1882). It was decided in 1905 that Australia should follow suit, a tardy action in the imperial context which reflects not only the weakness of Australian Home Rule sentiments, but the timidity of Irish Catholics in Australian public life—and the absence of Irish persons of the stature, confidence and vision of Moran. In 1905 H.B. Higgins moved such a motion, supporting Irish Home Rule, in the Federal parliament. It was seconded by McMahon Glynn (who must have changed or placed in abeyance his private feelings) and supported by the Prime Minister, Alfred Deakin: Deakin had told Redmond that the Australian people were under a debt of gratitude to the Irish Parliamentary Party for help with the passage of Australia's Commonwealth Bill. Higgins' motion, which he introduced with an attack on the Union, faced the predictable Orange opposition, but also those who believed—or said they did—that it would be an unwarranted interference in the affairs of the imperial parliament and might provoke interference back. Most members hoped the motion would somehow vanish, thus sparing them a decision on contentious ground, but Hugh Mahon ensured that it reached a vote—passed, 33:21. All the Labor members voted for it, harbinger of alignments to come. The motion's passage made no difference to the issue it concerned, Home Rule, but it did signify the appearance of an Irish matter, successfully, at the highest level of Australian affairs, something properly taken by its proponents as a notable advance, a boost to morale, and a signal piece of publicity.

Moran was delighted. Nineteen hundred and five had been a good year. But he took a public opportunity to justify this concern with Irish affairs. There had been some public Catholic criticism of the Home Rule collections undertaking of £2000 annually, on the grounds that charity began at home and Catholic Australia had enough local demands—particularly its schools—without supporting other distant causes, however just. Moran's response was that Ireland's was 'a Mother's appeal', a duty of a natural relationship. He did not, on this occasion advert to the principle enunciated so baldly by Father P.E. Hurley in 1887: 'I have never here yet met a bad Irishman who was not a bad Catholic too . . . When they forget the land of their fathers, the faith of their fathers vanishes too.' But it was a principle to which Moran (and after him Mannix) subscribed. In fact, from this time—indeed from much earlier—Irish and Catholic were two facets of the same personality. They were nothing split, in competition, but two integrated aspects of the same individuality, the one sustaining the other. Far from seeing the one cause or the other prospering from the absence of its rival for attention or money, the greater likelihood is that either, alone, would have been diminished. They fed on each other, a culture and a religion, both enlarged and more vital for the relationship. Or at least more secure, more confident, larger, richer in spiritual resources, each more assured in the fuller dimensions of being themselves—Irish Catholics in Australia, with each of those words of description, ideology, location and place, important, meaningful, and balanced with the others.

This unique mixture which had evolved since the 1880s was related to and interested in, what happened in Ireland, but also had an independent existence apart, or more exactly, separate from it. Its Irish elements were, particularly under Moran's tutelage, more generic, more absolute, more detached from circumstances, than contingent on what happened in Irish politics. It was a spiritual kinship, the closeness of distant cousins—which was often precisely what was in fact involved. One was interested, mildly, in their doings, and wished them well. In 1906 when the British election produced a Liberal government pledged to Home Rule, Moran's championship of the cause became more vigorous, but his enthusiasm made little wider impact. Neither did the tour of Australia in that year by the Irish politicians Joseph Devlin and J.T. Donovan. John Redmond, writing to Irish organisations in Australia, promoted this tour as a reward, as a due direct report back to loyal supporters, but it was a money-collecting mission for all that pleasantry. Devlin was member for West Belfast and Donovan the organiser of his Belfast victory: perhaps their selection was aimed at making a point in an Australia where Unionists were vocal.

This delegation was successful in raising funds—£22 000—but not enthusiastic interest. Surely the matter was settled? What was there to get worked up about? Conditions in Ireland had greatly improved. No longer did famine or evictions prompt the anger and

J. Devlin M.P. (seated) and J.T.
Donovan (standing) 1906

generosity of the colonial Irish. Had not the British at last come to their senses with such reform measures as the Wyndham Land Act of 1903 which effectively inaugurated the transfer from landlords to peasants? Furthermore, the Church had taken over the Irish cause in Australia, and the laity were as willing to allow the clergy to manage them in affairs Irish as in affairs spiritual. So, all Irish organisations in Australia were in decline. The memberships had faded away. No new lay leaders offered themselves as replacements for the veterans of the 1880s: how could they, given the dominance of the clergy? But above all, the Australian atmosphere was dominated by two great facts. One was the certainty that Home Rule must come, that all Ireland's problems were due to be solved soon, that the Irish cause was on the verge of vanishing. The other was that Moran utterly dominated the Sydney Irish scene. When John Redmond, as leader of the Irish Parliamentary Party, wanted an assessment of the disposition of the Australian Irish in 1908 it was to Moran that he wrote. He asked Moran if money for the party could be raised in Australia without the usual delegate's tour. Not unless there was some major development within Ireland itself, replied Moran, with keen perception of Australian Irish attitudes. Moran was Sydney's Irish voice: in 1910, on behalf of the 'assembled Gaels of Sydney' he sent Redmond greetings on St Patrick's Day 'the Empire Day of the Irish race'. The imperial Irish concepts and terminology were firmly established in Moran's vision.

Moran dominated Sydney, and it was there that Irish most closely equated with Catholic. The equation prevailed in Melbourne also, but there the Irish situation was freer and more complex, less constrained by clerical domination into a church straightjacket. It is possible to detect more clearly in the Melbourne scene those aspects of secular idealism and commitment to the imperial enterprise that, for elements of Irish Australia, were embodied in the Home Rule cause. Denied (and denying themselves) full or at least easy participation in the enterprise Federation designated for Australia, leading Irish Australians saw Home Rule as a type of cleansing of the imperial image which would allow their identification with it, and their absorption into the totality of a vision of a better world. For them, Home Rule was a test of the quality and principle of the Empire, a test on which depended their own future spiritual comfort in Australia itself. The fate of Home Rule was crucial because on its passage depended their vision of their own Australian future: they had invested Home Rule with a variety of Irish Australian hopes and aspirations. It could not fail.

These hopes and aspirations, these yearnings to contribute to the nation, the wish to give, to participate, to be accepted, valued, are not easy to comprehend long after the matter has been settled and the questions of the time now seem absurd. Basic to an understanding is the long habituation of Irish Australia to being regarded as inferior, indeed foreign. The Melbourne *Age* put this host attitude clearly in 1883: 'We are Englishmen, and this is an English colony . . . we do not intend to let a handful of "foreigners" . . . impugn our loyalties to the hard-won traditions of race.' The Irish were the 'foreigners'. But by the early twentieth century Irish Australians had come to reject that allotted role and to demand an equal part in the determination of the character of the new nation. The more confident assertion of Irish rights to influence Australia appears to have derived from several coincident factors—the Federation debate and the subsequent heightened sensitivity to questions of national character, the impact of the Gaelic revival on Irish pride in Ireland's own culture, the growth in the power and prestige of Catholicism under Cardinal Moran, with impressively intellectual Australasian Congresses in 1900, 1904 and 1909, and, of course, the presumption of the imminent passage of Home Rule. The focus of the new Irish Australian dynamic was Australia, not Ireland, and in 1908 the Melbourne *Austral Light* expressed exactly its spirit and direction: 'We have as much right to impress an Irish mark on the national character as they [bigots] have a right to stamp an English impression thereon . . . not the least of its needs is the high spiritual force of the Irish Celt—the saving leaven of its materialism.' This was a theme of which much, much more was to be heard.

The Melbourne Irish revival from 1900 had its origins in two events in that year—the formation of the Melbourne branch of the United Irish League in June, and the takeover by the Archdiocese of Melbourne of the formerly lay *Austral Light* in January.

The formation of the United Irish League, consolidated by the visit of the Irish politician William O'Brien in 1901, began the Victorian Home Rule revival, itself heavily dependent on the energies and enthusiasm of one man, Dr Nicholas O'Donnell. The league's formation signals a marked change in the temper of Irish Melbourne. Before that, since the Parnell split, there had been disappointment, then disgust, then dismay—O'Donnell's own descriptive terms were entirely appropriate. An idealist, a man of emotion, he saw things in terms of darkness and light, not as manoeuvres in practical politics: a good deal of the nasty in-fighting that comprised Irish politics was beneath his notice in the sense that he operated on a higher plane. Yet he was practical enough to see that, in terms of the support for Home Rule growing in 1902, the money collected (£750 in Victoria in the two years of the league) came from ordinary workers, and from 'natives'—the Australian sons of Irish fathers. This he, and O'Brien on his visit (a health trip), took as a gratifying sign of filial piety, but the process is not so readily explained: such subscribers made an identification with Irish causes beyond that of the groups that might be expected to give, the Irish wealthy and the Irish-born. Why?

Hostile observers such as the *Argus* and *Age* held that Irish immigrants would forget their old country if only pestilent agitators and delegates would leave them alone. That held some truth, if coupled with the other proviso—if only pestilent newspapers and anti–Home Rulers would do likewise. As soon as an Irish delegation appeared on the horizon, anti–Home Rule petitions were activated, correspondents (often non-Catholic Irish) beseiged the papers, saying that Protestants were persecuted in Ireland, and that the Irish were barbarians and rebels: professional loyalists and Empire-savers, sectarians and anti-democrats—the terms the Irish applied to them—sprang into action. Nor did it need an Irish delegation to trigger such avalanches of anti–Irish Catholic abuse. In 1903 in Australia it was Michael J.F. McCarthy's anti-clerical book *Priests and People in Ireland*, published in London and Dublin the previous year but giving comfort to Ireland's enemies worldwide. Each year it was something: the delegations were merely an extra stimulus to Paddy-bashing. Such criticism bore most heavily on Irish Australians, those most sensitive and least protected, those least sure of themselves. Wealth was admirable insulation, and was in itself implicit reply to those criticising the Irish as outsiders, rebels and so forth. The Irish-born had been inured to such attacks and were usually confident in their own identity. Those most vulnerable were the less successful Irish and the Australian-born, whose identity and achievements could most easily be called in question. They struck back in the only way they knew, by supporting Irish causes: if they were accused of injury to the community, they might as well add insult.

Yet there was far more to support for Home Rule than elements of negative backlash. In 1906 the *Age* described the oratory of the Home Rule delegate Joseph Devlin as 'cloudy rhetoric'. The *Austral Light* saw it very differently: 'his subject was heroic with the heroism of the issues underlying those facts. The eternal principles of liberty and justice involved in a people's struggle to be free shone through . . .' It was 'a noble cause presented with the adornment of noble oratory'. This was classic *Austral Light* rhetoric of the period but it reveals a very real and important dimension of the support for Home Rule, indeed of Ireland generally. It was a cause which engaged the idealism, the quest for recognition of high principle, present within the Irish-Australian community; it tapped resources of poetry as well as the impulses of self-praise. This very point had been put into verse by Dr O'Donnell in 1890, contrasting the historical sterility of the Australian scene with the myth-encrusted richness of the Irish:

> The hills of my country are stern and lovely,
> Its foliage bright and its rivulets fast;
> But painfully real one sentiment only
> Pervades, 'Tis the present, and never the past.'

> No history excites, and no stimulant potion
> Of legend rides Fancy on dalliant wing;
> But that little isle in the northern ocean
> Has cradled my race, and to it will I sing.

In this pursuit of Irish fancies, the *Austral Light* was itself central. When the Church took over this monthly magazine in 1900 it became markedly more Irish. The educated laity in Melbourne were pro-Irish, but (save for a few enthusiasts such as O'Donnell) not markedly so. Not so the clergy who moved into the *Austral Light* as contributors: their Ireland was a holy place and a dreamland, their championing of it, spiritual, romantic and extravagant. The Gaelic revival in Ireland had developed a religious dimension whose productions these priests fell upon with delight—and with reprints and reviews. Fr Michael Phelan was vastly impressed in 1900s with Mary E. Butler's *The Ring of Day*, a novel of the Gaelic revival which 'attributes to the air of Ireland the power of checking the animal appetites, and quickening the spiritual perceptions'. The idea of Ireland as a holy place, in which not only were the people good, but the land itself was holy—spiritual, ancient, consecrated, mysterious, clean—permeated the imaginations of many Gaelic revival enthusiasts of the lesser calibre, and these notions were imported into Irish Australia by the *Austral Light*. So Sir William Butler on 'Ireland's Destiny' reprinted in the issue of February 1908: 'if ever there has been placed by the hands of the Creator An Entirely Complete Piece of World Structure, a bit of earth-entity designed and fitted to become the home of a strong, sentient, and successful race of human beings ...' it was, of course, Ireland. With such compliments as these, and Cardinal Moran dispensing similar encomiums ('the most enlightened, the most progressive, the most virtuous people at the present day'), it is small wonder that the dispossessed of the Australian earth were beginning to rise up to claim their due—or at least, demand recognition of their existence and of their rightful place in a spectrum of national endeavour.

By 1908 the celebration of St Patrick's Day in Melbourne was well into a phase of revival. Sixteen or seventeen thousand were at the sports, which were attended by Lord Northcote, the Governor-General. The street procession was the longest ever witnessed in Melbourne, watched by 100 000 in the streets. Archbishop Carr was much in evidence, the traditional drinking booths at the sports were abolished, and for the first time the Gaelic revival was evident in public: Dr O'Donnell gave a speech in Irish. The Melbourne celebration of St Patrick's Day in 1909 was even more triumphal. The Governor-General, Lord Dudley attended: he was a former Lord Lieutenant of Ireland. The organisers were delighted, seeing this as symbolising their acceptance by Australian society; Unionist and ultra-Protestant elements reached the same conclusion and were very angry. The celebrations were much larger than the previous year and saw the first appearance of 1500 Catholic school military cadets, 'the gallant little army' just brought into existence by the Military Training Act: as the organisers saw it, this gave the lie to the charge that Catholic schools were separatist and non-Australian. (Particularly sensitive to such imputations, in 1910 Archbishop Carr advised young Catholics to form an Irish regiment for the defence of their country, not in factious competition but in friendly rivalry. He was fifteen years behind Cardinal Moran, who, in November 1895 chaired the meeting which led to the formation of the NSW Irish Rifle Regiment, with the motto 'Faugh-a-ballagh' (Clear the way). By 1898 it had 305 enlistments. Twenty-three members of this regiment fought in the Boer War: in 1930 it was merged into the 55th Battalion NSW Rifle Regiment.) The school cadets at the 1910 St Patrick's Day celebrations proclaimed the whole message of the occasion: Australia is ours too. Such a claim required some sacrifices. Speakers played down the theme of injustice to Ireland. They were fulsome in praise of Lord Dudley, not a Home Ruler but a Unionist who believed that, given appropriate reforms, Ireland could be well governed without resort to Home Rule. This could be forgiven of a man willing to proclaim, as he did, that no man would be a worse Australian because he was a good Irishman, and that the chief danger of disruption to the Empire lay in the abandonment of old-world viewpoints. This kind of multi-culturalism, coming from such an elevated quarter, was a marvellous boost to Irish egos and totally anathema to that body of Melbourne opinion represented by the *Argus*. That paper maintained the righteous theory that the introduction of old-world politics into Australia was divisive and unnecessary, which in practice amounted to the demand that all conform to its (British Protestant) views.

Since the 1880s the Irish in Australia had been engaged in a protracted set of discussions and debates among themselves and with others as to who they were, and how they related, or should relate, to the Australian scene. Increasingly they moved towards assertive self-praise. Whereas the apologias of mid-century were defensive, Irish-oriented, and focussed on minimal fitness to dwell in Australia, by the 1880s they begin their claim to have contributed their share to the Australian national enterprise. A.M. Topp's series of articles in the *Melbourne Review* of 1881 mark a convenient point to mark the end of the phase of virtually unhindered denigration, though its themes, of course, continue—essentially that the Celtic Irish were of vastly inferior racial stock, that they had all the vices of their servile position (moral and intellectual deficiencies of all kinds), and that they needed strong English government for their own good. Topp saw the Irish as crafty, cunning liars, and advanced the propositions:

> That the Irish people as at present governed are a purely baneful influence in an English community; that they are, as Lord Lyndhurst strongly but truly put it, 'aliens in feeling, in religion, and in blood,' and are, as a race, distinctly inferior, morally, socially, and intellectually, to Englishmen; that they have corrupted and are ever corrupting our political institutions and our public and private morality; that they have no patriotic feeling towards the empire to which they belong; that they alone cling to a religious organisation that is year by year falling more behind the aims and needs of advancing civilization; that our only hope is to destroy the power of this organization and assimilate this alien race . . .

The only way to deal with them was to enforce the secular Education Act and concede them nothing.

Lest Topp's be considered the nadir of anti-Irish polemic, an example of other contemporary scurrility bears citing. A Dublin cobbler went for an unaccustomed walk in his city's Phoenix Park. 'Being there, the poor man found the fresh air so unusual to him that he became overcome and fainted.' All efforts to revive him failed until an old woman suggested 'Go and stick his head over a sewer, and sure one whiff of *his native air* will bring him to again'. This kind of racialism, fashionable at the time, leading to convenient political conclusions, invited, by way of response, the kind of inflated counter-racialism—Irish triumphalism—that Irish Australia produced from the late 1880s. J.F. Hogan's *The Irish in Australia* almost coincided with an article by Gavan Duffy in the January 1888 *Contemporary Review*, both of which celebrate Irish achievement as a part of an Australian totality. Hogan's thesis was essentially that the Irish were an integral part of the new and exciting colonial enterprise, and that Australia's freedom liberated the natural genius of the Irish to allow of their outstanding success. Hogan's technique was to prove that success by providing lists of famous and powerful Irish in Australia, a device followed by many other apologists after him, most notably at book length in P.S. Cleary's *Australia's Debt to the Irish Nation-Builders* in 1933. That technique was open to obvious objection, particularly when pursued to exaggeration by the coralling of any famous Australian name with tenuous Irish connections, and in 1889 Hogan's book, and Duffy's article, came under fire from A. Patchett Martin in *Australia and the Empire* and B.R. Wise in the *Centennial Magazine*. Martin scoffed: 'According to these authorities, it is the Irish who have done everything of record in these so-called British colonies.' And he pounced on what was a consistent feature of the 'famous Irishmen in Australia' lists; they were mostly Anglo-Irish, members of the 'English garrison' whom the Gaelic Irish wanted out of Ireland. Martin's acidulous conclusion was that he agreed that the Celtic Irish had advanced themselves in

Australia, but it was themselves alone: they had contributed little or nothing to the common good. The fabled generosity praised by Hogan was to themselves, and they had hived themselves off from 'the principle that we are one people'. Wise's argument was similar in a political context. He claimed that the Irish race had two salient characteristics, a tendency towards isolation from other nationalities, and a tendency towards cohesion among its own members. There was an Irish vote, directed by the Church. Of course this was hard to prove, he conceded, but the general belief was that it was so, and such a widely held conviction must have basis in truth. Hogan and his like should stop this beating of the Irish drum, which was needlessly divisive and isolationist. And they should stop putting Ireland first. Wise's 'Irish vote' allegations were a permanent feature of Australian political history which nothing could dislodge, a fundamental departure point for both foe and friend. In 1898 G.W. Rusden took consolation in the heavy and growing involvement of the Irish in Melbourne municipal government, where he thought a wide and low suffrage to be a healthy outlet for the Irish: 'While they are grinding at the local government mill they are not likely to be plotting . . .' Others had less confidence in that likelihood. And as for the myths of friends, according to John Redmond's biographer in 1910, '. . . municipal elections in Sydney are fought on the Home Rule Question'. Was this myth? No: Irish involvement in local politics had begun early. Small areas and local issues lent themselves to the kind of intimate and personal contact politics at which the Irish were adept. Their economic and social position may have denied them, initially, their quota of big public names and potential colony-wide political figures, but they were numerous and strong in just these areas relevant to local politics—hotelkeeping, contracting, real estate, small business, unions.

Both Hogan's claims for the Irish, and the hostile responses they evoked, make points beyond any of the particular issues or facts therein canvassed. Hogan was claiming respectable tenure of Australia for the Irish. The real point of compiling lists of famous, influential, or wealthy persons deemed 'Irish' was to deny, with examples, the validity of anti-Irish stereotypes, and to urge a general claim for equal participation in the credit for building a new nation: to be intelligible this claim had to be couched in the then accepted language of success—fame, power and wealth. But Hogan's real message was a simple affirmation—we belong. And the responses amounted to rejection of this—you don't.

They did. It was no accident that J.F. Hogan should have written, eight years before *The Irish in Australia*, a perceptive essay on 'The Coming Australian'. This archetype would be informally dressed, interested in sport, independent, irreverent, unambitious, insular, not religious, and uninterested in matters of the intellect, or art. 'In fine, the coming inhabitant of the southern continent will be peaceably disposed and sportively inclined; rather selfish in conduct and secular in practice, contented and easy-going, but non-intellectual and tasteless.'

The whole matter of what might be the character and destinies of Australia was a question which was a constant feature of the Irish-Australian disposition. This interest, to the degree of dedication, went back to the beginnings of settlement, appearing in a variety of expressions and forms. It can be seen in Daniel Deniehy, son of convict parents, with his 1860s vision of an independent republican Australia, egalitarian, humane, the good home of small men. It can be seen in the disproportionate strength of the Irish in the Australian Natives Association from its founding in 1871. It is reflected in the support for the idea of federation—Smith O'Brien as early as the 1850s; Gavan Duffy; down to Cardinal Moran's

Donovan, Hazelton, Redmond, 1911–12

candidature for the Federal Convention in 1897—and past that to injunctions such as that of Rev. Patrick Dowling's October 1901 address to the Catholic Young Men's Societies Union on Owen Roe O'Neill: Dowling swung effortlessly from praise of that seventeenth-century Irish hero to 'Be loyal to this young Commonwealth of Australia. Work for it, strive for it, toil for it, aye, and if necessary, die for it'. And if one was looking for an ideal embodiment of the virtues of Irish Australia, one existed, a public figure from the 1880s to 1912—that Tasmanian-born Anglo-Celt, E.W. O'Sullivan, democrat, patriot, state socialist, idealist, a man tolerant and liberal, the advocate of compromise and reconciliation, 'a positive and creative spirit, always seeing and seizing the good and building with what materials he had to hand'.

The drift of the Home Rule movement towards what appeared to be inevitable success in the early years of the new century created an atmosphere conducive to further Irish identification with Australia: the Irish were moving into the Australian world in time and in tune with Home Rule: Ireland would be itself; they would be themselves. The paeans of self-praise became louder, more confident, more able to convert liabilities into assets. By 1903 Rev. J.A. Knowles was claiming for the Irish the lion's share of credit for Federation, arguing that the frustration and denial imposed by Irish circumstances produced unparalleled bursts of energy and commitment in Australia. By 1908 the slur that the Irish had 'the gift of the gab' (facile, mere talkers) was being paraded as their virtue in Australian politics and law. As to the fact that so many were labourers, or policemen, they were 'physically ... the finest people' who had come to Australia, men of superb quality whose work was superior to all others. And they had much more sentiment and imagination than other people, thus their success in journalism and literature. But the boasting had its pathos in that it was still necessary, still a plaintive appeal to be noticed, accepted, brought in from the cold.

Home Rule seemed to be the vehicle on which these Irish Australians, together with the Irish in Ireland, would ride, in comfort, into the warm welcoming heart of the Empire. It was this euphoric confidence in imminent victory, of at last coming home to the bosom of the imperial family—given an edge of relish by the increasing bitterness of Ulster Unionist opposition—that made the visit of the last of the Home Rule delegations such a great success. In 1911–12 John Redmond's son, William, Richard Hazleton and J.T. Donovan raised £30 000. It seemed inconceivable, whatever the opposition from Ulster, that Home Rule would not come in some form, and by 1913 many Irish-Australian organisations were making arrangements to send representatives to the anticipated opening of the Irish parliament in Dublin. Nineteen fourteen was full of premature celebrations of the total resolution of all Ireland's problems—and uneasy anger at the obduracy of Ulster Unionists.

From the distance of the colonies and with the fall-off in Irish immigration from the 1890s as a source of first-hand knowledge, the complexities of Anglo-Irish relations were not comprehended. Nor was the strength of Ulster's determination to reject Home Rule. By 1914 Home Rule for the Australian Irish was a cause, a slogan and a symbol: matters such as the degree of Irish self-government, the spheres in which it would operate, its timing, and, of course, the area to which it would apply, which were vital questions in Ireland itself, seemed, from Australia, lesser questions. What mattered was the principle. But that principle was, for the Australian Irish in 1914, more a religious one than a nationalist one. It does not appear to have occurred to Cardinal Moran that his involvement with Irish causes could have been a liability to them, hardening Protestant opposition, confirming the spectre of Rome rule, making a national appeal in its widest sense impossible. The religious takeover of the Irish question in Australia dated, on the Catholic side, from Cardinal Moran's initiatives in the 1890s; on the Protestant side it may be dated from the formation of the Australian Protestant Defence Association in June 1901. Its leader was the dynamic demagogue the Rev. Dill Macky, an Irish Presbyterian minister who had been brought up in Derry, where he had been a member of the Prentice Boys' Club. Certainly many Ulster immigrants eschewed such organisations, and Orange Lodges as well, seeing no need for them in Australia. A nonsectarian Ulster Association of New South Wales was formed in Sydney in 1909, with David Storey MLA as president; a Victorian Association was already in existence. Hearing of it, Cardinal Moran was deeply suspicious, but Storey was at pains to point out to him its non-sectarian and indeed anti-sectarian nature, and that it invited Catholic speakers: it simply sought to bring together those of Ulster birth or descent for social purposes. In fact its members tended to be prominent Ulstermen above the social level of Orange Lodge membership—and above militant sectarianism.

This was not the case with those Ulstermen, and Irish Unionists, and Australians who took up Ulster's cause in Melbourne early in 1914. A meeting addressed by Rev. W.H. Fitchett, Sir Robert Best, and Rev. Dr A. Leeper heard that the Empire was about to be destroyed, Ulster Protestants coerced, and Rome would rule via Dublin: it was the standard religious case against Home Rule. Dr O'Donnell and Morgan Jageurs of the United Irish League responded to this in a pamphlet both denouncing and minimising Ulster's irreconcilables as unscrupulous and bigoted. Their stance was dismissive and abusive, in keeping with the simplistic orthodoxy which by then sustained the Australian Home Rule argument. This was that Home Rule was innocuous; Ireland would be getting merely what Australia already enjoyed, that is, democratic self-rule. Imperial experience proved that the bond was strengthened rather than weakened by self-government: the Empire stood for liberty. It was a great moral force and Ireland's position in it was an aberration soon to be remedied.

The trinity of Australia, Empire, and Home Rule Ireland was the holy totality advanced at the monster meeting at the Sydney Town Hall in June 1914, which the Premier, W.A. Holman attended: he was a convinced Home Ruler. And it infused the great demonstration in Melbourne in May, where there were 25 000 people (some reports said 45 000) and three sets of speakers in different sections—including Andrew Fisher and W.M. Hughes, in fact thirty-one parliamentarians. But this vision of the Empire embracing a Home Rule Ireland was delusory, not only in terms of Ulster intransigence, which Irish Australia might be excused from failing to comprehend, but in relation to direct Australian experience. The whole concept of the British Empire and loyalty to it had been taken over in Australia from 1900 by the British Empire League. By 1905 it had secured the observance of Empire Day in schools, a celebration of Englishness, imperialism, Protestantism, and Anglo-Saxon ideas and institutions. Irish Catholics were sufficiently awake to what this meant to respond with an Australia Day for their schools in 1911. By 1914 in Australia, the notion of the Empire had been narrowed to the Protestant and the Tory, and no Home Rulers need apply.

Whatever it had been in earlier phases, by 1914 Irish-Australian support for Home Rule had direct domestic relevance. Home Rule had become the test of the character of the Empire and the issue on which would be decided who would govern and how. The standard argument that Home Rule meant that Ireland would then be like Australia had a double edge—what would Australia be like if Ireland did not get Home Rule? Like Ireland? And where would the Irish in Australia be then—under the Tory and Protestant heel? The intensely self-interested hopes and fears that underlay the Home Rule movement in Australia in 1914 leap out of one of the advertisements for the Melbourne monster meeting in May. It was imperative that Irish Australians 'born in this free, self-governing Commonwealth' attend—in their own interests: no sentimental plea for Ireland here. Why?

> The same gang that hate Ireland and the old race at home, for sectarian reasons, hate you equally, and would carry this hatred effectively into the ordinary business of life if they ever achieved supremacy here. Home Rule for Ireland will mean another spoke in their coffin . . . Come, democrats of all creeds and colours, and all sexes. The Irish question has aroused in its train questions reaching far beyond self government . . . shall the hungry, ill-paid, ill-fed masses at last have a chance of becoming unfettered and emancipated throughout the United Kingdom?

Questions reaching far beyond self-government. For the Australian Irish, the Irish question had come to mean; shall we here, in Australia, be condemned to live our futures in the shadow of servitude? Their sense of the matter had come to this: while Ireland was in any semblance of chains, could they ever feel themselves fully free?

C H A P T E R
S I X

R E B E L S

The clerical takeover of Irish nationalism in Australia, completed by Cardinal Moran in the 1890s, linked the two causes—Ireland, and Catholicism in Australia—in such a way as to render them the one cause, its elements distinguishable, if at all, only in terms of emphasis. That they were in fact distinct causes is best illustrated by the champions of the Home Rule cause in the doldrums of the mid-1890s—in Victoria, the Congregational minister Rev. W. Currie, a Home Rule fanatic, or that formidable Presbyterian contro-versialist, Rev. Dr Rentoul. But by 1914 it was Catholic, and very respectably Catholic at that. By the outbreak of war, Home Rule was on the British statute book, suspended by agreement for the duration of the war, the problem of Ulster's refusal shelved, but with colonial Irish opinion equating Ireland with a Home Rule future. The identification of Australian Catholicism with Ireland became of national significance during the First World War and immediately after for two reasons. In 1916 Ireland ceased to mean Home Rule and came to embody rebellion. And Irish Catholics in substantial numbers publicly qualified their willingness to accept Australian society as it then was, and took up attitudes of difference, challenge and hostility to the prevailing social orthodoxies. To separate these two reasons in this way is—deliberately—to stress the element of coincidence. Events and processes in Ireland and in Australia interacted and fed on each other, but Australian events had their own separate life and character: what happened coincidentally in Ireland exacer-bated the Australian situation and ensured that the language of conflict be Irish. But the questions at issue in Australia were Australian. The questioning was Catholic-led in that its leaders were mainly Catholic clerics, notably the Archbishop of Melbourne, Daniel Mannix: it was Irish-led in that these clerics were exclusively Irish-born, and some were intensely nationalist in an Irish context. The issues were Catholic in so far as they related to the place of Catholics in Australian society and to demands for aid to the Catholic education system; they were Irish in so far as they related to the question, posed in Australian wartime society, of allegiance to all the policies of the then British government, and particularly Britain's treatment of Ireland. Mass support for this agitation was Catholic in so far as, by 1914, under 2 percent of the Australian population was Irish-born. That is, by that time, at most two in ten Catholics had been born in Ireland. It could be said to be 'Irish' in that these Catholics were almost exclusively of Irish descent and reared in an Australian version of an Irish cultural tradition, and in that, small though the Irish-born percentage was, it had power and influence far beyond its numbers: clerical leadership was Irish; the Irish-born were heaviest in the older age groups and thus stronger in the most prominent and influential sector of the Irish Catholic community; and the militant republican complexion of developments in Ireland itself tended to draw out, in the Australian scene, the support of the Irish-born and more recent immigrants.

Another powerful influence highlighted what was Irish in Australia. In its own defence, the Australian establishment found it expedient to concentrate on and exaggerate the Irish elements in the forces which challenged it. These forces could then be fitted into traditional frameworks, eliciting longstanding prejudices and hostility to come into play against them: here were these Irish troublemakers again as they had ever been, since convict days. And as allegedly 'Irish', criticism and non-conformity could be depicted as disloyal, foreign, seditious, charges particularly damaging in wartime.

Despite the public prominence of Irish issues in the turmoil which overtook Australian society between 1916 and 1921, the undoubted strength of these issues was more symbolic than real. Whatever the appearances of events, the basic matters in contention were ones internal to Australia; the big Irish questions in Australia were the ones that raised Australian questions. And it was Catholic rather than Irish energies which sustained the widespread minority agitation among Irish Catholics. Despite superficial appearances—an Irish veneer—Australian society's Irish Catholic elements overwhelmingly shared the same selfish, inward-turned characteristics discernible in the nation as a whole. The style and the symbols differed. So, naturally, did the objectives, for the interests were not the same. But it is realism not cynicism which sees, not Ireland at stake, but the character and destiny of Australia.

This conclusion can be sustained most obviously by a glance at those organisations in Australia which were most patently and radically Irish nationalist. They were thin on the ground. In the aftermath of the Easter 1916 rebellion in Dublin, the Melbourne Home Ruler Morgan Jageurs lashed out at those Irish who demanded that the old Irish organisations now accept the rebellion. He described them as

> a section of Irishmen whose names are not to be found on the membership rolls of Irish associations, and seldom, if ever, on the subscription lists of any Irish political movement with which Dr O'Donnell has been the leader. Yet these malcontents have the audacity to expect him to stand up and calmly witness the destruction of his life's work in this city. The same intolerant factionist spirit is also responsible for similar work in the old country ...

A little later Jageurs described the support for armed insurrection in Ireland as coming from 'a few irresponsible youths not long resident in Australia, of little knowledge of the political history of their own country and considerably less of that of the land of their adoption'. The description was largely accurate and the last phrase an indication of Jageurs' own priorities. Indeed it would have been amazing had the situation been anything different given the tiny size of the revolutionary movement in Ireland itself and its initially hostile reception by the mass of the Irish population. It was simply that events in Ireland had rendered the Home Rule movement less relevant and focused attention on a very few and unimportant extremists, inflating their own sense of importance but failing to convince others of it. The collapse of the Home Rule movement in Australia was to be followed not by the rise of republicanism, but by nothing. Or rather, by a period of intense turmoil in which the name of Ireland was much bandied about, and then by nothing. With Home Rule the relevance of Ireland to Australia comes to an end. Whereas in Ireland, as W.B. Yeats perceived it, all was changed, changed utterly by the rebellion, in Australia all that was really changed was the news from Ireland. And that, from an Australian viewpoint, was unrelievedly bad until 1921. No terrible beauty. Just terrible. Only for some very few was that change important for itself. For most, its importance was in what it signified for Australia—which was bad news, conflict, uncertainty, hostility. The nature of things Irish in Australia had not changed: but events in Ireland ensured that the environment in which they operated had. The clergy still ruled, time was continuing to erode what was Irish, moderation was the primary inclination—and such new radical republican organisations as sprang up remained small, powerless and irrelevant, just visible enough to cause trouble. For five years Ireland became a cause which had to be defended in Australia, but the experience confirmed Irish Catholics beyond any doubt in the conviction that had long drifted in and out of their consciousness, that Ireland was a liability they could well do without.

Of those organisations in Australia dedicated to the new republican Ireland, by far the largest and most significant was the Irish National Association of New South Wales formed in Sydney July 1915, following on a preliminary public meeting of eighteen people in the Catholic Club. The initiative came from a young man of twenty-seven, Albert Thomas Dryer. Dryer had an Irish mother, and an Australian-born father of German descent. He had never been to Ireland and was never to go there, in a lifetime of dedication to the INA; he died in 1963. Nor was he interested at all in Irish affairs until, early in 1914, he read Alice Stopford Green's book *Irish Nationality*. (Dryer was not the only Irish Australian to be influenced by this book: Hubert Murray, son of Terence Aubrey Murray, Lieutenant Governor of Papua, passed it on to Hugh Mahon. Murray, an extraordinary if insecure man, held the theory that those half-Irish were more fiercely patriotic than full-bloods. A commanding officer in the NSW Irish Rifles since 1898, he had served in the Boer War though opposed to it, so as to gain experience. By 1905 he was learning Gaelic and subscribing to the Irish paper *Sinn Fein*: in 1925 he was still a member of the Gaelic League. He did not know Dryer, but they were both members of a singular if eccentric Irish-Australian company.) The message of this book—that a rich diverse and heroic Irish culture stood at last on the verge of a natural and fruitful independence—burst on Dryer as a revelation, and he turned to an intensive study of Irish history and culture, and to championing Ireland's independence. His enthusiasm, at first cultural, led on to political conclusions, sharply intensified by his reaction to the outbreak of the First World War in August 1914.

Established Australian Irish opinion did not regard the war as altering the Irish question. John Redmond had pledged, in the House of Commons, Ireland's support for Britain in the war: Irish Australia joined in the great surge of loyalty. Home Rule was the final answer, suspended until the war was won. In Australia, the leading Home Rule families were unquestionably pro-British, to the degree of giving their sons: among those who enlisted early in the war were the sons of Dr McCarthy, Dr O'Donnell, Samuel Winter, Thomas Fogarty and Morgan Jageurs. John Davitt Jageurs was killed at Gallipoli. Other prominent Irish Catholic families sympathetic to Home Rule were similarly involved. A stained-glass window in St Mary's Cathedral, Sydney, commemorated Second Lieutenant Brendan Lane Mullins, killed in action in France in June 1917: two of Sir Thomas Hughes' sons were killed. The Irish Catholic community was as heavily committed to the war as any other sector of Australia. Of Irish revolutionary movements it was hardly even aware.

Not so a powerful element of American Irish opinion, which was strongly pro-German and committed to an Irish republic completely independent of Britain. Dryer became aware of this through reading the New York weekly *Irish World* in the Sydney Catholic Club's reading room. He quickly adopted a similar position. There seems little doubt that Dryer's response was influenced by his German as well as his Irish descent, an unusual heritage in Australia. He was unusual too in that his intellectual disposition—he was a university graduate in arts—predisposed him to intellectual conversion, while his warm, sensitive and generous temperament lent itself to total enthusiasms. The cause of Irish independence filled needs of commitment in Dryer to a degree where his dedication went beyond that of any of the Irish-born in Australia: their knowledge of Irish reality could not compete with the intensity of his dream. There was also a negative dimension to his conversion. Dryer was a Catholic of Irish-German descent in an Australia which, in 1915, was hysterically anti-German and traditionally anti-Irish and anti-Catholic: he felt a strong sense of social oppression and exclusion. He suffered Ireland's wrongs and took up her grievances as if they were personal to himself.

So too, in a much milder way, did Australia's Home Rulers, but Dryer—suddenly with a new and inspiring purpose in his life—was blind to this. What he saw was dismaying—total Irish-Australian commitment to Britain's war, undisturbed faith in the limited self-

Albert Dryer in 1919

government of Home Rule, Irish culture ignored, the ideal of full Irish independence unrecognised. Nothing Irish existed in Australia 'further than the annual chanting of the "Wearin' o' the Green" on the 17th March'. No Irish organisation in Australia embodied the ideas and attitudes he had come to believe in so strongly. He decided to start such an organisation himself.

In June 1915 the Sydney *Freeman's Journal* published a letter from Dryer under the heading 'An Appeal to Irishmen. Be Irish'. This letter was prompted by the discontinuance by the Hibernian Society of its annual donation to school scholarships and prizes in Irish history. (Reflecting clerical pressure, the money had been diverted to an ecclesiastical bursary at St Patrick's College, Manly—Dryer's criticism would not have endeared him to the clerical establishment.) In his letter Dryer made clear that, although he was Australian-born, his adopted identity was totally Irish. When he wrote, 'a close study of our history is the sole antidote for the anglicising poison which has permeated and is permeating our national system', he was referring not to Australia, but to Ireland. Australia no longer existed for him. Residence there was merely accidental: the reality of his life was its Irish derivation. 'The fact that the Eireannach speaks a foreign language or was born in a foreign country need not deter him from co-operation with his compatriots at home, for he should be able to assess these linguistic and geographical accidents at their true value'. Australia was a 'foreign country'; Ireland, which he had never seen, was his home. Irishmen, and their descendants, in Australia were 'the exiled sons of Erin'. No, worse than exiles, they were slaves: their very presence on foreign soil was testimony to Irish weakness and degradation. And nothing was more revealing of that enslavement than use of the English language, to Dryer who had no Gaelic, 'that badge of subjection which is burned into our very souls'.

Dryer's message was that Irishmen in Australia, unless they be utterly degraded, must act in common with the new initiatives of Irishmen in Ireland and America, not in the weak Home Rule tradition, but in relation to the new emergent wave of Irish nationalism. His models were the Gaelic League and Sinn Fein in Ireland, and Clan-na-Gael in America, and he saw in the resurrection of Ireland and of Irish culture, less a political program than a strong moral imperative, a direct means of furthering virtue and religion. He was familiar with the objectives and activity of the Irish Volunteers (formed in 1913 as an anti-Ulster Unionist defence force) through their newspaper, but he did not look to the paramilitary Irish bodies for a model. Dryer's orientation was cultural, seeing an Irish revival in Australia in terms of the Gaelic language, history and drama, as part of a worldwide rebirth of Irish values.

All this was highly unusual in the Australian Irish scene, but Dryer's case illustrates frontally both the new and radical thinking that had grown in the nationalist movement in Ireland itself, and the extreme to which the Australian Irish would never go: if Dryer could have been transported to Ireland he would have been nothing unusual in the camp of the new nationalists; in Irish Australia he was a crank. And a most unwelcome one—though the leaders of Australian Irish orthodoxy contrived not to notice him, an easy enough task. Dryer's belligerent Irishry, and his utter disregard for any Australian environment, were not only repugnant to them, but simply absurd. They saw their future, and Irish Australia's, successfully merged with the general Australian community, and Ireland happily merged, through Home Rule, with the British Empire. Surveying the Melbourne Irish scene in 1915 Dryer saw nothing more than convivial Home Rule-ism, itself almost expired in expectation of imminent success. The leading organisation was the Celtic Club:

'It takes an active interest in all things Irish (especially the whisky) and all the leading Irishmen of Melbourne, whether R.C.s or not, are members of it.' The Shamrock Club was merely social, the United Irish League was inactive, and the Irish Pipers' Band, merely that. Jageurs and O'Donnell were the big Irish names, as they had been since the 1880s. And Melbourne Irishry was stronger than anywhere else.

Dryer's ideas for an Irish nationalist organisation represented a totally revolutionary break with Irish-Australian tradition. Knowing this, he proceeded prudently, but prudence was not enough. The Hibernian Society provided rooms free of charge and a respectable backing. The Irish National Association's objects, 'to assist Ireland to achieve her national destiny and to foster an Irish spirit among the Irish portion of the community' were tame and vague dilutions of Dryer's personal convictions. But it was Dryer's other efforts to compromise with reality which came to grief. He sought, with a non-sectarian clause, to bridge the religious divide between Irishmen, accepting the proposition that a Catholic Irish society would not be a truly national one. But Archbishop Kelly's idea of an Irish society was one under clerical patronage, and he concluded that in not seeking this, and declaring itself 'non-sectarian', the INA was implying that Catholic societies were sectarian: Catholicism could never be sectarian, for it was the enduring truth. Kelly's public hostility did grave damage to the INA from its beginnings and the rift with the hierarchy was never healed. Still, the problem with Kelly was not merely the 'non-sectarian' clause: the Archbishop was not disposed to tolerate any lay initiative whatever, and particularly not from the nonentities that comprised the INA. His later comment that 'he did not know who these people were' carried a message of disdain which his power could translate into their ostracism within Catholic circles.

It also conveyed the reality of another fact of Australian life—that the influence of an organisation commonly related to the social standing or prominence of its officers. Its provisional chairman told the INA 'there was no use in members nominating any member for positions who did not hold some status in society'. The difficulty was that very few members did: to quote a member in 1916, they were 'mainly of the working class and not much in the councils of the great'. It is hardly surprising that militant Irish nationalism in Australia drew such support as it had from that quarter: pro-Irish motions frequently surfaced after 1916 at Labor Party and trade union conferences. But having in the nature of things no friends in high places, no well-known officials, the INA cut itself off from its natural mass source of power and influence by what amounted to a self-denying ordinance not to become involved in local party politics. This probably had the same constricting paralysing effect on potential membership as did the non-sectarian clause, but more importantly it isolated the association from an avenue whereby its opinions and initiatives might have reached a wider audience or found their way into corridors of power: for all that the INA was a tiny organisation, Albert Dryer was an enthusiast of extraordinary force and dedication whose impact may have been considerable had he had access to a wider Australian stage. (Still, it is doubtful if this made much difference, given that Labor itself had no intention of becoming a vehicle for Irish causes. J.H. Catts, who was sympathetic, explained why in the Brisbane *Worker* in November 1920: 'To do so would not only be a base betrayal of the economic interests of the Australian masses, but it would soon wreck the movement.' Against this, not to do so, at least by way of gesture, might wreck the movement also, which accounts for the belated and by then safe endorsement of Irish self-determination of the ALP Conference in June 1921.) The reason for a self-denying political ordinance was obvious and valid enough on Dryer's view—not to import Australian divisions into a society whose total concern was Ireland, but this made an assumption which was itself unreal, that members would, or could, shed their Australian identity for the benefit of the INA. In an environment in which Irishness had become identified both with support of Catholicism and support of the Labor Party, to opt out of both these allegiances was to repudiate what were regarded in Australia as the natural concomitants of Irishness. Catholicism and Labor politics had become the dominant social characteristics of the Irish-Australian clan, and it was impossible to abstract from them successfully to distil what was purely Irish. Or rather, it was possible, but the pure Irish residue thereby isolated in the refining process was tiny, insignificant. The formation of Dryer's INA resembled a laboratory experiment in finding the Irish gold in the Irish-Australian dross: it was a most excellent measure of what was really Irish in Irish Australia—virtually nothing.

That measure was in, first, the size of its membership. For its first few months, the association's committee 'endeavoured to render the weekly meetings popular by means of a large measure of social amusement, with the object of augmenting the membership list'. In addition to frequent social gatherings, euchre parties, dramatic impersonations of Irish patriots, an Irish wedding, a harbour excursion and so on, every business meeting was followed, and usually overshadowed by, Irish music and dancing. By January 1916, six months after its formation, the INA had 211 members.

In terms of the then Irish population, this was a tiny few: there were over 22 000 Irish-born living in Sydney and its suburbs, and around 150 000 of Irish descent. At the peak of its membership in 1919, the INA had attracted about 1500 of these. Even this is a gross exaggeration of the support for Irish militancy. Dryer had grave misgivings about building the INA through its social program. The features he wanted did not develop: the membership had joined for social reasons. When, eventually, a Gaelic teacher was found, few members were interested. The committee affirmed the desirability of establishing a co-operative store to stock Irish goods and manufactures: nothing was done. Nor was anything done about classes in other Irish cultural activities—history and the like.

Dryer had informed the Gaelic League in Dublin of the formation of the INA, and a response from the general secretary, Sean T. O'Kelly, strengthened his misgivings about building up membership through providing society and amusement. O'Kelly stressed the imperative necessity of the revival and spread of the Irish language, the study of Irish history and support for Irish industries, and put to Dryer that it was 'better to have a small band of earnest and sincere workers who know what is required of them than to have a large body of indifferent people . . .'. Dryer was aware of this problem, but not aware, it seems, of other Australian contacts with the Gaelic revival in Ireland: the fragmentation of what was already a small Australian response reduced its significance even further. Dryer had not made contact with Melbourne Gaelic enthusiasts, presumably because of their Home Rule politics; perhaps it is understandable that he was not aware of Hubert Murray in Papua; but there were enthusiasts in his own city of whom he seemed also unaware. The Franciscan priest T.A. Fitzgerald had become a convert to the cause of the Gaelic language. In 1909 he had translated from the Irish some of P.H. Pearse's Connemara stories for publication in the Sydney *Catholic Press*. At that time Pearse himself had revised the stories in proof form and, either then or later—1914 or 1915—Fitzgerald had met Pearse in Ireland. In either of those later years, Fitzgerald, together with William Burke of Paddington in Sydney (a 'thorough Irish-Irelander') had attended a banquet to commemorate the summer break-up of Pearse's St Enda's College in Rathfarnham. (Fitzgerald observed: 'those patriarch patriots the Hon. John Meagher and Bernard Gaffney, and many others from Australia, would have been delighted at the scene'.) Fitzgerald republished the Pearse stories in book form in Sydney in 1921 and remained lyrical about Ireland's achievements and future: 'Gaelic Ireland is a new and glorious Ireland ...' That Dryer and Fitzgerald and Burke and others in Sydney should be active in Sydney separately makes another comment on the Australian scene: jealousies, class and social divisions, and sheer selfish lack of interest in others' efforts, as well as laziness and incompetence, reduced what was of narrow interest to less significance still.

But probably the main feature which distinguished Dryer's Gaelic enthusiasm from those of others in Australia was his radical political dimension. Taking O'Kelly's advice to push for an Irish National Association which would be a small elite of devotees of Irish independence, on 17 April 1916 Dryer secured an amendment of the objects to include the recognition and pursuit of Ireland's 'sovereign nationhood', thus rendering the objects no longer open to a Home Rule interpretation. The effect of this on membership was never tested, for exactly one week later the rules of all Irish games were changed utterly. On 24 April the INA's monthly ceili dancing was abandoned, as the minutes put it, 'in sympathy with the patriots who lost their lives (being murdered after the Irish insurrection) to satisfy the blood lust of the champion of small nations'. In the early months of 1916 the INA had been taking on an increasingly radical complexion. Suddenly, events in Ireland conferred on its ideals and aspirations, in their most extreme form, the accolades of according with Irish reality: inevitably the Irish rebellion injected new life and purpose into this tiny, distant mirror. But would this new Irish reality generate a genuine and sympathetic response from Irish-Australian reality?

The INA was the only organisation in Australia whose immediate response to the rebellion was sympathetic. Among prominent Australian Irish organisations and personalities, reactions ranged from emotional denunciations, and fervent declarations of loyalty to the Empire, to saddened regret and repudiation. Archbishop Clune of Perth said it was 'insane', Archbishop Carr of Melbourne said it was 'an outburst of madness, an anachronism, and a crime', Dr McCarthy of Sydney said it was 'sectional pro-German rioting', the Melbourne Hibernians condemned the 'lamentable folly of extremists', and the 'abhorrence and disgust' of Broken Hill Hibernians was a stock phrase of which other such organisations produced variants. Archbishop Mannix was the least censorious, but even he initially regarded the rebellion as 'truly deplorable', 'lamentable', and its leaders as 'misguided'.

This virtually unanimous condemnation sprang from feelings much more basic, and selfish, than traditional loyalty to Home Rule. The Home Rule solution to the question of Ireland's political status suited the Australian Irish perfectly: Ireland would become, like Australia, free within the British Empire. The leaders of Irish Australia felt a certain amount of pride and satisfaction in that Ireland would be, in a sense, following their path as Irish Australians, but the main attraction of the Home Rule scenario was that it allowed Irish Australians to reconcile, without difficulty, their various loyalties, old and new: they could be loyal to Australia, Ireland and the Empire all at once, in a piece, without conflict or tension. The Easter 1916 rebellion destroyed this harmony by posing loyalty to Ireland and loyalty to the Empire as alternatives. Irishmen, aided in part by Germany, had taken up arms against Britain, which was fighting Germany with Australian aid. The howl of anguished repudiation which arose from Irish organisations throughout Australia, the torrent of denunciation they poured on the rebels, testified to their dismay that Irish affairs should call in question their Australian and imperial loyalties, to their feeling that the rebellion prejudiced their comfort, security and reputation in Australia, and generally, to their awareness that the question of the position of the Irish in the Australian community had now become a very sensitive and precarious one.

That this indignation sprang from a sense of personal betrayal was made quite explicit by the United Irish League of Melbourne: 'Such fanatics betray gross ingratitude for the benefits Ireland received through the long agitation and generosity of the Irish abroad, as well as the valuable help rendered by the British and other democracies.' It was to take a little while for Australian Irish to realise that these 'fanatics' were distinct from the visible Home Rule Ireland they had known and supported, and that gross political errors had been made in what had been presented to them as Irish reality by the Irish Home Rule machine. Part of the Australian Irish anger stemmed from being taken so unawares, made to look such fools: it was no comfort that there were ample and prominent fools in Ireland as well. But Archbishop Clune explained much of the emotional intensity of the Australian Irish response when he declared that those of Irish birth or sympathy looked on the rebellion with shame. Reacting to this shame and humiliation, smarting under the disgrace of some few of their countrymen having betrayed Britain, the Australian Irish—Catholic hierarchy, Hibernians, Irish National Foresters, United Irish League, Irish associations and clubs in every State—loudly asserted their loyalty to Britain, to the war, and to the Irish Parliamentary Party. They sought to depict the rebellion as an insignificant riot, and—most important in explaining the direction taken by subsequent Australian Irish reaction—they searched for someone to blame for their predicament.

Hostility to the rebellion's leaders was immediate, but when the initial shocked fury had passed, this began to be seen for what it was—willingness to accept the discreditable proposition that Irishmen alone were to blame for what had happened. Some organisations had already baulked at that from the beginning, citing British provocation. With the execution of the leaders their availability as potential scapegoats for Australian Irish hostility and frustration ceased: their role became quite other. Soon the same impulses that had led to the denunciation of the rebellion—pride, aspirations to community acceptance, a sense of what was right and honourable—made an anti-Irish interpretation of the rebellion unacceptable: soon, most Irishmen in Australia moved on to place the blame elsewhere, on Britain.

Within a month of the rebellion the weight of opinion was moving from the position that the rebellion was 'madness', 'insane', to the stance that it was a response, however deplorable, to provocation, a reaping of what Britain had sown. Soon the segment of Irish-Australian opinion critical of, even hostile to Britain, became overwhelmingly preponderant. It was even more important that this division, and swing toward its anti-British pole, appeared, and remained, among the Catholic hierarchy and clergy, that is, among those who moulded and led the Australian Irish community. Within a few weeks of the rebellion it was possible to find support among the Catholic hierarchy and clergy for the whole range of possible attitudes to the rebellion and the revival of Irish republican nationalism that followed it. The decisive influence of the episcopacy on Irish nationalist organisation and commitment is evident from Albert Dryer's observation from Sydney to Maurice Dalton in Melbourne in November 1917: 'As to a meeting here, I do not think it would be possible without the aid of Dr Mannix. We have very few laymen capable of addressing such a meeting here. There are a number of clerics who, they say themselves, could not take the platform on account of the attitude of that old contemptible seoinin, Archbishop Kelly, a notorious recruiting sergeant.' Kelly, deeply conservative, had a vigorously repressive effect on Irish republican sympathies in New South Wales. Mannix stimulated them in Victoria—and once liberated and encouraged there, they were impossible to repress totally elsewhere in Australia. Without Mannix, in a situation in which 'Irish' life was clerically dominated, it seems likely that the issue of Irish independence would have received small attention in Australia. Most Australian Irish would have preferred to avoid it.

Mannix made this impossible. His championship of Ireland's cause provided leadership, but leadership of a peculiar kind. It was inspiration of the reluctant, and Ireland was the least attractive, least real, aspect of his appeal. While Ireland remained, for the Catholic masses, a symbol of their own oppression and exclusion, they followed a Mannix to whom Ireland's plight was not symbolic but real. When, after 1921, Ireland ceased to have any Australian resemblances, Mannix lost his local 'Irish' tribe virtually overnight: they would not follow him out of their Australian environment into the darkness and complication of civil-war Ireland. But in 1916 his public statements expressed what many thought, but did not wish to say for reasons of peace or comfort—or lacked the wit to phrase, or opportunity to promulgate. Mannix, like the Home Rule delegations of the 1880s, made the issues unavoidable. Like them he was virtually unassailable—they, because they were itinerants passing through, he because of his position. Both acted as the conscience of the Irish: it might be resented, but it told the truth and a good man would be grateful for it. It was both stimulus and irritant; Mannix amounted to an Irish delegation that would not go away as the others had done, a permanent outside force that made Irish issues unavoidable. Once they were forced to face these issues, even those who disagreed with Mannix's frontal methods had to concede their substantial agreement with his conclusions. Archbishop Kelly was such a case. And those bishops who disagreed with Mannix, if only on tactical grounds, could not attack or repudiate him, for to criticise his belligerent Irishry would be to court a reaction from their own laity and perhaps prejudice, even gravely, the unity of Catholicism in Australia. Nor, for the same reason, could they discipline too harshly those of their own clergy who came out in support of Mannix's position. For all that Dryer—correctly—assessed Kelly's power, the Archbishop sought, without notable success, to quieten the vigorous and spectacular INA priest, Dr Tuomey, and the equally explosive pro-republicanism of the rector of St John's College of the University of Sydney, Rev. Dr Maurice O'Reilly. Yet the Sydney situation makes clear what would have been the Australian state had it not been for Mannix: repression of the whole Irish question and particularly republicanism. To a very large degree, Irish republicanism was a mushroom growth, which sheltered and flourished under the Mannix umbrella. The mere presence of this remarkable personality both allowed and forced developments whose relative extremism was abnormal to the Australian situation.

Dr Mannix's character and motivation have been much discussed, though much still remains mysterious. Suffice to say that Mannix elected to take a stand sympathetic to the 1916 rebellion and critical of British policy in Ireland, a position he advanced reasonably but with increasing impact on, and interaction with, the two extremes of his supporters on the one hand, his detractors on the other. What has not come under scrutiny are the reasons for his extraordinary popular support, it being assumed that this was somehow natural to Irish Catholics. The reality is more complex and relates less to the Irishness that Mannix espoused than to his social role as a hero.

The demand for a hero was a constant in Irish Catholic life in Australia from its foundations—Michael Dwyer, Fr Therry. This took curious and diverse forms—Caroline

Les Darcy in the ring

Chisholm, Ned Kelly—and even reversed into anti-heroes, people they loved to hate, such as J.D. Lang, and Henry Parkes. Its sporting manifestations were continuous and marked, but the biggest names were in boxing, Larry Foley and Les Darcy. Sport allowed the creation of instant heroes to fill the psychological need of a subordinate group for self-esteem: boxing ritualised fighting, physical violence, demonstrating power and venting spleen and frustration vicariously. Les Darcy from Maitland came to Sydney and to fame in 1914. Helped by a priest, of Australian birth but Irish stock, Darcy emerged as a pure and simple hero, a good boy who loved and looked after his mother, went to daily Mass, said the rosary—and won: 'the power in his fists came straight from God.' World fame, and money, lay outside Australia, but in 1916 passports were being refused men of military age. Darcy secretly boarded a ship to America, where his career was obstructed by various authorities and individuals. He collapsed and died in Memphis in April 1917 aged 21, but his body was returned to Australia to be buried in East Maitland after a vast funeral testified to his extraordinary veneration among Irish Catholics: there were murmurings about Australia's first saint. In life and death Darcy's career generated legends which told more about Irish Catholics than about Darcy, full of ambivalence, contradictions, half-truths, piety and invention. The myths came to this: here was a decent Irish boy, the flower of Australian manhood, on his way to being world champion. He was willing to enlist freely as a true hero should, but he decided to defy authority and escape conscription to fight in America to win fame and fortune and provide for his mother. For this he had been persecuted and vilified in Australia, by the jingoes and anti-Irish, and betrayed by his mate, E.T. O'Sullivan, that Dublin jackeen: was it not typical of us that he should be crucified by his own countrymen, Irish included? And then martyred in his prime, poisoned, by those rich and greedy Yanks, dying in his fiancée's arms in American exile, cheated of success and money by Ireland's enemies and by—ah, dear God—that last enemy death, come too soon.

But a new hero was at hand. Darcy died in April 1917 in what might be best called an atmosphere of hysteria. His popular heir was Mannix, adored because he was a fighter too, with words; superb in sparring with the establishment, knocking them out with his verbal punches, dazzling with his footwork in avoiding their lumbering counter-attacks, the master of the quick and telling jab. Prodigiously out of place in a slow, conservative church, Mannix combined the hallowed virtues of religion, and the role of leadership thereby conferred, with the legacy of Darcy. From the popular Irish Catholic viewpoint, Mannix was wholeheartedly on their side—a shining Mick—he was a fighter, and most of all he was a winner: his wins, against the enemies of the Irish, were there to see and savour, up there in the biggest public arena there was. Mannix was the Irish sportsman's dream. And it was his swinging of Irish pugnacity away from sport and into politics that made him so formidable and dangerous to the establishment.

The executions of sixteen of the leaders which followed the Easter 1916 rebellion in Dublin had a sharp and pronounced effect on Australian Irish opinion, but not for the reasons that obtained in Ireland. The surge of bitter resentment engendered by the executions sprang, not from sympathy with the rebels or their cause, but from alarm and concern about the local implications. John Redmond had appealed for clemency and a number of Australian Irish organisations and churchmen had supported this with cables. These appeals had been ignored. The executions, followed by violence, martial law and mass deportations, branded the Irish—wherever they were—as traitors and criminals, and arraigned them all by association, as potentially disloyal, a charge much more serious in the sensitive Australian environment than in the Irish or the American. Besides, there seemed flagrant discrimination, in that the British policy of executions in 1916 contrasted sharply with the treatment of other situations—the Ulster crisis, and South African rebels. English policy came to be seen as a calculated and vicious affront and humiliation, cruel repayment for Irish and Irish-Australian loyalty to England, to England's war. So the real significance of the Easter rebellion in Dublin was not that it of itself alienated the Australian Irish from the British government (and consequently, to a lesser extent, from the Australian government) but that the British reaction seemed to them to show that government to be ruthlessly and vindictively alienated from the Irish. This dismay and resentment were most intense among not the poor Irish, but their leaders, those of public and social standing who had long sought to demonstrate their loyalty and assimilation: naturally, the impugning of Irish loyalty to the Crown hurt those who valued and professed it most. Brutally, what had happened in Ireland following the rebellion compelled the established leaders of the Australian Irish to consider if they had been fools, naive idealists, to have believed British rhetoric about justice, fair play, decency and the rest. It is not too strong to suggest that for many of the respectable Australian Irish, the British reaction to the Irish rebellion gravely damaged, if it did not destroy, an innocent world-view based on trust of Britain and the virtues of her civilisation. The shattering of this dream formed an ideal seedbed for the growth of fellow feeling with Mannix's cynicism: they would never trust Tory Britain, or Tory Australia, again. Some saw this as undermining their former trust in the goodness of the Empire, others as having disastrous implications for Australia. What worried Archbishop Duhig most was the damage British policy would do to what he regarded as a major element in the progress of Irish integration into Australian life—enlistment in the armed forces. He need not have been concerned. By 1916 the wide-eyed idealists had already joined and those who remained probably already had, as members of the working classes, a healthy scepticism unlikely to be further affronted by England's Irish policy.

A segment of one of Mannix's typical audiences

What had developed among moderate and conservative Australian opinion was a dual repugnance: it liked neither what had happened in Ireland or how Britain had dealt with it. This is evident in the motion of an interstate Hibernian Society conference on 16 May to 'publicly condemn the late lamentable folly of extremists in the old land, but deeply deplore the ruthless retaliatory measures of the home government'. As these measures continued, the drift of such injured opinion took Irish Australia into increasing alienation from Britain's Irish policy, but it did not take other than a very small minority into support for Irish republicanism. However they might feel, or talk among themselves, very few Irish in Australia were prepared to commit themselves to Irish nationalist causes. Most of that very few were Irish-born, and fairly recent immigrants. But the rule was what a Melbourne Gaelic Leaguer told Dryer in 1916, that 'the real nature of so-called Irishmen's sincerity for Irish freedom' was 'lip nationalism . . . [A] man or woman leaving Ireland . . . [is] lost to her cause; with very few exceptions . . . they are not prepared to stand by truth and right; but rather with the Empire policy'. The Australian Irish en masse would listen to and applaud Irish nationalist sentiments, but they did not want these to prejudice or interfere with their Australian life. By 1920, certainly by 1921, this wish to be rid of the local embarrassments that flowed from the Irish question had reasserted its predominance. This norm may have prevailed earlier—or never been departed from—had it not been for a few spectacular clerical partisans of Irish nationalism, for the involvement of Irish issues with the question of Catholic status and claims in the Australian community, and for the intense exacerbation of the loyalty issue in the deep social divisions occasioned by the conscription referenda of 1916 and 1917.

And had not the rebellion itself struck a responsive chord in the Australian Irish. However much they might wish to repress or deny this, the rebellion brought a thrill of excitement, of identification. The intensity of the outrage and indignation expressed against British policy was part composed of a repressed instinct to take the rebel side. Repudiation of the rebellion had been genuine, but as a reaction it was only the top layer of a complexity in which the affirmation 'I will not serve' lay very deep. For some, the rebellion and the British reaction prompted voyages of self-discovery with surprising results: the rebellion 'stirs up rebel instincts that I thought had perished', as a *Catholic Press* columnist put it. This reaction extended to every social level: the wealthy Mrs E.M. Freehill remarked to Archbishop Kelly in August 1916, 'one thinks of the way our people are treated in Ireland (and as an Irish-Australian I must say it does not bear too much thinking) . . .'. John Dillon's comment in the British parliament that the rebels had been foolish, but he was proud of them, pleased many and led to increasing criticism of what John Meagher MLC called 'the sycophantic messages cabled to Mr Redmond by our self-appointed Irish leaders and some of our so-called Irish societies in Australia', and of 'the timid counsel of Dr McCarthy and Dr O'Donnell'. Obviously, opinion was moving rapidly away from the old Home Rule order in Australia, but that process of movement was action enough: nothing practical needed doing. Confronted by the need to think through, in relation to themselves, what was happening in Ireland, this became a sufficiently absorbing reactive task to be enough in itself.

So, while Australian Irish opinion deserted the Irish Parliamentary Party very rapidly, this desertion was much more a bitter disillusionment with its policies and their Australian outcome than conversion to Sinn Fein. The Sydney lawyer Neal Collins, long prominent in the Home Rule cause, wrote to the *Catholic Press* late in June 1916 to express his disgust with reports that the party had agreed to the partition of Ireland, which he took as demonstrating that the party had been outmanoeuvred again, this time by Ulstermen: 'Was it for a mockery of this kind that the Irishmen and women of Australia and their friends (not to mention America) have for years parted with their hard-earned money to envoys or chosen delegates sent here to plead the cause of a national parliament for a united Ireland . . .? To sum up the situation, John Redmond and his party failed utterly when the supreme test came'. Collins and men like him felt cheated and betrayed—by an Irish Party patently powerless to affect events or policies. Had the party handled affairs properly, Irish Australians would have been spared the sharp and humiliating social discomfiture of being identified with failure and stupidity, of being accused of disloyalty to the Crown, of becoming the objects of suspicion, contempt and ostracism, and of now seeing the ultimate humiliation of Ulster winning, getting its own way and destroying Irish viability in the process. Incompetence and failure could hardly be more complete than that. Australian Home Rulers had, as it were, paid Redmond (as well as trusted him) to harmonise the interests of Ireland and the Empire, and to conduct Ireland's affairs with dignity and care, so that they might live in comfort and self-esteem with themselves in Australia. He had completely failed to do his job.

Anger and disillusionment with the Parliamentary Party did not lead to enthusiasm about the rebellion. The respectable Irish had no wish to be associated with any violence. Besides, these rebels were the cause of all the problems, and many still thought of them as betraying Redmond and Ireland's chance of Home Rule. Perhaps few thought of them as did Geoffrey Hughes in France, facing imminent death: 'scum' he called them; the 'real' Irish were in the trenches with him, fighting against despotism and for Christianity. Anyhow these rebels had failed, their rebellion had been crushed, and themselves executed. It was another of those abortive incidents in Irish history which did only harm: would that it could be swiftly forgotten.

There was another reason for repudiating this rebellion: it was not genuinely 'Irish' in the nationalist sense. The image of the rebellion which reached Australia in the first few months that followed it had strong tinges of working-class revolution: James Connolly and the Irish Citizen Army figured dominantly in this version of events. This made it very popular with some of the more militant Irish Catholic members of the Labor Party who, in the words of the East Woollahra Labor League in Sydney, saw an uprising of 'the Irish militant workers . . . endeavouring to secure self-government for their countrymen'; or in the words of the Brisbane Catholic *Age*, it was 'a revolutionary movement', directed against 'capitalistic sweaters, landed aristocracy, the governing classes, all those who fattened on the work of others, the craven place seekers'. While an asset among the ranks of the militant working class, such a reputation was the kiss of death not only among the respectable but among clerics, without whom nothing Irish in Australia happened. At first, conservative Catholic publicists freely bracketed Sinn Feiners with the then most dreaded anarchic socialist bogey in Australia, the IWW (Industrial Workers of the World), a linkage perpetuated (and later embellished by the addition of Bolshevism) in the pro-conscription campaigns of the Prime Minister, W.M. Hughes.

So at first the 1916 rebellion bred among the Australian Irish disgust, division, uncertainty, confusion, and simple dismissal as being an unfortunate event now over. As in the 1860s Fenian Prisoners' Dependants Fund, inauguration by the INA in mid-June of an Irish Relief Fund, for the dependants of those who lost their lives in the rebellion, bred division. The money was to be sent to the Archbishop of Dublin, but Archbishop Kelly would have nothing to do with the INA—'some people who set themselves out as an Irish National Association'. As to the appeal, it was associated with terrible events in Ireland, whereas Kelly expressed the hope that the Australian Irish would support the constitutional party. The INA tried to circumvent Kelly's obstruction by circularising the clergy direct, asking them to appeal to their people for donations to the fund, but it grew very slowly.

However in August there was an appeal from Ireland, approved by the Archbishop of Dublin, to which all the Australian bishops, including Kelly, responded. The bishops took the central role in large public meetings attended by prominent politicians (usually Labor) and civil dignitaries. As previously, donations salved Irish Australian consciences, and imparted a glow of solidarity. But further, on this occasion such fund-raising shifted attention away from the rebellion itself towards the distressful condition of the Irish people, a by-product of the lives lost and destruction wrought in the suppression of the rebellion. This was a concern in which most Australian Irish could unite while ignoring the issues raised by the rebellion. Indeed the rebellion itself was being rapidly lost to sight in the manoeuvres of the respectable Irish. In the view of the Hon. J.D. Fitzgerald—and it appears to have been a representative one—the purpose of the Sydney meeting for the Dublin Relief Fund was to 'protest against the betrayal of Ireland in regard to home rule and the establishment of martial law there': the rebellion did not appear in a picture which had Ireland fighting in Britain's war on the promise and expectation that it would get Home Rule but its reward had been martial law instead. The rebellion was more than a profound embarrassment. It was potentially a dangerous and divisive influence in Australian affairs—which is why many Catholic leaders and labour politicians wanted to pretend it had not taken place, or was insignificant, or better still, should be buried immediately under the granting of Home Rule. To simply ignore the rebellion, or treat it as basically irrelevant, seems absurd only in the hindsight of the processes of Irish independence it was later seen to have initiated. In 1916 many saw it, particularly from an Australian distance, as another of those abortive risings which littered Irish history, another extremist failure which merely strengthened the force of moderate demands for reform.

The anxiety that the contagion of Ireland not spread to Australia was expressed at its height in a resolution of the Federal parliament in March 1917, urging the granting of Home Rule. For some parliamentarians this was a matter of principle, for others a matter of politics and pelf. Prime Minister Hughes believed settlement of the Irish question was essential to any improvement in Australian recruiting and made that clear to Lloyd George. Other politicians were more concerned with personal interests than national, and feared that divisions over Irish matters might have adverse effects on their own fortunes. They wanted Great Britain to resolve a matter outside Australian control but potentially disruptive of Australian tranquillity.

Meanwhile, the degeneration of affairs in Ireland into increasing confrontation, and the polarisation of opinion on the issue in Australia, made a noncommittal or conservative Irish stance less and less tenable. Despite himself, Archbishop Kelly moved towards sharper criticism of British policies, exasperated by recurring allegations that the Irish priesthood was responsible for the rebellion. Kelly, and conservatives like him, would like to have forgotten the rebellion, but loyalists and super-patriots would not allow them to. Attacks produced defence even from conservatives, and defence took the form of justification and increasing refusal to accept blame. Under this insistent hostile pressure, Irish-Australian orthodoxy gradually came around to some degree of acceptance of the rebellion and the assertions of Irish independence that followed it, and increasing alienation from British policy in Ireland.

In this transformation, no one was more influential than Tighe Ryan, editor of the *Catholic Press*. Ryan's brilliant advocacy of Ireland's cause, until his death in 1922, was central to Australian Irish opinion for several reasons: he saw its Australian implications, occupied a position of reasoned moderation which supported, but did not share the extravagances of Mannix's apparent extremism, and he offered a solution to the problem of conflicting loyalties. Ryan's starting point was that the positive response of Britain's dominions to the war was their assumption that there would be Home Rule. Now (August 1916) the problem of divided or diminished loyalty had arisen. 'God forbid that the Irish in Australia should blame the people of England, or lose interest now in the common cause for which we are fighting.' Ryan saw that the strongest local impulse, confronted by this problem of conflicting loyalties, was to avoid it. So nothing had been done to express the righteous anger that British policy in Ireland had generated: 'The reason why no public meeting has so far been called to give expression to Irish-Australian indignation is because our people desire to do nothing that would divert attention from the war'. They had been very restrained. But the fact remained, Ryan insisted, that thousands of Irish Australians were fighting in Europe for freedom, the liberties of small nations, while that small nation most dear to them was despotically oppressed by Britain itself. This, Ryan maintained, was foreign to the spirit of the British Empire and repugnant to the British people. Who, then, was responsible for this malfunction? Reactionary English Toryism, or as Mannix was to put it, 'a few Orangemen in Ireland, and a knot of Freemasons in England', to whom self-government had always been anathema. The whole sentiment of the dominions, claimed Ryan, was in harmony with Ireland's aspiration and against this 'brutal antiquated Tory spirit'.

So Ryan resolved the problem of conflicting loyalties by postulating a democratic concept

Tighe Ryan, editor of the
Catholic Press

of Empire enshrined in the dominion situation, representing the mass of the ordinary people, and at odds with Toryism. This approach had been used before, indeed for a generation, to argue for Home Rule, but Ryan now applied it to an actual situation and offered it as a solution to a pressing problem. The essentials of his liberal democratic approach became prominent features of Australian Irish arguments, not only because this allowed the influential and respectable to support the cause of Ireland's freedom while still professing adamant imperial loyalty, but because the argument was congenial as well as convenient. It was the best moral ground, allowing the Australian Irish to occupy a position on the nature of the Empire which could be urged as enlightened, progressive, liberal, democratic, expansive, human. Thus the numerous demands from organisations and public meetings all over Australia for an end to martial law in Ireland and immediate Home Rule were invariably couched in terms of the claim that this would serve the best interests of the Empire and of effective and patriotic furtherance of the war. Certainly this blend of fervent imperial loyalty and support for Ireland's freedom was difficult to maintain in the Australian situation. The loudest supporters of the war defined the imperial cause in an authoritarian, anti-democratic, non-liberal, 'Tory', sense, and were furiously insistent that Ireland's behaviour had been treacherous and disloyal—and that the Irish must admit this in shame and humiliation. But Ryan's interpretation circumvented this. If the Australian Irish were on unpopular and besieged ground it was nonetheless firm: it was a legitimate and defensible concept of Empire in which the occupants could feel reasonably comfortable under fire.

Morally comfortable, but certainly under threat. The worry that lay behind the Australian campaign for Home Rule became more intense: if the Empire had no room for a free Ireland, indeed if Britain would coerce her with martial law, would it have room for Irish identity within Australia? The question was too sensitive to ask. In September 1916 Archbishop Mannix asked and answered it: 'if he could not be loyal to the commonwealth and to the empire without forgetting his own people in Dublin and Ireland, then he was no longer loyal to the commonwealth; no longer loyal to the empire. The hypothesis was, of course, absurd.' To say it was absurd was not to state a fact, but to make a debating point: the Australian establishment in politics and press did not think it absurd, for they had no other loyalty than the Empire. Mannix did nothing to conciliate such critics: 'Our loyalty is freely questioned. The answer is that Irishmen are as loyal to the empire to which, fortunately or unfortunately, they belong, as self-respecting people could be under the circumstances.'

So, while the questioning of their loyalty caused some Irish Australians to evade the question, or prevaricate, others—and some in prominent public positions—openly championed the Irish rebels and made no apologies for it. But only when they were pushed. The Queensland Minister of Justice, John Fihelly, asked—and it was regarded as a great provocation—'Why should the Irishmen of Queensland care whether their motives were misinterpreted and misconstrued?' The Brisbane branch of the Irish National Association, formed in September 1916, was in a similar mood. It rejected a motion that representation be made to the proper authorities to stop the insulting remarks made by recruiting sergeants with regard to the Irish people and their loyalty. The majority felt 'that the epithet of "disloyalty to England" hurled at the Irish and Irish-Australians should not be regarded as an insult but with feelings of pride'. The later months of 1916 were to see operative again an old law of Australian Irish history: if the Irish were pushed into a corner and constantly berated with charges of disloyalty, some would react not with defence but with some form of counter-attack. But a better indication of the growth of Irish republican intransigence might be the fortunes of the INA in Sydney. In January 1916 it had

Mannix at the opening of the parish hall, Oakleigh, Victoria, 28 July 1918
Melbourne Diocesan Historical Commission

211 members, in December just under 600. Small branches had been established in Brisbane and Melbourne. Subsequent events were to indicate that only seven INA members had any revolutionary tendencies. The remainder of this small membership was not regarded, even by police and military authorities infected by the hysteria of the time, as constituting any threat whatever: so much for the power of the Irish question in its own right.

But linked with the issue of conscription, or the activities of Archbishop Daniel Mannix? These are quite other questions, but the answers are not as simple as the traditional orthodoxies suggest. Both contemporaries and historians have assumed that from Easter 1916 Irish affairs had a profound effect on the mood of Irish Catholics in Australia, in such ways and extents as impinged vitally on Australian history: the older traditions had Ireland determining the outcome of the conscription referenda of 1916 and 1917. Detailed research has demolished this theory, but the shadow of events in Ireland seems to cling to the period in some vaguely deterministic fashion: Ireland must have been important. However, the grounds for so thinking would seem to be superficial—the spectacular public prominence of the Irish crisis itself, and of its champion Archbishop Mannix, who was also opposed to conscription, and the devotion and antagonism which focussed on the Archbishop. The storms that raged around the Irish Dr Mannix, at a time of Irish rebellion on which he had sympathetic views, seem to make it obvious that Ireland was important in Australian affairs. Yet this assumes that Mannix's influence derived from his stand on the Irish question, a most doubtful proposition. It assumes also, by implication, that Irish affairs first burst on to the Australian scene at Easter 1916: for their critics, yes (they would pay attention only when Ireland was troublesome), but Ireland's friends had been long accustomed to relating Irish matters to their Australian lives and had long established the priorities of an accommodation—Australia first. And the further unspoken assumption behind the thesis of Irish importance is the implication that Irish Australians viewed Ireland and its rebellion with enthusiasm. The evidence suggests quite otherwise—that the rebellion turned out to be a barely tolerated last straw. To predicate Mannix's enthusiasm as general is to presume that his audiences shared it: their support was given for other reasons—Catholic, Labor, tribal, the mood of the occasion.

Of course, the very assumption, then and later, that Irish events could be and were of vital importance in moulding Australian history is mythology of major importance. It reveals the tremendous heat which could be generated in Australia, not so much by Irish issues, but by the presence in the Australian community of elements actually Irish-oriented or deemed to be so. It illustrates the demands by the press and political arbiters of that community for ideological homogeneity—and the sectional rejection of that demand. But it also illustrates the tendency of complex and confused political and social situations to polarise themselves, in a public search for simplicity and intelligibility, around the most obvious dramatic positions. To be for or against Ireland, Mannix, conscription, Catholic causes, satisfied the need for grand symbols and heroes on the one hand, and bogeys and scapegoats on the other.

Ireland was one of the matters subject to bitter debate, and the terminology of Ireland—particularly 'Sinn Fein'—one of the languages of controversy, but however prominent in the Australian public forum were the affairs of Ireland they do not appear to have been a decisive factor in the great questions of the day. Recent research supports the conclusion that the rejection of conscription had very little if anything to do with events outside Australia, but was an Australia-wide, inward-turned reaction of a simple materialist kind:

earlier analysis which suggested that a self-interested farmers' vote was decisive has been broadened into the general proposition that what carried the day against conscription was a nationwide selfish impulse towards non-involvement in the European war, given point by fear of personal inconvenience and economic disruption.

Did a scepticism generated by Britain's treatment of Ireland contribute to this atmosphere? Did Mannix and Ireland influence public opinion towards change, or merely polarise further divisions that already existed? Did the Irish issue alone change people's minds? If so, which people, and did such changes, for and against, cancel each other out? Such questions are greatly complicated by the entanglement of the Irish question with Catholic and labour movement issues, but some elements of the answers are clear.

The assumption that Irish Australians opposed conscription because of their feelings on the Irish issue is closely linked to the obvious chronology in which the Easter 1916 rebellion preceded the conscription referenda: sequence in time (as so often in history) has been taken as a causal link. Yet the weight of the evidence, stretching back long before 1916, points to their being motivated by local, Australian grievances: that is, hostilities and divisions which long pre-dated both the 1916 rebellion and the conscription referenda, and which had nothing, at least directly, to do with Ireland. Furthermore, to assign decisive importance to the 1916 rebellion is a deceptive anachronism: for some considerable time—perhaps until 1918—it seemed to have been a clear failure; then its status remained obscure, until it could be seen from the vantage point of the Anglo-Irish Treaty of 1921 to have been the starting point of a process that had culminated in independence. At any time before 1921, but particularly in its immediate aftermath, the historical status of the Easter 1916 rebellion was uncertain indeed: John Wren's publication of a set of pictures of the Easter Week heroes was more an addition to Irish political martyrology than any celebratory gesture. A scenario which has the Irish in Australia acting, in 1916–17, in an atmosphere of gloom, despondency, defeat and despair would better reflect the Irish actualities of that time: how much emotions might have affected Australian decisions is an imponderable, but presumably the balance is towards negativity—no, to conscription.

But the truth is that the Irish in Australia did not need any Irish lessons, or any British lessons imposed on Ireland in 1916, to teach them anything: what happened then simply reinforced, drove home, old lessons from Irish history and, more to the point, fairly old—half a century—lessons from Australian history. They were moved by attitudes derived from a deep conviction formed in the long struggle over education, which itself fed an experience of prejudice as old as Australian settlement, all confirmed by the recent history of the Irish struggle before and after 1916, that the dominant forces in Australian society sought to exclude or demean Catholics of Irish origin. In fighting conscription, but also in his whole critical social stance, Dr Mannix led what amounted to a crusade against these dominant forces, a crusade whose supporters saw conscription as a summation and symbol of a history of manifold oppressions. Conscription seemed to them to be, in microcosm, the enslaving program of the ascendancy party: the terminology is deliberately Irish, for an ascendancy party is what Irish Catholics in Australia had always most dreaded as a possibility, and always fought, back to the exclusives of the 1820s. Their history had resounded with affirmations that they would never allow the tyranny of Ireland to reappear in Australia: conscription was another attempt to establish it. To that extent, Ireland influenced the conscription campaign, in that the total Irish Australian experience, in both Ireland and Australia, disposed many to react strongly against the whole idea of conscription, and what it symbolised by way of authoritarian rule.

Of course not only Irish Catholics saw conscription as potential tyranny, but a massive section of the whole population came to the same conclusion for reasons which had nothing whatever to do with Ireland. A flock of existing Australian divisions and dissatisfactions, fears and hatreds, with all the bitter and violent emotions they had spawned and fed, came home to roost on that single issue. This situation had the curious effect of drawing Irish Catholics into the centre of Australian affairs in a way they had never been before: the enemies they had in 1916–17 were hardly new—merely their traditional opponents revived—but now as one aspect of a victorious anti-conscription movement they had new friends with whom they had made common cause. Far from distancing Irish Catholics from Australian affairs, the period of most intense Irish disruption coincided with most intense Australian involvement—involvement in contention certainly, but Australian contention, not Irish. The nature of the anti-conscription movement also had the general effect of integrating Irish Catholics much more firmly into the labour movement. And crucially, into the Labor Party. The Labor Party split in 1916 into pro- and anti-conscription elements. The purged anti-conscription Labor Party that remained contained, by virtue of the defections, a much higher proportion than before of those of Irish Catholic origin, a stake in the party's power and Australia's future which they have never lost. And a source of lasting misapprehension. The conjunction between Labor Party and Irish Catholics masked the truth that, in Australia, there was no necessary connection between underdogs and radicalism: British presence in Ireland had produced a distortion. In themselves the Irish were poets and politicians, not political theorists or revolutionaries. They were ideologically unadventurous, and their dominant religion, Catholicism, was conservative in social disposition: they had no abiding wish to overturn the system, or devise a new one, only to use the existing structures more to their own advantage. There is ample evidence for suggesting that, for Australian reasons, the period of Irish crisis marks the beginning of full Irish Catholic integration into the power centres of the Australian community.

What gave the Irish situation its wider force in the Australian situation was its local application as a model, as a salutary example of the potential extremes to which tendencies within the Australian community might develop. Both Dr Mannix and those who opposed him made much of the Irish situation as a grievance and a battlecry, but it was an extra grievance, a secondary one, among many. Mannix told an anti-conscription meeting the truth late in 1917 when he observed 'Sinn Fein has nothing to do with us at present'. But it was an ideal term of abuse, with its foreign sound and connotations. In his 1917 avalanche of anti-Mannix pamphlets published by Critchley Parker, Rev. T.E. Ruth exhausted the clichés of depiction of hydra-headed menaces: 'Russian Bolshevism is own brother to Irish Sinn Feinism and they are both brothers to German Prussianism . . . with a little sister in England, the screaming suffragette . . .' The sister is an unusual addition: more central to the stereotype is the IWW bomber. The point remains: Sinn Fein, Ireland, are simply some of the many faces of the forces of disintegration and anarchy. This multiformity in the faces of menace is contrasted with the beauty of oneness, unity. The basic position of Irish Australians was the claim that they were more Australian than anyone else: the *Church of England Messenger* (7 September 1917) replied with the charge that the 'hyphenated Australian' was less than an Australian; 'With the coming of the hyphenated there comes to Australia a conflict of ideals and a contrast of methods, the national ideal and the alien, the foreign or the sectarian ideals.' (Irish Catholics had their own hyphen construct— 'Brit-Huns'.) Yet all this dispute was over Australian ground. Even the criticism of 'Irish Australian' was an advance, in that it conceded the appellation 'Australian' to those who, twenty years earlier, were 'Irish'. Undoubtedly the Irish issue had tremendous potential for arousing emotion, a potential exploited by public figures in Australia to attach feelings of additional passionate intensity to causes much closer to home—the place of Catholics in the community, the state recognition of Catholic educational claims, the conduct of the war effort within Australia. To this utility might be added another. To refer to Ireland offered a wider stage which flattered the self-importance of propagandists on both sides: it offered the wider vistas of mankind as the context of Australian parish pumps. And there were those individuals, such as W.M. Hughes, who believed, mistakenly, and obsessively, that Irish affairs were very important in Australia and that improvement in the Irish question was essential to any improvement of recruiting in Australia. Such people could never grasp that in Irish Australia Ireland had become a convenient allegory, the medium through which local points were made, the public language of inner feeling, a way of working home things out.

And what is the evidence that Ireland was the medium, but not the message? When the fire of local Australian issues subsided after the defeat of the second conscription referendum in December 1917, so did interest in Ireland. It diminished sharply, although the situation there was deteriorating rather than approaching resolution. The reaction to the Irish Catholic agitation of 1916–17 under Mannix's leadership, a reaction which continued with great intensity and bitterness into the mid-1920s, was predominantly a sectarian one, anti-Catholic rather than anti-Irish. The distinction which needs to be made between a real and committed concern with the Irish situation itself—a concern which was small and narrowly based—and the very large and powerful local issues which convulsed Australian society in 1916–17, is clearly visible in the affairs of the Irish National Association, the sole bastion of Irish republicanism in Australia. These reveal the reality in contrasting ways. The Queensland branch of the INA was vehemently anti-conscriptionist—for Australian working-class reasons. The Sydney parent branch was convinced that only a complete abstraction from local affairs would preserve the purity and strength of its devotion to the cause of Irish independence. Accordingly, it decided to hold no functions under its auspices in the later six months of 1916 because of 'the unsettled condition of local politics'. It was determined to avoid the conscription issue as one of 'the shoals of local politics' on which it might perish. This Irish isolationism was incomprehensible to the mass of Irish Australians. Australian affairs, not Irish, were their main concern, and identification with and concern for the wrongs of Ireland would continue only so long as these wrongs seemed to symbolise their own.

There is another measure by which the strength and character of Irish sentiment can be gauged. On 17 June 1918, seven members of the Irish National Association were arrested and detained on the ground that they were members of what the acting Prime Minister, Mr Watt, described as 'an Australian division of an organisation known as the Irish Republican Brotherhood' which 'had been secretly and systematically organised, and its object was the establishment of an Irish republic independent of Britain'. These arrests were made under special regulations of the War Precautions Act, gazetted in March 1918, proscribing 'Sinn Fein' and any advocacy of the independence of Ireland, regulations whose impetus came from events in Melbourne, and which were aimed at Dr Mannix. The St Patrick's Day procession of 16 March 1918, with Mannix as central figure, a float depicting the 'martyrs of the Easter rising', and Sinn Fein banners much in evidence, brought loyalist reaction to Mannix and the Irish question to a pitch of fury: Mannix was alleged not to have acknowledged the National Anthem. A loyalist protest rally on 21 March sent a delegation to Prime Minister Hughes who agreed to act against 'Sinn Fein'. The natural first target was the INA, and its premises and homes of members in Sydney, Melbourne and Brisbane were raided and documents seized in a protracted operation which began in March and ended with the arrests in June of Albert Thomas Dryer, Edmund McSweeney, Michael McGing, and William McGuinness, all of Sydney; Maurice Dalton and Frank McKeown of Melbourne and Thomas Fitzgerald of Brisbane. All except Dryer were Irish-born.

The announcement of these arrests was received remarkably quietly in Irish Australia: the INA was regarded as a fringe organisation of little consequence or relevance to the mainstream. Nevertheless, by association, that community's reputation was in question and it responded with a Defense Fund and the best legal counsel. The inquiry too was a low-key affair, not only because of the tiny size of these secret Irish machinations, but because the full extent of their activity was not revealed, and particularly because of the ingenious way in which Dryer had organised the defence to make light of their intentions: the whole business had been play-acting, romantic dreams, so he suggested.

What the inquiry revealed was that a tiny group of IRB sympathisers—the organiser, John Doran had left for America—had been using the INA not only as a cloak for their own activities, but as a recruiting ground, without the knowledge of the bulk of the members. This group was no bigger than the number detained—seven—and the number of INA members they judged as potential IRB members no more than fifty in Sydney and many fewer in Melbourne and Brisbane. The detainees were hardly sinister, cunning and dedicated revolutionaries, but rather men of militant Irish disposition and outlook but of questionable competence or efficiency. Indeed they had no real title to description as IRB men save their belief that the IRB was the kind of organisation to which they would have liked to belong. They had no connection 'with any enemy person resident in the commonwealth' and the inquiry also confirmed that their contacts with Irish revolutionary movements were infrequent, indirect, and tenuous—and all through America. The most that could be discovered against them was that they had evaded the ban on the entry of Irish republican newspapers by using Irish seamen on the Australia–America run as couriers, had been in contact with American Irish organisations, and wanted to help the republican forces in Ireland. All they had actually done, was that 'they collected moneys in Australia for the purpose of assisting armed rebellion in Ireland against the British government' and that 'this money was expended in the purchase of warlike material from Germany'. This last conclusion is speculative. And although the principle was no doubt in breach of law, the amount remitted was hardly of major revolutionary importance—£20.

What the inquiry did not discover was that in 1916–17 the Sydney IRB had established a secret military training camp in the Blue Mountains. It was merely a few tents, and the handful of men who attended had no firearms—and service was to be in Ireland itself—but in the hysterical anti-Irish climate of the time, any exposure of such arrangements to train men to fight against Britain seems likely to have led to what the government at one stage contemplated—a charge of high treason against Dryer. Practically, the idea of sending men from Australia to fight in Ireland proved not to be feasible. The hope had been to get aboard a ship (as Les Darcy had done in November 1916) bound for America, and thence to Ireland. Nor did the inquiry discover the full truth about the revolutionary intentions or backgrounds of the detainees. It was correct in attributing a central role to Dryer, but haphazard in its insights into the roles of others. Maurice Dalton, a 73-year-old pensioner, was the most obvious revolutionary. He claimed to have been an IRB member and to have

The I.R.B. prisoners in Darlinghurst Gaol, 1918

taken part in the 1867 Fenian rebellion in Ireland. He boasted of this in his correspondence and it was his carelessness that provided the Crown with most of their documentation. But the inquiry had no knowledge whatever that William McGuinness had genuine, recent, and impeccable IRB expertise. He had been sworn in in Belfast in 1906 and had Sean MacDermott, one of the executed leaders of the 1916 rebellion, among a considerable Irish revolutionary circle of friends.

Justice Harvey confirmed the detentions. The 'Irish seven' were held until December 1918, when all but Dryer were released. He was held until February 1919, a delay which related to the fact that the government would not act in the matter without reference to Britain. Dryer himself attributed it to spite. He was dismissed from his position in the Customs Department and had great subsequent difficulty in getting employment. Engaged in 1915, he did not marry until 1933: he enrolled as a medical student in 1929 and graduated in 1937. To his death in 1963 he remained the backbone of the INA.

There is little doubt that the government move against the INA was inspired, at least in part, by the hope that Mannix would be in some way found to be implicated in Irish revolutionary activities. In fact the INA had written to him, but he had not replied. The four-month delay between the seizure of INA documents and the arrests is open to various constructions and the course followed by the official inquiry is hardly less mysterious. Judge Harvey, far from wishing to pursue the manifold questions raised, appears to have sought to damp down the whole affair, to diffuse it. Perhaps the Crown had anticipated, with maybe as much fear as hope, that it would discover through the INA a hideous web of

Albert Dryer at the I.R.B. training camp in the Blue Mountains 1916–17

The Irish Seven in Darlinghurst Gaol 1918.
Standing: *F. McKeown, W. McGuinness, M. McGing*
Seated: *E. MacSweeney, M. Dalton, A.T. Dryer, J. Fitzgerald*

Irish plotting leading to that arch-fiend Mannix, and directed towards that seldom spoken of, but then ever-present spectre—civil war. And then, finding instead what seemed to be a few silly Irishmen playing revolutionary games, they wanted rid of the fiasco as quickly and quietly as possible. In fact, dedicated Irish plotting was indeed afoot, but it was the tactics of the plotters to remain silent in the inquiry and to ridicule and belittle themselves through their own lawyers. There did exist the determined nucleus, however tiny, of a secret Irish army, but it was of the nature of that secrecy that it should, if possible, continue to be maintained.

Yet the whole IRB conspiracy did come close to farce. They were too few; it was too small; the organisation was an imitation, not the real thing. The utter sincerity and complete seriousness of Albert Dryer, and the very few like him, compelled the authorities to take them seriously—but not too seriously, for they represented only themselves. As an insight into Irish Australia, what is remarkable and significant about the internment of the seven alleged IRB members is its failure to arouse any considerable public reaction. Certainly the case provoked an immediate newspaper sensation with its suggestions of revolutionary plot and conspiracy, but this was very short-lived. The response of the Irish-Australian community in an instinctive reaction of defence was based on the belief that the charges were persecuting fabrications. Labor politicians, led by Frank Brennan and Frank Tudor, demanded a full trial, not an inquiry. Leading Irish Catholic lawyers volunteered their defence services free. All this was on the evident supposition that the charges were totally outlandish: it was testimony to the distance that mainstream Irish Australia was from Ireland that it seems not to have even occurred to local leaders that there might be substance in the charges. What they were used to were persecuting lies and distortions, and obviously this IRB business was just that—another baseless smear. That was the defence line at the inquiry—'purely Irish imagination . . . It was a mere tongue war they wished to wage'—to which Judge Harvey added, with devastating percipience, 'Unfortunately, this sort of thing led to Easter Week'.

All Irish Australia was interested in was its pacific reputation. Efforts by the INA to build a release campaign around its interned martyr heroes met with little response: postcards bearing a photograph, smuggled out of jail of the 'Irish Seven', made no impact: protest meetings were small; representations to the government were few, half-hearted (they were made reluctantly by the respectable) and ineffective. When Albert Dryer, the most celebrated of the detainees, was released he emerged to no vast demonstration, but to fifty INA members at the gaol gates. The detention of the seven champions of Ireland's independence was an obvious and ready-made cause for the expression of a massive Irish-Australian declaration of support for their ideas and ideals. No such declaration was made because such support did not exist. A limited sympathy perhaps did, but not to the degree of active protest. The majority of Irish Australians did not feel involved in the cause of the internees because that cause was an Irish cause of an extreme kind—and thus irrelevant to Australia. The same may be said of the non-Irish and the anti-Irish: perhaps the most striking testimony to the Australian irrelevance of the IRB case to local concerns is its relative failure to generate extravagant denunciation and expressions of hysterical alarm. It was the declarations of Daniel Mannix, with their sharp Australian applications and their backing by the Catholic proletariat, which prompted widespread enthusiasm, hero-worship, outrage and protest, all with Irish reference, implications and explicit association. Yet the discovery and detention of a group of Irishmen allegedly engaged in a conspiracy to further Irish independence by force of arms created less concern than detached sensationalism. This tiny group and its alleged activities were felt to be irrelevant to the real and very great concerns that agitated and divided Irish and non-Irish Australians: these were Australian concerns basic to the future character of that country and the lives of its citizens. At bottom there was consensus among those involved in the great Australian conflicts and debates, that the IRB detainees were cranks, and their cause of no real local application or importance.

Ireland generally, however, still was. By 1919 the old slogan of 'Home Rule' had given way to the terminology of the Versailles Treaty makers—self-determination—and support for that principle being applied to Ireland was coming from the Irish-Australian social and political level that had formerly led the campaign for Home Rule. Ireland had become respectable again, and it was appropriate that the year should begin with a Melbourne demonstration in favour of Irish self-determination at which the leader of the Federal Labor Party, Frank Tudor, and the Premier of Queensland, T.J. Ryan, spoke. The Queensland government (which had two Irish-born cabinet ministers, John Fihelly and William Lennon) had a reputation of support for Ireland much heightened by the 'Warwick Egg' incident of 29 November 1917. (At the railway station at Warwick, the Prime Minister W.M. Hughes was hit by an egg thrown by Paddy Brosnan, and inadequately protected by Sergeant Kenny: Queensland was obviously, on the strength of such surnames, in the hands of Sinn Fein, and Hughes established the Commonwealth Police Force as a consequence of this incident.) The intensity of this Irish orientation in Queensland, and its support by leading citizens, is perhaps best illustrated by a Brisbane meeting in May 1918 which protested against the British intention to introduce conscription in Ireland. The motion was moved by Archbishop Duhig, seconded by T.J. Ryan and sent to de Valera officially by the Queensland government. This was a bold and unusual step of commitment and intervention, somewhat diluted and confused by being accompanied by a demand for the establishment of 'Home Rule'. But then, not only was Australia well behind in its comprehension of Irish developments, but 'Home Rule' of some kind represented the limits of its imagination in regard to Irish freedom. It was not in the minds of any but a very few Australian Irish (and those the nonentities) that Ireland could or should do more—or was it better?—than themselves: as they saw it, some variant on Home Rule should be the limit of the march of a nation. Nor was Irish Queensland inherently radical: the opposite. As to 'loyalty', Fihelly's question of November 1916 revealed his priorities, and that of most of his Australian compatriots. 'Why not build up a great nation here', he demanded, rather than 'stick to a wet little island' on the other side of the world? He meant England, but Ireland also shared that climate and distance, and his message was abundantly clear—Australia first, what amounted to the Australian Irish Catholic slogan. Fihelly's reaction was typical of those volatile Irish Australians who believed that flag wavers were trying to push Union Jacks down Irish throats. Such insistence overlooked a basic fact—that Australia's Irish Catholics had been freed from the authority of British tradition by Irish origins and working-class affiliations: they would accept or reject such authority on criteria distinct from that of the general community, and they would resist such compulsions as did not concede that they marched to different drums. The mere fact that automatic pro-British commitments were assumed of them was enough to alienate and enrage some Irish temperaments otherwise moderately disposed. Such blatant Irish identifications as the conscription in Ireland motion, and various other Sinn Fein flag wavings (those at the 1919 St Patrick's Day parade got ample notice), had the air of Queensland snoot-cocking in defiance of the Federal government rather than genuine commitment. Probably it was both, but the Irish issue was certainly a convenient way in which Queensland could affirm not only Ireland's freedom, but Queensland's.

What returned Ireland to the ranks of the respectable in Australia was the end of the war and the theoretical principles to be pursued by the peace. Whatever the legacy of division and distrust, November 1918 liberated the Irish question to be itself again, as distinct from a complication in the war effort. It was exactly a year before Australian caution was overcome: the Irish Race Convention was summoned in Melbourne in November 1919, by Archbishop Mannix, at the request of the hierarchy and the Irish societies of Australia. That nothing had been done earlier by way of mass demonstration of solidarity with the Irish cause was explained at the time as due to the prohibition of public meetings during the influenza epidemic. A more basic explanation lies in the disinclination of the Australian hierarchy to become too identified with the Irish independence movement. However, events in Ireland and America, and changed circumstances in Australia, prompted the Australian bishops to take action. The Irish events were the Sinn Fein election landslide—destroying the old Home Rule party—in November 1918, the establishment of a de facto Sinn Fein government in Ireland itself during 1919, and a swing among the Irish bishops towards acceptance of this situation as being the path of the future. Patently the old Home Rule order was dead and something had to be done about relating to the newly emergent one. And there was American example—the Irish Race Convention in Philadelphia in February 1919.

What was changed in Australia was the Irish Catholic mood, now notably more radical. Mannix's leadership had done a good deal to contrive that, but so had the liberation from the constraints of a war situation, and, most importantly the developments in Ireland which indicated that the 1916 rebellion might not have been a disaster, but the beginning of a successful freedom movement. Nineteen nineteen saw an Irish Catholic community much more confident and aggressive than the one that had entered the war five years before. They had had some remarkable victories—over conscription, twice—had discovered an exciting and charismatic leader in Mannix, and through the fortunes of the Labor Party they had become powers in the land: they were prominent in the Federal Party, they owned Queensland politics—how the lowly had risen! Now Ireland looked like succeeding as well, something in which they wished to share. The Irish Race Convention, attended by almost the entire hierarchy, with bishops and priests ubiquitous and dominant among the thousands of delegates assembled from all over Australia and New Zealand, was another in the long series of clerical devices to maintain control of Irish Catholic sentiment, to reassert clerical initiative, to keep that sentiment Australian, and to ensure that it did not slip away down paths of extremism. The few delegates of militant Irish organisations, with whose dreams Irish reality was now beginning to catch up, societies such as the Irish National Association, were buried by the big battalions of prominent clergy, Hibernians and the rest. And they were quite lost in the mass demonstrations of enthusiasm which focussed, not so much on the principle of Irish independence as on the hero of the hour, Daniel Mannix. With an entourage of bishops and clergy, he opened the convention with High Mass: 'No monarch ever received a more loving demonstration from his subjects' was one journalist's description of the reception accorded Mannix. In Australia Mannix was Ireland, or at least Ireland enough.

In essence, the convention amounted to an expression of Mannix triumphalism and an exercise in clerical determination to remain the arbiters of Irish sentiment in Australia: with its ranks of dignitaries, and its very size, it also proclaimed the strength and respectability of Irish Australia. Mannix defined its purpose as supporting Ireland's claim to self-determination and her chosen leader, de Valera. The convention chairman, T.J. Ryan, ex-premier of Queensland and leader of the Federal Labor Party, stressed that British democracy was in favour of Ireland's claims. Supporting resolutions were moved by archbishops and seconded by prominent Irish Australian Catholic politicians. A fund was set up to help the cause.

The Irish Race Convention was an enormous success—or so it was felt to be by participants and sympathetic observers, largely because it gave them a warm feeling of solidarity and a sense of importance as being involved in large events. It was squarely in the Australian Irish tradition, clerically orchestrated, full of predictable oratory, highly respectable, witness once again to the transitory emotionalism, local orientation, and dominant clericalism of Irish Australia. Its notability lies in its being more any of those things than any previous manifestation: it was bigger, more clerical, more prestigious, more localised in its focus and enthusiasms—Mannix. And there was another local implication. The convention was another instance of drawing together in the face of local hostility.

Yet, while the convention had the effect of submerging and rendering powerless the left wing of Irish republicanism in Australia, it did not satisfy or please the conservative right wing of Irish nationalist support. The champions of traditional honour and principle in old Irish Australia were not about to desert their positions lightly, or merely because of some spectacular events in Ireland. The core of the Melbourne Celtic Club had always been composed of ardent Home Rulers, committed to the degree of a virtually self-contradictory fanaticism: they espoused a moderate policy in an extreme way. In 1914, Major T.M. McInerney as Club president responded to Ulster's threats to Home Rule by cabling Asquith, the British Prime Minister, a message which ended, 'if required can send assistance to quell criminal conspiracy Ulster'. Fighting words. Precisely what 'assistance' the Celtic Club envisaged itself as providing was unclear, but the intensity of its feelings was evident and it clung to the causes of Home Rule and the Irish Parliamentary Party long after the tide of events, and the sympathies of most Irish Australians, had turned towards republicanism. The Club was not invited to the 1919 Irish Race Convention, nor would it attend because of what its then president, Morgan Jageurs claimed was the convention's 'republican character'. These developments both revealed and intensified policy divisions which amounted to a split within the Club from 1918 to 1922. Lives lived for Ireland at a distance, as Jageurs' had been, could not always be instantly and painlessly readjusted to new, upstart, and unfamiliar demands from home. Home? Jageurs was nearly sixty and he had lived in Australia since the age of three.

As the Anglo-Irish war developed in intensity in 1919–20, so did the organs of public opinion turn increasing ire on advocates or supporters of Irish independence. Their tack had changed since the war: their focus was now not the good of Britain and the Empire, but of Australia. The *Sydney Morning Herald* of 19 June 1920 was relatively restrained in denunciation of those who 'endeavour to antagonise Australians among themselves in a matter which is not Australia's concern ... There is no room for the perpetuation of old-world feuds; here we are all Australians whatever the land of our birth. If any section or clique finds the atmosphere of goodwill to Britain unpalatable ... it is not under any compulsion to remain in Australia ...'.

The reference to goodwill towards Britain was apposite in 1920, for Britain's own goodwill was very much in question following the introduction of the 'Black and Tans' as military auxiliaries in Ireland early in that year. This marked a further degeneration in the Anglo-Irish war, that armed conflict between the forces of Irish independence and the British military forces that dragged on from 1919 to 1921. That war, in which the Australian press was more pro-British than the British—there was no equivalent to the misgivings of, say, the *Manchester Guardian*—was a profound embarrassment to Irish Australia. According to the Australian press, the fate of the Empire hung in the balance (and without the Empire Australia could not exist), the loyalty of Catholics was still in question, and their religion was again proved to be seditious and violent, and the appalling atrocities perpetrated by the so-called fighters for Irish freedom proved what the Irish were really like. So the Australian Irish were brought to book once again by what was happening in Ireland. But by this time too, a good deal of pro-Irish republican lecturing and pamphleteering was under way in Australia, mostly by priests: their circumstances allowed them the travel which brought the immediacy of personal experience. The Australian-born but Irish-educated Carmelite priest P.J. Gearon had returned from Ireland in 1919 and made a lecture tour in 1920, telling his audiences 'The Truth About Ireland'; this was published in 1921, with an appreciation by the Melbourne doctor Gerald R. Baldwin. The first printing sold out within a month, the second within two months. Rev. M.D. Forrest MSC was also a popular reportage pamphleteer. In a widely circulated series of pamphlets in 1920–21—*Atrocities in Ireland*—*What An Australian has seen; Ireland's Deathless Agony. Reflections for St Patrick's Day;* and *Ireland's Darkest and Brightest Year*, Forrest linked his personal experience of the Black and Tan campaign in Ireland in late 1920 with historical observations (particularly on the Penal Laws) to produce a bitter indictment of British policy and rule as that of injustice, oppression and atrocity. To him 'the soldiers of the Irish Republican Army, many of whom I had the honour of meeting personally, are the most virtuous and chivalrous young men the world could hope to produce'. In contrast were the atrocities of the Black and Tans: 'On my honour as a Catholic priest, in full accordance with the evidence I have, I now declare the following facts:—'; thereafter followed details of 'Cold-Blooded Murders'. This type of clerical testimony had a deep influence on Australian Irish attitudes, but little practical outcome: there was little opportunity or point to being critical of Britain and most who acquired such information and attitudes merely stored them away. That such hostility was there is clear in such instances as the singularly unpolitic appointment of Sir Matthew Nathan as governor of Queensland in 1920. Nathan had been under-secretary for Ireland in 1916 and effectively in charge of British government there during the Rising. His civil administration had been superseded by martial law, but inevitably, by association, he shared the odium of executions and repression. He was received with intense suspicion by Queensland's Irish Catholics during his five-year governorship.

The traditional inhibitory processes continued to work in the Irish Australian community to damp down enthusiasms for Ireland's distant causes, but by 1921 they had acquired a new local liability—or at least, a radical narrowing of their sectional appeal. Police reporters in the Sydney Domain in 1921 found Irish matters, particularly in the form of denunciations of British policy in Ireland, stock fare with revolutionary socialist speakers. Agitators from a variety of socialist and communist factions were at one in condemning British action as an attack on the Irish working class, and in praise of Mannix: their newspapers and pamphlets—often raided by the conservative press for stories to shock and horrify the respectable citizenry—carried the same messages. The impression of a united Irish-socialist front was further reinforced by the appearance of socialist speakers and ALP left-wingers such as Percy Brookfield MLA on INA platforms, and those of the Irish Freedom and Self Determination League. The tensions between moderates and militants in such situations were so strong as to be clearly evident to police reporters, but what was not so evident was the effect on the Irish issue of the socialist kiss of death. Not only were the well-to-do alienated, or at least rendered inactive, but so was the Church and those likely to heed her teachings: in the aftermath of the Bolshevik revolution anything touched by that contagion was regarded with the deepest mistrust.

It seems probable that this dimension of attempted socialist takeover was one of the reasons why the local Australian repercussions of Irish affairs 1920–21 were not more explosive. There were incidents enough—and serious enough—to have aroused extreme tensions. The most spectacular of these centred on Archbishop Mannix. On 8 August 1920, the ship on which he was travelling to Ireland was intercepted at sea by a British destroyer and he was taken off, forbidden to land in Ireland, or to visit those British cities with large Irish communities, Liverpool, Manchester and Glasgow. There were large protest meetings in Australia, but their concern was more with Mannix the Catholic archbishop than with Mannix, champion of Irish independence: thus the Sydney meeting was sponsored not by Irish societies, but by the Catholic Federation. Again, it was mainly religious sensibilities that were aroused by the proposal—on which the government took

Mannix in 1920, New York

some initial action—to require Dr Mannix to take an oath of loyalty on his return to Australia in July 1921. But the government decided not to proceed in this, and the danger of possible conflict passed. The chameleon Mannix was the ideal embodiment of Irish Australia—citizen and churchman, Catholic and Irishman. When was he which? When the government wanted rid of the seditious Irishman, obviously he was church prince. Irish Australia played the same game, appearing in whichever guise suited the convenience of the time: the uniform of 'Australian Catholics' was one which better suited 1920–21 than any parading of green colours. It fitted better too—more themselves, whatever the older suits left in the wardrobe.

Hardly less potentially contentious than the treatment of Mannix were the local consequences of the 74-day hunger strike—to the death—of Terence MacSwiney, Lord Mayor of Cork, in Brixton Prison, from August to October 1920. Hugh Mahon, Labor member for Kalgoorlie, attempted to raise this as a matter of urgency in the Federal parliament but was gagged. Then on 7 November he addressed a Melbourne demonstration organised by the Irish Ireland League, attended by a crowd variously estimated at 3–10 000. Mahon delivered a savage attack on British policy in Ireland, labelling it a 'bloody and accursed despotism' and describing the police as 'spies, informers and bloody cutthroats'. The meeting went on to pledge its support for the establishment of an Australian republic. On 13 November, the Prime Minister, W.M. Hughes, moved, on the basis of this speech, Mahon's expulsion from parliament, claiming that he had 'by reason of seditious and disloyal utterances been guilty of conduct unfitting him to remain a member of this house'. There were protests against this expulsion—carried on party lines—but nothing massive, and they soon ceased. Mahon dropped into obscurity and another potential cause around which the Australian Irish might have rallied disappeared.

Another available cause existed in Sydney from January to March 1921, in the person of Mr Osmond Thomas Grattan Esmonde. On arriving in Sydney, Esmonde, claiming to represent an Irish trade mission, but suspected of being an official representative of the self-proclaimed Irish Republic, was refused permission to land in Australia until he took an oath of allegiance. He refused to do this and eventually left. Again the Australian Irish failed to respond sufficiently to make a significant issue of the incident.

They were, however, prepared to support the Irish Self-Determination League of Australasia established in Sydney in February 1921 by Miss Kathryn Hughes of Alberta, Canada, to organise support for Irish self-determination. Miss Hughes, billed by local Irish as a lady well known in the American literary world, was in fact an international organiser for de Valera, a role she kept semi-secret to avoid deportation. The league was an international venture but it produced its own Australian propaganda to cope with what was obviously its main stumbling block—revulsion at the escalation of violence in Ireland. In this it revealed something of its own Irish-Australian Eureka mythology:

> But it is a salutary thing for us Australians to remember, when we are tempted to be horrified at the killing of the police and military in Ireland, that we ourselves gave them a bad example. For, when we felt the galling effects of an unjust regulation, put in force, as it was, in a truculent fashion, we raised for the first time the Australian flag—five stars on a blue field—formed a provisional government, and took up arms against the forces of the Crown.

This was a highly inflated view of what had happened at Eureka, particularly coming from the respectable league: the prominent Sydney lawyer Neal Collins was president and the officers were other public figures. The league sought, fairly successfully, to absorb the

Mannix welcomed on his return in 1921, at the train at Seymour, Victoria
Melbourne Diocesan Historical Commission

various small Irish groupings in a large movement, had strong American links, and published a journal, *The Small Nation*. It fitted the traditional Australian pattern in offering an outlet for moral and financial support for Ireland. And it was active, forming 119 branches in New South Wales, and sending P.S. Cleary, editor of the *Catholic Press*, and Rev Dr M.J. O'Reilly to the Irish Race Conference in Paris in January 1922. O'Reilly had been in the forefront of Irish causes since 1916, converted by the execution of the leaders of the rebellion. A natural enthusiast who relished controversy ('life without an enemy is a life without purpose') O'Reilly the indifferent versifier, the visionary dreamer, is an excellent example of the commitment Ireland could generate, the distance Irish Australia was from Irish reality, and the profound difficulty such people had in reconciling their beliefs and expectations with the shock of encountering the less edifying aspects of Irish affairs. This encounter began for O'Reilly at the Paris Conference. He returned apparently as chipper as ever. 'I was never a disloyalist,' he declared, 'but I was always a rebel and I am glad to have come back a perfectly impenitent rebel.' Perhaps. The press lapped up this cavalier Irishness. In fact, the real Irish in Paris had criticised O'Reilly for a 'slave mentality', because he had said 'Irish Australians, the very backbone of Australian democracy, accepted unequivocally allegiance to the Australian Government'. O'Reilly believed this and it was true: so much for the prince of Irish Australian fire-eaters. An unexpected gulf had begun to yawn: the overseas Irish had at last admitted to themselves that they were happy citizens of successful societies different from—and superior to—the deprived Irish. In private, O'Reilly wrestled uneasily with encroaching disillusionment: he was aghast at the in-fighting among the Irish at Paris, astounded at their devious manoeuvring, and outraged by what he saw as totally unprincipled behaviour, particularly by de Valera, in efforts to gain support. This was a side to the Irish he had not ever imagined and, publicly, O'Reilly kept quiet about it. The problem was, that from the signing of the Anglo-Irish Treaty on 6 December 1921, the Irish in Ireland could not keep quiet about it themselves.

Hugh Mahon, M.P.

Rev Dr Maurice O'Reilly C.M.

The relative success of the respectable league, and the unwillingness of the Australian Irish to be provoked by incidents that might have been regarded as persecution of their race and principles, testify again to the unwillingness of the Australian Irish to go beyond that point where active sympathy with Irish causes would involve them in direct and deliberate conflict with other Australians. This was something of a law of their history, but it had become firmer in its application, more proof against dislodgement. While in one sense the provocations offered to Irish sentiment during the years of the Anglo-Irish war 1919–21 were much more extreme than ever before—it was, after all, an outright war between guerilla Ireland and Great Britain with significant casualties on both sides—the factors working against any Australian Irish involvement were also much more powerful. First among these was an influence impossible to quantify or even assess accurately, since it consisted of an absence, a shrinkage, a quietening, in hostility, animus, denunciation—all those elements likely to provoke, anger, produce reactions, among Irish Catholics. These elements remained—prejudice, distrust, suspicion—but less, and less confident, and directed inward to Australia rather than arrogantly imperial in concern: Australia's loyalists no longer felt that the Empire depended on them; no doubt Australia did, but that was a local matter. The war, Bolshevik revolution, the influenza plague—by 1919 all of these remote disasters had taken up their local forms of deadly or disruptive residence: very few wanted Ireland's woes as well. The bloody violence of the IRA's campaign for Irish independence was a constant lurid feature of the Australian press, and while those who read the Catholic press could balance this off with reports of Black and Tan atrocities, Irish Australia as a whole was repelled by Sinn Fein terror and guerilla warfare. Very few Irish Australians wanted any association whatever with that aspect of the struggle for Irish independence which involved killing, maiming and destruction. This reaction, which became one of utter revulsion by 1922, began as early as 1919 to cause more and more of the Australian Irish to wish to opt out of active commitment to the Irish cause. It had become a considerable embarrassment. Sympathy with an abstract cause was very different from sympathy with the killing necessary to achieve it: the colonial Irish were used to identifying their cause with martyrs, not with murderers. Besides, all but the most fanatic, and there were few of these in Australia, had to some degree dual loyalties, dual cultural traditions, British and Irish. In the Anglo-Irish war, few Australian Irish could commit themselves to one side, without hesitation or reserve. For the overwhelming majority it was a painful situation which they ardently wished would end. The Anglo-Irish treaty of December 1921 seemed to have ended it completely, and satisfactorily.

A U S T R A L I A N S

The Anglo-Irish Treaty of 6 December 1921 ended the war between the Irish Republican Army and Britain and created the Irish Free State: twenty-six Southern Counties became a self-governing dominion within the British Commonwealth and the matter of Ulster's already operative determination to remain part of Britain was referred to the demarcation of a Boundaries Commission. This outcome—it is inaccurate to call it a settlement—was reached in circumstances of duress for the Irish delegates contrived by devious manoeuvre by Lloyd George: it fell short of granting Ireland the status of independent republic and it effectively confirmed partition—and it was to lead to civil war.

Irish Australia fastened on what the treaty did provide, not on what were its shortcomings. It created the Irish Free State. Surely this was Irish freedom. Ireland's political status had become equivalent, within the Empire, to that of Australia. That the 'Free State' was only part of Ireland seemed less important: it was, after all, most; surely the North would soon find itself not viable separately, and join the South. Irish Australia was not interested in the treaty other than as an honourable opportunity for it to escape from an involvement that had come close to being intolerable: the leaders of Irish Australia pounced on it with immense relief as the end of the Irish question. The reasons are clear in *Smith's Weekly*'s joking references in December 1921. The Irish question would be terribly missed. It had entered all aspects of Australian life and kept everyone on the jump. 'Certainly Australia was becoming a most distressful country . . . What with the Irish Self-Determination League, the King and Empire League, the Catholic Federation and the Protestant Federation, one was not safe in asking a man to have a drink, unless he was a Hebrew or an atheist.'

Irish Australian community leaders had, for long, not been amused. Archbishop Duhig's comment of January 1923 sums up how they felt: 'The settlement of the Irish question was a matter of great importance. In the past that question had kept the Irish people in Australia to a great extent divided from their fellow citizens. With a settlement of that question there could be no further division.' Indeed, even this is to exaggerate the treaty's local terminal importance, for the Australian Irish had already lost all enthusiasm for Irish independence by 1920 and were merely awaiting some decent point to signify severance with the matter. Even in 1918–19 indifference prevailed. As Dryer commented on the peak INA membership of 1919, 'there should be a hundred times the number', if Irish Australians had really supported it. That the tiny sparks of Irish republican enthusiasm in Australia had died even before the treaty is indicated by the fate of the ephemeral pro-republican organisations of the time. The Brisbane INA founded in September 1916 faded away in 1921. The Melbourne INA was not set up until September 1917: it died in 1920. A Melbourne Young Ireland society, set up at the end of 1916, with objects similar to those of the INA, expired in 1920. The Adelaide INA was formed in 1918 and lasted about a year. The multiplicity of Irish organisations in Victoria led nine of them to attempt to set up the Irish-Ireland League of Victoria (with Arthur Calwell as secretary); it failed. In 1919 Dryer set up an Irish book depot in Sydney to cope with what he expected to be a great demand for Irish history and literature. It could not afford him a living and he had to abandon it.

There are ample subsidiary explanations for this situation. Disunity was one problem, as various groups set up small distinct organisations impelled by factionalism and personality clashes. Policy conflict was another. Even up to 1920–21, Home Rule continued to be advocated by many, and many of the most influential, of the Australian Irish: Tasmania was particularly tardy in its desertion of Home Rule. And up to the Irish elections of December 1918, this advocacy often took the form, most notably in the United Irish League in Melbourne, of active and powerful efforts to frustrate the growth of republican societies in Australia. Moreover, the decline of those societies that espoused Home Rule did not mean that the membership had become converted to republicanism; rather did they depart from Irish causes altogether.

These were the superficial factors. The basic facts of Irish-Australian life 1916–21 are clearly demonstrated in a comparison between those organisations which survived the period intact, to continue to the present time, and those organisations which disintegrated or collapsed. The organisations which survived—not to mention of course the Catholic Church, in a sense the most Irish and most powerful of them all—were those without a primarily political orientation. The only exception was the Sydney Irish National Association which was very much a special case in that its continued existence substantially depended, as had many Irish societies before, on the extraordinary dedication of one man, Albert Dryer—and Dryer made the INA his life's work. But otherwise, the survivors consisted of the Hibernians, a benefit organisation closely linked with the Church; the Melbourne Celtic Club, politically moderate and formally unaligned, with a largish membership and an almost exclusively social orientation; and its Brisbane counterpart, the Queensland Irish Association. The organisational casualties were all explicitly political. The Home Rule societies died with their cause. The republican societies died because they could strike no real roots in Irish Australian soil: they were irrelevant. Their support came not from Australians of Irish descent, but from those of Irish birth, those of relatively recent—and sometimes very recent—arrival in Australia. These were very few, mostly young, predominantly working-class, with no influence or status in the Australian community. They were transients, either moving on to other places or becoming gradually absorbed in the Australian community. And their mental orientation was Ireland, not Australia. Of their itinerant nature, this group could not form a stable base for organisational growth in Australia, nor could their narrowly Irish cause win support in an Australian environment.

By 1921, those of Irish descent in Australia had been taught the lesson that close involvement with Irish politics was painful, embarrassing and damaging to them. The Home Rule cause had been taken up because it would make Ireland like Australia. Republicanism would not: at very best it was irrelevant. Some of those of Irish race were prepared to continue their acknowledgement of their descent, to seek each other's society, and perhaps to take some interest in Ireland's politics. But an interest is all that it would be, not an involvement. For those of Irish birth the situation was, or could be, different, dependent on the degree to which they conceived their identity to be Irish. After 1920 the Irish organisations in Australia which retained any commitment to Ireland's particular internal politics were small, largely ephemeral, and overwhelmingly composed of people of Irish birth. Irish Australia as a whole retired from such involvement, though at times prepared to acknowledge and honour its ancestry. Mary Durack put their position in its essence, and to its then residual extent: the Irish Australians were 'like the children of Israel, in that they carried with them the past of their race'. Or in the words of Dr Herbert Moran, though 'sheltered from Irish animosities' he 'always felt the call of race'. They accepted Ireland's history as their own, but not its contemporary politics.

This reaction was sharpened to the point of disgust by the Irish civil war of 1922–23 which dismayed and baffled Australian Irish opinion, even those of Irish birth. Archbishop Clune of Perth, who knew the Irish situation first-hand from a 1920 visit, in which he had been a go-between in truce negotiations, enquired in puzzlement of an Irish friend in January 1922, 'Don't you get practically all you would have as a republic?' 'The bickerings and recriminations' which followed the Anglo–Irish treaty 'made us sick' reported the Archbishop. This was before the outbreak of civil war, and from a source that knew Ireland well, and recently: such nausea was mild in comparison to the utter revulsion and incomprehension which greeted the actual fighting in June. The Catholic press had been confident there would be no civil war. It found it hard to endure the predictable taunts of its Protestant counterparts: 'Pat fighting with Mick and without outside interference or influence . . . showing the world . . . how well able to govern themselves the people of Ireland are.' Before that fratricidal depth had been reached, Irish Australia had time to sneak in its last hurrah—the 1922 St Patrick's Day procession in Melbourne. Held in spite of a city council prohibition, and perhaps a little uneasy and subdued, it was the last major demonstration of the militant Irishry that had grown after 1916. Isolated pockets of Irish Catholics might continue to sing out their defiance in the form of 'God Save Ireland' instead of 'God Save the King' into the 1920s, but they were voicing their anger and frustration against Irish realities as much as in favour of her cause. God Save Ireland—from herself. As Irishman killed Irishman in Ireland, they also killed what remained of Australian Irish enthusiasm for Ireland's cause—whatever that was. In November 1922 Bishop O'Farrell of Bathurst told an Irish friend, 'You can form no idea of the depression and humiliation in the sentiments of the Irish-Australians at the state of things in Ireland. If tomorrow there was complete peace in Ireland she will start her role as a nation under the severe handicap of loss of that sentiment and sympathy she had in Australia anyhow, I don't think anything will restore that'.

Only Archbishop Mannix remained a committed republican of de Valera's stamp. But even his charismatic leadership could not attract those who had once been his devoted followers into the republican camp. In March 1923, Rev F.M. O'Flanagan and Mr J.J. Kelly arrived, as Irish republican envoys, to tour Australia. Mannix welcomed them, but not so his clergy. The envoys met a discouraging reception from influential Irishmen and open hostility from most of the clergy. By the time they reached Brisbane their reception had so embittered them that they attacked the Australian bishops as a body, and particularly Archbishop Duhig. The envoys were arrested in April 1923 on charges of engaging in seditious enterprises and were deported in June. There was little protest for, in Australia, Irish republicanism was blamed for the civil war, which was inexplicable, repugnant and totally offensive to those who assumed the Irish Free State meant what its title said: 'No one wants to speak of the Irish question out here,' reported Bishop O'Farrell.

Archbishop Mannix's visit to Ireland in 1925 was an embarrassment to the Free State government and a popular success—in Ireland: in Australia it roused little feeling. By

1927 disillusionment in Australia had reached even those who had been Ireland's most vigorous champions. Monsignor Maurice O'Reilly wrote in February, 'As to poor old Ireland and how she stands, like most Irishmen abroad, I can hardly pretend to be interested. Possibly, I had idealised too much and have thus made more painful than needs be the inevitable disillusion'. But Ireland held more disillusion still. In July, Kevin O'Higgins, brilliant young vice-president and Minister of Justice, was gunned down in Dublin while walking to Mass, in circumstances both of atrocity and politics by murder. 'I am completely disillusioned,' wrote Bishop Barry of Tasmania in August 1927. 'This is not the Ireland of my youth and my dreams.' Therein was pronounced both testimony and epitaph. The testimony could have been only narrowly true: Barry's youth was in the Ireland of the Land War, where there was violence aplenty—the Phoenix Park murders

Archbishop Clune, with Archbishop Mannix and Bishop McCarthy, on board ship in Britain in 1920
Melbourne Diocesan Historical Commission

Father O'Flanagan and Mr J.J. Kelly, Irish Republican Envoys, deported in April, 1923

make something of a parallel with O'Higgins' assassination. What is revealing about Barry's comment is its explanation of a vital element in a century of Irish Australia: so much of it had been erected on clerical dreams, on the good things remembered, invented, wished, and—dare it be said?—demanded of psychological necessity to justify their own lives. One of the favourite concert pieces of the period was 'Fairytales of Ireland' a sentimental ballad in the indulgent Victorian genre: the Irish clergy of Australia had long been fabricating Irish fairy-tales of their own, a fantasy culture which took little account of the real Ireland. Nor were the clergy alone in this conspiracy of romance: involvement in Ireland's cause had been for many the pursuit of ideals, a search for lost youth, a quest for their dreamworlds. Distance had indeed lent enchantment, allowing Ireland to become the focus of a kind of personal utopianism, a symbol of noble aspirations realised far away in this happy isle, the home of holiness. But even the most determined dreaming was not proof against the repeated brutal assaults of Irish facts in the decade that followed 1916: Ireland had not merely fallen short of romantic expectations, it had pioneered new directions in terror. Irish Australia would have nothing to do with this: it would not exchange dreams for nightmares. Of course the Australian Irish were still generous in helping Irish distress. In February 1925 Miss Kathleen Barry and Miss Linda Kearns, delegates of the Irish Relief Mission, were very well received.

Reaction against the painful Australian Irish involvement in Irish politics also twisted inwards against that most potent Irish influence within Australia, the Irish clergy of the Catholic Church. The domination of the Church by Irish clerics had come under serious criticism since 1914, almost entirely from Australian-born priests who had studied at St Patrick's College, Manly: their argument was 'The mission of the Church in Australia is no longer to save the Irish exile but to convert the Australian race', but while although only five Catholics in a hundred were Irish, three priests out of four were Irishmen. Initially this argument was advanced in the form of stressing the positive advantages of a local Australian clergy. However, between 1919 and 1923, the very new concept of the Irish being 'foreign' crept into the debate, and openly anti-Irish lines of argument appeared. The idea of the

Irish as being 'foreign' was particularly important in unsettling and calling into question basic assumptions within the Church and the community it served. In this case, there was a good deal in a name. As far back as 1900 the *Austral Light* and the Sydney *Freeman's Journal* had a lively exchange on what Catholics in Australia should be called. The *Austral Light* saw them as Australian Catholics: to the *Freeman's Journal* they were Irish, and it was patent that the *Freeman's* felt threatened by the idea of 'Australian' Catholics. Rightly so: on the question of who these people were rested a whole range of matters of church policy, personnel, and future development. It was in the interests of the Irish clergy to keep their Australian people 'Irish' as long as possible—by assumption, pretence, contrivance, leadership, whatever methods were to hand. And now, from 1919, came these Manly priests with a proposition that came close to denying a central tenet of Australian clericalism, that good Irishman equals good Catholic and vice versa: the Manly proposition was, that close involvement of Australian Catholicism in Ireland's political cause was detrimental to the interests of religion. Further, some Manly priests contended that Irish priests were unfitted by their detestation of England to minister effectively to a people whose loyalties were broadly English, or, at least, who saw no direct reason to hate England. Such critics also suggested that the Irish priests' concern with Irish problems was a distraction from their priestly duties, and took them away from what should be their first concern—Australia's religious problems.

This criticism aroused antagonism, but little practical response: the Irish government of the Church was not going to abdicate in favour of the locals. It was compelled to do so by Rome's insistence on native-born clergy. The appointment of two Australian-born, Manly-trained, bishops to minor dioceses began the gradual loosening of the Irish hold on the episcopacy. With Archbishop Gilroy's succession to Sydney in March 1940, Australianism had effectively arrived: the long episcopates of the Irishmen Drs Mannix and Duhig, ending in the 1960s, were the protraction of an earlier phase. However, the influence of Irish Catholicism on Australian Catholicism had been so long continued, so profound, that it remained an integral part of the Australian developments that followed the end of its dominance. Its influence remained in an Irish style of religion—clerical, authoritarian, non-intellectual: it was Australian Catholicism, with a brogue.

Through the 1920s and thirties a generalised Irish racial and religious sentiment remained, a kind of residual disposition to acknowledge Irish origins and to feel most at home with things and people of Irish derivation. An Irish-Australian climate prevailed among Catholics, sustained largely by the Church and by the strong community ties—of a common separate education, and a common political allegiance to the Labor Party—notable among Catholics. In part this distinctive Irish-Australian atmosphere was real, but it was increasingly a phantom of the perceptions of outsiders who exaggerated the 'Irishness' of what they opposed or considered threatening or contemptible. The idea that Labor Party politics and trade union organisations were dominated by incompetent 'Hibernian windbags', corrupt time-serving Paddys and Mickeys, disloyal priest-ridden shirkers, became a commonplace of anti-labour propaganda of the 1920s and thirties, focusing particularly on the administrations of Theodore in Queensland, Lang in New South Wales, and Scullin federally. The typical scurrilous pamphlet of the period *Rafferty, King of Australia*, detailing the alleged Irishness of such Australian politics, carried such chapter headings as 'Irish Politicians', 'Gathering of the Kernes', 'Bhoys and Blackthorns'. In such polemic it was regarded as sufficiently damaging merely to list the Irish-derived surnames of office- or job-holders: Celtic lists were condemnation in themselves.

And racial typology was still in use, with Irish reference, in the 1920s and thirties as Ireland sought to enlarge its dominion status: these Irish were still 'a peculiar people' in the estimate of a press convinced that Irish actions to insist on greater independence were a threat to the unity of the beloved Empire: denigration of Ireland remained one of the ways in which loyalists could define their position. That denigration intensified from 1932 with the replacement of the moderate Cosgrave government by the republican de Valera, with his rejection of British sovereignty, his economic war against Britain, and his declaration of a new Irish constitution. De Valera was irrational and fanatic: 'the godfather of the fairies of illusion' the *Sydney Morning Herald* called him in July 1937, in a phrase of traditional dismissive contempt.

Yet the *Herald* was not alone in its presumption of an Irish fairyland. For all that its more perceptive commentators saw Ireland as the healthily restless dominion pioneering the way for the future in imperial and then Commonwealth relations, Australian Irish Catholicism clung generally to a highly idealised, indeed utopian Ireland, a great nation with a proud past which Australian Catholics shared. This romantic vision was perhaps best and most consistently sustained in the *Irish Review*, a monthly launched by Arthur Calwell and his wife in 1933, and continuing to be published from Melbourne until 1953. It would be too harsh to say that the *Review* had little to say about the real Ireland, and even less to say about its Irish-Australian context, but such a jibe captures something of this publication's studied unreality. As carrier of information on Ireland, the *Review*'s news was all good, its stories all positive, its pictures picturesque—which was what was wanted in Irish Australia. Ireland was the measure of Australian Catholicism, whose self-esteem demanded that Ireland be glorious, pure, good, holy, historic. What else did Australian Catholics have?—a minority existence in a drab and soulless Anglo-secular society. Irish illusions were vastly preferable to that—or so it then seemed. But the cost of harbouring illusions, or visions, or dreamworlds of truth and decency was sniggers, sneers.

So the stigma attached to being Irish-Australian lingered on—it exists in some places still—a legacy useful to detractors of that culture and religious allegiance, a bolster to their own needs to feel superior and to justify their own beliefs, attitudes and behaviour. The term 'Irish Catholic' was a label designed to separate and distance those of that tradition from the mainstream of Australian life, to imply that they were foreign and apart, inferior of course, not truly of the real Australia, having interests and loyalties distinct from that of the majority. It was a label which carried with it an historical load of old divisions and prejudices, too old or too silly to be openly reactivated, but there as shadows on the mind, to darken the reactions of those to whom 'Irish Catholic' meant people who were distinct, different, not understood.

Nor could new and non-Irish directions within Australian Catholicism change this external image. The intellectual awakening of Australian Catholicism in the 1920s and thirties had English, European and American roots, evident in the names of its new organisations—the Campion Society, Catholic Evidence Guild, Newman Societies, *Catholic Worker*, Knights of the Southern Cross, the Ladies of The Grail; even the name B.A. Santamaria makes the point. Yet the Movement, and later the Democratic Labor party, still acquired the malodorous repute of being 'Irish Catholic', an ethnic party: absurdly Mannix's green touch, despite his own stress on the necessity of fostering what was Australian, was sufficient contamination to make 'Irish' an organisation locked in mortal combat with other 'Irish' labour forces, particularly obvious in the machine politics of New South Wales. Was this 'Irish' fighting 'Irish', ancient faction-fighting in up-to-date guise?

By the 1920s, Irish immigration had dwindled to a selected few. Emigrant families posed on the wharf in Belfast, 1929
Ulster Museum

When would being 'Irish' ever end? When the term ceases to have utility as a mode of denigration, as a weapon, or as the refuge of the intellectually incompetent and lazy.

And when there is absolutely no basis for the distinction it implies. The disadvantaged position of Irish-descent Catholics, particularly in the cities, remained a continuing legacy, bequeathed to their children, and to subsequent generations. A century after the arrival of the original immigrants, their positions of poverty and lesser social attainments continued to be noted by demographers in the 1970s in the significantly less advantaged situations of their descendants.

The cause of this might be simply explained as the results of the poverty trap whose forces were self-perpetuating and from which it was difficult to escape. But because an Irish descent and tradition was common to many of those so entrapped, the culture of such poverty developed an 'Irish' tinge which tended to affirm and assert, often truculently, 'Irish' features, not because they were 'Irish' but because they were theirs—a distinctive identity among otherwise few possessions. It would be wrong to characterise this 'Irishness' as false, in the sense of being some kind of pretence or imitation: it was genuine, true to the people involved, but 'Irish' only at a remove, a double remove of time and place, with little to do with Ireland now. Take the illustration of attitudes to Britain. The Australian Irish were not really anti-British: or, more exactly, they were only anti-British because, and to the extent that, the Australian establishment was pro-British. It was an Australian reaction. So was acceptance of the tag 'Irish working class', a phrase of dismissal and contempt adopted with belligerent pride by many of those to whom it was applied. They were, in fact, nothing like the Irish working class, which was weak, poorly unionised, hardly class-conscious and, until recently without significant political expression: in contrast, the 'Irish'-Australian working class was strong, heavily unionised and attached to a powerful political party. But it was a label they accepted, sometimes gloried in, because it captured a crucial aspect of their solidarity, a sense of historical apartness. The movement of the Australian Irish up the socioeconomic scale was retarded, complicated and con- ditioned by the commonality they valued and sought as well. They felt comfortable with the Irish clergy's interpretation of themselves as the glorious and indomitable poor, loved by God in their suffering. Moreover group solidarity and security was most readily available at the bottom. To rise was to become more alone, more isolated, less at ease with others. Indeed, 'poor' Irish made sure that upstart recreants were isolated for moving out of orbit. The historical ethos of the Australian Irish, forced together in common exclusion from society's higher echelons, worked to sustain itself: there was a tug in all Australian Irishness pulling back towards the human comforts of society's bottom levels, or at least to settle for not too far up, not too distant from familiar origins.

The Catholic Australian community of Irish descent which stabilised its character in the late 1920s after the turmoil which had spilled out from Ireland had quietened, was distinctively Australian in its concerns, if still patently Irish in its derivation. It was determined that it alone was 'Irish' in Australia: for the job of being Irish, no other than Catholics need apply./Birthplace or descent was insufficient qualification, such as that of the Anglo-Irish or Ulster Protestants: such persons could be conscripted for the purpose of sustaining such celebrations of Irish Australian achievement as P.S. Cleary's 1933 compilation *Australia's Debt to the Irish Nation Builders*, but were otherwise excluded, not only by want of Catholicism, but by 'class', from the living operation of this culture. It was not only Catholic, but poor, and these two features were further confirmed in the crucible of the 1930s depression. It was a culture of extraordinary human resource and religious depth, but harsh and narrow and limited in its ambition. It was a popular culture which constantly promoted its own virtues in its speech-making, sermonising and newspapers, but lacked any intellectual dynamics even within the dimensions of the culture it claimed as its own. In Melbourne in 1927, H.B. Higgins was considering ways in which he might encourage the study of Celtic literature, a subject of which he was not a scholar, but which he was convinced had 'some unique value—spiritual value'. He proposed bequeathing £20 000—a vast sum for that day—to found a chair of Celtic literature, in the University of Melbourne, But he doubted whether such a chair would be a success: 'who would be students, and for what purpose?' Higgins eventually gave the money to the Royal Irish Academy in Dublin. An obscure proposal that there should be an Irish-Australian Cultural University in Melbourne surfaced briefly in the 1930s. The basic problem of Irish-Australian popular culture was that that was all that it was—popular, without dimensions which would give it relevance and vitality that would sustain it when the generations it had supported had gone.

The 1940s saw the emergence, from among the young of Irish Australia, of those who could see no relevance in Ireland whatever. In 1946 Rev. A. Cleary 'asked a young friend of mine what he thought should be done about Irish history and sentiment in Australia. "Forget about them," he replied at once with a smile'. Cleary would have none of this. Writing in the *Advocate* he argued that if one was of Irish origin nothing could change that fact, and it could not be ignored, in the way a parent could not be ignored: justice was demanded by one's origins. He conceded that many ignored or downplayed their Irishness because they were ashamed of it as allegedly inferior, looked on with contempt by the rich and powerful: this attitude was a problem of the slave mind. Cleary's argument was based on the propositions that 'Catholicism in the concrete is necessarily identified with race and blood', and that abandonment of the Irish tradition too often led to a rootlessness ripe for conversion to communism: the number of ex-Irish Catholics prominent in the ranks of the Australian Communist Party had not escaped the notice of clerical commentators.

Cleary advocated imperative re-education in things Irish. But he, and other Ireland enthusiasts, had a major problem even greater than Australian apathy or resistance—the quality of Ireland itself. In the postwar world, some Irish priests in the antipodes were casting 'resurgent Catholic Ireland' 'as a weapon for Christ's Church and the civilisation of the West now mortally threatened by the anarchistic nihilism of the East'. These idealists saw Ireland in the role of the spiritual super-power that would win the Cold War for Christ. But, regrettably the spiritual quality of Irish emigrants was lacking: how could a new world be built with such rubbish? Their minds were 'filled with Irish party politics rather than with true Gaelic values, ideals and traditions'. By the late 1940s even Ireland's friends in Australia were highly critical of the new Irish republic proclaimed in 1948. It was simply not doing its job in educating its sons and daughters in the Gaelic tradition. Its emigrants were liabilities not assets in the matter of religious practice: instead of improving the quality of Australian Catholicism they formed another missionary problem. Nor was Ireland sustaining its cultural superiority, but rather, resting on ancient and outworn laurels and failing to adapt and promote its message to a modern world. Nor did it really care for, or about, its emigrants whom it simply abandoned to the secularism of the countries to which they went.

The disillusionment of the 1940s was final, adding to the rejection of Irish politics that had taken place in the 1920s, a rejection of the myth of Irish moral superiority: Ireland could no longer be sustained comfortably as a model, as the measure by which Irish

Australia could be assessed—unfavourably, or at least less than as an equal. The older generation found this Irish colonial mentality of deference to Dublin, a habit difficult to shed, so long had they been tutored in it. And the young of the 1940s and fifties kept their scepticism quiet, preferring to ignore rather than to openly question and attack an Irish orientation still regarded as a necessary part of an ordered and religious world by the older generation. But the facts of Australian life were rapidly telling against the Irish connection. The immigration explosion from 1947 carried a very small Irish element: the 1954 census revealed that 0.53 percent of the Australian population were Irish-born, and about a fifth of those were from Northern Ireland. And from 1962–65 the Second Vatican Council began a process of change in Australian Catholicism which effectively destroyed the old cultural order in religion: what was Irish was swept away with the rest. Perhaps not swept away, but gradually eroded, diminished in sacred power, isolated as antiquated. Yet not until the late 1960s did the descendants of the Irish in Australia become sufficiently free of the authoritarian seriousness of their heritage to be able to poke fun at it. This exercise was first performed, with considerable comic skill, by the novelist Thomas Keneally in *Three Cheers for the Paraclete*, published in 1968, in which traditional Irish Catholic culture receives perceptive satiric treatment. In 1971, the attempt by the alleged Fenian, O'Farrell, to assassinate the Duke of Edinburgh in Sydney in 1868 was made the subject of a largely lighthearted song-and-dance play. The tendency to evaluate the Irish Catholic cultural tradition through the means of farce was even more extravagantly demonstrated in Barry Oakley's *The Feet of Daniel Mannix* staged before packed and hilarious audiences in Melbourne in 1971. Oakley's explanation of the play's genesis illuminates the process of which he is representative:

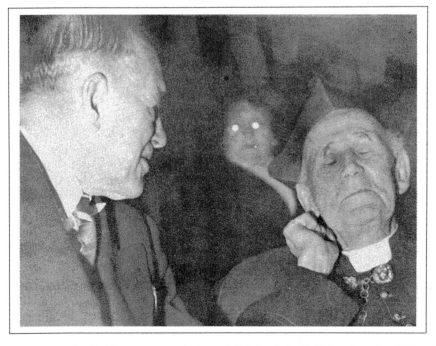

Dr Mannix enthralled by Victorian politics. With John Cain M.H.R., Premier of Victoria
Melbourne Diocesan Historical Commission

Why Mannix? Because he is a central figure, not just of Catholicism, but of Australia itself. For too long he dominated the antipodean scene in a way that was bad for him and bad for Australia. He's the father figure of Irish-Australia, and the embodiment of all that's good and bad in that combination: authoritarian—yet an incorrigible meddler in politics. I grew up in that stimulating, monolithic, controversial atmosphere, and the play is an attempt to slough it off, and shed a skin through the convention of comedy.

Irish Australia in retrospect made good theatre, and more serious dramatic encounters with it marked the mid-1970s—John O'Donoghue's *A Happy and Holy Occasion* in 1974, and perhaps the most successful and powerful evocation of the religious aspects of that culture, Ron Blair's *The Christian Brothers*. The passing of the old Irish-Australian Catholic culture continued to stimulate literary efforts—novels and reminiscence mainly—of which the extremes bear noting. At the popular level of million-dollar bestseller was Colleen McCullough's *The Thorn Birds* (1978) whose setting was old Irish Catholic Australia, exaggerated to novelistic absurdity and fittingly mythologised into a saga of heat, dust, drought, bushfires, and kangaroos, populated by stereotypes of clerics and brogues, passions and plotting. At the other extreme of Irish orientation at an intellectual and artistic level, lay Vincent Buckley, Melbourne poet and essayist, with his idea of Ireland being his 'Imagination's Home' and his exploration of this theme in poetry and prose. Perhaps more Australian in his vision of the Irish connection was the thematic return (to the degree of fascination) of the painter Sidney Nolan to the subject of Ned Kelly: the strange helmeted figure of Ned is a recurring mystery at the heart of Nolan's brilliant enigmatic work.

Another force was at work in the 1950s to render Irish Australia a matter of history—the disintegration of the half-century-old alignment between Irish Catholics and the Australian Labor Party which followed the split in that party from 1954 over the issue of Catholic power and policies within it. The destruction of this traditional political identification, and the profound and bitter disputes to which it gave rise, stimulated a widespread revaluation of the old modes of Irish Australia, already out of step with improvement in the socioeconomic status of Irish Catholics. The public concentration of attention on the continued disruption of Labor's old political order, and the appearance of the new Democratic Labor Party with largely Catholic support, tended to resurrect the traditional concept of 'Irish Catholic' as something of importance in Australian politics. This had been so, but the explosions and realignments of the 1950s signalled its departure at least with any Irish reference. From then on, 'Irish Catholic' became merely a derogatory label to apply to Australian Catholics, and was used in the political controversies of the 1950s and sixties in an attempt to stigmatise Catholics by association with a tradition commonly alleged to be poor, ignorant, divisive, inferior and somehow foreign to Australian life—the ancient canards of Australian history levelled again. In present journalistic usage, these elements remain, with some shifts of emphasis: 'Irish Catholic' is the same dismissive pejorative label, but with further distance in time from any direct Irish background and the growth of fashionable non-belief, its connotations (unless used as a vague category devoid of all meaning) are those of clannishness and obscurantism, inferior peasant origins, and devious, if not corrupt, Labor politicking.

All this labelling and soul-searching took place very much within an Australian context and with Australian reference: nobody bothered to make any comparisons with Ireland or suggested the presence of any links with it in the imbroglios of the 1950s and sixties. It was simply irrelevant. Australians made clear distinctions between relations with the Irish political state—the Republic of Ireland—and their fellow Australians of Irish extraction: curiously, Irish reality for them was not the small state of three million people that stood off the island of Britain, but the nineteenth-century heritage that lived on in a section of the Australian scene. 'Irish', in common Australian usage, now more often meant of Irish background than of Irish birth. This was a function of the tiny numbers of the Irish-born—44 813 in 1947—and of political shorthand for describing the Catholic segment of the Labor movement. It was also a result of the determined efforts of the Irish Free State to break the constrictions of its dominion situation to grasp full independence. By 1937 it had effective autonomy, styled itself 'Ireland', behaved as a republic, and remained neutral during the Second World War. The neutrality was not popular among Australian loyalists, but it did not become an issue within Australia, and together with the other aspects of Ireland's stance confirmed the image of Ireland as separate and 'foreign', if uniquely so. In the postwar world, both Ireland and Australia were small powers seeking much wider international recognition and greater prestige. The idea of opening diplomatic relations with Ireland was particularly attractive to Australian Labor governments, and to Arthur Calwell in particular, the Minister of Immigration and long active in Irish-Australian causes. It was also appealing to Dr H.V. Evatt, Minister of External Affairs, for political reasons: he sought to confront Britain and to appear on the world scene as the champion of small nations, and he saw support for Ireland as popular within his own party. In April 1946, Mr W.J. Dignam, a Sydney barrister who was an active ALP member and a friend of Dr Evatt, was appointed Australian High Commissioner to Eire (the Gaelic form of the name of the island). The Liberal and Country Party opposition questioned the cost and need for such representation in a country, in their view, of such minor importance. In September 1946 the Irish government appointed Dr Thomas J. Kiernan minister plenipotentiary in Australia. He arrived with his wife (well known as the ballad singer Delia Murphy) and family in October to a warm welcome. This appointment appears to have been an expression of de Valera's (he was then Taoiseach—Prime Minister) policy to engage overseas Irish opinion in support of his campaign to bring an end to the partition of Ireland. Kiernan made it clear that his mission was primarily a cultural one. He sought to inform Australia on all aspects of Irish affairs, but particularly scholarship and the arts, and for the next several years lectured widely on Irish culture and history, presented Irish books to public libraries and made significant original contributions himself to the study of the history of the Irish in Australia.

Kiernan was a successful image-maker, but he also had another task—to attempt to get the Australian government to accept him as ambassador for 'Ireland' not 'Eire': the terminology was crucial, as its implications were to reject Britain's sovereignty over the six counties of the province of Ulster which Britain called 'Northern Ireland'. The device was also part of an Irish campaign to remove itself from the Commonwealth, something incomprehensible to Ireland's friends in Australia, who envisaged closer, not looser Irish–Commonwealth associations—another of the continuing examples of the incapacity of the pro-Irish elements in Australia to understand the realities of Irish affairs. Kiernan used various devices to stress Ireland's claim to distinctive foreignness—or at least, non-Britishness: the use of Gaelic in the Embassy letterhead was one, calling his mission the 'legation' was another. But the Australian Labor government mixed politeness with unwillingness to be used against Britain and the Commonwealth in this way: it would do nothing effective to help Ireland's efforts to advance its independence. Even the most enthusiastic proponents of closer ties with Ireland saw these in terms of gratifying their own sentimental inclinations and affirming their heritage, not as serving the interests of contemporary Irish politics—particularly any bid to leave the Commonwealth club.

The facts of Irish-Australian life were clearly demonstrated in relation to the visit to Australia in April–May 1948 of Eamon de Valera. Briefly out of power (his Fianna Fail party held government 1932–48, and again 1951–54, 1957–73), de Valera, and his former Finance Minister, Frank Aiken, embarked on an overseas tour to arouse the Irish diaspora in support of his anti-partition crusade. Much to the surprise of the organisers, they accepted Archbishop Mannix's pro-forma invitation to attend the Melbourne archdiocesan centenary celebrations, guaranteeing de Valera a large audience assembled for the occasion: the 15–20 000 people who crowded the Melbourne Exhibition Hall were there for Mannix, and de Valera was an additional attraction. His Sydney audience, variously estimated at 7–13 000 is a truer guide to his appeal, although it too was a Catholic occasion crammed with bishops and priests, the rearguard of clerical Irish Australia. It was not the mammoth rally for which Dr Albert Dryer had hoped. The 1947 census indicates that there were 11 134 persons of Irish birth living in Sydney, but Dryer had expected a massive response from the hundreds of thousands of Irish descent. But at least the crowd was substantial: de Valera's public meeting in Hobart incurred a financial loss. The prevailing Irish-Australian mood, faced with de Valera, was indifference or embarrassment, and even those who took the trouble to hear him found his political style disconcertingly different from the Australian. A Brisbane Catholic journalist described him as 'a public figure who believes . . . that it is his country's high duty to teach the world the might of moral beauty and stamp God's image truly on the struggling soul'. This was not the language of Australian politics, and by 1948 very few Irish Australians believed that Australia had anything to learn from Ireland.

Nor did they believe they should become involved in Irish politics. De Valera, recognising in Albert Dryer the true believer, charged him with the task of organising, as secretary, the Australian League for an Undivided Ireland, the anti-partition organisation which de Valera wished to see rising spontaneously from the Australian Irish to pressure Britain to relinquish its hold on the North. Dryer invested a great deal of his time and energy in efforts to float this organisation: over the next five years he wrote about 5000 letters all over Australia—in vain. The South Australian response illustrates his problems:

Dr and Mrs T.J. Kiernan with de Valera in Canberra, 1948

*Eamon de Valera in Irish Australia, with the backdrop of the Union Jack at the Melbourne
Archdiocesan centenary celebrations, Xavier College, May 1948*
Melbourne Diocesan Historical Commission

it took him nine letters and seven months to raise a reply from the champions of Ireland in
Adelaide. The league never lived. By 1953–54 it was quite dead. Its brief existence had
been plagued by internal disputes between State organisations, incompetence, even by
hostility from the Catholic clergy: the Archbishop of Hobart requested that the league be
not organised in Tasmania. To end the dismal tale, the league was suspended, to avoid its
remnants being taken over by local branches of Sinn Fein, the political wing of the IRA.

Shortly after de Valera's departure, in November 1948, Ireland declared its separation from
the Commonwealth and asserted independence as the Republic of Ireland. Australia joined
other Commonwealth countries in passing legislation preserving Ireland's previous
favoured status, a decision not welcomed by the opposition, whose position was that
Ireland should be punished for withdrawing from the Commonwealth. With the election of
a Menzies Liberal-Country Party government in December 1949, this markedly less
sympathetic attitude to Ireland became official policy, and the matter of Ireland's title, the
name of the Irish state, became deadlocked: Australia refused to use 'Ireland', Ireland
refused to accept 'Eire' or 'Republic of Ireland'. Because of this impasse, throughout the
1950s, diplomatic exchanges were sporadic and junior. In 1951 the Irish-born Labor
member Dan Minogue began a campaign, which was to last until 1964, to have a full
ambassador appointed to Dublin: his annual questions on the matter became a

De Valera's welcome in the Sydney Stadium, April 1948

parliamentary ritual, garnished with salty interjections such as 'Get back to the bogs' and fulsome oratorical evasions by government ministers. Eventually the matter of diplomatic forms of address was resolved in a way commentators at the time regarded as 'Irish', but which might be more accurately described as an ingeniously diplomatic compromise which saved all faces and satisfied everybody. In the exchange of ambassadors Ireland would use its legislative styles and titles, which implied its claim to government of all thirty-two counties of Ireland, including the North, and Australia would use its styles and titles, which recognised the Irish Republic and implied recognition of Britain's government of Northern Ireland. And it was agreed that neither government, Irish or Australian, would attach the significance to these titles that was accepted as being attached to them by the other party. Or simply, the Australian forms recognised Irish partition, the Irish forms did not, and both governments agreed to ignore this. It was on this basis that the first two full ambassadors were exchanged. Dr Eoin MacWhite, a career diplomat, became Irish ambassador in Canberra in 1964; and early in 1965 Mr Hugh Roberton, formerly a senior cabinet minister, became Australian ambassador in Dublin. Both appointments were eminently successful, leading in particular to closer trading and cultural ties, and resulting in the growth of the importance and prestige of both posts to a level worthy of the energies and imagination of the most reputable level of career diplomats.

Until 2 April 1974. On that day the Whitlam Labor Government, seeking to solve internal political problems, appointed Mr Vincent Gair, a former premier of Queensland and then a senator of the Democratic Labor Party, as ambassador to Dublin, a move that required the precipitate removal of the highly successful then incumbent ambassador, Mr Keith Brennan. This was an act firmly in the central traditions of Australia's diplomatic relations with Ireland since 1946, a tradition in which misunderstanding, hostility, contempt, crude political considerations and cynical opportunism might seem to be more active and more obvious than is usual in such matters. For most of this time these relations had been conducted by Liberal-Country Party governments, but this action by the Whitlam Labor government in 1974—seen by many commentators as a first step in its downfall—emphasises a basic commonality in the political dispositions of all parties towards Ireland. Labor was much closer to Ireland in its spirit and the background of its members and supporters than the Liberal and Country parties, but politics is the art of power and manoeuvre, and not the domain of sentiment. Besides, Ireland was determined to be 'foreign', not part of the British Commonwealth, a policy which distanced it from even the sentiment of Labor members of Irish heritage, which could not understand, as their fathers had not understood, why what was good enough for Australia should not satisfy Ireland too.

By the 1950s the old Irish Australia, that of heritage and sentiment, had been almost totally absorbed in its Australian concerns, with merely an occasional nod to its origins. But a new Irish element was appearing in Australia. In 1933, there had been 78 653 persons of Irish birth in Australia. By 1947 this had almost halved to 44 813, and almost half of these were over sixty years of age. But from 1948 there began an influx of young Irish immigrants, some direct from Ireland, but many after a period in England. By 1954, the Irish-born sector of Australia's population had risen to 47 673, a substantial inflow increase on 1947 given the decrease natural to the aging 1947 Irish group. By 1961 this increase had steadied off to a then figure of 44 685 Irish-born, but about a third of these had arrived in Australia since 1947. The presence of these young Irish—mainly men—was evident in various construction sites, particularly in the Snowy Mountains project, and in a big revival in Gaelic sports, mainly hurling. It also began to have an impact within existing Irish organisations, particularly the INA and the League for an Undivided Ireland. This became evident in 1952–53 when they moved into these organisations demanding that the old and Irish-Australian give way to the young and the Irish—and enforcing their will through intimidation and stacked meetings: 'arrogant, aggressive larrikins' Dryer called them. He had all sorts of explanations for their character—they had been corrupted in England, the worst of the Irish emigrated—but he was eventually forced back to the conclusion that 'the best and most ardent workers for the cause of Ireland I have ever met are either Australian-born members of our race, or are native folk from Ireland who have resided here for half a lifetime. In other words the present generation of Irish people is hopeless'. It was a familiar complaint, and of course that 'present generation' in its Australian manifestation regarded Dryer and his like as hopeless too. Different they certainly were. The Irishness of the old generation, even in such clerically unfavoured organisations as the INA, was still intensely clerical. If it had any Irish politics at all, they were mainstream conservative and usually out of date. The new Irish-born generation had little contact with either church or clergy and derived its Irishness from militant nationalism or socialism: a typical expression was its formation in Melbourne, in May 1964, of a Connolly Association, on the British model, named after the Irish socialist executed after the 1916 Rebellion, which sought to raise Irish issues within the ALP and unions. Its politics were often those of Sinn Fein, the political wing of the IRA, and it had close and frequent contact with the left wing of Irish affairs through new arrivals and airmail correspondence and literature. For one of their characteristics Dryer and others of the old order could be grateful: their employment was changeable and often remote, which meant that their impact on existing organisations tended to be sporadic and disruptionist, rather than that of complete and permanent takeovers. They lacked staying power, thought Dryer. And they often preferred to set up their own organisations rather than struggle with the old generation for theirs: Sinn Fein organisations appeared in both Sydney and Melbourne in 1955.

A recent study—that of J.J. Grimes on Irish friendship patterns in Sydney in the late 1970s—illuminates what was the same, and what was different, about the new Irish immigrants. What was the same was their heavy concentration in labouring employment, to the degree of virtual monopoly of certain kinds of navvying work, for instance, drain-laying and installation of underground cables. The same too was the function of certain hotels (such as the Freemason's in Burwood) as social, entertainment and employment centres. And the mobility: many were constantly on the move, searching for bigger money, spending a spell in the city, another in the bush, avoiding taxation with cash in the hand, living out of suitcases. The Gaelic Club membership changed up to 50 percent in any one year. And they were, as before, young and mostly unmarried, with a strong sense of locality and county loyalty in regard to their Irish origins.

But the differences from their forebears were no less marked. Where before the sex ratio was remarkably even, the new migrants were heavily male, and nursing, rather than domestic service, was the main female occupation. And there was a new element of professional and business people, small in number but significant in diversity. As before, they were well dispersed over the city, but stronger in the inner western suburbs. Burwood attracted the tag, 'Little Ireland', but the whole string of railway suburbs between Central and Strathfield attracted the Irish, and in the 1970s there were concentrations further out, at Parramatta, St Mary's and Penrith as well as Concord. This dispersion, so unlike the tight locational groupings of some other national groups, made the Irish appear assimilated, but this is deceptive. Inquiries showed that many of the new Irish had few or no Australian friends after ten years' residence: it was in fact a closed network in which newer immigrants had little contact with older and even less with the Australian-born. These new immigrants tended to set up their own social and sporting clubs, and to overwhelm the older and the Australian-born in the existing organisations: in 1975 the Irish National Association/Gaelic Club combination in Sydney, with a total membership of 1530 was nearly 70 percent Irish-born. These differences reflect the communications revolution. Where before distance compelled Irish immigrants to make a permanent commitment to Australia, with all the social and individual attitudes that entailed, now the options were much wider—travel on elsewhere, return to Britain, or Ireland itself. The notion of Australia as providing a working holiday of indeterminant length replaced the concept of permanent migration: in some cases the idea of integration, assimilation, simply did not arise.

One conflict neatly encapsulates the difference between old Irish Australia and the new young Ireland. Dryer had always, in his idealism, opposed the seeking of a liquor licence for the INA. Weakness for drink he believed was the Irishman's vice and a licence would be both a potential source of shame, and the subversion of the cultural developments he sought to foster. In a special INA meeting in December 1962, those of Dryer's mind were defeated by eighty-two votes to thirty-five. The meeting was packed by recent young Irish immigrants. 'They are utterly and absolutely destitute of even the slightest sentiment of patriotism,' Dryer wrote in disgust; 'they are even apt to ridicule Irish sentiment and culture.' Sacrilege. Dryer did not see that the culture he venerated was dead—if in fact it had ever really lived, for it was a construct, an abstraction generated by the Gaelic revival movement, an Irish make-believe. The young Irish had not the slightest sentiment of this kind of patriotism, to which they were in reaction, and their tendency to ridicule came from their rejection of an artificiality which purported to be a culture which they believed was not their own. Who was Dryer in Australia, an old man who had never seen Ireland, to tell them what Irish culture was? It was what they said it was, and they knew, because they were Irish.

And they said it was what Ireland was—now. Not what it might have been in some distant past. Not some fairyland forlorn. Not some haven for saints, scholars, and plaster nationalists of yesteryear, but this week's news from Dublin and Belfast, airmail. These were the Irish in Australia who were directly and consistently interested in the re-emergence of the Northern Ireland question from 1968. Among those of Irish descent, any involvement with or support of organisations related to this new Irish crisis, tended to be cautious, reluctant, narrow and fluctuating. Initially, in 1968–69, when that crisis had the complexion of a civil rights agitation, Irish Australian support was open, strong, and prestigious—with bishops, professional men and academics prominent on aid committees. Yet it was a sign of the Irish-Australian times that the traditional Melbourne St Patrick's Day procession was discontinued in 1970. The emergence, early in 1970, of the IRA as a factor in the struggle in Ireland, and its massive bombing campaign, abruptly terminated or radically narrowed this Irish-Australian support, which extended to civil rights, but not to violence, and particularly not the indiscriminate terror of 1971. The Irish-Australian mood became one of detachment, mixed with revulsion—and with some sympathy with the British Army as it was introduced as a peace-keeping force from August 1969. But the killing of thirteen civilians by British paratroopers in Derry on 30 January 1972 swung opinion against the army, and British policy generally—but not towards the IRA; such support as the IRA had in Australia, in such organisations as the Sean South and Fergal O'Hanlon Society, and, perhaps, Noraid, was small (perhaps 1000 throughout Australia), greatest in Melbourne, and almost exclusively made up of recent Irish immigrants (or so it seems: such organisations did not reveal their strength). As before, the role of those of Irish descent, as distinct from those of Irish birth, was largely that of providing financial assistance to Irish—Northern Irish—distress; but that assistance seems to have been very limited given the continuing claims that such money was used to assist the IRA, and that the dominant Irish Australian reaction has been the belief that what is happening in Northern Ireland has nothing whatever to do with them. They wished to dissociate themselves from it. Certainly, the focus on the issues provided by the Maze Prison Hunger Strikes of 1981 generated a wave of sympathetic interest, and hostility to the unrelenting intransigence of the British government, but the nature and dimensions of this reaction was hardly distinguishable from—indeed much milder than—the protest demonstrations of other ethnic minorities in Australia against events in their countries of origin. One factor in this has been the attitude of the Irish government in Dublin, its hostility to the IRA, and its series of negotiations with Britain to devise a joint policy towards, and solution of, the Northern problem. This attitude, injected into the Australian atmosphere and official climate by an active and able embassy staff in Canberra, has tended to suppress and isolate the small movements of radical Irish nationalism that exist in Australia and to confirm the moderate majority opinion in preferred attitudes of benign and distant friendliness. So, the first visit of a president of Ireland to Australia in May–June 1985, together with the Foreign Minister, was a harmonious, low-key occasion, a pleasant ritual of state visits, meeting the Australian Irish—and the Irish in Australia—and predictable exchanges of speeches, with clichés about distinctive 'contributions', 'source people' and the national ethos: all true, and matter of fact. And the President also visited the headquarters of the Australian Society of Genealogists, an appropriate acknowledgement both of the family past and the increasing Irish Australian interest in it. More facts.

But the Irish President Dr Hillery also visited that place where facts intercut with dreams, the strange and beautiful monument in Waverley Cemetery, Sydney, where Michael Dwyer and his wife are buried and which commemorates those violent rebellions against English rule which began the Irish peopling of Australia. Carved in this stone are the names of Irish heroes to whom Australia meant nothing. They came here nonetheless, famous ghosts who journeyed across the world in the minds and hearts of Ireland's exiles. That they should merit a monument at the other end of the Irish world speaks their power to transcend facts of space and time, and to capture the imaginations of humdrum people of ordinary life settling a vacant place. Ireland in Australia was both fact and dream. Its dimensions of fact coincide with the boundaries of the continent, but its dreams were unbounded, spanning the world—and more than the world. No man can fix the boundaries of the nation of the mind and heart. Least of all the soul. Nor call their territories complete. On 19 September 1803, a time at the beginning of Australian civilisation, Robert Emmet in Dublin concluded thus his speech to his executioners: 'When my country takes her place among the nations of the earth, then, and not till then, let my epitaph be written.' The monument at Waverley is inscribed with the names of a heroic Irish legion—save one. It is innocent of the name of Robert Emmet.

B E I N G I R I S H

I N A U S T R A L I A

By 2000 Emmet was irrelevant, his rhetoric swept aside. In the swirl of Irish events this no longer fitted Irish circumstances. It was on the agreement and consent of a majority that the future depended. Ireland had taken her place among the nations of the earth, though not in the manner or form that Emmet might have expected or desired. People rather than territory would take their place at the heart of Irish constitutional law and the principle of freely given consent—North and South—would alone determine the destiny of Emmet's Nation. In December 1999 the Irish government renounced its historic constitutional claim to sovereignty over all of the island of Ireland, including the North, declaring its recognition that, at present, the majority of the people of Northern Ireland wished to maintain the Union with Britain. The British government repealed the 1920 Government of Ireland Act, and, taking a similar position, accepted that the future of links with Northern Ireland depended on the consent of a majority of its people. It devolved many of its powers over Northern Ireland to a newly elected power-sharing Assembly in Belfast. Both governments agreed that future relationships within the island of Ireland would be a matter for the people of Ireland—Irish Republicans would no longer die for Irish freedom. They would instead, through dialogue and negotiation, work for Irish unity—become persuaders for Irish reconciliation. That Assembly, with limited executive powers, met for the first time in December 1999, though events soon suggested that this may have been, not a false start, but optimistic in timing: ancient antagonisms and distrust still held destructive powers. Whatever of that, the new arrangement posits a startling positive innovation in definitions of identity, a move away from stagnant notions of nationhood and sovereignty towards a society in which identity is seen as a shared process, a gradual evolution, rather than some static conclusion. As in so much else in its modern history, the island of Ireland has become the crucible for the fashioning of modernity.

In Irish Australia these were developments viewed from afar, certainly of interest, importance, but essentially world affairs, foreign, good news it seemed—but nothing of immediate relevance. Ireland's North was of major interest only when it exploded. Far more to the local point were complex changes in the character of Irish Australia: character was becoming characters in ways which abraded each other and pulled differently, though not apart. Old Irish Australia, that of pre-1960s immigrants, stretching back to 1788, had ideas and ideals focused on a vanishing Ireland, a dream-place which somehow captured their imaginations and emotions. There *should* be a place, called Ireland, which was theirs. But did the present actuality meet their requirements? The new Ireland, that of the Celtic tiger economy, increasingly secular and hard-nosed, home point of reference for recent Irish 'emigrants' (the self-styled 'ex-pats'), was in complex tension with the old Australian Ireland. Complex, because by the late 1990s the term 'emigrant' had lost any useful meaning in explaining the character of the Irish encounter with Australia. In 1997–98 there were 776 Irish migrants, that is, those intending on settlement. But there were over 16 000 Irish visitors, and nearly 8000 on work visas (backpacking, and the like). So, an annual influx of 24 000, increasing massively; with 20 000 (perhaps as many as 50 000) visitors, plus probably 10 000 on working-holiday visas, predicted for the period of the Olympic Games. The permanent 'migrant' figures remained low and stable, at around 3 percent of the annual Irish influx. And in the 1996 census the total Irish born, including from Northern Ireland, was 74 510, a drop of 3000 from 1991. The figures make the obvious point. The Irish born were less than half of one percent of the permanent Australian population, and, at any one time, roughly a third of the Irish in Australia are moving through, in some form of visiting transit.

Set that potential intricacy, discontinuity, confusion, variety of allegiances, in the context of those who came before. What was the stance of that massive proportion of Australians with some degree of Irish descent—estimated at a quarter to a third? To the extent that they were at all interested in their origins (and most of them were not), as Irishness diminished with time and distance from social practice, the 1990s saw it re-invented by enthusiasts as 'social memory' or 'collective consciousness' or 'historical self-image'—as heritage. There emerged, as the new recent Irish drifted—consciously or unconsciously—towards an ethnic Irishness identified with modern Ireland, some Australians of Irish descent who were re-inventing, resurrecting the remnants (selective and sanitised) of an Irish culture which had long gone and, in part, never was: the old cult of an unreal, superseded, partly manufactured, mythological nation was revived, strengthened.

In the absence now of the coercions of the old social hierarchies and structures, weakened or destroyed in a modern world, individuals compose and construct the culture, the living space and values which suit them. All this can be assembled without effort from the bits and pieces readily to hand: in this case, from the residuum of Ireland—past and present. But which?

The setting for this situation has been, and is, multiculturalism; this policy of government social engineering, embarked on from the 1970s, had curious and unintended side-effects. The upshot was to encourage problems and confusion about what 'Ireland' meant. New, or old? Multiculturalism had the effect of encouraging both, but as divergent and not as a continuum. And, in the view of the new Irish, the old Irish had become involved in, identified with that mainstream environment in which the new Irish found themselves, and with which they found themselves in tension.

Criticism by the new Irish was of a kind and level very different from that which had given the old Irish their galvanic effect in Australian history. It was now a question of irritations and impatiences rather than of rebellions against constrictions on their liberties. The new Irish believed that the 1990s Australia was in a 1960s time-warp, was infuriatingly conservative, lacked dynamism, was not like America, was addicted to outmoded fooleries such as Anzac Day and the monarchy, inhabited by people who did not know who or what they were, and who had the unfinished business of reconciliation with the ancient people of this land.

It was a formidable list of discontents, in which the basic premise was that Australia should emulate modern Ireland. Immigrant expectations had reversed: Australia should follow them and the new Ireland. The old Irish came to Australia to learn, to stay, to insist on adequate room and recognition for themselves in a society in which they were committed to stay—and re-make, to include their own dimensions in that totality. The new Irish were far less so disposed. They were under no compulsion to either stay in, or give themselves to the wider society into which they had entered. They remained Irish; detached, ambivalent, committed or uncommitted—to what? Irishness? But what was that? Asked how he felt about Ireland in December 1999, a young Irish salesman in Sydney said he missed the idea of the place more than the place itself. The feeling that Ireland, as Ireland, was the measure of one's essential identity, was to arrive at a present balance in an old dichotomy, which had been oppositely decided in the past. It is not only that the new Irish had the usual young problems in merging with old generations of Irish Australians, it is that they remained essentially Irish, an identity sustained by the devices of modern technology. There was not only ease of travel, but cheap telephone rates, the availability of video recordings of family and sporting events in Ireland (even live, satellite coverage of All-Ireland finals), Irish newspapers by air or daily on the internet, e-mail—all the apparatus to keep in close touch with home.

Meanwhile, the old Irish Australia, that segment of it which retained consciousness of Irish heritage, lost itself in an extraordinary enhancement of the image and influence of the 'Irish' factor in Australian life. Australia had become much more 'Irish'. One of multiculturalism's unintended side-effects was to gradually make Irishness respectable: by 2000 the days of its being a social liability were well over. But this was Irishness of a certain kind and within limitations. And it created a false environment for newcomers: this was Irishness for Australians, not for Ireland, engendering misunderstanding and impatience amongst the new Irish.

How did this come about? Old Ireland, the Ireland before 1916—the Ireland that had celebrated its founding contribution to Australia with that bold declaratory monument to 1798 in Sydney's Waverley Cemetery—had made its profound and enduring Australian mark by the time of the Second World War. Like the monument itself, its Irish and its Irishness had weathered storms and settled into the Australian earth. They had become part of the features and texture of the human landscape, so much so as to be virtually indistinguishable as Irish, save for assumptions generated by their names and usual—if sometimes very residual—Catholicity. In all else they were simply a variety—not even that, an integral element—of the ordinary Australian scene. It was entirely proper and appropriate that the refurbishment of that imposing and beautiful 1798 monument should, in 1999–2000, be undertaken with the advice and assistance of Australia's National Trust.

The new Irish were very different. They had come in a trickle from 1947, many from Northern Ireland, or via Britain, swelling into significant numbers in the 1970s and, particularly, the 1980s: the 1990s were to see even greater numbers, but many more as visitors and short-term workers, than as migrants proper. Albert Dryer, that idealistic devotee of Old Ireland (he died in 1963), was baffled and angered by those he encountered of the new breed. The difference was not merely generational. There was indeed a new Ireland. Indeed, there were at least three—a Northern Ireland which had been going its own divided way since 1920; a large Irish element in Britain (a significant source of Irish migrants to Australia); and the Irish Republic, emerging by the late 1950s from an economic and social somnolence that Dryer, and older Australian lovers of the idea of Ireland, had long taken to be the 'real' Ireland. This is to neglect, as beyond classification, a fourth Ireland: those on the move, from all parts of America, from Africa, the Middle East, those wandering, enterprising Irish scholars of mankind, whose itinerancy put them eventually in Australia, to work, have fun, move on.

All these modern Irelands were to a greater or lesser degree incomprehensible to those Australians of Irish heritage whose view of Ireland was bogged in a make-believe nineteenth century of thatched cottages, pious peasants and beloved parish priests. That Ireland, fostered by the Irish Tourist Board, had become the folkways persona of a new economic Ireland of the 1960s and 1970s, presided over by de Valera as continuity with the past, but in fact led by Prime Ministers Sean Lemass and Jack Lynch into hard-headed technological change and increasingly close ties with Europe. Having applied for

The rear wall of the 1798 monument, inscribed with the names of Irish patriots—with a blank space for Robert Emmet

membership in 1961, Ireland was admitted to the EEC in 1973, beginning (or rather returning to) an orientation that was simply incomprehensible to old Irish Australia, which could not conceive of an Ireland otherwise focused than on the relationship with Britain. The fact that Ireland would play a major role in Europe, and from 1975 take its turn to be the chair of the European Community, was beyond the structural imagination of the traditional Irish Australian experience.

Furthermore, the population decline which had begun with the Great Famine was halted, for the first time in over a century, in 1966: emigration had by no means ceased, but, staying in Ireland was becoming a thinkable possibility for the young. There were population ups and downs but the stage was to come, in 1999, when Irish labour demand well-exceeded supply and Ireland (with a population of 3.7 million) was importing European labour, and pleading for qualified migrants to return. As to the young, they were, increasingly, university graduates, a highly educated workforce available to the multinational companies attracted to Irish investment by generous taxation and locational incentives.

To this Ireland of social and economic revolution, the North added a new, and violent, political twist. There, the discriminatory stagnancy that had prevailed since the foundation of the Northern Ireland state was disrupted by civil rights agitation from 1968, leading on to political crisis and the continuing rule of violence and counter-violence. If the geography of terror and death was confined mainly to the North, its repercussions affected the Irish everywhere, generating passion and division—or bewilderment and avoidance. And more than that. One of the great imponderables of recent Irish history lies in the impact on the Irish psyche, at home and abroad, of the brutal inroads of the North. That fundamental assault lay not only in any contagion of violence which might harden minds and hearts, but in its generation of division, in its erosion of trust, and in what it did to lay siege to the ideal of unity on which had rested the traditional assumptions of Irish nationalist history. The North had the capacity to poison all things Irish, near and far.

Did its hopeful settlement, in December 1999, have the capacity to undo damage, reconcile, and make new? That very settlement marked the achievement of remarkable progress in realism, compromise, negotiation, of acceptance of difference, of tentative, cautious trust. Whatever the crises and difficulties of the future, the momentum and the weight of new vested interests lay on the side of peace.

Here indeed was a new Ireland—and new Irish. These not only inhabited their own transformed environment but the wider global world of the 1960s and after, brought into Ireland by television in 1961 and made physically accessible by air travel and sufficient prosperity within Ireland to use it. Increasingly, those who came from the new Ireland took on a very different character from their straitened predecessors of the ocean age of sail and steam. They were not in the mould of their nineteenth century ancestors, not in the tradition of permanently intentioned settlers, destined never to return. Nor were they pioneers in inclination, nor grateful escapees from crippling destitution. Nor did they have that acquisitive eye for the land characteristic of their predecessors: as before, many could be found in remote work-places—the Snowy, Mount Isa, and around Western Australia—but most sought the cities.

Neither were they the aggressive social dynamic their forefathers had been, nor any force for social ferment. Indeed, they were a minority now dwarfed to insignificance in size by the major ethnic elements that were pouring into Australia after 1947, from the

Mediterranean, from the Middle East, from Asia. That they stood tall in the public view sprang not only from the colour, largeness and self-confident stridency of the new Irish psyche but also from the firmness of the Australian Irish shoulders on which they stood: their ancestors had helped to build a sympathetic, congenial environment which was disposed to welcome them.

But these Australians, even those Irish who had left Ireland prior to the 1980s, did not understand the younger newcomers. In joining the modern material world, the new Ireland had also fallen prey to its manifold discontents and problems, its ambitions and dissatisfactions, disappointments and indulgences. As in Western-type societies everywhere, the young Irish would not accept old modes and limitations. Dynamic prosperity had its reverse coin. While reflecting the vitality, optimism, and assurance of the new Ireland, some few of the young carried away with them its seething restlessness and disgruntlement.

Not all was new. Old patterns of Irish immigration reappeared in new forms. Many did come to stay, looking hopefully for permanent opportunity. Where once had been individual, casual labourers, there were now the modern equivalent of the classical navvies—small contractors, skilled, mechanised, working in efficient groups. A significant number in the 1970s—those from Northern Ireland—were essentially refugees, Catholic and Protestant, fleeing from a society whose level of violence and structures of discrimination and unemployment had become intolerable. There were even, as there had been in the nineteenth century, relocated Irish informers given new identities, and—less identifiable, the subject of rumour—terrorists on the run, and their pursuers. And, although the employment profile had changed radically with Ireland's educational revolution and transformed technology, some traditional avenues renewed their Irish enclaves (nursing, journalism, law enforcement, hotel management).

But the new Irish influx lacked an element central to the old immigration—the religious. It did not include that powerful and pervasive missionary contingent of bishops, priests, nuns and brothers that had firmed and formed the old rank and file of Irish immigration and their descendants—and had given it its coherence, leadership, and aggressive bite. Many of the new Irish left their religion behind them; or they brought its legacy in the form of the openly expressed conviction that religion was what was wrong with Ireland. They contended that the people were priest-ridden, and that the law as it affected personal morality, on contraception, divorce and abortion, was hypocritical, oppressive and outmoded.

The 1990s seemed to them to confirm the correctness of their rejection of the Irish Church. It was beset by a continuing procession of much-publicised scandals: clerical, even to episcopal, sexual misbehaviour, sexual and physical abuse in Catholic schools, misappropriations, swindles, thievery—all given ample space in the Irish Australian press.

This was hardly anything new, in the sense that most Western countries had preceded Ireland down that path much earlier. But it was new for an Ireland in which the church had held, traditionally, such power and prestige. These waned rapidly in the 1990s. The young, in particular, were often indifferent and sceptical, attitudes which found ready acceptance among the substantial ex-Catholic elements in old Irish Australia.

There was also the proposition that sectarianism was the basic cause of the problems of the North. All this reflected an old strand of anti-religion and anti-clericalism in Ireland itself, especially among the educated, but not common—or at least little voiced—in old Irish Australia.

Both groups, new and old, coalesced in the swing to what was Irish in the tradition-al Irish–Catholic amalgam. They emphasised, perhaps exaggerated, the folk elements of that extraordinary culture, raising for the future those imponderables: were the Irish without their old brand of religion really Irish?

For fifteen hundred years that religion had been entwined with Ireland's totality of life—society, culture, politics. It continued to provide much raw material for Irish—and Irish Australian—literature, memoirs, drama. But, past tense. Ireland had joined the rest of the Catholic world in seeking some different accommodation between spir-itual life and a secular society and state. In the political world, where Irish national-ism had been a traditional anchor and focal point for Irish identity, the developments in the North, formalised in 1998–99, demanded some profound readjustments of atti-tude and response. No less challenging was the religious erosion, the questioning of old certainties, the decline of church authority and power. That, too, went to the heart of the traditional Irish identity. That, too, demanded reappraisals, new definitions of the Irish self. Daunting tasks both, but within the proved capacity of Irish ingenuity—and generosity.

Daunting, but not impossible long term. After all, the 'traditional' Catholic Ireland was a post-Famine invention. From 1850 Cardinal Cullen transformed a situation in which religion was relatively weak and its practice confined and erratic (less than a third attended mass), into a situation by the 1880s of firm and pious Catholic practice. Even then the church remained constantly challenged by the old beliefs, by revolutionary nationalism, by violence, and by refusal to accept its authority. With all of which it reached accommodations, truces, and convenient (or compassionate) blindnesses. The Irish encounter with religion was to be as 'crazily tangled as the Book of Kells', and is likely to remain so.

The change in tone and temper, and the stance critical of religion, is hardly surprising, for these new Irish were the educated: surplus professionals and skilled products of an increasingly prosperous, secular state. It was those at the lower levels of employment status who travelled most contentedly. And it was precisely those less well-qualified who were disadvantaged, discouraged, excluded by Australia's points system immigra-tion policies, which heavily weighted skills, qualifications and higher education: will-ingness, enthusiasm, commitment to stay, in themselves, carried no weight at all. Those best educated, well-qualified in profession, business or trade were most prone to dissat-isfaction at their situation and ready to move elsewhere. Firmly self-confident, even convinced of superiority in their identity, abilities and accomplishments, these were often out of sorts both with an Ireland which had not found a place for them, and impa-tient with what they saw as Australian insensitivity and resistance to dominance in what some regarded as a subject Irish colony.

Taken all in all, what distinguished the new from the old Irish in Australia was prin-cipally their attitude to their presence in that place. There were, of course, historical reversions and parallels. Some of the educated elite harboured an arrogance, which was redolent of the old Irish priesthood, though without their faith or grace. Some,

professional or commoner, saw Australia as milch-cow—though in that they had
ample local tutorship, not least from some of their own ancestral tradition: it was the
goldfields mentality again, with a much harder edge. What was most different, was
the extent and degree of commitment. As suggested in my *Vanished Kingdoms*—the
title embodies the point—the new Irish from the 1950s to 2000 were not the imperial successors of the great wave of the 1830s to the 1880s, of those that had so transformed the Australian enterprise so as to accommodate them. These later arrivals did
not seek to invest their energies in the creation of the new, or see beyond the well-
being of the individual.

Rather were they sojourners, visitors, casuals, hived off and happy inhabitants of their own
particular division of multiculture: they were a microcosmic reduction of what once had been, minus the
conquering aggression and ambition, content to be permanently Irish while resident in Australia. These
new arrivals, airborne, with money, and a ticket home in their heads if not their pockets, educated, with
a republic of their own, self-confident in their identity and proud of their culture, were much like other
Europeans, even the British. They were far distant in character, outlook, mission from those Irish whose
Ireland predated 1916–1921.

This is to take a positive view. There were also those Irish who were in Australia reluctantly—as had always been so—and whose reaction to their deprivation was sharper,
more hostile than anything readily contemplated in the days of no possible return. In
May 1991 a sixteen-year-old Kerry girl who had been in Sydney for four years wrote to
the Irish community monthly, the *Irish Exile:*

One letter that was published in your last issue stated that 'today's Irish in Australia are
here through their own freedom of choice'. Although this is true and the choice is ours to make, but that
'freedom of choice' stated was also a choice of necessity for a lot of people. My parents didn't really have a
choice, it was either emigrating or joining the dole queue which is seen as a last resort.

Although Australia is a good country and it has given us employment that our own country couldn't, if we had a 'choice' many of us would not be here today. I know I wouldn't!

It was such Ireland-orientated dispositions—the idea that Irish circumstances had banished their unwilling victims to distant foreign estrangement—that sustained the choice
of the name the *Irish Exile* for the Irish community newspaper, founded in December
1988. The name was deliberately taken from that of the first Irish newspaper in
Australia, the *Irish Exile and Freedom's Advocate*, published in Tasmania in 1850 by
Patrick O'Donohoe, one of the 1848 rebels transported there as gentleman prisoners—
men who were in Australia undoubtedly against their will, saw themselves as temporary
exiles, and sought to escape as soon as they could. The implications of the choice of such
a name for the 1988 newspaper generated a heated controversy which bubbled along in
that paper's correspondence columns until, in April 1992, the name was dropped, and
Irish Echo substituted. But the change was not one of direction or emphasis. The *Echo* was
still a reverberation of Ireland, though sounding more cheerful. The name change
brought no editorial reference to any Australian commitment or dimension, but was a
concession to those elements in the labelling controversy that had argued that the word
'exile' 'conveyed a negativity that has no place in the modern image of Ireland or the
Irish' and that it was 'inconsistent with the content and style of the newspaper'. Later,
the paper came up with the self-description 'Authentically Irish, uniquely Australian',

which begs all possible questions, as did its subtitle, 'The Voice of Irish Australia'.

To pursue further the complexities of the differences between *Exile* and *Echo*. Initially, the Irish pubs which began to mushroom in Australia's cities in the 1990s might have testified to loneliness, as in London; an attempt to cope with foreign isolation by seeking the company of one's fellows. By 2000, the character of this hotel proliferation had changed from something socially negative—a retreat—to something socially positive, aggressive even, something not apologetic or recessive, more assertive, stridently self-confident; but no less, even more apart. The terms and balance of social engagement had reversed. Now it was the Australians who were the outsiders, the welcome foreigners, in the fluid bastions of a lively and colourful Irish host culture: Guinness, *craic*, music, *céad míle fáilte*.

The sheer dimension of this Irish pub imperialism is impressive. In the early 1990s Sydney's only hotel to be popularly known as 'Irish' was the neutrally named Mercantile. In 1999 the *Irish Echo* sought nominations Australia-wide for the best Irish pub of the year. There were 150 nominations, and Durty Nelly's in Paddington, Sydney, was declared winner.

These new Irish-style bars were of three types, all invented for the demand, most equipped with names thought to suit: Scruffy Murphy's, Paddy Shehanigans, Fenians, Kitty O'Shea's, even The Bog. The first Guinness Australian Pub Guide in December 1999 provided details on fifty: ranging from backpacker bars, through the craze of Irish-theme pubs, to older pubs metamorphosed into 'authentic' Irish drinking-places, sometimes even—to the disgust of the old, authentic patrons—with new Irish names. Some few catered for Irish drinkers mainly, but most focused on giving an Irish 'feel', or atmosphere, to Australians—and not simply Irish Australians. What was an Irish 'feel'?—the stage props (pictures of Ireland on the walls, the wooden bars, Gaelic lettering) said it all, plus lively music. But cultural confusion reigned. Asked to comment on the success of Durty Nelly's, the Australian proprietor said, 'It's like the [American]

The Sydney Mercantile's Irish music program, 2000

TV show "Cheers". Everybody knows everyone else's name . . .'. Indeed, who cared if it was ersatz Irish or manufactured American? It worked, it was fun, it was friendly, alive. And many Australians, repelled by the yuppy bars, or those silent (or crudely rowdy) Australian drinking tombs, chose 'Irish'. As did the young Irish. There they met their own kind, looking for accommodation, work, girls, company, music, someone to talk to. And in this 'Irish' environment, they, and not their host country, called the tune.

Durty Nelly's, Irish pub of 1999

The dimension of this 1990s boom in the 'Irish' pub phenomenon is suggested by the import history of those distinctive products on which it is based—mainly Guinness, and Jameson's whiskey. The growth in sales of Guinness (it is mainly brewed under licence in Brisbane, with some lines imported from Ireland) over the decade from 1990, was 181 percent. The consumption of Jameson's, and other Irish Distillers' labels, has undergone an even more prodigious increase. In 1988, 1400 cases of Irish whiskey were landed in Australia: in 1999 it was 50 000 cases. It is a cultural irony that, although the Australian management of these companies is Irish—effectively, indeed brilliantly so—neither of these Irish liquor flag-bearers is Irish-owned. Guinness is a dimension of the giant United Kingdom-based international food and drink conglomerate Diageo PLC; Irish Distillers is owned by a similar giant, the French company, Pernod Ricard.

The Irish pub phenomenon offers Australia a contradictory Irishness, to the extent that it is real rather than make-believe; though, of course, the act, the performance, the shamrock trappings—all are part of the reality. There is a sense in which these pubs isolate their Irish patrons from Australia. For some—the backpacker invasion, in particular—such hotels are their social world, the focus of their identity and meaning: an Irish home away from home. To that extent they foster isolation in Australia. But to the extent that such pubs are commercial ventures, seeking and successfully attracting a patronage wider than the Irish born, they act as environments for familiarisation between Irish and Australians. But not as forces for assimilation. Indeed, the mixing process seems to confirm the participants in their separate identities: both see the other as being other. Logical enough. They are visiting as backpackers and one-year working visa-holders. No need for them to assimilate.

A parallel explosion in the numbers of Irish associations, clubs, and other activities makes even more evident the decision, or preference, to remain apart, or at least to protect or encourage the Irish elements of the 'immigrant' persona. Some few of these organisations have made known their reluctance to accept Australian members, but in any case the nature of their concerns or rationale often is not of Australian application or relevance, except locationally. In the 1960s Australian Irish organisations amounted essentially to the Celtic Clubs in Melbourne and Perth, the Queensland Irish Association, and the Sydney Irish National Association. In 1992 the Embassy of Ireland in Canberra was in touch with 90 centres of Irish activity in Australia; in 2000 there were 198. There were 76 Irish associations spread over, not only the major cities, but the regional centres as well: Gold Coast, Bendigo, Geelong, Darwin, to name a few. Plus nine major clubs. Irish radio programs had grown to 20 in 2000. Such was the impact of *Riverdance* (half-a-million Australians bought tickets) that, from three in 1992, the number of Irish Dancing Associations listed by the embassy in 2000 had become 40. The GAA (Gaelic Athletic Association) was well-established in all States by the 1990s, but the following decade saw a major expansion of sporting activities. And Irish businessmen in Australia were becoming increasingly active in associations to further Ireland's—and their own—commercial interests: in 1999 Australian imports from Ireland passed the billion dollar mark. All these indicators bear witness to the extraordinary surge of Irish energy, enterprise, and self-confidence that transformed Irish Australia in the 1990s. In part, this was an astonishing Irish achievement—ourselves alone—the self-liberation of people who had long had a unique proud identity and were now proclaiming it; happily, and separately, in a society not their own. But, in part, that burgeoning was a product permitted, welcomed, encouraged, by the environment in which it took place: in fundamental ways, Australia—and particularly Irish Australia—had changed. It had become a place which could tolerate, within limits, those who wished to remain apart.

Happy apart. It would be false to cast the old Irish as instant integrators, but their movement, be it sometimes slow, or reluctant, was in that direction. And it was that failure to make that movement of the mind and heart, away from Ireland, into Australia, which distanced the new Irish from the old in a way not experienced previously in the procession of immigrant generations. True, the virtual cessation of Irish emigration to Australia across the long period from 1921 to 1947 had made for a protracted break in continuity. That break was also radical, in that it saw Irish Australia and Ireland take divergent political directions. Australia remained happy within Empire and Commonwealth; Ireland strained and agitated to leave. At the beginning of that long period of little contact, Ireland had engaged in civil war, inexplicable and repugnant to Australians. At the end it had asserted neutrality in a war in which Australians were heavily engaged, and then in 1948 proclaimed republicanism, neither of which actions attracted much Australian approbation. For Ireland it had been a period of asserting and building independent nationhood, pursuing its own identity and problems, externally often in circumstances of conflict with Britain and things British. Things British included Australia, insofar as Australia retained ties with Britain, especially in its requirement of those seeking citizenship that they take an oath of allegiance to the monarch.

This was not changed (to omit the queen) until 1994, when some long-term Irish residents made a public occasion of taking up citizenship. However, this was an addition, not a renunciation. They maintained dual citizenship, retaining their Irish. It was understandable that, despite the change in wording, the Irish mind-set did not rush to embrace even a less obviously monarchical society. The derivative atmosphere and some of the trappings remained.

It was, of course, such an oath of allegiance which had been a major issue in Ireland's civil war, and such a connection with the British crown that had been finally severed in the declaration of an Irish republic in 1948. For many of the new Irish, becoming permanent residents of Australia, even after the change, was too much to swallow. About half became citizens (rather more than the proportion of English). Some of these did so for reasons of advantage or convenience, but reluctantly. Amongst these, and amongst the half that did not take Australian citizenship, was an element that favoured and supported the movement for an Australian republic, although, as it transpired in the 1999 referendum, to no avail.

To the extent that this disposition derived from antipathy to Britain (and that motivation appeared strong) explanation may lie in the obvious: the long history of Irish oppression, and current events in Northern Ireland. But the question is complicated—as is the whole area of Irish immigrant attitudes to Australia—by the matter of the number of Irish who came to Australia after living in Britain. Visa applications to Australia's London embassy suggest that this is a significant number, perhaps a quarter, but it may be considerably more, given that many who applied from elsewhere may have had previous British experience. The question is not merely of unresolved statistical interest. There are many studies of the Irish immigrant presence in Britain which indicate negative experience, intensified particularly in the 1970s as the British public, press, and judicial system reacted to the IRA campaign of violence carried into Britain itself. Hatred, ostracism, racial obloquy, prejudice and outrageous injustice drove many of the Irish into ghettoes of the mind, if not physical ones. As community and as individuals, they were subjected to a protracted, popular and official campaign of hysterical denunciation, manipulated with unscrupulous cynicism.

Did those who escaped therefrom to the Antipodes carry the injuries and the resentments with them, to be revived and irritated by the residues of Britishness surviving in the once-colony?

And is this part explanation—if not by direct British experience, then by disparate British legacies—of the distance, reserve, even polite dislike, that sometimes seems to underlie the bonhomie that links Irish with Irish Australians? After all, the Australian Irish were Home Rulers almost to the cliché man, that man being Dr Mannix, whose Irish republicanism was the only issue on which his massive devoted following would not follow him. Mannix's brand of Irish politics was the exception, as were the Australian incidents in the republican tradition, such as 1804, or Eureka: the overwhelming weight of the Irish Australian disposition lay in the British imperial, colonial home-rule tradition. As Cardinal Moran, speaking publicly in Dublin in 1888, said of Australia's Irish: 'none but a fool would be disloyal amongst us. The imperial flag is the symbol of our strength and unity - of justice, prosperity, and peace'. And '. . . we are impelled', Moran said, 'not by hatred of England, but by love of Ireland'. It was a crucial distinction—and an unwelcome one to those who were unable to make it. In 1988 an American Irish commentator concluded 'that Australian Irish really want to be accepted as British gentlemen' and that, in consequence, 'the career of Australia's Irish has been less than heroic and worthy of but limited praise'. Politely put: others in the Irish republican tradition, or just those whose experience of Britain had been less happy than the distant Australian, would have chosen harsher words—shoneens, traitors. So, while the 'Irish' Irish might find the super-Irish drum-beaters of America ridiculous and an embarrassment, the Australian Irish raised an opposite problem: they appeared soft on the Britain issue, less than adequately Irish. Certainly, an anti-British dimension is evident in the *Irish Exile*'s swingeing criticism, in May 1990, of Anzac Day, whose celebration was described as disturbingly obsessive, beyond anything evoked in Irish nationalist fervour, suggesting, it was claimed, that Australia 'craves more conflict in her past'—and was, in this general regard, sick, disordered, and infantile, in need of experienced Irish tutelage.

Even more repugnant, and bewildering, was Australia's rejection of republicanism in the November 1999 referendum. The dominant—or at least most publicised—stance of the new Irish was pro-Labor, and particularly pro-Paul Keating, in national politics. They made no disguise of their anti-Coalition political position. Keating's moves towards a republic were particularly welcome. Following his defeat in 1996 (inexplicable, for there was no Irish notion of the depth of public hostility Keating had generated), when the Coalition decided to resolve the issue by placing it before the people in a national poll, a common assumption among the new Irish was that the outcome was a forgone conclusion. The *Irish Echo* poured scorn on the monarchists as being out of touch with the mood of the Australian people. However, the referendum campaign took unexpected directions. Irish offers of help were declined by the Australian Republican Movement, which saw any Irish prominence as a liability. Early opposition to the republican movement had branded it, falsely, as a Keating-Irish-Catholic-Fenian conspiracy: its proponents were anxious to offer no basis for this slur. The eventual proposal was not to new Irish liking: they wanted direct election of a president, as in Ireland.

Commenting on the rejection of the republican option, the *Irish Echo* expressed disappointment on behalf of 'the lost generations of Irish emigrants', claimed that the uniquely Australian traits of a fair go and resistance to authority were Irish, and lamented the lack of Irish input into the debate. The politicians and manipulators had 'conspired to rob us Republicans of an empowering new dawn', in which the queen's head would have been 'chopped off' the new currency, the flag purged of the Union Jack, and so on.

The impression was abroad among some of the younger Irish that they owned the 'real' Australia: it was essentially an Irish creation. U2's lead singer Bono captured this, if only in jest, when the band visited in 1993: 'It's good to be in a place where the Irish are truly in charge'. Perhaps the Irish names and the warm welcome conveyed that impression, but the reality was otherwise. Australian 'Irish' politicians and personalities were very conscious, in ways the new Irish were not, of the preferences and demands of the non-'Irish' majority, of a multicultural society and of the values of being themselves. Coming from a homogenous society, in a country whose concerns focused on the identity of varieties of itself, the new Irish had little experience of the multiculture that was Australia. Indeed, in common with other ethnic groups in Australia, they tended to see themselves as the *only* ethnic group, having little consciousness of others, other than to be envious, believing they had superior claims.

Which raises the question of the new Irish as 'ethnics'. Until the late 1980s it had been simply and generally assumed, without much thought, that, since the Irish were historically a major element of Australia's original white population, newcomers would be merely added, absorbed. The idea of the Irish as distinct, separate, 'ethnic', did not come to mind. Ethnic community leaders (say, Greek, Italian, eventually Vietnamese) took this position. The Irish were simply part of the Anglo-Celtic majority. The new Irish were increasingly ambivalent about this. On the one hand, it was satisfactory to be identified with major strands in the historical evolution and power-broking of the country. On the other, the very substantial assistance funding available to ethnic communities—for cultural and welfare purposes—was increasingly attractive. The funding of St Patrick's Day celebrations offered a case in point. The government should substantially assist, either because it should act as an 'Irish' government, or it should help the Irish as a recognised ethnic community. The same with welfare. There were three welfare services to assist Irish families in financial and social difficulties: in Melbourne in the 1980s, in Sydney and Wollongong in the mid-1990s. The Irish government contributed, but only about one-third of the budget: essentially the community helped itself. And it took enormous effort to get even a small voice in ethnic radio or television.

Frustrated, elements among the new Irish in the 1990s became increasingly convinced that their future lay in being 'ethnic'. After all, with the emergence of interest in Gaelic and the establishment of a significant number of language classes, plus the explosion of dancing classes following *Riverdance*, and the popularity of every other thing Irish, they were convinced that they qualified.

A Gaelic street sign in Brisbane

What is more, they felt a growing sense of being apart, their contribution unrecognised, that Irish Australia had let them down. The illusion that they in some way owned old Irish Australia was severely challenged by the outcome of the November 1999 referendum. Commenting on the 'Yes' campaign generally, one of the old Irish-born, a 1950s immigrant, remarked that casting the queen as a 'foreigner' was a grave mistake: the ordinary Australian knew who the *real* foreigners were. Certainly, the new Irish had no appreciation of the complex, subtle ambivalences and carelessnesses that marked Australian attitudes towards the monarchy.

For a long time the more restless elements among the new Irish had been working towards, and acting on the presumption of building common cause with Irish Australia. The Queensland Irish Association had, for instance, 5000 members, many of them very powerful in politics, the professions, commerce. Alliance with this had obvious appeal. The American Irish model constantly beckoned—Kennedy, Tip O'Neill. Thus the infatuation with Prime Minister Paul Keating. Undoubtedly, Keating was a friend of Ireland, in very practical ways. His government contributed to the international Fund for Ireland, and he did much, both as prime minister and treasurer, to promote and facilitate Australia–Ireland trade and investment links. He took a personal interest in the problem of the North. Yet a perceptive glance at his position would have signalled

Memorials.
Left: the Pikeman's dog, Ballarat.
Right: the Irish workers on the Snowy River Scheme

the realities long before they were recognised: friendly when possible, and convenient, but his ambitions were Australian, his foreign focus—Asia. That he should be welcoming to the Irish president, Mary Robinson, when she visited Australia in October 1992, or that he should visit Ireland a year later, is hardly surprising, and not particularly remarkable in the political and diplomatic way of things. Nor were the predictable and florid acknowledgements of Australia's debt to the Irish, which were trotted out (appropriately, and with sincerity) on all occasions; given the extraordinary invasion in the 1990s of Irish politicians, cultural ambassadors, celebrities, *et al*, these were very frequent. Add to this Australia's own major Irish occasions: all the blossoming activities associated with St Patrick's Day, Bloomsday, conferences, fundraising dinners and monument dedications. In the four years prior to 2000 the Irish ambassador attended the formal dedications of twelve memorials—in Sydney and Melbourne to the Great Famine, in Ballarat to the Pikeman's dog, to the Irish in the Snowy, the Duracks, Mannix, O'Connell (in plaque and in glass), the Young Irelanders in Tasmania, and to a legendary policeman in Queensland. Was there anything left in Irish Australia uncommemorated? All of these were occasions for appropriate speeches.

Affirmation, celebration of origins, proclamation of shared identity. As has been widely observed, 'public memorials are more often about the politics of the time than of the events or people commemorated'. Irish Australia had arrived, and was in the process of demonstrating that it had, to Australia in general—and to the new Irish as well. But it was not Irish. It was Irish Australian, and that was a different matter.

By the end of the 1990s the new Irish had become convinced of the constrictions and shortcomings, from their viewpoint, of their position in Australia. The first issue of the *Irish Echo* in 2000 drew some, by then obvious conclusions and pointed to a new path—an emphasis on the pursuit of distinct ethnicity. What was to be done? It was a matter of cultural identity. The first thing was to recognise the distinction between the Irish born and Australians of Irish background, something long-productive of irritation to activists: the hope had been to overcome such a distinction. (In fact, the assumption that the Irish born was a single category was false. The older elements, with long residency and professional and commercial standing, while disposed to be hospitable, were often strongly opposed to, and critical of newer, younger arrivals, on the grounds of being arrogant and irreligious, but particularly on Irish political grounds: anything suggestive of extreme republicanism was unacceptable to many old Irish.) The push by the new Irish towards common cause with the Australian Irish had been patterned on—derived from—American experience. There, key members of the wealthy Irish community had created an 'Irish lobby' for political purposes. The result was an Irish social and political impact far beyond actual Irish numbers.

A consultation with the Sydney Irish Tourist Board would have offered some relevant comparative lessons and implications. American Irish tourists in Ireland preferred organised package tours in coaches, using hotels and with guides, booked perhaps a year ahead. Australians preferred self-drive cars, determining their own destination and itinerary, casual bed-and-breakfasts, booked immediately before or taking pot luck. Australians imbibed Ireland on their own terms. The American model also blinded the Sinn Fein leader Gerry Adams when he visited, after being long denied a visa, in February 1999. Misled by the warmth and enthusiasm of his reception, he called for Australia to 'replicate' the United States support base which raised funds for Sinn Fein.

The suggestion disappeared without trace. Australians welcomed him because it was thought he should be given 'a fair go'. They listened with interest, but with some caution, to the story of others at some distance who appeared not to be getting a fair go.

The new Australian Irish seemed not to be alive to American Irish facts: that American-Irish politicians looked on Ireland as an object for both their local vote-catching and their benign, patronising imperialism. They would put money in, teach the Irish how things should be done, and, by interference in Irish affairs, they would insist the Irish do it—they would, in fact, compromise its sovereignty in the nicest possible way. Uncle Sam's avuncular interest came at a price—at least in Ireland itself. The Australian Irish, and Australian governments, had neither the means nor, more importantly, the inclination to act in that way.

The *Echo* regretfully concluded that in Australia the American strategy was 'possible only up to a point'. Why so, it asked? It believed that Americans were secure in their own identity. Australians were not, but still working out what it meant to be an Australian. Besides, even many Irish born were unhappy to be regarded as 'ethnics', which, in Australian usage, had distancing and at times contemptuous connotations. But the *Echo*'s position for 2000 was that the new Irish in Australia must be an ethnic group, whose main task was 'to adopt, absorb and communicate the new Ireland to the general populace'. It was the educated young—working visa holiday-makers and recent emigrants—who held the future; the challenge to Irish groups and associations was to harness their energies to 're-invent' Irish Australia to reflect the new Ireland. The problem with this plan was that it assumed that the young were interested, and such a challenge would be accepted by existing Irish organisations. Problematic indeed.

Gerry Adams speaking at the University of New South Wales

The historical causes of the divergence between Irish born and Australian born lay both in Ireland and Australia. Since 1891 the character of what was Irish in Australia had changed rapidly from the dominance of the Irish born to the preponderance of those who were their Australian descendants. What was indisputably Irish, if only in some past tense, were the Irish born. This was a permanent population element that was both declining in numbers and aging in character. Its dominance rested on its occupancy of positions of authority, in the Catholic community in particular, and in the influence it could exercise over those of Irish descent, mainly through church and school. Numerically, the Irish born in Australia were at their peak presence, with 222 696 people, in 1891 By federation in 1901, the number of Irish born had dropped to 184 085, in a population of 4.5 million, roughly 4 percent. By 1921, it was 105 033, bottoming at 44 813 in 1947, when the Australian population was 7.5 million. Post-war migration produced a slight increase in total numbers of Irish born—47 673 in 1954, 50 205 in 1961—but the major impact was on the age structure of the Irish-born population. In 1947 almost half the Irish-born population was over 60 years of age. New Irish arrivals replaced, but did little more than replace, the attrition by death of the old Irish. This was in the context of a migrant avalanche which pushed the Australian population from 7.5 million in 1947 to 15.5 million in 1986, 17 million by the early 1990s, 19 million by 2000. The figure of 69 962 for the Irish born in 1986 was about the same as the number of Poles and significantly below that of Vietnamese: around 0.4 percent of the population. Nor did this alter much by 2000: at fewer than 80 000 permanent residents.

Such figures provide a misleading indication of the extent and strength of the Irish presence. In themselves, they disguise the transformation of the Irish-born element from old to young, with the consequent potentiality of continuance by descent. Nor do they take into account the extraordinary growth in Irish consciousness that had developed among Australians of Irish origin. Taking the statistics available from the 1981 census, the demographer C.A. Price has estimated the ethnic origins of the Australian population at the time of the 1988 Bicentennial. His calculation revealed nearly 3 million (2 810 430) Australians of Irish origin, that is, 17.24 percent of the then population of 16.3 million—by far the largest minority, in relation to an English majority group of 43.92 percent. While earlier censuses do not give access to ethnic origins, it is highly doubtful if such Irishness would have been a matter of acknowledgement and pride in, say, the 1950s or indeed much later. The late 1980s witnessed developing ethnic openess among Australians of Irish descent, even the abandonment of postures of denial and disguise among some public figures: it had become acceptable, even advantageous, to be Irish in origin. In some ways this brought tentative closer relationships and associations between those of Irish heritage and the new Irish, under various broad Irish banners—social, cultural, financial—but it did not abolish or even blur the distinctions: both the Australian Irish and those of Irish birth recognised the differences and kept their removes; distant cousins, not brothers.

But the census figures also diminish the Irish reality in another way. From the mid-1980s a remarkable increase occurred in short-term Irish migration to Australia, of such duration as to have been and gone within census periods: family visitors, those on working holidays (working-holiday visas for those under 26 years of age were particularly important), those on fixed employment contracts. The Bicentennial was one particular magnet, then the 2000 Olympics, with the international publicity these generated, but there were other factors: generally, the 1980s economic boom; specifically, limitations on visas for entry to the United States. Figures from the Australian embassy in Dublin indicated that, whereas 5270 visas had been issued (only 940 for permanent immigration) in 1984–85, this number shot up to 14 390 in 1987–88, with 13 360 the following year. Most of these were for brief visits or working holidays and the number fell sharply in 1989–90, but the Dublin figures probably represent only about half the total, as Irish applications to other Australian embassies, notably London and Washington, need to be added. While the Dublin figure for 1989–90 is 9190, the overall official figure for Irish entries into Australia in that year was 18 346. But this is from the Republic only. Many Irish nationals living in Northern Ireland hold dual nationality, and apply for Australian entry using their British passports. Taking all this into account, the total Irish intake in 1989–90, as agreed between the Canberra Irish embassy and the Australian Department of Immigration, stood at 27 000 entries. Using this basis for rough calculation, the total Irish immigration to Australia for the six years 1984–90 would be about 180 000, of whom about a quarter would be migrants with intentions of staying permanently; but by far the greater number, around 130 000, would be short-term visitors. The number of illegal Irish immigrants—over-stayers— was significant, but not disproportionately so: the Canberra Irish embassy estimated 6000–8000 in 1991: it remained constant thereafter.

The statistics point to other obvious characteristics of the new Irish: their constant fluidity and mobility as a rapidly changing group, their continuing physical interaction with Ireland, and their view of Australia as an experience in the short term, essentially an exotic tourist destination. As the introduction to the Irish 'definitive guide to Australia' ('mainly for young people, but for any middle-aged adventurer') put it, 'Australia is, these days, the "in-place" and by the time 1988 has drawn to a close, we'll all be heartily sick of hearing and reading about the place or we'll be packing our bags to go there'. It was the latter which occurred: Australia became the flavour of the 1990s amongst Irish backpackers, and those with relatives there. That Australia should be seen by the Irish as a new focus for tourism, adventure and backpacking is a historical irony in a relationship once governed by the horrors of transportation and the traumas of exile. There is particular irony that in the same decade as the affluent Irish joyfully discovered anew Australia the marvellous the Australian descendants of their forebears were flocking back to Ireland to inspect and wonder at the melancholy wastelands and ruins from whence their ancestors had sadly departed. By the 1980s Australians were accepting the Irish Tourist Board's insistence that Northern Ireland's troubles were indeed in the North, and, as droves of Americans had done before them, were following Ireland's heritage trails. The increase in the number of Australian visitors was dramatic: from 27 000 in 1983 to 69 000 in 1990, and 124 000 in 1998. Again, the mid to late 1980s were the pivotal years. In general, these saw the mushrooming of interest in genealogy among older Australians: for the first time many ordinary Australians developed an interest in family history and in the times and places from whence their ancestors had come. Those of Irish heritage who had the means to do so began to visit Ireland on trips of sentimental discovery, sometimes little more than fond, general tourism, but often on quite specific searches for relatives and places of origin. The process was fostered and assisted by the Irish Tourist Board. Few Australian visitors were less than enthusiastic, either charmed by the genuine clichés of an Irish welcome, or struck by the eerie recognition on first sight that part of them, buried deep, had been there before. And then, in 1989, a bonus for Australian travellers to Ireland, a free extension of their London air ticket, on to Ireland. Nor was it only older Australians who went. In 1994 the Irish embassy in Canberra issued 14 Irish working-holiday visas. In 1999 it was 1200. With 30 000 job vacancies, the new Ireland welcomed short-term Australians: backpacking traffic worked both ways.

What was the Irish Australia from which the new Irish-born discovered themselves distanced despite, and in the midst of a great and unprecedented Australian explosion of interest in, and popularity of things Irish?

The idea of being 'Irish' has undergone a remarkable recent transformation from being identified, historically, with poverty, ignorance, low social and occupational status, sectarian Catholicism, drunkenness, disorderly behaviour. It has recently become a fashionable asset, representing charm, sociability and conviviality, mild social radicalism, fun and entertainment, possessing some of the essential ingredients of the popular Australian self-image. By 1995 it was politically correct to call the Irish 'delightful'.

All this was a product of Australia's swing to multiculturalism. That set of affirmative government policies fostered the public expression of ethnic identity; but it also had the effect of encouraging—compelling even—the host majority population to some degree of derivative ethnic affirmation. In part, too, this was a response to genuine rediscovery of Australia's Irish past in the late 1980s; in part, it was a growing interest in, and awareness of Ireland's own cultural renaissance, particularly in literature, drama and music. Accordingly, those who formerly denied and distanced themselves from anything Irish have come to embrace and affirm it, to seek it out. Even persons whose Irish origins were remote and tenuous, searched for what little they could find, across many generations of intermarriage, to offer as proof of Irishness: it had become a liability *not* to be Irish. And, historically, the substantial numbers of Irish immigrants, their strong tendencies towards mobility, and towards marriages out of their own culture—all meant that a very large proportion of Australia's population could claim some Irish connection in their past.

Of course, this had always been the case. What was new in the 1980s and 1990s was the willingness to acknowledge it, become conscious of it, take pride in it, boast of it.

There were many, a majority of the Australian population perhaps, who neither knew nor cared about their ethnic origins. They saw this as irrelevant, unimportant, of no personal consequence; but a significant number of those who thought the matter meaningful chose to be 'Irish'.

The question was, and is: what did that mean? It varies, and that greatly. For those Australians of some immediate Irish parentage it might be a kind of comfortable symbolic ethnicity, a feeling of identification with a desirable national community, which is achieved without effort or cost, by virtue of mere birth into it, requiring more effort to renounce than accept. With others, removed by generations from any Irish influence, it might be a case of capitulation to the implicit pressures of multiculturalism: every Australian ought really to be something else, from somewhere else, which has a *real* history and aboriginality. Some constructed a virtual ethnicity—a rag-bag of Irish bits and pieces, idiosyncratic collections, say, a sentimental song, green for St Patrick's Day. In some cases it takes very little to sustain a sense of 'Irishness'; for some few others it is a demanding commitment, requiring support of Irish organisations and causes, and stimulating Australian activities celebrating Irish heritage.

All this grew out of the stimulus of multiculturalism (or, as some prefer, polyethnicity). Devised as a policy to recognise differences within homogeneity—thus, one 'multiculture'—arguably, the effect of multiculturalism was to foster cleavage; even, in the case of the Irish, to divide those who demanded a new Ireland from those who preferred the old. At the same time, they had multicultural needs in common: to create a mythology and share a common history. Multiculturalism, whatever its positive virtues, had also inherent dangers: those of embedding static cultures, over-emphasising coercive homogeneity, and repressing divergence. Worse still, it tended to foster competition in misery. Those whose histories suggest they have endured the most injustice, deprivation, and suffering, those who constituted the most wronged and exploited minority, somehow were superior, more socially deserving. Even better if this victim-people had triumphed over appalling adversity to achieve prosperity and power: the achievement is all the greater, more worthy of praise and self-satisfaction.

It would be difficult not to detect some of these forces operative within recent Irish Australia, and not to see the confusion and misapprehension they produce. The commemoration of the Irish Famine is a case in point. While avoiding the worst excesses of the American Irish, some of the Australian reaction was no less innocent of recent Irish research on the subject, and continued the nineteenth century hyperbolic dramatisation of John Mitchel, whose purposes were to generate rebellion against Britain. That dimension did not sit well with the Australian Irish: it was a myth that all Irish were anglophobes. But some of these Australian Irish did entertain the recent proposition that the Famine was equivalent to the Holocaust, one of those competitive ethnic comparisons.

Irish Australia remains a contradictory, vague and vacillating creation. Until very recently, backward knowledge was unimportant to most people. They were too busy getting on; still are. But one of the by-products of affluence was the luxury of indulging in a past. That was partly a manufactured commodity. The politicians and the heritage business and tourist boards were interested in creating a simple, convenient, and profitable past. Descendants usually did not know who their ancestors were, or why they had left their homeland, and they accepted explanations and images derived from a mixture of bits of popular history, rhetoric, fiction, film, television, journalism, whatever lay to hand. 'Ireland' was an idea very vague and various in content. Only in the later 1990s were efforts made to give that idea professional academic discipline and content: major Irish Studies centres and chairs were in process of foundation in Melbourne, Perth and Sydney, though some individual academics had long given university courses in Irish areas.

Irish Australian university conferences had begun in 1980: the 2000 one in Fremantle was the eleventh. And there were important exchange and visiting appointment arrangements of both staff and students between several Australian and Irish universities, going back to the 1970s but stabilising and expanding in the 1980s and 1990s. The balance of academic enquiry and activity is likely to remain what it is now, a matter of interest, even close interest, rather than commitment or involvement in things Irish. To reiterate, being Irish Australian is a way, not of being Irish, but Australian.

In this way. The essential Ireland was created distinct from Britain and in continuing assertion of its difference and unique character. From the Bicentennial, Australians became increasingly conscious of a similar urge—to be themselves, whatever that was.

Ireland seemed to have achieved this, offering something that seemed to be heading along the same direction, and with familiar echoes and resonances for some Australians, particularly those influenced residually by the traditional Catholic culture. An Irish orientation enabled them to, in the fashionable jargon, 'inhabit landscapes of memory', a country not real or authentic, but composed of images of Irishness in which they felt they could easily belong. Ireland seemed to offer wider dimensions of themselves, more depth, more emotional scope than the great Australian ordinariness. It gave them a greater sense of connection to world history, of being vicariously involved in great and dramatic events. Ireland filled the gap created, for some, by the collapse of the state of British imperial belonging. Hence the astounding popularity of Irish TV shows and films, visiting pop groups, singers, novelists, touring drama companies, *Riverdance* (the most extraordinary of all), even the Book of Kells—indeed, everything Irish. Of course, this was a world-wide phenomenon: what is at issue here is its peculiar Australian variant. Here it was more than cut-price, brief, armchair tourism: it ministered to real emotional needs; it filled, if only for a moment, undernourished lives. But, when the curtains came down, Australians returned to their own ordinary world of home.

This process had specific illustration in the increasingly frequent exchange visits of politicians. From the 1980s with Bob Hawke and Charles Haughey, politicians could be found regularly beaming with genuine pleasure and saying all the right things in various parts of both countries. Then they went home and got on with domestic business. Behind the smiles and the pleasantries was genuine good will but also hard-headed realism. Any tendency to interpret the contemporary Ireland–Australia relationship as entirely light-hearted or sentimental needs to be offset against the non-Irish orientation of Australia's non-Labor parties, and the hard facts of economics.

Trade has been increasingly, and is now massively, in Ireland's favour. In 1970 trade between the two countries was small, and roughly of equal value: Ireland exported goods to the value of $2.6 million to Australia and imported $3.7 million worth of goods. In the 1980s there was an explosion of Irish trade. In 1985 the value of goods Australia imported from Ireland was $130 million but of those exported, only $7.5 million. But this was as nothing compared to what happened in the late 1990s: in 1999 the value of Irish exports to Australia topped $1 billion, Australia sending only $183 million worth in return (significantly, featuring wine). Australia had become a significant Irish market.

Here was the strong economic base for one very significant aspect of the new Irish presence in Australia. A range of major multinational companies, particularly in computing and pharmaceuticals, established production in Ireland in the 1980s. So it came about that the Australian financial and commercial boom was underlaid and processed by office technology marketed by the computer giants, but made in Ireland. At the same time, Ireland's tertiary education policies were producing a surplus of highly trained professionals, in a historical echo of the situation of the 1850s, when Ireland had populated professional life in colonial Victoria. These professionals were ideally fitted to the demands of new technological and managerial skills, which emphasised computer-based commerce and accounting. This, and their English language, made them desirable employees, and at the height of Australia's financial boom of the 1980s some Australian firms were recruiting direct from Ireland. At the same time, the pressure of limited opportunities in Ireland was pushing out such professionals to opportunities wherever they could be found: Australia was an obvious destination. But such employment was often on contract, of short- to medium-term, and, with recession from 1990–91, many such professionals went elsewhere, or returned to Ireland, itself experiencing a labour shortage which became acute by 2000. However much their economic and social value at the time, inevitably the outcome was a superficial degree of engagement with the permanent and settled elements of Australian society.

Indeed, these, mainly young Irish might be better described as members of a transnational class of what has been called 'Eirepreneurs', a tertiary-educated middle-class elite associated with the culture of the global economy.

It was natural for such professionals, transitory by compulsion or inclination, to consort with similar sojourners. Within Australia they tended to move within the Irish-born and professional community as their social world: from there their external links and orientation were with Ireland itself, and their outlook, in keeping with both the possibilities and exigencies of their professions, international. Again, this was a curious reversion to phases historical. As the gold-seeker had moved from Victoria to California, or the nineteenth century labourer from Sydney to Auckland, in search of riches or just a wage, so were the new Irish elite itinerant, and with much more ease. Yet, there was a significant historical difference. Whereas the nineteenth century Irish immigrant had been typically unskilled and among the first to be affected by downswings in employment opportunities, as recession bit deep into the Australian economy in 1991 both the Canberra embassy and Irish community sources agreed that the Irish were not unduly affected. Indeed, their skills and education were such that most found little difficulty in gaining employment within the constricting labour market of that time. A 1995 survey suggested that Irish immigrants were better educated, and had higher incomes and lower unemployment than the Australian average.

All this may suggest untroubled homogeneity. Not so. The Irish community's factions are focused in on themselves, often in tension, sometimes in conflict. The divisions are predictable, with ample historical precedent—between generations, counties, geographic locations, political orientations, class, wealth, education, personality. So, the long-established (1915), Sydney city Irish National Association and Gaelic Club weathered (but only after vigorous criticism) waves of takeover bids and the establishment of competing Irish venues in the suburbs.

The control of Sydney's St Patrick's Day celebration became from the early 1990s a matter of bitter dispute and division, as new Irish fought with older immigrants. The Sydney-based Irish national newspaper the *Irish Echo* (founded in 1988) prospered, moving from a monthly to a fortnightly, and printing a healthy 16 600 an issue by the year 2000. Its wide circulation (though it had less impact outside Sydney) attracted a massive advertising content, particularly from Irish hotels and clubs.

Melbourne Irishism still lived obsessively under the austere shadow of Mannix's ghost and legacies: the new Irish were a lightweight irrelevance in that dour, embattled climate. Even there, the hallowed and ancient Celtic Club experienced financial problems, formal enquiries, and internal difficulties.

In sunny Queensland and balmy Perth the Irish had long won established and harmonious place, again less likely to be ruffled by the transitory concerns of upstart newcomers. Only Sydney was a sufficiently open city—with its Irishism absorbed into

Labor's right wing and its political concerns, and its multiculturalism in chaos—to offer anything, everything, and nothing to the initiatives of the new Irish.

Other differences and divisions abounded. At the top of the Irish social tree was the Australian branch of Dr A.J.F. O'Reilly's international Ireland Fund, with its objective to raise money ($130 000 in Australia for the year 1987–88) from the overseas Irish and their friends, to aid peace, culture and charity in Ireland. This has been mildly contentious since its Australian establishment in 1987, for reasons social and political. Aimed, logically enough, at the higher echelons of Australian 'society', who might have significant money to donate, its list of supporters included the names of many Australian public persons not formerly known for their friendship to Ireland; some, indeed, renowned for the contrary. Remembered anti-Irish contempts, natural egalitarianism and hostility to the world of formal dinners, garden parties and period dress favoured by the Fund—all generated hostility and some picketing of functions. In that, Irish republicans of Sinn Fein sympathy were the most prominent, as was their Adelaide-based newspaper the *Irish People* strident in criticism of the Fund. They contended that the Fund was biased against any Northern Ireland community project which might be associated even remotely with Sinn Fein—a charge that did not sit well with bizarre public allegations, from other quarters, later withdrawn with apologies, that the Fund was financing the IRA. But then the *Irish People* republicans were at odds with the Canberra embassy in their belief that the Irish government had sold out to Britain and essentially abandoned claims to Northern Ireland.

As to the Ireland Fund, this continued to raise very substantial amounts of money in Australia for Irish purposes, for instance in the 1998–99 year, $347 000. In 2000 it agreed to donate funds to the UNSW Chair of Irish Studies Endowment.

Sinn Fein sympathisers, and those supportive of the IRA, continued as a tiny, shadowy and anonymous presence, surfacing only vaguely and briefly in organising the visit of Gerry Adams to Australia in February 1999. They were careful to adopt a low profile, particularly given the fact that their Irish politics were detested, and themselves viewed with hostility and contempt, by many of the older, well-established, Irish-born. Numbers? Informed guesstimates suggest about 300, Australia-wide.

To Irish born and to Irish Australians, the Irish embassy in Canberra represented the official focus of their Irish world. The Australian Irish revival of the 1980s and thereafter was overseen and to a remarkable degree stimulated and co-ordinated by a sequence of extraordinary ambassadors, each in his own way innovative, extremely hard-working, personable and popular. Prodigiously peripatetic, as demanded by Australia's dispersed geography, these ambassadors had responsibilities that took in also New Zealand and the Pacific Islands. As interest in Ireland and its activities—and trade—boomed, so did demands on its embassy increase. It was not until 2000 that this was recognised with the establishment of a consulate in Sydney. This shared a Sydney presence with the arms of Irish government most in Australian demand: the Irish Tourist Board as well as Enterprise Ireland and the I.D.A. (Ireland's trade and investment arms).

Strangely, it was the re-emergence of violence in Northern Ireland in 1968, its development and continuance, that was the initial catalyst for the rehabilitation of the Irish image in Australia. Beginning as it did in 1968 with a protracted phase of civil rights agitation by Catholics, protesting against injustice which was patently long-standing,

gross, intolerable and indefensible, the Northern Ireland crisis could not be represented convincingly at a distance (as Irish disturbances had traditionally been depicted by
Britain) as unreasonable and irrational behaviour in the face of a benign, just and long-
suffering mother country, unquestioned defender of all human rights and liberties.

Events in Northern Ireland contributed to the further decline of Britain's reputation
in Australia. From the fall of Singapore in 1942, but inescapably from Britain's over-
tures to join the European Economic Community in the early 1960s, Australians experienced a sense of abandonment, betrayal. To this disillusionment Northern Ireland
added a further dimension of cynicism. What happened in British political and economic policy in the 1960s at first shocked, then permanently unsettled, then eroded,
the whole edifice of Imperial assumptions: it shifted and redistributed the traditional
categories of blame and praise. Formerly reprobate Irish Catholics became the wronged
victims, meriting sympathy if not support; Protestants and the British became the
wrong-doers, the one through their intolerance, intractability, and violence, the other
through incapacity and incompetence. This fundamental reversal of dominant images
had established itself in Australian consciousness—albeit suppressed or reluctantly
acknowledged in many cases—before the civil rights situation of 1968 was complicated by the major intervention onto the scene of the IRA in 1971. By that time too much
of the old facade of Protestant and British moral superiority had fallen victim to the
odium of its response to events and to the intransigent and unacceptable extremism of
Rev. Ian Paisley. For all that the IRA presented a convenient target on which to vent
anti-Irish sentiment, this was not the essence of what occurred. This was rather that the
IRA, both Officials and Provisionals, and the various Protestant para-military groups
were placed in a separate category of mad terrorists, to be lumped in with the PLO and
other murderous crazies of the day, hardly specifically Irish at all, merely a local manifestation of international derangement.

All this—and particularly Britain's disgraceful Irish performance (proven policies of
torture, Mrs Thatcher's willingness to allow Irish hunger strikers to die in 1981, fab-
rication of evidence and imprisonment of the innocent, shoot to kill)—cleared the way
in Australia for a new view of the Irish scene and its multiform complexities.
Moreover—though this was hardly voiced—as multiculturalism and Aboriginal
claims began to trouble old Protestant Australia (and, for that matter, old Catholic
Australia), and to call its narrow assumptions and wilting hegemony into question, the
once-despised, once-excluded Catholic Irish did not seem nearly so undesirable: they
were more like 'us' than those ethnic others, possessing dynamic character and colour
the threatened 'we' could parade as its own—'Anglo-Celt'. So, when it came to a murderous IRA error which bore direct Australian relevance—the shooting in Roermond
in the Netherlands, in May 1990, of two young Australian tourists in mistake for off-
duty British soldiers—the massive Australian media coverage focused narrowly on the
IRA as incompetent terrorists, and 'scum'. Little attention was paid to any possible
Australian IRA dimension. The nearest that could be found was the Australian Aid to
Ireland organisation, a merger of various organisations in 1983, which sought to assist
republican prisoners' families. It was reputed to send $100 000 a year to Ireland for
this purpose, but few suggested this was untoward, or would be misdirected towards
purchase of arms. Moreover, the wholesale condemnation of the IRA was set amid a
consciousness of British mistakes—and Protestant terrorist barbarities, when they
became known.

Such was the political background to the radical transformation in the image of the Australian Irish which took place in the 1980s. From 1969 to the early 1970s, civil rights in Northern Ireland had been a popular and agitated cause amongst some Australian-born Irish, notably in Melbourne. However, the revived IRA's entry onto the Irish field of events in 1971 changed this, and most such supporters backed away sharply from the violence that dominated the Northern Ireland scene in the 1970s. By the 1980s, for all its continuing reality, Northern Ireland had been rendered distant and remote—a hopeless imbroglio best forgotten. This cleared the way for the emergence into public view of that sea-change that was to overtake the general estimation of the Irish in Australia, a transformation that was to flow from the interaction of people, events and an increasingly receptive intellectual and social climate: things Irish became first tolerable, then acceptable; then fashionable.

It is easier to detail the Irish Australian resurrection of the 1980s than to explain it; easier, too, to make sense of its component parts than to assess what they might add up to, or mean, or signify for the future. As to explanation, that lies, in part, within the climate and pre-echoes of the Bicentennial celebrations, but also within the development of a broader obsession with identity, coincident in both Ireland and Australia. For Ireland the stimuli lay in the questions raised by the North, the amazing cultural and economic renaissance, and by an awakening to the implications of its own diaspora; for Australia the process stemmed from the challenges of Aboriginality and multiculture. By the 1980s, matters of identity, or at least identification, concerned two varieties of Australian Irish: the Irish *of* Australia, those of Australian birth; and the Irish *in* Australia, the Irish born. For all the overlap and interaction their concerns were essentially different.

The main shared concern was public image. From the late 1980s, the general media became increasingly receptive to things Irish, stimulated by the sheer quality of the increasing number of Irish political and cultural visitors.

These were impressive. Both Irish presidents of the 1990s were women of the highest international calibre. The visits of Mary Robinson in 1992 and Mary McAleese in 1998 left Australians in no doubt that Ireland was a country to be taken very seriously in world affairs, and that the charm, poise and ability of these Irish leaders testified to a country of singular character. So did the frequent visits of Irish taoiseachs, cabinet ministers and politicians. Within the Australian federal parliament the response to Ireland was, by 2000, extraordinary: over half of all members belonged to the Australia Ireland Parliamentary Friendship Group.

There was a change in media attitudes, with the media now being invigilated and disciplined to curb its tendency to disseminate malicious Irish 'jokes'. This change was typified by the national broadcaster. Traditionally cautious, indeed resistant, in matters Irish, the ABC broadcast a radio series in 1984 on the Irish hunger strikes, the beginning of an Irish love affair which peaked in 1999 with the enormous popularity of the TV series 'Ballykissangel'.

At another cultural level, the romance with Ireland, and recognition of its centrality to the Australian experience and imagination continued to emerge in the writing of significant Australian writers.

Then there was the revival of the public demonstration of Irishness. The people's day was St Patrick's, lapsing Australia-wide by the 1970s (earlier in Sydney), lapsing as what had long been, since the 1890s, a triumphal affirmation of the strength of

Catholic church and school. When it was revived in Sydney in 1979, it re-emerged without church connection, but with the Saint and emblems of popular Irish religion in clear evidence. It was a family day, an Irish counties day, a picnic outing for ordinary people with plenty of folk music and Irish dance. Above all, it was a day, not for Australian vestigials, but for the genuine Irish. And, as with any people's day, a bit rough at the edges: a few drunks, the procession a little amateur—but great fun.

And it attracted increasing dispute over its control and nature. Here was a parade symbolising Ireland. But what Ireland? Younger new Irish contended that it ought to represent modern Ireland: the dynamic, secular, Celtic tiger, of which they were proud; well-constructed, affluent, efficient. It seemed to them a tatty assemblage of ancient and outmoded stereotypes and clichés. Whatever, it contained that deliciously warm hint of self-mockery that spoke so powerfully to the Irish imagination and spirit—that wandering stream of genuine Irish consciousness.

It was also curiously uncertain, slightly ill-at-ease in the streets, lacking the arrogant, swaggering possession exuded by the confidence of St Patrick's Day parades in New York. In Australia, here are people who do not quite belong—or do not want to belong. Or who have not made up their minds.

Bloomsday. Here, since 1989, are people who do belong, but are not sure that their inherited culture—their high culture—does: celebrating, by a reading marathon, the Dublin day of 1904, chronicled in James Joyce's masterpiece, *Ulysses*. Featuring in the

The Taoiseach speaks on the Irish peace process at the University of New South Wales, February 2000

main those socially and culturally ill-at-ease with the more plebeian and at least residually religious character of St Patrick's Day, here is secular, generic Irishness—Irish and
Australian—in praise of Ireland's international cultural archangel, affirming his mild
bawdiness in testimony to their own freedom from Ireland's religious and sexual
restraints. Their identity is, thus, implicitly proclaimed—from that rich, word-spinning tradition, civilised, culture-steeped, true heir to . . . what? Hardly the ancient Irish
tradition (as understood by medievalists), more the gospel post-Yeats.

The evolution of these contrasting orientations was exemplified in the two Irish
community publications of the 1980s, *Irish Voice* and *Irish Exile/Echo*. The *Irish Voice*
(1983–87) was a quarterly magazine in the traditional expatriate Irish mould: sentimental, with old-style literary, historical and travel articles, mostly reprints from
Irish authors; bland, with little news or live politics, it was reminiscent of the
Melbourne *Irish Review* of the 1930s. It paid affectionate homage to a remote and
essentially irrelevant Ireland, fondly and proudly remembered. The *Irish Exile* (from
1988, or *Irish Echo* from 1992) was very different. It was full of current Ireland, its
problems and grievances—politics, scandals, unemployment, emigration, contraception, abortion, an errant clergy. Relatively little on the North: the balance of the
paper reflected the way ordinary opinion in the South of Ireland had drifted away
from interest in Northern Ireland or from any feeling that its traumas had much to
do with them. And it was highly commercial: half the pages were devoted to display
advertisements for immigration advice, travel to Ireland, and Irish community pub
and club life. Sport—mainly sport in Ireland—was covered extensively: the *Echo*
knew that most of its audience was still very much part of the Irish sports world. In
Australia the new Irish, significantly more than their Australian forebears, were heavily into hurling and Gaelic football, and the outer suburbs of Australian cities saw
sports grounds entirely Irish, supported—sometimes owned—by enthusiasts both
affluent and dedicated.

The *Echo* was not entirely an ethnic closed shop. True, it was deep into today's Ireland,
but ambivalently so. After all, whatever the degree or kind of coercion, if only self-generated, the new Irish had chosen to leave. And in the early 1990s, after consideration,
and under strong pressure, the Irish government refused to allow an emigrant vote in
Irish elections. That it should have been forced to even consider this points to emigrant
unhappiness and restlessness in their foreign locations. It also underlines the new Irish
wish to be a continuing power factor in what they still regarded as their home; to matter in, and to Ireland—to belong, if at a distance. They, or some of them, were caught
in the classic emigrant predicament: they belonged neither to the society they had left,
nor to the society they had joined. It was that situation they resented, and felt uncomfortable with—from time to time, to a greater or lesser extent.

Were these Irish 'ethnics'? The answer is Irish enough: yes and no. But the question
is misleading. The Irish were not either/or, but both; part of the mainstream culture *and*
a distinctive group. And some were more mainstream while others were more distinctive; a polarity which drew different groups in different directions, as did their other
polarities, of birthplace, class and wealth, cultural interest, religion or not.

Besides, being 'ethnic' (if Australian society is to maintain any cohesion at all) tends
to be a short-term destiny. Place, time, success, children—for residents, all these are
potent forces for assimilation that cannot be escaped. The melting pot operates, if slowly,

imperceptibly, even against the will. Being 'ethnic' can only intensify and prolong the immigrant agony, only sap the immigrant pride, only shrivel, limit and frustrate the immigrant achievement—and paralyse and stultify the wider community.
A verse from John Hewitt's 'An Irishman in Coventry':

> This is our fate: eight hundred years' disaster,
> crazily tangled as the Book of Kells;
> the dream's distortion and the land's division
> the midnight raiders and the prison cells.
> Yet like Lir's children banished to the waters
> our hearts still listen for the landward bells.

In earlier Australian Irish history those landward bells have been too distant to be heard, until the technology and the discontents of today have amplified their insistent tolling. Until now Lir's banished children have, perforce, sailed free on their desert waters—or drowned. Now the options are far less clear, the freedoms greater and, thus, more wrenching, troublesome.

For the Irish born, their Australian Irishism stems in part from the old loneliness and yearning, the wish to be with one's own special kind. But its context is radically different. It is now possible to entertain return as a practical possibility, much more than the vague dream that haunted emigrants of Ireland's past. Club life—indeed, pub life—with its modern inclusion of women, of wives and families, can offer a satisfying social world in Australia, but not of it. Historically, the Australian Irish have always eschewed the physical ghetto. They have always lived dispersed, with a diversity of neighbours. They still do. But again, the context has changed. Neighbourhoods have ceased to be communities, become dormitories. The car, the telephone, and internet join all locations, offer the immediate society of one's own. It is possible to opt out of Australia.

This mean prospect goes against the generous Irish grain, and the loyalties of Australian-born children. As before, if now perhaps more painfully and with a greater sense of both loss and gain, the Irish who stay in Australia, and are not merely passing through, will become the Irish of Australia. Not that history suggests that to be that is any final destination. Since the mists of Brendan—before—the Irish have been voyaging: 'There is a distant isle around which sea-horses glisten . . .'; so is tempted Bran, in the eighth century. And though they are sustained in love by the constant hope of home-coming, their journeying is their true tale, and travelling their true occupation.

That is a poetic way of appraising the new Irish. There are ways more prosaic, more painful. Commenting on the displaced searchings of the new Irish in New York, a sympathetic commentator lamented, 'And they still haven't found what they're looking for.' Nor had they. Nor would they, for they did not know what that was. Recognition? Acceptance? Something more than mere affluence, if they indeed found that. There seemed no escape from the harsh conclusion that Ireland, as it hurtled into an astonishing, transformed future, had flung them out, brushed them aside, found them no space within itself. Perhaps that could have been endured when Ireland seemed a stagnant backwater. Now it is bursting with modernity, ridding itself of its backward-looking past. Small wonder that so many of the new Irish will not accept that they have left, will not see their futures as other than with Ireland.

Irish Australia, in the sense of the Irish echoes which sound within the Australian, is no less voyaging in its search for self-discovery. That journeying is close to home, a mode of exploration of what a colony is; how it is the same but different, how it can be a derivation but uniquely itself and none the lesser. In 'September 1913' W.B. Yeats announced, 'Romantic Ireland's dead and gone, / It's with O'Leary [the great Fenian] in the grave'. He remains wrong. Romantic Ireland remains very much alive among Ireland's descendants overseas. If, as in Irish Australia's case, it can sustain something of a search for self-awareness and impart a sense of belonging to a wider world, its unreality may be immaterial. What matters may be the reality of the illusion. It may be a benign and therapeutic necessity, a firming framework: Ireland as both idea and ideology.

So long, perhaps, as it is recognised for what it is: a contrivance, a self-identifying myth, a gloss on the search for self.

All these concerns may seem limited matters of passing interest, of no broader or future consequence. The matter of Ireland and the Irish is a facet—large for some, tiny for others—of the never-ending quest for some tenable identity. For Ireland the question is not only the basic one of working through with its people, North and South, towards new understandings of nation and religion, it is also the problem of relating to its peoples overseas in ways which are positive, creative, and diplomatic. This was a need recognised by Mary Robinson as Irish president, by the placing of an 'Emigrant Light' in the window of her state residence. But nothing has occurred beyond that symbol. In Ireland for the past two centuries the percentage of the population that emigrated was greater than in any other European country. Yet Ireland has traditionally neglected both its emigration problem and its emigrants. Modern, prosperous Ireland has the means and ingenuity to better confront and handle the enigmas of emigration: the modern world offers immigrant structures which would facilitate this, even insist on it.

That a significant number of Australians find some identification with Ireland points to their need to relate to some wider and deeper historical world. Their own is too short-lived, too starved it would superficially seem, of the great human dramatic issues and dimensions. Particularly is this so in the wake of the decline of Britain and of the collapse of the great Empire in which Australia found purpose and meaning. And for those of recent Irish Catholic heritage, there is another area of structural dissolution and felt deprivation. Since the 1960s the universal certainties of the Catholic world, once so much taken for granted—triumphally—by Australia's Irish Catholics, that firm system of belief, culture, and social practices with which they had defined their meaning and identity, had faltered, weakened, and in part fallen away. Aside from that, the Australian cultural imperatives were inner-focused, seeking to find identity and significance either within Australia itself—in its deserts, its bush, its emptiness, its silence—or escaping to self-discoveries in places overseas. The romantic involvement with Irish culture and history, particularly as it has impinged on Australia, may suggest other modes in which a multiculture may understand itself—not only where it is in space, but where its elements may have been in time. Our selves are not only where we are, but where we have come from. The enthusiasm—even infatuation—with Ireland and the Irish points, as example, towards a pioneering evolution of an eventual multiculture which will perhaps not fragment society, but may issue in assimilation in diversity, acknowledging the shared tenancy of space, but holding differing tenancies of time. That is to draw a long bow. Whether that will represent sufficient commonality for a workable, cohesive society may be the question of the future.

The present condition of Irish Australia makes some of the problems clear—but also the remarkable possibilities. The prospect of a global identity—or identities—may be daunting and remote, but technology has made it no longer fanciful. The alternatives are problematic, disquieting—new Irish Irish who will drift into being a tiny element in a querulous multiculture? old Australian Irish discovering a vanished Irish world of bygone insurrections, catastrophies, injustices and laments? And settling for that? No. Things, of their nature, fall apart; but, in this Australian case, the centre will hold, the essential, happy dynamic will remain, despite the betrayals and contempts. The impulse towards some sense of national community and the desire to create a continuing identity both unique and worthy of respect, which the Irish elements within Australian history have always exhibited, survives still in mainstream Australia.

S E L E C T E D

F U R T H E R   R E A D I N G

A NOTE ON SOURCES

Much of this book is based on primary and archival material. Of its nature, this has been diverse and scattered, and usually of small quantity in any one place or collection: the Australian Irish have been favoured with few major collections of their historical materials. Such as there are, are often dimensions of the archives of Australian Catholicism and for those I refer the researcher to the note on sources and the bibliography in my *The Catholic Church and Community. An Australian History*. The sources list appended to my *Letters from Irish Australia 1825–1929* illustrates the dispersion which is their feature within the one archive: sixty-four collections of Australian relevance are listed for the Public Record Office of Northern Ireland in Belfast (and there are others there in addition, not drawn on for that particular book). In these circumstances, and given the standards of professional expertise and information now available in major archives and libraries, it is both impossible in terms of length and unnecessary in terms of the excellence of advice available on the spot, to do more than list the general location of such materials as were consulted.

These were as follows, with particularly significant collections noted in brackets. In Dublin: National Library of Ireland (the Redmond Papers, Monteagle Papers); All Hallows College; Dublin Archdiocesan Archives; Trinity College, Dublin (the Lecky Papers); Department of Irish Folklore, University College, Dublin; the State Paper Office. In Belfast: Public Record Office of Northern Ireland; Queen's University (W.M. Brady Notes and Quinn Letters). In Rome: the Irish College. In Australia: Mitchell Library, Sydney; National Library of Australia (Dryer Papers, Corrigan Papers); State Library of Victoria; State Library of South Australia; New South Wales State Archives; Melbourne Catholic Historical Commission; St Mary's Cathedral Archives, Sydney.

The files of the following newspapers were consulted: *Advocate* (Melbourne), *Australasian Chronicle* (later *Morning Chronicle* and *Sydney Chronicle*) (Sydney), *Catholic Press* (Sydney), *Cork Examiner*, *Freeman's Journal* (Dublin), *Freeman's Journal* (Sydney), *The Gael* (Sydney) 1906, *The Gael* (Sydney) 1929, *Galway Vindicator*, *Irish Exile and Freedom's Advocate* (Hobart), *Irish Review* (Melbourne), *The Irishman* (Dublin), *Nation* (Dublin), *Weekly Irish Times* (Dublin), *Weekly Freeman* (Dublin). Extensive use was made of newspaper clippings held personally and in St Mary's Cathedral Archives, Sydney. For the more recent period I have used the *Irish Exile* and *Irish Echo*.

What follows is a brief list of selected books for the general reader, arranged first according to the chapter topics, then by other topics. This present guide does not include those many books on Australian Catholicism which have Irish dimensions. My emphasis has been on key books and the numerous conference proceedings, with the wide variety of contributions they provide. The state of the subject is such that much of the research literature is in article form in learned journals or is a subordinate aspect of wider studies. In the 1987 and 1993 editions of this book there are substantial academic bibliographies, to which a specialist reader may refer.

PRISONERS

Adam-Smith, P. *Heart of Exile. Ireland, 1848, and the seven patriots banished ....* Melbourne, 1986.

Costello, C. *Botany Bay. The Story of the Convicts transported from Ireland to Australia, 1791–1853.* Cork, 1987.

Davis, R. *William Smith O'Brien: Ireland – 1848 – Tasmania.* Dublin, 1989.

Davis, Richard. *Revolutionary Imperialist. William Smith O'Brien 1803–1864.* Dublin, Sydney, 1998.

Davis, Richard (ed.). *'To Solitude Consigned?' The Tasmanian Journal of William Smith O'Brien.* Sydney, 1995.

Holt, J. *A Rum Story. The Adventures of Joseph Holt. Thirteen Years in New South Wales (1800–12).* Edited by Peter O'Shaughnessy. Sydney, 1988.

Kiernan, T.J. *The Irish Exiles in Australia.* Melbourne, 1954.

Mitchel, J. *The Gardens of Hell. John Mitchel in Van Diemen's Land, 1850–1853.* Edited by Peter O'Shaughnessy. Sydney, 1988.

Patrick, R. and P. *Exiles Undaunted. The Irish Rebels Kevin and Eva O'Doherty.* St Lucia, Qld, 1989.

Reece, R. (ed.). *Irish Convicts: The Origins of Convicts Transported to Australia.* Dublin, 1989.

Reece, [R.] Bob (ed.). *Exiles from Erin. Convict Lives in Ireland and Australia.* Dublin, 1991.

Shaw, A.G.L. *Convicts and the Colonies. A Study of Penal Transportation from Great Britain & Ireland to Australia & other parts of the British Empire.* London, 1966.

Sheedy, K. *Upon the Mercy of the Government. The story of ... Michael Dwyer ....* Dublin, 1988.

Silver, L.R. *The Battle of Vinegar Hill. Australia's Irish Rebellion, 1804.* Sydney, 1989.

Whitaker, Anne-Maree. *Unfinished Revolution. United Irishmen in New South Wales 1800–1810.* Sydney, 1994.

IMMIGRANTS

McClaughlin, Trevor (ed.). *Irish Women in Colonial Australia.* St Leonards, 1998.

O'Mahony, D. and Thompson, V. *Poverty to Promise. The Monteagle Emigrants 1838–58.* Sydney, 1994.

SETTLERS & UNSETTLERS

Campbell, Malcolm. *The Kingdom of the Ryans. The Irish in Southwest New South Wales 1816–1890.* Sydney, 1997.

Currey, C.H. *The Irish at Eureka.* Sydney, 1954.

Durack, Mary. *Kings in Grass Castles.* London, 1959.

Forth, Gordon. *The Winters on the Wannon.* Deakin University Press, Warrnambool,

1991.

Ingham, S.M. *Enterprising Migrants. An Irish Family in Australia*. Melbourne, 1975.

McQuilton, J. *The Kelly Outbreak 1878–1880*. Melbourne, 1979.

Mecham, F. *'John O'Brien' and the Boree Log. A biography of Patrick Hartigan, 'John O'Brien'*. Sydney, 1981.

Molony, John. *An Architect of Freedom. John Hubert Plunkett in New South Wales 1832–1869*. Canberra, 1973.

Molony, John. *Ned Kelly*. Penguin, 1982.

Molony, J[ohn]. *Eureka*. Penguin, 1989.

'O'Brien, John'. *Around the Boree Log*. Illustrated by Patrick Carroll. Sydney, 1978.

Park, Ruth. *The Harp in the South*. Sydney, 1948.

Ryan, P.A. *Redmond Barry: a colonial life 1813–1880*. Melbourne, 1980.

Waldersee, J. *Catholic Society in New South Wales 1788–1860*. Sydney, 1974.

NATIONALISTS

Amos, Keith. *The Fenians in Australia*. Sydney, 1987.

Evans, A.G. *Fanatic Heart. A Life of John Boyle O'Reilly 1844–1890*. Nedlands, W.A., 1997.

McKinley, B. *The First Royal Tour 1867–68*. Adelaide, 1970.

Travers, R. *The Phantom Fenians of New South Wales*. Sydney, 1986.

REBELS

Gilchrist, M. *Daniel Mannix. Priest and Patriot*. Blackburn, Vic., 1982.

Kiernan, C. *Daniel Mannix and Ireland*. Melbourne, 1984.

Santamaria, B.A. *Daniel Mannix. A Biography*. Melbourne, 1984.

AUSTRALIANS

Buckley, Vincent. *Cutting Green Hay. Friendships, movements and cultural conflicts in Australia's great decades*. Melbourne, 1983.

Buckley, Vincent. *Memory Ireland*. Melbourne, 1985.

Kavanagh, P.J. *Finding Connections*. London, 1990.

Kerry Murphy's Memoirs. The Diaries of an Irish Immigrant. Petersham, 1998.

Windsor, G. *Family Lore*. Sydney, 1990.

Windsor, G. *I Asked Cathleen to Dance*. St Lucia, Qld, 1999.

THE IRISH WORLD-WIDE

Akenson, D.H. *The Irish Diaspora. A Primer*. Toronto, Belfast, 1993.

Fitzpatrick, D. *Irish Emigration 1801–1921*. Studies in Irish Economic and Social History 1. Dublin, 1984.

O'Sullivan, Patrick (ed.). *The Irish World Wide. History, Heritage, Identity* (6 vols). London, 1992–97.

GENEALOGY

Irish Tourist Board. *Tracing Your Ancestors in Ireland.* Dublin, n.d.

McClaughlin, Trevor. *From Shamrock to Wattle. Digging up your Irish Ancestors.* Sydney, 1985.

Reid, R. *The Heritage Trail. Ireland.* Sydney, 1986.

Trainor, Brian (ed.). *Researching Irish Australians.* Ulster Historical Foundation, Belfast 1998.

CONFERENCE PROCEEDINGS

Bull, P., McConville, C. and McLachlan, N. (eds). *Irish-Australian Studies: Papers delivered at the Sixth Irish-Australian Conference, Melbourne (July 1990).* Bundoora, Vic., 1992.

Davis, Richard *et al* (eds). *Irish-Australian Studies: Papers delivered at the Eighth Irish-Australian Conference, Hobart (July 1995).* Sydney 1996.

Grimes, S. and O Tuathaigh, G. (eds). *The Irish Australian-Connection: Proceedings of the Irish Australian Bicentenary Conference, University College, Galway (January 1988)* [this contains two articles in Gaelic]. Galway, 1989.

Kiernan, C. (ed.). *Australia and Ireland 1788–1988. Bicentenary Essays.* Dublin, 1986.

MacDonagh, O. and Mandle, W.F. (eds). *Ireland and Irish Australia. Studies in Cultural and Political History.* London, 1986.

MacDonagh, O. and Mandle, W.F. (eds). *Irish-Australian Studies: Papers delivered at the Fifth Irish-Australian Conference (Canberra, 1988).* Canberra, 1989.

MacDonagh, O., Mandle, W.F. and Travers, P. (eds). *Irish Culture and Nationalism 1750–1950.* London, 1983.

O'Brien, J. and Travers, P. (eds). *The Irish Emigrant Experience in Australia.* Dublin, 1991.

Pelan, Rebecca (ed.). *Papers Delivered at the Seventh Irish-Australian Conference (July 1993).* Sydney, 1994.

Richards, E. (ed.). *Poor Australian Immigrants in the Nineteenth Century. Visible Immigrants: Two.* Canberra, 1991.

Richards, E., Reid, R., and Fitzpatrick, D. (eds). *Visible Immigrants. Neglected Sources for the History of Australian Immigration.* Canberra, 1989.

LETTERS

Fitzpatrick, David. *Oceans of Consolation. Personal Accounts of Irish Migration to Australia.* New York, Melbourne, 1995.

O'Farrell, Patrick. *Letters from Irish Australia 1825–1929.* Sydney, Belfast, 1984.

GENERAL

Campion, Edmund. *Australian Catholics.* Penguin, 1987.

Cleary, P.S. *Australia's Debt to the Irish Nation Builders.* Sydney, 1933.

Dixon, Miriam. *The Imaginary Australian. Anglo-Celts and Identity – 1788 to the Present.* Kensington, 1999.

Hogan, J.F. *The Irish in Australia.* Melbourne, 1888.

Hogan, M. *The Sectarian Strand. Religion in Australian History*. Penguin, 1987.

Jupp, James (ed.). *The Australian People*. Angus & Robertson, 1988.

McConville, Chris. *Croppies, Celts and Catholics. The Irish in Australia*. Melbourne, 1987.

MacDonagh, O. *The Sharing of the Green. A modern Irish history for Australians*. St Leonards, 1996.

O'Farrell, P. *Vanished Kingdoms: Irish in Australia and New Zealand. A Personal Excursion*. Kensington, NSW, 1990.

O'Farrell, Patrick. *The Catholic Church and Community. An Australian History*. (3rd edition) Sydney, 1993.

O'Farrell, Patrick. *Through Irish Eyes. Australia and New Zealand Images of the Irish 1788–1948*. Melbourne, 1994.

O'Hearn, D.J. *Erin Go Bragh – Advance Australia Fair. A Hundred Years of Growing 1887–1987*. The Celtic Club, Melbourne, May 1990.

Wannan, Bill. *The Wearing of the Green. The Lore, Literature, Legend and Balladry of the Irish in Australia*. London, 1965

INDEX

language (300)
§ J. Letter
letter
§ finish terms.
§ finish terms
patterns
patterns